Utah's

Incredible Backcountry Trails
(2nd Edition)

Queen's Garden Trail, Bryce Canyon (page 431)

WARNING:
HIKING INVOLVES RISK!

Hiking is a sport, not a pastime, and like all sports it involves an element of risk. There have been several instances in recent years of people suffering injury while hiking in Utah's backcountry and then filing a lawsuit against a person or organization that gave them information about the hike. This is a disturbing trend with serious implications for everyone involved in the sport.

The author and publisher of this book will not assume responsibility for any mishap that may occur as a result of information present or not present in this book. It is assumed that anyone attempting any of the hikes described in the following pages is already aware of the potential risks, has made all the necessary preparations, and has had sufficient experience to assume responsibility for himself.

Furthermore, while the author has done his best to assure that the information herein presented is accurate, he cannot guarantee its accuracy. Hikers using the information in this book should make allowance for the possibility that it may not be correct.

Utah's
Incredible Backcountry Trails
(2nd Edition)

Text and Photography
by
David Day

White Pine Lake, Bear River Range (page 28)

Rincon Publishing Company
1913 North Skyline Drive
Orem, Utah 84097
www.utahtrails.com

Library of Congress Control Number: 2012902811
ISBN: 978-0-9660858-5-3

Other books by David Day:

Malaysia in Colour (1979)
Singapore, Gateway to the Far East (1986)
Java, Island of Antiquities (1988)
Malaysia, Gemstone of Southeast Asia (1990)
Thailand and the Kingdoms of Siam (1991)
Utah's Favorite Hiking Trails (1998)
Utah's Favorite Hiking Trails, 2nd Edition (2002)
Canyonlands National Park, Favorite Jeep Roads and Hiking Trails (2004)
Utah's Incredible Backcountry Trails (2006)
Colorado's Incredible Backcountry Trails (2009)

Printed by Art Printing Works, Kuala Lumpur, Malaysia

Published by:

Rincon Publishing Company
1913 North Skyline Drive
Orem, Utah 84097

(801) 377-7657
www.utahtrails.com

For Darleen,
my most loyal
hiking companion
for the past 30 years.

Contents

Southern Utah

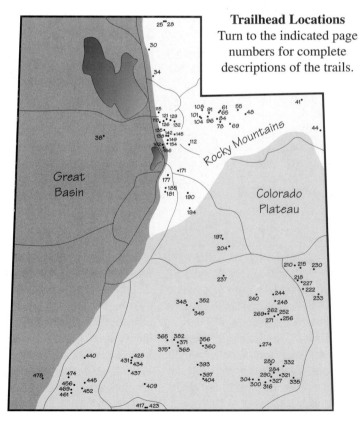

Trailhead Locations
Turn to the indicated page
numbers for complete
descriptions of the trails.

Preface

The publication of my book, *Utah's Favorite Hiking Trails*, in 1998, marked what I thought would be the end of a six-year project to document all of the best hiking trails in Utah. But as the reader replies began to come in I soon realized that many interesting trails had been left out. This led to a revised edition four years later, and then another revision, and finally to the present book. At this point I must admit that my original goal of documenting all of the best trails in this amazing state will likely never be met, but I do hope I have not omitted too many of your favorite trails. As Edward Abbey once said, there is enough wild backcountry wilderness in Utah for a lifetime of exploration.

In selecting the trails for this book I have focused primarily on those hikes that do not require any special equipment and can be accessed with an ordinary passenger car. There are a few exceptions, the most notable being three trails in a remote corner of Canyonlands National Park. This amazing national park contains many other great hiking opportunities besides the few described here, but most of the trailheads cannot be accessed without a four-wheel-drive vehicle. You can read more about those trails in my book, *Canyonlands National Park Favorite Jeep Roads and Hiking Trails*.

As with my other books, I have attempted to rate each of this book's trails on a scale of one to five stars according to how much I personally enjoy that hike. The best rating of five stars ☆☆☆☆☆ is reserved for those trails that, in my opinion, are the ten best hikes in the state. I am open to suggestions, and I hope to hear from you if you disagree with my ratings. I would especially like to hear from you if you have a favorite hike that is not included in this book.

A companion website to this book can be found at *www.utahtrails.com*. This site has links to many other useful sites where you can obtain information about local weather forecasts, river flow rates, road conditions, rules and regulations for backcountry camping, and more. Other hiking guide books can also be purchased at this site as well as the popular National Geographic *Trails Illustrated* trail maps of Utah, all at discounted prices.

May there always be wild places for us to explore!

David Day
Orem, Utah
davidday@utahtrails.com

Introduction

In the past fifty years the state of Utah has emerged as one of the premier hiking destinations in North America. Situated as it is in the heart of the American West, it combines the rugged splendor of the Rocky Mountains with the colorful sandstone canyons of the Colorado Plateau and the remote deserts of the Great Basin. And many of the most scenic spots can only be reached on foot.

In addition to magnificent scenery, many of Utah's hiking trails also provide fascinating glimpses into the region's colorful past. A few of the trails retrace the footsteps of the Mormon pioneers who settled the state in the mid-1800s. Some trails pass by turn-of-the-century mining and cowboy camps, and others visit homestead cabins from the early 1900s. But perhaps the most interesting artifacts are the 800-year-old Anasazi Indian ruins in the canyons of Southern Utah. There are more Anasazi archeological sites in Utah than any other state, and when hiking in these canyons it is hard not to feel the presence of the ancient ones who once called them home.

Another factor that makes hiking in Utah so attractive is the presence of so much wide open space, uncluttered with fences, roads, and other man-made obstacles that inhibit one's freedom. Utah's population is still relatively small, and only a tiny percentage of the state's 84,899 square miles is privately owned. In many areas hikers can literally walk for days without seeing any sign of man at all. Sixty-three percent of the state is owned and administered by the federal government, with most of the best areas being preserved in five national parks, seven national monuments, and thirty-three wilderness areas.

Left Fork of North Creek, Zion National Park (page 461)

Unfortunately not all of the best areas are currently protected. Although the total acreage of Utah's designated wilderness was increased by nearly a third during the 2005-2009 tenure of Governor Jon Huntsman, Utah still has fewer acres of protected wilderness than any of the other ten western states. The state's economy and population have increased dramatically since the original Wilderness Act was passed in 1964, and many residents have long opposed limiting the expansion by imposing more regulations on the state's publicly owned land. The mining, logging, and ranching industries are especially sensitive to such regulation, and as a result of their lobbying efforts Utah now accounts for only 1.1 percent of the total land protected by the American Wilderness Preservation System.

Geology

Geologically, Utah can be divided into three broad provinces: the Colorado Plateau, the Rocky Mountains, and the Great Basin. Each of these three geologic areas includes a large swath of land that spans across several states, but Utah is unique because it contains all three. The three regions meet at a vaguely defined point somewhere near the center of the state, with the Colorado Plateau occupying the southeastern sector, the Rocky Mountains occupying the northeastern sector, and the Great Basin lying in the west.

The Colorado Plateau

The Colorado Plateau is Utah's most famous geologic province. It is a large, mostly desert, region covering parts of Arizona, New Mexico, Colorado, and Utah that was uplifted and eroded some ten million years ago to its present elevation of 3,000 to 6,000 feet above sea level. It was named after the Colorado River, which drains most of the region. The plateau is composed almost entirely of sedimentary rock, predominantly sandstone, that has been cut into a myriad of deep, meandering canyons by the Colorado River and its tributaries. The best

known of these canyons are Arizona's Grand Canyon and Utah's Zion Canyon, both of which are now national parks.

Like most of the southwestern United States, the Colorado Plateau is an arid region, receiving an average of only about ten inches of rain annually. As a result, a great deal of the plateau's bedrock is exposed, and to a large degree it is the exposed sandstone that makes the scenery so dramatic. Perhaps Edward Abbey described it best in his book, *Desert Solitaire*:

> . . . here all is exposed and naked,
> dominated by the monolithic forma-
> tions of sandstone which stand above
> the surface of the ground and extend for
> miles, sometimes level, sometimes tilted
> or warped by pressures from below,

Devil's Garden Trail, Arches National Park (page 210)

*carved by erosion and weathering into
an intricate maze of glens, grottoes,
fissures, passageways, and deep narrow canyons.*

*. . . each groove in the rock leads to a
natural channel of some kind, every
channel to a ditch and gulch and ravine,
each larger waterway to a canyon bottom or broad wash leading in turn to the
Colorado River and the sea.*

All of Utah's national parks are located
on the Colorado Plateau: Zion, Arches,
Bryce, Canyonlands, and Capitol Reef.
And about half of the hikes in this book are
located there. It is a naturalist's paradise,
filled with strange and wonderful rock formations, frequently called Utah's Redrock

Country because of the ruddy appearance
of the stone. The shades of red, pink, and
yellow are created by tiny particles of
iron oxide trapped within the rock. The
colors are usually subtle, but become very
pronounced in the reddish light of the late
afternoon. Early morning and late afternoon
are the "golden times" for desert hiking, as
desert scenery that may appear harsh and
unappealing in the middle of the day can
become surprisingly beautiful when the
sun is low.

The Rocky Mountains

The Rocky Mountains in Utah consist
primarily of the Wasatch Range and the
Uinta Range in the northeastern corner of
the state. It is an area about as different
from the Colorado Plateau as one
can imagine, with high alpine lakes,
glaciated valleys, and snow-capped
peaks being the dominant features
of the landscape.

The Wasatch Range is a long
narrow range of mountains running
for about 180 miles in a north-south
direction from the Idaho border to
the center of the state. The western
side of the range, known locally
as the Wasatch Front, is one of the
state's most prominent landmarks.
Here the mountains rise dramatically above the western desert with
very few foothills in between. Most
of the ski resorts for which Utah is
so well known are in the Wasatch
Mountains, and the Wasatch peaks
are popular hiking destinations.

Most of Utah's major population centers are located along the
western side of the Wasatch Front;
hence the trails in these mountains
are well traveled. Several of the
state's wilderness areas are located
in this range, with four of them lying

Death Hollow (page 382)

Unnamed lake on Ryder Lake Trail, High Uintas Wilderness Area (page 65)

in the forty miles between Provo and Salt Lake City. Residents of this area are blessed by their close proximity to several hundred miles of Utah's finest hiking trails.

Unlike the Wasatch Range, the Uinta Mountains run in an east-west direction parallel to the Wyoming border. They span a distance of about 150 miles, finally ending in the Wasatch Range east of Salt Lake City. The Uintas are particularly interesting because they are so high. The area above timberline in the Uinta Mountains exceeds that of any other range outside Alaska in the United States. The hiking trails seldom dip below 9,000 feet, and many of the range's hundreds of alpine lakes remain partially frozen well into August. Kings Peak (13,528 ft.), the Uintas' most famous summit, is the highest point in Utah.

The centerpiece of the Uinta Mountains is the 456,705-acre High Uintas Wilderness Area, which was created by congress in 1984. An extensive network of trails in the wilderness area make it possible to walk for days without ever coming to a road. The longest route, the Highline Trail, is over sixty miles long. It follows the east-west summit ridge, remaining more than 10,000 feet above sea level for most of the distance.

The Great Basin

Immediately to the west of the Wasatch Mountains lies a vast, dry desert province known as the Great Basin. It is one of the most prominent geologic features in the West, occupying an area of nearly 200,000 square miles and extending all the way through Nevada to the Sierra Nevada Mountains in California. The Great Salt Lake, which lies on the eastern edge of the Great Basin, is a remnant of the huge prehistoric Lake Bonneville that once covered most of northwestern Utah. But today there are few sources of fresh water in the province; hence few people live there.

The Great Basin is mostly barren land, but it is certainly not featureless. Interestingly, the flat desert country is broken up by a large number of small linear mountain ranges, all oriented in a north-south direction. Most of the mountains have no permanent rivers, and, with a few notable exceptions, none exceed 10,000 feet in elevation. An old geological survey likens the ranges to "a group of caterpillars, all crawling irregularly northward". Surrounded as they are by desert, the small mountain ranges form biological "islands", and many contain unique species of plants and animals. Consequently, they are of great interest to evolutionary biologists.

The arid nature of the region and the general lack of population mean that there are few established hiking trails in Utah's Great Basin. Some hikers enjoy the solitude of the area so much that they don't mind the lack of water and the long dusty drives to the basin's interior desert ranges, but the most popular hiking opportunities are in two less isolated areas near its eastern boundary. Good trails can be found in the Stansbury Mountains, about 40 miles west of Salt Lake City, and in the Pine Valley Mountains, between Saint George and Cedar City.

Ecology

The Deserts

Utah, with its average annual precipitation of only 13 inches, is essentially a desert state. The only state in the U.S., in fact, that receives less rainfall is Nevada. Most of the hikes in this book lie within a desert ecological zone known to biologists as the Upper Sonoran Life Zone that extends across the Colorado Plateau and the Great Basin. The zone is characterized by plants resistant to drought and salty soil. On the valley floors one can find a variety of desert grasses intermingled with cactus, shadscale, greasewood, Mormon tea, rabbit brush and saltbush, and growing at slightly higher elevations is that ubiquitous western shrub, the sagebrush.

In areas where the annual rainfall exceeds 12 inches you might also find scattered groves of pinion pine and juniper along with the resident squirrels and chipmunks that feed on the pinion nuts. Other Upper

The Chocolate Drops Trail, Canyonlands National Park (page 269)

Row Bench Trail (page 112)

Sonoran animals include prairie dogs, kangaroo rats, desert cottontails, jackrabbits, skunks, and coyotes. Mule deer are quite common, and occasionally you might be lucky enough to see a pronghorn antelope or a bighorn sheep. There are also bobcats and mountain lions in the desert canyon country, but they are rarely seen. The Upper Sonoran Zone is a favorite habitat of rattlesnakes, so be on the lookout for them when hiking in these areas.

The Foothills

The Upper Sonoran Life Zone normally extends to about 5,500 feet, above which lies the Transition Life Zone. This region defines the transition between the desert and the mountain ecosystems. Open forests of ponderosa pine are usually common in the Transition Zone, with pinion pine, juniper, and sagebrush scattered between. In Northern Utah, however, the ponderosa pine are more often absent—a fact that has long puzzled botanists.

In the canyons one is likely to find dense thickets of Gamble oak, scrub maple, and mountain mahogany. At the higher elevations, the pinion pine and juniper are replaced by Douglas fir. Squirrels and chipmunks also thrive in the Transition Zone, along with cottontails, jackrabbits, skunks, coyotes, mule deer, and the occasional mountain lion.

The Mountains

Above about 8,000 feet the Transition Life Zone gives way to an ecosystem known as the Canadian Life Zone. This is the zone that contains most of the hiking trails in the Wasatch and Uinta Mountains. Here the forests are usually dominated by Douglas fir, although in the Uintas lodgepole pine prevail. Deer, elk and moose can often be seen grazing in the meadows of the Canadian Zone and, among the smaller animals, gophers, marmots, and pikas are common.

As one goes higher in elevation Engelmann spruce and subalpine fir begin to dominate. Then above 10,000 feet one enters the Hudsonian Life Zone, where a short growing season and harsh winter conditions prevent the trees from reaching full size.

The only trees that can generally be found in the Hudsonian Life Zone are stunted Engelmann spruce, sometimes reaching only a few feet in height. Timberline, the maximum elevation at which trees will grow, varies a great deal from mountain to mountain, but in Utah it rarely extends much over 11,000 feet.

History

Prehistoric Cultures

The ancestors of the American Indians resided in Utah for at least ten thousand years before the arrival of the first white men, and the remnants of their most recent cultures can still be seen along many backcountry hiking trails. The most notable artifacts belonged to the Anasazi Indians, who left behind hundreds of archeological sites in southeastern Utah. Almost every major canyon in this part of the state contains traces of prehistoric Anasazi occupancy.

Archeologist have divided the Anasazi culture into six distinctive periods: the Basketmaker I, II, and III periods and the Pueblo I, II, and III periods. The Basketmaker II period, which began around the time of Christ, marks the time when the early nomadic Indians first began to learn the secrets of agriculture. Corn, introduced by other Indians living in Mexico, was probably their first crop. During the Basketmaker III phase they farmed extensively and lived in large, subterranean pit houses. It was also during this time that the bow and arrow were invented.

The Pueblo I, II, and III periods, lasting from about 700 until 1300 A.D., mark a time of increasing technological skill in building above-ground stone houses. It was during the last 150 years of this time, the Pueblo III period, that the famous Anasazi cliff dwellings were built in the four corners area of Arizona, New Mexico, Colorado, and Utah. The best preserved Pueblo III ruins are now located in Colorado's Mesa Verde National Park, but Utah has a greater number of Anasazi sites than any of the other three states.

There must have been many thousands of Indians living in southeastern Utah at that time, because now it seems that almost every canyon in the region contains at least one or two Anasazi ruins. Discovering these ancient structures while traveling alone in the wild canyon country of Southern Utah, far away from the tourists, park rangers, asphalt trails and interpretive plaques of the national parks, is an awesome experience. Some of the most interesting hikes in this

Anasazi ruin behind Polly's Island in Grand Gulch (page 290)

book are in the canyons where the Anasazis once lived.

North of the four corners area you may occasionally come across remnants of the Fremont Indians. These people occupied parts of eastern Utah from about 700 to 1250 A.D. There were particularly large concentrations of them along the Green River and the Fremont River, after which they were named, but there numbers were never as large as the Anasazis. Nor were they as advanced. They lived in caves and simple shelters, and, although they did build stone granaries, they never developed the elaborate cliff dwellings that distinguish the Anasazis.

All of the prehistoric Indian cultures of Utah—the Anasazis, the Fremonts, and the Archaic Peoples that preceded them—produced prodigious quantities of rock art. Most of it is in the southeastern part of Utah where the Indian populations were largest, but some rock art can be found in almost every corner of the state. The largest rock art panel in the United States is in the Horseshoe Canyon section of Canyonlands National Park, near Hanksville. Here, decorating the smooth canyon walls, are a series of intriguing red, brown, and white ghostlike pictographs that may be as much as 8,000 years old.

Early White Settlers

The first known Europeans to enter Utah were a group of Spanish explorers led by Francisco Vasquez de Coronado in 1540, and for nearly three centuries the territory was claimed by Spain. After Mexico achieved its independence from Spain in 1821 most of what is now the southwestern

United States became part of Mexico, but the huge territory was lost 27 years later after Mexico's defeat in the Mexican-American War. Utah became an official territory of the United States with the signing of the Treaty of Guadalupe Hidalgo in 1848.

Before the mid-1800s there were very few non-Indians living in Utah, but the last half of the nineteenth century saw a massive influx of pioneers from the eastern and midwestern states. The Mormons, led by Brigham Young, first arrived in what is now Salt Lake City in 1847, and almost immediately began fanning out to settle the rest of the state. The following year gold was discovered in California, and soon there was a huge exodus of people traveling westward through Utah in hopes of getting rich.

In 1849 alone some 6,000 wagons journeyed through the state carrying an estimated 40,000 people to the west coast. The new Mormon settlers made a thriving business of selling supplies to the wagon trains, and many cattle and sheep ranches got their start during that time. A number of the trails in this book pass by the remnants of this early ranching activity.

Indian and cowboy petroglyphs along the Escalante River (page 393)

Tips for Hikers

Dozens of books have been written telling hikers and backpackers in great detail what they should wear, what they should eat, where they should sleep, how they should walk, what they should carry, and a thousand other minutia. But let me assure you, you don't have to be a scholar to enjoy this sport. Hiking is really just an excuse to get out and enjoy the great outdoors, and the most important prerequisites are nothing more than common sense and a love of nature. If you have never done any hiking I suggest you get out and do some now, and read the books later. Start with the easy trails first. Then after you have completed a few hikes go ahead and read what the experts have to say.

Having said that, let me now caution you that successful hikes require a large amount of planning. Before you set out try to think through what the journey entails. How long is the trail? Is the route well marked? How long will you be gone? How much water will you need? What kind of clothing should you wear? Most of these questions can easily be answered with a modicum of common sense, but it is important that you ask them. Make the entire trip in your mind before you actually start, checking to see that you have packed what you will need for each phase of the journey. The longer your hike is the more adversely you will be affected by your mistakes, so be sure to try a few easy ones before you go for the big ones.

The Hot Pots (page 171)

Access

The first thing to consider in planning a hike is how to get to the trailhead. An ordinary car is all you need most of the time, but occasionally a good four-wheel-drive vehicle can come in very handy. In some cases you can avoid the necessity of a 4WD by using a mountain bike for the last few miles to the trailhead, and some-

Mount Nebo (page 181)

times, if the roads are dry, a 2WD with high clearance will do nicely. There are only three hikes in this book that you absolutely cannot do without a 4WD vehicle: The Maze, The Chocolate Drops, and the Green and Colorado River Overlook, all located in the Maze District of Canyonlands National Park. These hikes require seven hours of off-highway driving, the last 14 miles of which are extremely rough. If you don't have a 4WD vehicle with high clearance you won't make it.

Quite often a hike does not end at the same trailhead where it started, and in these cases you will need a plan for getting back to where your vehicle is parked. Again, a bicycle is often a good solution. Of course the best way to handle this situation is with two cars, one parked at the end of the hike and one at the beginning, but this is often inconvenient. If you are a serious hiker I suggest that you invest in a bicycle rack and carry a mountain bike on your car on all of your backcountry trips. You will be surprised how often it comes in handy.

Finally, let me point out that there are a few items you should always carry in your car when driving to remote trailheads:

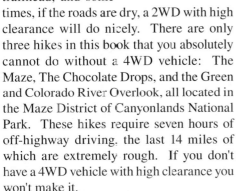

- several gallons of extra water
- a hundred feet of rope
- a good spare tire
- a bicycle pump
- a few basic tools
- a shovel

When driving to an unfamiliar trailhead for the first time I also like to carry a logbook with me. It is useful to write down the odometer reading at various points along the way so you can keep track of where you are and how far you have come.

Clothing

The most important item of clothing on a hike is, of course, your foot wear. Your shoes must be comfortable and durable, and they must give your feet the protection they need. Many of the trails in Utah are very rocky, and on these trails boots are the only practical thing to wear. Some trails, however, are over slickrock or sand, and on these many people prefer to wear sneakers. When planning your hike be sure to find out if it will be necessary to wade across any streams. If so, you should wear some sort of wettable shoes. Walking for long distances

Governor Dern Lake (page 78)

your head warm. The most practical kind of headgear is a cheap, wide rimmed, foldable, canvas hat.

A special mention should me made here about the hazards of skin cancer in Utah. This state has one of the highest incidents of skin cancer in the United States. Since exposure to the sun is the largest single cause of skin cancer, hikers should choose clothing that will minimize their exposure and use a high SPF sunscreen lotion on those parts of the body that cannot be covered.

with wet feet can cause blisters, but on hikes that require a lot of wading there may be no other alternative.

Some hikers carry an extra pair of shoes in their pack for use around the camp or for wading streams, but for me it is more important to keep my weight down. Carrying extra socks, however, is a very good idea. A clean pair of socks each day will go a long way toward preventing blisters.

Walking generates a lot of body heat, especially if you are climbing. So you will probably want to wear jackets and sweaters that you can easily take off and put back on. Most hikers prefer to wear several layers of clothing rather than a single heavy jacket, but on long trips the weight of additional sweaters and shirts can add up fast.

In my opinion, shorts are impractical in most hiking situations. Your legs need protection from brush, from insects, and from the sun. If there is any doubt about what the trail conditions are going to be like always opt for long pants. I also prefer to wear a long sleeved cotton shirt, even in summer, just for the protection it offers. Never go hiking without a hat. In hot weather it protects you from the sun and in cold weather it keeps

Drinking Water

Water is one of the most important items to consider when planning a hike. Water is necessary for almost all of our body functions, and without it we cannot survive for more than a few days. When it is hot our bodies need prodigious amounts of water to function normally—a gallon a day or more in Utah's desert country in the summertime. This is not a problem on day hikes, but on longer hikes water can become a matter of serious concern. Fortunately it is usually possible to find water along the trail, so it need not all be carried from the trailhead. But caution is advised. There is always a possibility getting sick from ingesting contaminated water.

Opinions vary widely on the subject of when water is safe to drink. If you listen to the rangers in our national parks you will come away with the opinion that untreated water is never safe to drink. Yet I have known people who routinely drink from desert potholes, filled with tadpoles and mosquito larva, with no ill effects. Some people use inexpensive halogen tablets to treat their water in the backcountry, and others, claiming that the pills cause cancer, insist on carrying expensive filter pumps with them wherever they go. Again, common sense is the key. No one can guarantee that you will never get sick, but there is no need to be paranoid about the possibility. With a little common sense the risk can be minimized significantly.

First, it is important to remember where the germs that carry human disease come from. Generally, they are carried by other humans and animals that associate with humans—i.e., cows, sheep, horses, pigs, cats, dogs, etc. Beaver should also be included in the list, since they have been known to carry the microbes that are responsible for giardia. Second, bear in mind that most microbes can't swim very far; hence they are only likely to be found downstream from the contamination point. Knowing this, we can formulate a few basic rules:

- The closer you get to the source of a stream, the safer is the water.

- Stream water should be treated if humans or their animals frequent areas upstream in the watershed.

- Running water is safer than still water, since microbes tend to be washed downstream before they can multiply.

- Always treat the water if there are signs of beaver in the area.

Untreated spring water can be consumed with very little risk, but you should always treat the water you get from ponds and lakes. On rare occasions, especially in the desert, you may come across water that is contaminated with naturally occurring, sometimes poisonous, minerals such as salt, sulfur, or even arsenic. This is generally not a problem, since the taste of contaminated water is usually so bad no one would want to drink it anyway. But if you are in doubt check for insects or frogs living in the water.

Devils Garden, Arches National Park (page 210)

If the water is lifeless and has a peculiar taste, don't drink it under any circumstances.

There are three commonly used ways of treating water to kill or remove microbes: halogen tablets, boiling, or filtering. Using halogen (iodine or chlorine) tablets is the most convenient and inexpensive method. As stated earlier, some studies indicate that prolonged use of these tablets can cause cancer, but for short term use the risk is infinitesimal. If you are boiling the water, be sure to boil it for at least several minutes. Above 8,000 feet you should boil it for a full five minutes, since at higher elevations water boils at a lower temperature. If you don't mind spending the extra money and carrying a little extra weight, filter pumps are probably the best way to purify your drinking water.

Finally let me say that in my opinion the danger in drinking untreated water in the wild has been vastly overstated. Even if you drink indiscriminately, the chances are good that you won't get sick. And in most circumstances, even if you do get sick it will not be a life threatening illness. On the other hand, dehydration can easily lead to a life threatening situation, especially in desert areas. If you are threatened with dehydration a muddy pool of untreated water could well save your life.

Minimum Impact

There was a time in the West when there were so few people using the backcountry that human impact was not a problem. That is no longer the case. The detrimental effects of man on the environment are becoming increasingly obvious, and it is up to each one of us to minimize them as best we can.

Probably the greatest amount of environmental destruction by hikers and backpackers is caused from incidents involving campfires. Many acres of prime forest land in the West have been destroyed by people who were careless with their fires. But fires adversely affect the environment even when they are carefully tended. The ugly marks from fires built in arid areas can last for years, and in places where wood is scarce campers often ravage the land for firewood, burning everything in sight. A much better solution is to carry a small camp stove. They are inexpensive, convenient, and weigh only a pound or two. Furthermore, open fires are now illegal in many of our national parks and forests. A small camp stove should be an integral part of every backpacker's standard equipment.

Another area of concern is garbage. There is nothing more disheartening to a nature lover than to walk through a pristine wilderness area that has been littered with

The Wave (page 423)

Little Wildhorse Canyon (page 237)

trash. The slogan "Pack it in, pack it out" is a good one to follow. Some organic material, such as unwanted food or body wastes can be buried, but only if it is deposited at least six inches below the surface and covered with well packed dirt. But do not bury your toilet paper. Furthermore, nothing should be buried near a lake or in a stream bed where it might pollute the surface water.

Utah's desert areas require special consideration from backcountry hikers. Most people don't realize how fragile the arid ecosystems are, but it can take years for the desert to recover from the impact of a careless hiker. Old campfire sites, refuse deposits, and even foot prints seem never to go away. Desert soils are filled with an array of dry, thread-like microscopic plants that nitrogenate the soil and bind it together, and once these plants are crushed or burned it can take up to twenty years for them to grow back. Without this component of the soil, called the cryptobiotic crust, the desert would be a barren place indeed. Most shrubs and grasses cannot thrive without it. So when hiking off-trail in the deserts of Southern Utah try to stay on the slickrock or in the sandy bottoms of washes as much as possible.

One of Southern Utah's greatest treasures is the incredible prehistoric cliff dwellings that were left behind by the Anasazi Indians some 700 years ago. It is impossible to describe the thrill of discovering one of these archeological gems, far from any road in a wild desert canyon. Yet the ancient ruins have received more abuse than any of Utah's other backcountry attractions. Most of the damage was inflicted many years ago, when indiscriminate excavation and pot hunting were legal, but even today the ancient dwellings are still being abused. Occasionally they are intentionally vandalized; more often damage is inflicted as a result of carelessness. If you visit one of these ruins remember that they are very fragile and can be easily damaged. Do not walk over them or climb on them. And do not remove any pottery shards, corn cobs, or other objects from the sites. Treat them just as you would treat an exhibit in a museum, because that is exactly what they are.

Maps

There is no substitute for a good map of the area in which you are hiking. The maps provided in this book should be sufficient to complete the described hikes, but if possible you should take along a more detailed map of the area you plan to visit. Part of the joy of hiking is exploring and taking side trips on your own that may not have been part of the original plan, and it is much easier to do this if you have a good map with you. Also, it is sometimes useful to know exactly where you are on the trail. A good map will help you plot your course with greater accuracy.

The best topographic maps available are the 7.5 minute series, published by the United States Geological Survey. They are large scale (about 2.6 inches per mile with contour lines at 40 foot intervals), and they are widely available in ranger stations, national park visitor centers, and stores that sell camping supplies.

Unfortunately, many of the 7.5 minute USGS maps do not accurately depict the trail locations. The best trail maps are the *Trails Illustrated* maps produced by National Geographic in Evergreen, Colorado. Most of the *Trails Illustrated* maps are drawn to much smaller scale than the detailed 7.5 minute maps, but they do give better information about the hiking trails and trailheads.

You will find your map much more useful if you also carry a compass and a watch. The watch will help you estimate how far you have gone since the last landmark (most people walk about 2 miles per hour on level ground), and the compass will help you locate landmarks. When using your compass to determine a direction, bear in mind that the magnetic declination throughout Utah is generally about 15 degrees east. In other words, your compass needle will always point about 15 degrees east of true north.

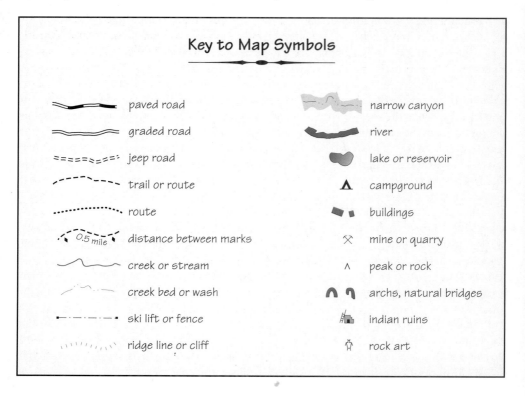

Key to Map Symbols

paved road		narrow canyon	
graded road		river	
jeep road		lake or reservoir	
trail or route		campground	
route		buildings	
0.5 mile distance between marks		mine or quarry	
creek or stream		peak or rock	
creek bed or wash		archs, natural bridges	
ski lift or fence		indian ruins	
ridge line or cliff		rock art	

Naomi Peak

Mount Naomi Wilderness Area
day hike

Distance:	6.4 miles (round trip)
Walking time:	4¹/₂ hours
Elevations:	1,920 ft. gain/loss
	Tony Grove Trailhead (start): 8,060 ft.
	Naomi Peak: 9,978 ft.
Trail:	Good trail most of the way
Season:	Midsummer through mid-fall. Parts of the trail are usually covered with snow from November until the end of June.
Vicinity:	Near Logan
Maps:	Naomi Peak *(USGS)*
Information:	http://www.utahtrails.com/naomipeak.html *(Utah Trails)*
	http://www.fs.usda.gov/uwcnf/ *(Uinta-Wasatch-Cache Nat. Forest)*
	phone: (435) 755-3620 *(Logan Ranger District)*

Drive north from Logan on Highway 89 toward Bear Lake. After 22 miles you will see a sign directing you to Tony Grove Lake and Campground. Turn here and follow the signs for 6.9 miles to Tony Grove Lake. There is a parking area at the end of the road just above the lake, and the trailhead is on the north side of the parking lot. No permits are required, but you will be charged $5.00/day for parking at the trailhead.

Naomi Peak is the highest point in the Bear River Mountains of Northern Utah and Southern Idaho. While the limestone range is not very high it is extremely rugged, and the views from the top of Naomi are outstanding. Many of the most interesting peaks in the range can be seen from the summit.

If you are hiking in late July you will also be able to enjoy another highlight of the Bear River Range: wildflowers. A colorful display of geraniums, paintbrushes, columbines, lupines, daisies, and mountain sunflowers stretches for miles across the meadows north of the Tony Grove Trailhead. It is a shame that these meadows were not included in the Utah Wilderness Act that created the Mount Naomi Wilderness Area in 1984. Snowmobile operators frequent the area in the winter, and they lobbied successfully to have the

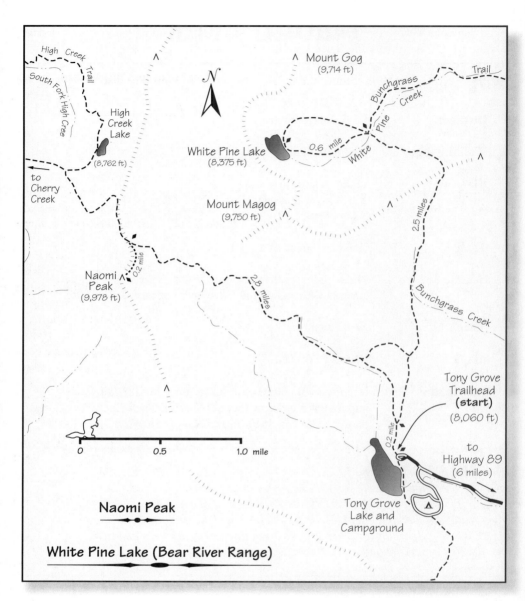

High Creek Trail

South Fork High Cree

∧

N

∧ Mount Gog
(9,714 ft)

Bunchgrass Creek

Trail

High
Creek
Lake

(8,762 ft)

White Pine Lake
(8,375 ft)

0.6 mile

White Pine

∧

to
Cherry
Creek

Mount Magog
(9,750 ft)

∧

∧

2.5 miles

Bunchgrass Creek

Naomi ∧
Peak
(9,978 ft)

0.2 mile

2.8 miles

∧

Tony Grove
Trailhead
(start)
(8,060 ft)

0.2 mile

to
Highway 89
(6 miles)

0   0.5   1.0 mile

Tony Grove
Lake and
Campground

Naomi Peak

White Pine Lake (Bear River Range)

watershed east of the peak excluded from the bill. This hike touches only briefly on the eastern boundary of the wilderness area.

From the trailhead at Tony Grove Lake the path climbs gently uphill for about 400 yards and then comes to a junction beside a forest service signboard. Bear left here, following the trail as it goes into a long west-

ward turn toward Naomi Peak. The profusion of wildflowers continues for another 0.5 mile beyond the junction, but then the grade gets steeper and the rocky soil becomes less supportive of ground cover.

As the trail ascends toward the summit ridge you will climb onto two narrow benches, each about 250 feet above the preceding one. The path climbs out of the meadow and onto the first bench about 0.8 mile from the trailhead. Then, after a brief respite, the route becomes steep again until the second bench is reached 0.8 mile farther along. From the second bench the trail makes its third and last steep climb up to the summit ridge just north of the peak.

Once you reach the summit ridge it will be necessary to leave the main trail and strike out along the top of the ridge on a less distinct trail for the last 0.2 mile to the peak. The Mount Naomi Wilderness Area boundary line also follows the ridge, and you will see a Forest Service sign at the boundary just before the point where you must leave the main trail. It is an easy ten-minute scramble along the summit ridge to the top of Naomi Peak. The peak is only 140 feet higher than the pass, and there is no vegetation to impede the way.

The view from the top of Naomi Peak is striking. Smithfield Canyon, a deep gorge through the mountains, dominates the view to the west. The dome-shaped peak 1.5 miles to the northwest, on the other side of Smithfield Canyon, is Cherry Peak. Cherry Peak is easily accessible from the Cherry Creek Trail which you can see about 400 feet below its summit. The distinctive peak one mile east of Naomi Peak is Mount Magog. White Pine Lake, lies just out of sight on the north side of Mount Magog.

High Creek Lake

If you still have energy to spare after climbing Naomi, you might want to visit the nearby High Creek Lake . This side trip will add 2.4 miles to the hike's total distance and about a thousand feet to the elevation gain and loss. To get there just continue west on the trail below Naomi as it crosses the summit ridge. After 0.9 mile the trail splits again, with the right fork leading to High Creek Lake and the left fork leading to Cherry Creek. High Creek Lake is a small but very scenic lake nestled against the steep western side of the summit ridge. There are several groves of large Engelmann spruce around the lake, and a few fine camp sites along its southern shore.

Naomi Peak Trail

White Pine Lake (Bear River Range)

★★   **day hike**

Distance:	6.6 miles (round trip)	
Walking time:	4¼ hours	
Elevations:	1,250 ft. gain/loss	
	Tony Grove Trailhead (start):	8,060 ft.
	highest point:	8,840 ft.
	White Pine Lake:	8,375 ft.
Trail:	Good trail all the way	
Season:	Summer through mid-fall. Parts of the trail are usually covered with snow from November until early June.	
Vicinity:	Near Logan	
Maps:	Naomi Peak *(USGS)*	
Information:	http://www.utahtrails.com/whitepinelakebear.html *(Utah Trails)*	
	http://www.fs.usda.gov/uwcnf/ *(Uinta-Wasatch-Cache Nat. Forest)*	
	phone: (435) 755-3620 *(Logan Ranger District)*	

Drive north from Logan on Highway 89 toward Bear Lake. After 22 miles you will see a sign directing you to Tony Grove Lake and Campground. Turn here and follow the signs for 6.9 miles to Tony Grove Lake. There is a parking area at the end of the road just above the lake, and the trailhead is on the north side of the parking lot. No permits are required, but you will be charged $5.00/day for parking at the trailhead.

This is one of the most scenic hikes you will find anywhere, especially if it is done around the first of August when the wildflowers are at their peak. The first two-thirds of the trail pass through a series of alpine meadows that are filled with acres and acres of pink, blue, purple, yellow, and white flowers. No other trail in this book offers the abundance of wildflowers you will see on the White Pine Lake trail. You might want to stop at the Forest Service Ranger Station in Logan and buy a guide to the wildflowers on your way to the trailhead. As you leave Logan you will see it on the right side of Highway 89 just 2.1 miles after you leave Main Street.

Given the natural beauty of White Pine

see map
page 26

White Pine Lake Trail

Lake and its environs, it is unfortunate that it is not a part of the Mount Naomi Wilderness Area. The lake lies about a mile outside of the wilderness area's eastern boundary. It is a popular destination among snowmobile sportsmen during the winter months, and it was their lobbying effort that led to its exclusion when Ronald Reagan signed the Utah Wilderness Act into law in 1984. White Pine Lake is still pristine, but there is no guarantee that it will not be developed in the future.

From Tony Grove Lake the trail climbs gently uphill for a quarter mile to the junction with the Naomi Peak trail. Turn right here and continue climbing for another 1.9 miles until you reach the highest point on the hike, some 780 feet above the trailhead. Up to this point the trail goes through open meadows with occasional groves of Engelmann spruce and limber pine. The limber pines are the trees with large clusters of needles near the ends of the twigs that look almost like tufts of fur. They get their name because the branches are so limber they can be bent double or even tied in knots without breaking. Finally, 2.1 miles from

the trailhead the trail starts down into White Pine Basin. The prominent peak west of this point is Mount Magog and, although you cannot see it yet, the lake is located just north of this peak. When you reach the bottom of the basin you will come to a 4-way trail junction where you must turn left for the last half mile to White Pine Lake.

The lake itself is small and very shallow, but the beauty of its setting makes up for its deficiencies. It is situated directly between two 9,700-foot peaks, Mount Magog and Mount Gog, with a fine stand of spruce on one side. There are a number of good camp sites above the eastern shore, and if you have the time it is a very pleasant place to spend a night.

Bunchgrass Trail

Turning right at the 4-way junction mentioned above will put you on the Bunchgrass Trail, a 6.6 mile trail that ultimately leads back to Highway 89. The Bunchgrass Trailhead is located on the west side of Highway 89 just 0.5 miles north of the turnoff to Tony Grove Lake. Few hikers use this trail, but it is popular with mountain bikers who occasionally ride to White pine Lake from Tony Grove and return to the highway via the Bunchgrass Trail.

White Pine Lake

Wellsville Ridge

Wellsville Mountain Wilderness Area
shuttle car required
day hike

★★

Distance:	7.5 miles (plus 6.5 miles by car or bicycle)
Walking time:	5³⁄₄ hours
Elevations:	2,960 ft. gain, 2,520 ft. loss Deep Canyon Trailhead (start): 5,420 ft. Stewart Pass: 8,380 ft. Wellsville Cone: 9,356 ft. Coldwater Canyon Trailhead: 5,860 ft.
Trail:	Good trail all the way
Season:	Summer through mid-fall. Parts of the trail are usually covered with snow from November until mid-June. Also, the road to Coldwater Canyon Trailhead is unmaintained and inaccessible in wet weather.
Vicinity:	Near Wellsville and Logan
Maps:	Honeyville *(USGS)*
Information:	http://www.utahtrails.com/wellsvilleridge.html *(Utah Trails)* http://www.fs.usda.gov/uwcnf/ *(Uinta-Wasatch-Cache Nat. Forest)* phone: (435) 755-3620 *(Logan Ranger District)*

Take Exit 364 from I-15, 55 miles north of Salt Lake City, and drive east past *Brigham City on Highway 89 toward Logan. After driving 17 miles you will come to the junction with Highway 23, where you must turn left toward Wellsville and Mendon. You will arrive at the farming community of Mendon after 7 miles. Turn into Mendon and find the corner of Center and Main Street, then drive south on Main Street. After 0.5 mile the road crosses the highway again, and another 200 yards will bring you to a sign that says "National Forest". Turn right onto a gravel road and continue following the signs to the national forest. 1.2 miles after leaving the pavement you will pass the national forest boundary, and 2.2 miles later you will reach the Coldwater Canyon Trailhead at the end of the road (a total of 4.0 miles from Center Street in Mendon). This is where the hike will end and where you must leave your shuttle. (Note: the last two miles of the road to the trailhead are very rough, but with care they can usually be negotiated with an ordinary car.)*

In order to get to Deep Canyon, where the hike begins, you must drive west out of Mendon on 3rd North. After 3rd North crosses the highway it continues almost due west for 2.0 miles and ends at the trailhead. The road is graded gravel – much better than the road to Cold-water Canyon. There is a small parking area at the end of 3rd North but, unfortunately, no signs to let you know where the trail is. You will see two primitive roads leaving the parking area: one continues west along the fence, and the other forks off to the south. Walk down the road to the south, and within a few hundred yards it will end where the trail begins.

The Wellsville Ridge is very well known among Utah's bird watchers. It is probably the best place in the state to see birds of prey such as the Cooper's hawk and the red tailed hawk. These raptors are especially prevalent on windy days during the fall migration, when they can be seen riding the updrafts along the western side of the ridge. There are also a number of fine views from the top of the narrow summit ridge. The fertile Cache Valley lies below the mountains on the east side, with its settlements of Logan, Mendon, and Wellsville. On the west side the meandering Bear River makes an interesting picture as it winds its way lazily toward the Great Salt Lake.

The people who live below the Wellsville Mountains should be remembered for their valiant efforts in the early 1940s to save their beloved mountains. At that time the grass-covered ridges were suffering from decades of overgrazing, and much of the vegetation in the lower canyons had been burned out. In 1941 a few concerned citizens in Cache County formed the Wellsville Area Project Corporation, and soon, even as the United States was becoming embroiled in World War II, private contributions to save the mountains began to accumulate. The money was used to purchase land that was then deeded over to the Forest Service for protection. The Wellsville project was a huge success, and in 1984 a final tribute to its participants was paid by the U.S. Congress with the creation of the Wellsville Mountain Wilderness Area. Now 20,988 acres of wilderness stand as a monument to a group of people who, fifty years ago, cared deeply about their environment and their children's heritage.

From the trailhead the trail climbs steadily up Deep Canyon for a distance of 3.2 miles, finally reaching a small saddle on the summit ridge after an elevation gain of 2,700 feet. The trail splits at the saddle, with the southern branch going to Stewart Pass and the northern branch proceeding along

Coldwater Canyon Trail, below Wellsville Ridge

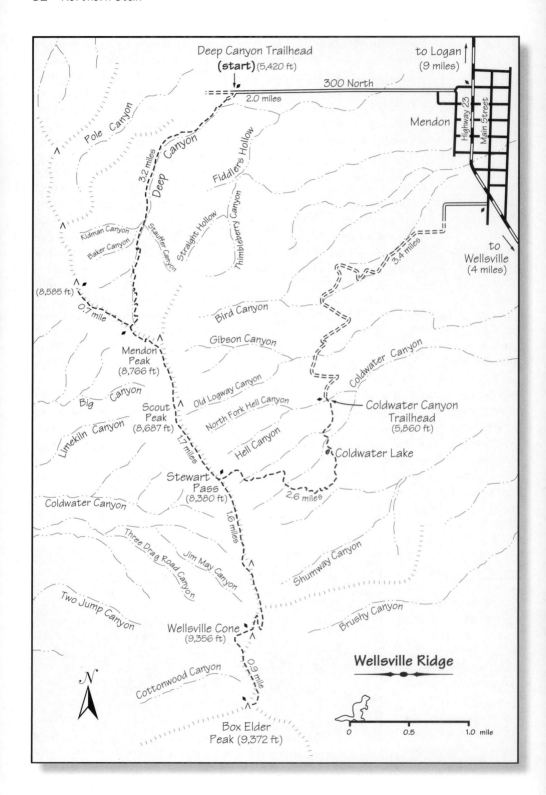

Deep Canyon Trailhead (start) (5,420 ft)

to Logan (9 miles)

300 North

2.0 miles

Mendon

Highway 23

Main Street

Pole Canyon

Deep Canyon

3.2 miles

Fiddlers Hollow

to Wellsville (4 miles)

3.4 miles

Kidman Canyon

Baker Canyon

Stauffer Canyon

Straight Hollow

Thimbleberry Canyon

(8,585 ft)

0.7 mile

Bird Canyon

Gibson Canyon

Mendon Peak (8,766 ft)

Coldwater Canyon

Coldwater Canyon Trailhead (5,860 ft)

Big Canyon

Scout Peak (8,687 ft)

Old Logway Canyon

North Fork Hell Canyon

1.7 miles

Limekiln Canyon

Hell Canyon

Coldwater Lake

Stewart Pass (8,380 ft)

2.6 miles

Coldwater Canyon

1.6 miles

Three Drag Road Canyon

Jim May Canyon

Shumway Canyon

Two Jump Canyon

Brushy Canyon

Wellsville Cone (9,356 ft)

0.9 mile

Cottonwood Canyon

Wellsville Ridge

N

Box Elder Peak (9,372 ft)

0   0.5   1.0 mile

the ridge to the top of a small unnamed peak 0.7 mile away. This peak is supposed to be an especially fine place to watch the hawks, but in fact if the conditions are right they can be seen almost everywhere along the ridge.

The Wellsville Ridge is surprisingly devoid of vegetation. Perhaps the dry winds that blow across the mountain from the Great Basin desert leave the rocky soil too dry for the forest to flourish. Whatever the reason, the absence of trees along the ridge makes for some marvelous views of the valleys below.

From the saddle above Deep Canyon the main trail proceeds southward for 1.7 miles to Stewart Pass. Along the way the route traverses around the west side of Scout Peak (8,687 ft.), another good place for hawk watching. There are no signs to let you know when you arrive at Stewart Pass, but there is a stone monument marking the place. This is where the ridge trail intersects the Coldwater Canyon Trail, and where you must start your descent back to your shuttle car. Stewart Pass is the lowest point on the Wellsville Ridge between Scout Peak and the Wellsville Cone.

The hike down through Coldwater Canyon is much like the hike through Deep Canyon, except the trail is slightly steeper. You will loose 2,500 feet in 2.6 miles. About 0.6 mile before you reach the trailhead you will pass by Coldwater Lake, a small pond about 100 feet long.

Wellsville Cone

If time permits, you really should make a side trip to the top of the Wellsville Cone before starting down the Coldwater Canyon Trail from Stewart Pass. The Wellsville Cone is 1.6 miles from Stewart Pass, over an excellent trail with an elevation gain of 980 feet. The side trip to Wellsville Cone and back will add about 2½ hours onto your total hiking time.

Wellsville Cone, which can be clearly seen from the top of Stewart Pass, looks like an old volcanic cinder cone with its northern side eroded away. The mountain is made of sedimentary limestone, however, so the cone could not have been formed by a volcano. The cone has two summits with the eastern peak being the higher one. The ridge trail passes between the two peaks. You will probably see another faint trail coming up through the bowl below Wellsville Cone on the west side of the mountain. This trail originates at the bottom of West Coldwater Canyon, but it is little used now and hard to follow.

For still more ambitious hikers it is only another 0.9 miles from the Wellsville Cone along the last part of the ridge to Box Elder Peak (9,372 ft.). Box Elder is the highest point in the Wellsville Mountains, but the views are not much different than the views from the summit of the Wellsville Cone.

Looking north along the Wellsville Ridge from Wellsville Cone

Mount Ogden

★

Distance:	10.0 miles (round trip)
Walking time:	7 hours
Elevations:	4,730 ft. gain/loss Malans Peak Trailhead (start): 4,840 ft. Malans Peak: 7,080 ft. Mount Ogden: 9,570 ft.
Trail:	There is no trail for most of the last mile. Furthermore, this part of the route is very steep, gaining 1,600 feet in one mile. It is a very strenuous climb.
Season:	Summer through mid-fall. The upper parts of the trail are usually covered with snow from mid-November through mid-June.
Vicinity:	Near Ogden
Maps:	Ogden *(USGS)*
Information:	http://www.utahtrails.com/mountogden.html *(Utah Trails)* http://www.fs.usda.gov/uwcnf/ *(Uinta-Wasatch-Cache Nat. Forest)* phone: (801) 625-5112 *(Ogden Ranger District)*

Drive east on 27th street in Ogden until the road ends. The trail begins just beyond the barrier at the end of the pavement.

Mount Ogden is a popular hike primarily because it is so close to the city of Ogden; the trailhead is only a three mile drive from Weber State University. The lower part of the climb, across Malans Peak and into Upper Waterfall Canyon, is very pleasant, but beyond that the route to the top of the mountain is extremely strenuous. There are some gorgeous views from the peak, not only of the city of Ogden, but also of the Snow Basin Ski Resort and the Pineview Reservoir. Unfortunately, however, the summit is now marred by the presence of microwave transmitting towers. Mount Ogden can also be reached from its east side by way of a jeep road that ascends

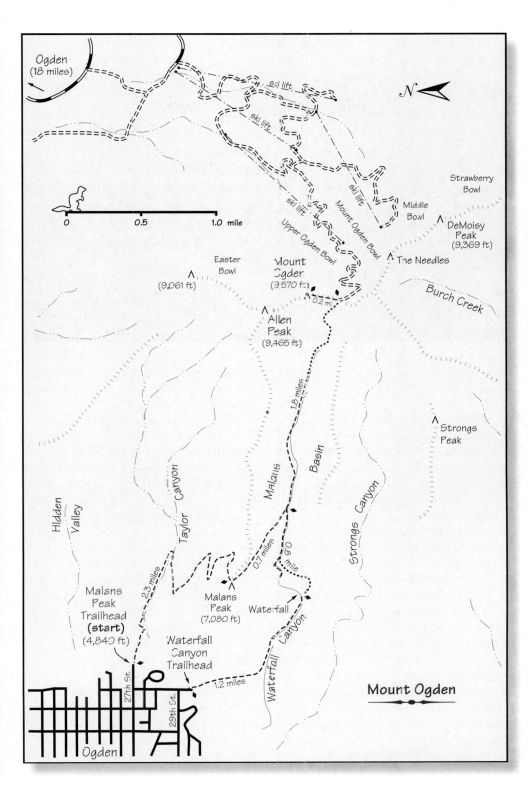

Mount Ogden

Mount Ogden Trail

from Snow Basin to a saddle 0.2 mile south of the peak.

There may be some confusion near the trailhead because of the existence of many intersecting ATV and motorcycle trails. Just make sure that the path you choose heads east, toward the obvious mouth of Taylor Canyon. After you enter the canyon, 0.3 mile from the trailhead, you won't encounter any more ATV roads.

The trail follows a picturesque stream through the bottom of Taylor Canyon for about 0.5 mile before turning south to begin its ascent up Malans Peak. Next, a series of wide switchbacks ascend through a forest of Douglas fir to an elevation of 7,000 feet, where the trail finally reaches the top of the ridge separating Taylor Canyon from Waterfall Canyon. As it crosses the ridge the path passes by the summit of Malans Peak. From this perspective you can see that Malans is not really a peak at all, but rather just a prominent knob on the end of a long ridge coming down the western slope of

Mount Ogden. From Malans Peak the trail continues south into the bottom of Upper Waterfall Canyon.

Once you reach Waterfall Canyon turn east and follow the drainage all the way to a saddle on the south side of the summit. For the first mile you will be walking on a primitive trail along the left side of the stream, but at about the same time the water disappears the trail also disappears. From there on it is a steep, strenuous climb up the dry, rocky streambed to the saddle. Once you reach the saddle on the south side of the peak you will see a good 0.2-mile footpath that leads the rest of the way to the top. The summit is clearly visible for most of the last two miles; it seems so close while you are on the trail, but so far away when the trail runs out.

Lower Waterfall Canyon
An alternative to the Taylor Canyon-Malans Peak trail described above is to start the hike in Lower Waterfall Canyon. To reach the Waterfall Canyon Trailhead,

Mount Ogden

a notch in the side of the canyon wall, through which it is possible to climb out. The route is not technically difficult, but it is a strenuous hand over hand scramble, and the notch is filled with loose rocks. The greatest danger is being struck by a loose rock dislodged by another climber. Soon the scramble becomes an uphill walk, and after about 600 feet of elevation gain you will cross over a ridge and see Upper Waterfall Canyon below. In the bottom of the canyon you will find a primitive trail that leads upstream to a junction with the Malans Peak Trail.

drive to the end of 29th Street, then turn right onto a dirt road that leads to a large public parking area. The parking lot is on the east side of a high-rise apartment building. A sign at the back of the parking lot marks the beginning of a 1.2-mile-long trail to the Waterfall Canyon Waterfall.

This is a good trail as far as it goes, but once you reach the 200-foot waterfall you must exit the canyon and do some steep, off-trail climbing to get around it. About 100 feet to the right of the waterfall there is

Some hikers do a loop hike up Waterfall Canyon, across Malans Peak, and down Taylor Canyon, with Mount Ogden as a possible side trip. If you do this I recommend you go up Waterfall and down Taylor—not the other way around. It is much easier and less dangerous to climb up the detour around the waterfall rather than down.

Looking south from the summit of Mount Ogden

Deseret Peak

★

Distance:	8.4 miles (loop)
Walking time:	6³/₄ hours
Elevations:	3,613 ft. gain/loss Mill Fork Trailhead (start): 7,418 ft. Deseret Peak: 11,031 ft.
Trail:	Most of the trail is well maintained and easy to follow. A portion of the return path, however, is not well maintained and can occasionally be confusing.
Season:	Midsummer through mid-fall. The upper parts of the trail are usually covered with snow from November through late June.
Vicinity:	Near Grantsville and Tooele
Maps:	Deseret Peak East, Deseret Peak West *(USGS)*
Information:	http://www.utahtrails.com/deseretpeak.html *(Utah Trails)* http://www.fs.usda.gov/uwcnf/ *(Uinta-Wasatch-Cache Nat. Forest)* phone: (801) 236-3400 *(Salt Lake Ranger District)*

Drive west from Salt Lake City on I-80 for about 20 miles, then turn onto Highway 36 (exit 99) and drive south toward Tooele for 3.5 miles. When you reach Mills Junction, turn west onto Highway 138 and drive another 11 miles to Grantsville. On the west side of Grantsville you will see a sign directing you to South Willow Canyon. Turn left here and continue for 5.1 miles, then turn right onto South Willow Canyon Road. South Willow Canyon Road ends after 7.3 miles, the last 4 miles of which are unpaved. At the end of the road, just beyond the Loop Campground, you will see a parking area and a sign marking the Mill Fork Trailhead.

Most of the western third of Utah, locally known as the West Desert, lies in an interesting geologic province called the Great Basin. The Great Basin is a vast, semi-arid desert that extends from the Wasatch Front, across Nevada, all the way to the Sierra Nevada mountains of California. The desert is not unbroken, though. It contains a number of narrow, isolated mountain ranges, running mostly in a north-south direction and separated by long desert valleys. This hike will take you to the highest peak in the

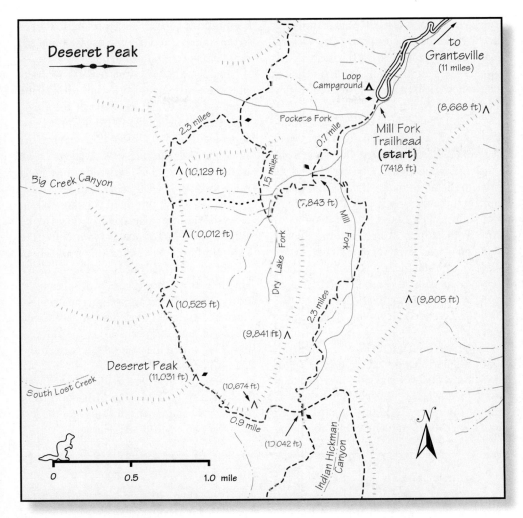

Deseret Peak

to Grantsville (11 miles)

Loop Campground

Pockets Fork

∧ (8,668 ft)

Mill Fork Trailhead **(start)** (7418 ft)

2.3 miles

Big Creek Canyon

∧ (10,129 ft)

0.7 mile

1.5 miles

∧ (7,843 ft)

∧ (10,012 ft)

Dry Lake Fork

Mill Fork

∧ (10,525 ft)

∧ (9,805 ft)

2.3 miles

(9,841 ft) ∧

Deseret Peak (11,031 ft) ∧

∧ (10,674 ft)

South Lost Creek

0.9 mile

(10,042 ft)

Indian Hickman Canyon

N

0   0.5   1.0 mile

Stansbury Mountains, a particularly promi-nent mountain range in the West Desert just west of Salt Lake City. The Stansbury Range rises an impressive 6,000 feet above Skull Valley in slightly more than four miles, and it is also one of the few ranges in Utah's West Desert with a good system of developed hiking trails. The uniqueness of the range was recognized in 1984, when it was selected for the creation of the Deseret Peak Wilderness Area.

From the Loop Campground the trail proceeds up South Willow Canyon for 0.7 mile to Dry Lake Fork. Here the trail splits, with the right path proceeding up Dry Lake Fork to the Willow Lakes and the left path continuing on to Mill Fork. Turn left onto the Mill Fork Trail. For the next 2.3 miles the path meanders up Mill Fork, crossing several picturesque meadows along the way with nice views of Deseret Peak, your destination. Finally, after an elevation gain of 2,200 feet, the trail comes to a saddle at the head of the drainage where you will see a 4-way trail junction.

The junction is only 990 feet below the summit, and there are few trees at this eleva-tion to block the view. The two trails on the left side of the junction lead to Bear Fork and

Antelope Canyon. You will want to turn right here to continue your climb up to the Deseret Peak summit ridge. The trail switchbacks up another 500 feet to the crest of the ridge and then follows it in a northwesterly direction for the last 0.4 miles to the summit.

Several of northern Utah's most prominent features can be seen from the top of Deseret Peak, including the Great Salt Lake and the Wasatch Front. Stansbury Island, 25 miles to the north in the Great Salt Lake, is thought to be an extension of the Stansbury Mountains. The island and the mountains were both named after Captain Howard Stansbury who first surveyed the area in 1850. To the southeast it is usually possible to make out Mount Nebo, the highest peak in the Wasatch Mountains. And to the west, 20 miles across Skull Valley, lie the Cedar Mountains.

After leaving Deseret Peak the loop trail continues northward, staying on the top of the summit ridge for about 0.4 mile and then dropping down 200-300 feet below the west side of the ridge. The trail is not as well maintained here and there may be some confusion at times. But there are few trees at this altitude, and you can occasionally see parts of the trail far ahead.

Finally, 1.6 miles after leaving the summit, the trail makes an abrupt turn to the right, crosses to the east side of the ridge, and starts down again toward South Willow Canyon. About 0.7 mile after leaving the ridge the trail intersects the Willow Lakes trail, where you should turn right. From that point the path is much more distinct.

As shown on the map, it is possible to cross the summit ridge and drop down to the Willow Lakes Trail about 0.4 mile before the main trail does so. Doing this saves about a mile of walking, but is unlikely to save any time as it is much easier to walk on the trail. You will recognize this alternative route because the Forest Service has placed an 8-foot-high juniper pole on the ridge at the point where the route departs from the main trail.

After you meet the Willow Lakes trail it is an easy walk back to Mill Fork, from where you can retrace your steps for the last 0.7 mile to the Mill Fork Trailhead.

Looking north from the summit of Deseret Peak

Little Hole

★

Flaming Gorge National Recreation Area
shuttle car required
day hike

Distance:	6.9 miles (plus 8.9 miles by car or bicycle)
Walking time:	3³/₄ hours
Elevations:	220 ft. loss boat ramp parking area (start): 5,780 ft. Little Hole: 5,560 ft.
Trail:	Very popular, well maintained trail. Because of its popularity with fishermen the Little Hole Trail has been designated as a National Recreation Trail.
Season:	Spring, summer, fall. There is often snow on the trail during the winter months.
Vicinity:	Flaming Gorge National Recreation Area, near Vernal
Maps:	Dutch John, Goslin Mountain *(USGS)* Flaming Gorge *(Trails Illustrated, #704)*
Information:	http://www.utahtrails.com/littlehole.html *(Utah Trails)* http://www.fs.fed.us/r4/ashley/ *(Ashley National Forest)* phone: (435) 784-3445 *(Flaming Gorge Ranger District)*

Drive north from Vernal on Highway 191 for 41 miles until you reach the Flaming Gorge Dam. Continue on past the dam for another 0.3 mile until you see a road leaving on the right near a sign that says "River Access". Turn here and continue another 0.9 mile to a large parking lot above the boat launching area. A short footpath descends from the parking area to the boat ramp, where the Little Hole Trail begins.

To get to Little Hole, where the hike ends, you must return to Highway 191 and continue driving north. After 2.3 miles you will come to a junction where the Little Hole Road begins. Turn right here and drive another 5.9 miles to the Little Hole parking area. This is where you should leave your shuttle car or bicycle.

The Little Hole Trail is an exceedingly scenic walk that winds through the bottom of Red Canyon on the north shore of the Green River. The canyon's brilliant

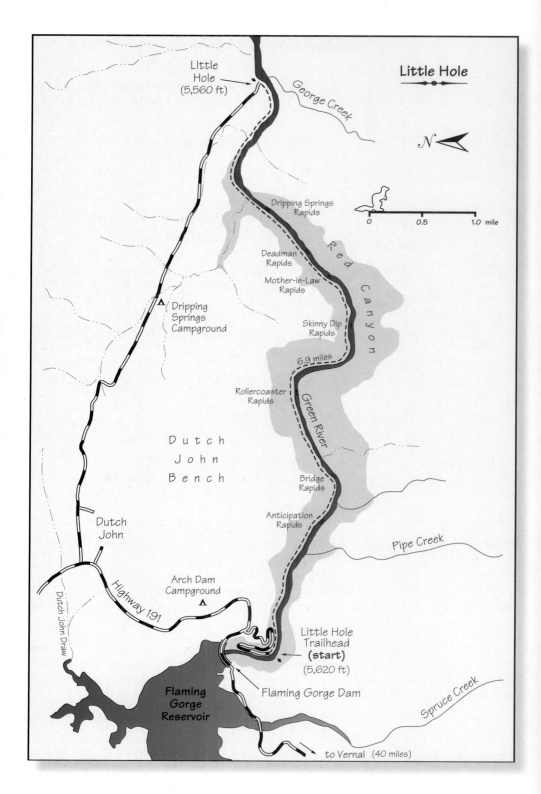

Little Hole
(5,560 ft)

George Creek

Little Hole

N

0   0.5   1.0 mile

Dripping Springs
Rapids

Red Canyon

Deadman
Rapids

Mother-in-Law
Rapids

Dripping
Springs
Campground

Skinny Dip
Rapids

6.9 miles

Rollercoaster
Rapids

Green River

D u t c h

J o h n

B e n c h

Bridge
Rapids

Anticipation
Rapids

Pipe Creek

Dutch
John

Arch Dam
Campground

Highway 191

Dutch John Draw

Little Hole
Trailhead
(start)
(5,620 ft)

Flaming Gorge Dam

Flaming
Gorge
Reservoir

Spruce Creek

to Vernal (40 miles)

Red Canyon of the Green River

From the boat ramp parking lot below Flaming Gorge Dam a sign will direct you to a small footpath, about 0.2 mile long, that descends to the boat ramp. You will find the Little Hole trailhead just beyond the boat ramp on the downstream side. The scenery starts almost immediately, as the red shale and sandstone cliffs of the Mancos Formation colors so impressed John Wesley Powell on his expedition down the Green River in 1869 that he named it the Flaming Gorge. A century later, in 1964, the 502-foot-high Flaming Gorge Dam submerged most of Powell's spectacular canyon with water, but a small section of it, Red Canyon, still remains below the dam to remind us of how the Flaming Gorge got its name.

In the past thirty years, since the creation of Flaming Gorge National Recreation Area, the Forest Service has developed Red Canyon as a premier sport fishing area, and you are likely to encounter dozens of fishermen along the Little Hole Trail. If you crave solitude this is the wrong hike, but, for me, watching the fly fishermen ply their skill is an added bonus. Few rivers offer a more perfect setting for fishing than the Green, and Red Canyon is kept abundantly stocked with rainbow, brown, and cutthroat trout. Trout as large as 22 pounds have been caught here.

This hike can be done in either direction. The west-to-east route described here is best if you are hiking in the afternoon, as the sun will then be at your back. If, however, you are planning a morning hike, you can avoid having the sun in your face by starting at Little Hole rather than the dam.

soar on either side of the river to a height of 600 feet. For the next four miles the elevation of the canyon rim steadily increases, finally reaching a height of 1,000 feet above the water.

A series of small rapids breaks the monotony of the clear water, with whimsical names like Rollercoaster, Skinny Dip, and Mother-in-Law. The rapids are usually not particularly hazardous, but it is fun to watch the boaters negotiate them. After the first two miles there is a noticeable decline in the number of fishermen, but their numbers begin to pick up again along the last two miles of the trail. Finally, after six miles, the river emerges from Red Canyon and widens somewhat as it approaches Little Hole.

Red Canyon of the Green River

Jones Hole

★★★

Dinosaur National Monument
day hike

Distance:	8.0 miles (round trip)
Walking time:	4³/₄ hours
Elevations:	540 ft. loss/gain Jones Hole Trailhead (start): 5,560 ft. Green River: 5,020 ft.
Trail:	Easy well-marked trail
Season:	Spring, summer, fall. Hiking is also sometimes possible in the winter, if the road is open.
Vicinity:	Dinosaur National Monument, near Vernal
Maps:	Jones Hole *(USGS)* Dinosaur National Monument *(Trails Illustrated, #220)*
Information:	http://www.utahtrails.com/joneshole.html *(Utah Trails)* http://www.nps.gov/dino/ *(Dinosaur National Monument)* phone: (970) 374-3000 *(Visitor Center)*

Drive east out of Vernal on 500 North Street. The road forks about a mile from town; take the left fork and follow the signs to Jones Hole. After six miles you will pass the turnoff to Island Park. Do not take this turn, but continue straight on the paved road for another 33 miles to the Jones Hole Fish Hatchery. The trail starts at the south end of the Fish Hatchery, about two hundred yards from the visitors parking area.

Jones Hole is the name given to a 2,000-foot-deep gorge that runs along the border between Utah and Colorado in Dinosaur National Monument. Jones Hole Creek, in the bottom of the gorge, is fed from a number of small springs at the head of the canyon and along its sides. The trail begins just below the first spring, at the Jones Hole Fish Hatchery, and winds pleasantly along the creek for about four miles to join the Green River in Whirlpool Canyon. The creek bed is a lush green oasis surrounded by the semiarid land of Dinosaur National Monument. At times the trail climbs away from the water into the sagebrush and pinion-juniper forest that surrounds it, but mostly it stays very close to the canyon floor where boxelders, cottonwoods, and other water-

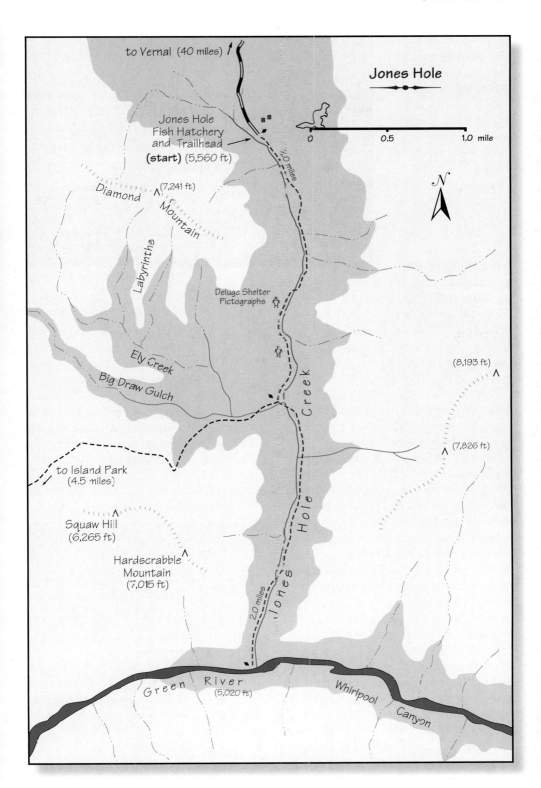

to Vernal (40 miles)

Jones Hole
0   0.5   1.0 mile

Jones Hole
Fish Hatchery
and Trailhead
(start) (5,560 ft)

1.0 miles

Diamond

Mountain

(7,241 ft)

Labyrinths

Deluge Shelter
Pictographs

Ely Creek

Jones Hole Creek

Big Draw Gulch

(8,193 ft)

(7,826 ft)

to Island Park
(4.5 miles)

Squaw Hill
(6,265 ft)

Hardscrabble
Mountain
(7,015 ft)

2.0 miles

N

Green River
(5,020 ft)

Whirlpool Canyon

hungry trees prevail. The creek is also an important source of water for the monument's wildlife, and it is not uncommon to see deer–especially in the early hours of the day.

Jones Hole Creek, above Ely Creek

From the visitors parking area of Jones Hole Fish Hatchery walk downstream for a few hundred feet, past the fish tanks, to the southern end of the complex. Here you will see a sign on the east side of the creek marking the trailhead. The trail stays on the same side of the creek for just over a mile. For most of the way the path is very near the water, although at one point it leaves the creek to meander briefly through the pinion-juniper forest on the left bank. The vegetation changes dramatically just a short distance from the water's edge.

After a half-hour walk the trail crosses a small footbridge, giving hikers the opportunity to see two interesting archeological sites on the west bank. Excavations at the Deluge Shelter site in 1965-67 showed that Jones Hole has been occupied intermittently by at least fifteen separate Indian cultures over the past 7,000 years. The cultural layers exposed by the excavation proved to be unusually well defined, and the information gained has contributed significantly to the puzzle of America's prehistoric past.

Both of the Jones Hole archeological sites contain well preserved examples of prehistoric Indian rock art that, although many hikers use this trail, are remarkably unvandalized. Enjoy the centuries-old art, but please watch that no one in your group does anything to deface the precious remnants of our past. Don't even touch them, as the oils in our fingers can cause significant damage.

Shortly after passing the second archeological site you will come to the confluence of Ely Creek and Jones Hole Creek. There is a small camping area here for overnighters. This is the only place in Jones Hole where camping is permitted, but permits must be obtained in advance from the Dinosaur National Monument Visitor Center. Ely Creek is also worth exploring. It flows out of an area known as the Labyrinths, a rugged maze of backcountry canyons, only about a mile northwest of the confluence.

Pictographs at Deluge Shelter

Sharp-eyed hikers may notice a change in the geologic structure of Jones Hole as they pass Ely Creek. Above this point the canyon cuts through the Weber Sandstone Formation, while below Ely the canyon floor enters an older formation of limestone and shale. This 200-million-year-old sedimentary formation bears testimony to the existence of an ancient sea that once covered the area, and fossil remains of the sea's inhabitants can often be found in the limestone.

The trail ends two miles below Ely Creek where Jones Hole Creek joins the Green River. If you are hiking in the summer you will probably see at least one party of river runners here. The Green River is very popular with rafters, and Jones Hole is a favorite overnight stop. There are several camp sites nearby, but the sites are reserved for rafters and are off limits to hikers.

Island Park

An interesting extension to this hike, for those wishing to sample the semidesert environment above Jones Hole, is the trail connecting Jones Hole to Island Park. This trail leaves Jones Hole from the backpacker's campground and follows Ely Creek for about a half mile. It then climbs 800 feet up the south side of Big Draw Gulch to the plateau above and continues in a generally southwesterly direction. Beyond this climb the trail is not difficult, but ample water should be carried as it is a hot, dry walk. The trail ends in Island Park near Ruple Ranch, 6.5 miles from the Ely Creek Campground. With a little advance planning a car can be spotted at Ruple Ranch

for the drive back to the trailhead at Jones Hole Fish Hatchery. An 18-mile-long gravel road leads from Ruple Ranch to the paved Jones Hole Road, and from there it is another 33 miles back to the fish hatchery.

The first two miles of the trail from Jones Hole to Island Park are well defined. Unfortunately, however, the Park Service no longer maintains the trail, and in a few places above Big Draw Gulch it can be difficult to follow. If you want to do this hike I recommend you take along a compass and a good map of the area (the USGS Jones Hole and Island Park quadrangles are ideal). The area is fairly flat and obstacle-free, so loosing the trail is not a serious problem if you have a compass and a good map.

One of the things that makes the Island Park hike so interesting is the extremely large number of deer in the area—especially in the spring. In the spring of 1995 I counted more than 50 deer (mostly doe with their newborn fawns) within a mile of Ruple Ranch!

One final note: Their seems to be a large disagreement over the distance from Jones Hole to Ruple Ranch. One Park Service signs says 8.0 miles, another says 4.7 miles, and a popular map says 7.7 miles. I stand by my estimate of 6.5 miles.

Island Park

Kings Peak

★★★★★

High Uintas Wilderness Area
4-day hike

Distance:	31.6 miles (round trip)
Walking time:	day 1: 5¼ hours
	day 2: 5¼ hours
	day 3: 8½ hours
	day 4: 4 hours
Elevations:	5,080 ft. gain/loss
	Henrys Fork Trailhead (start): 9,430 ft.
	Dollar Lake: 10,785 ft.
	Gunsight Pass: 11,888 ft.
	Anderson Pass: 12,700 ft.
	Kings Peak: 13,528 ft.

Trail: The trail is well marked and easy to follow as far as Anderson Pass. There is no trail, however, for the last 0.8 mile from Anderson Pass to the summit. The final assent to the peak requires a tiring scramble up about 800 feet of talus.

Season: Midsummer to mid-fall. The upper parts of the trail are usually covered with snow from mid-November until mid-July. The most pleasant time for the climb is late August, when the days are still relatively long but the meadows have dried out and the mosquitoes have abated.

Vicinity: North slope of the High Uintas Wilderness Area, near Evanston, Wyoming

Maps: Gilbert Peak, Bridger Lake, Mount Powell, Kings Peak (*USGS*) High Uintas Wilderness (*Trails Illustrated, #711*)

Information: http://www.utahtrails.com/kingspeak.html (*Utah Trails*)
http://www.fs.usda.gov/uwcnf/ (*Uinta-Wasatch-Cache Nat. Forest*)
phone: (307) 782-6555 (*Mountain View Ranger District*)

Drive east from Evanston, Wyoming, on I-80 for 35 miles, then take exit 39 south onto Highway 414. Drive south on Highway 414 for 6 miles to the town of Mountain View, where you must turn right on Highway 410 toward the farming village of Robertson. 6.8 miles from Mountain View, just before you reach Robertson, you will come to a junction where

Highway 410 makes an abrupt bend to the west and a wide gravel road continues straight ahead to the south. Continue south at this point on the gravel road. 12.3 miles after leaving the highway you will come to a major fork in the road. The right fork leads to China Meadows while the left fork leads to Henrys Fork Trailhead. Bear left at this point and continue for another 10.7 miles, following the signs to the Henrys Fork Trailhead.

As you probably know, Kings Peak is the highest point in Utah, and as you might imagine, this hike is a very popular one. According to Forest Service estimates the Henrys Fork Basin receives about 5,000 visitors annually. Many come for the express purpose of climbing Utah's highest mountain, but many more come just to enjoy the abundant scenic beauty of the area and perhaps do a little fishing in the basin's half dozen lakes. Late summer is the most popular time to visit Henrys Fork, but some visitors also enjoy cross country skiing in the basin during the winter months. Henrys Fork Trailhead is one of the few trailheads on the north slope of the High Uintas that is accessible all year round.

The mountain was named after Clarence King, who in 1878 became the first director of the U.S. Geological Survey. Interestingly, it wasn't until 1966 that the USGS determined Kings Peak to be the highest peak in Utah. Before then it was thought that South Kings Peak, 0.8 mile further south and 16 feet lower was the higher of the two.

Although the climb to the top of Kings Peak is very strenuous it is not technically difficult, and about the only requisite for the trip is good physical condition. Furthermore, the view from the top is extraordinary. Even if it were not the highest point in the state, the assent of Kings Peak would still be one of Utah's best hikes.

Henrys Fork is the closest trailhead to Kings Peak; hence it is the most popular place to begin the hike. But many varia-

Kings Peak, viewed from Anderson Pass

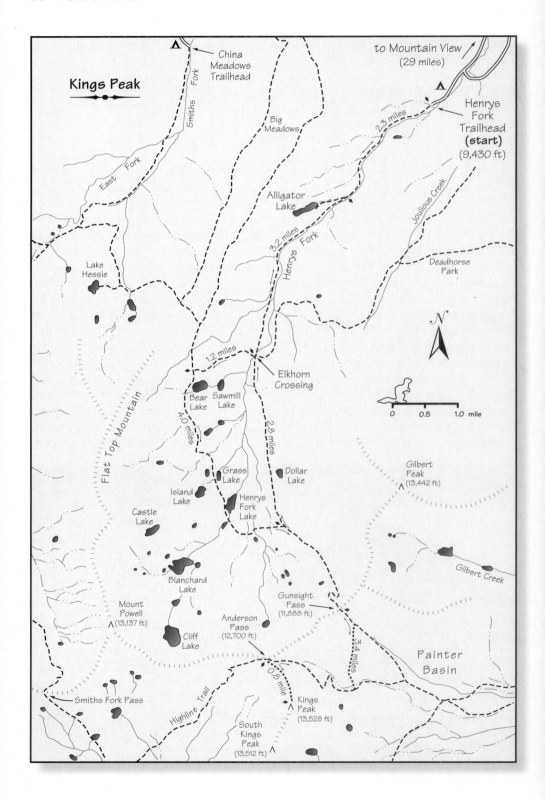

Kings Peak

China Meadows Trailhead

to Mountain View (29 miles)

Smiths Fork

Big Meadows

2.3 miles

Henrys Fork Trailhead **(start)** (9,430 ft)

East Fork

Joulious Creek

Alligator Lake

3.2 miles

Henrys Fork

Deadhorse Park

Lake Hessie

N

0   0.5   1.0 mile

1.2 miles

Elkhorn Crossing

Flat Top Mountain

Bear Lake

Sawmill Lake

4.0 miles

2.8 miles

Gilbert Peak (13,442 ft)

Grass Lake

Dollar Lake

Island Lake

Castle Lake

Henrys Fork Lake

Gilbert Creek

Blanchard Lake

Mount Powell (13,137 ft)

Gunsight Pass (11,888 ft)

Anderson Pass (12,700 ft)

Cliff Lake

3.4 miles

Painter Basin

Smiths Fork Pass

Highline Trail

0.8 mile

Kings Peak (13,528 ft)

South Kings Peak (13,512 ft)

Henrys Fork Basin and Gunsight Pass

ten minutes from the trailhead. Watch for a large pile of rocks on the south side of a wooden boardwalk that crosses a small drainage. At that point you will see the trail to Alligator Lake branching off to the right of the main trail. The lake is 0.4 mile up the drainage at the end of the spur. Alligator is a surprising large lake— about 600 yards long by 150 yards wide. There are a number of fine campsites on the lake's south shore, and it is a good place to spend the night if you are getting off to a late start.

5.5 miles from the trailhead the trail breaks out of the trees onto the northern end of a large meadow. There is a major trail junction here between the Henrys Fork Trail, which runs south along Henrys Fork, and the North Slope Trail, which crosses it in an east-west direction. The junction is called Elkhorn Crossing.

From Elkhorn Crossing you can either proceed south on the Henrys Fork Trail or you can turn right and follow the North Slope Trail for a short distance to the West Side Loop Trail. The two routes converge again just below Gunsight Pass; hence you can get to Kings Peak by following either trail. For the sake of diversity I suggest you take the West Side Loop Trail on your way up the peak and use the Henrys Fork Trail for your return trip. If you choose to do this turn right at Elkhorn Crossing and proceed west on the North Slope Trail (Forest Service Trail #105).

About half an hour after leaving Elkhorn Crossing you will arrive at the West Side

tions of this hike are also possible. If you spend an hour on the summit in mid-August you will probably meet other climbers who have walked up from every direction. Many hikers approach Kings Peak from the south slope along Yellowstone Creek or the Uinta River. Others come from Hoop Lake or Spirit Lake on the eastern side of the Uintas. And a surprising number of people begin their hike at Mirror Lake, 40 miles to the west. Looking down from the top with a good pair of binoculars you can usually see hikers far below inching their way east or west along the Highline Trail toward Anderson Pass, just north of the summit.

Day 1 (7.1 miles)

From the trailhead parking area the trail follows along the west side of Henrys Fork, climbing ever so gently at a grade you will hardly notice. The creek, usually about 20 feet below the trail, is pristine, and the forest is densely wooded with lodgepole pine. It is a very pleasant walk.

The first major point of interest along the way is Alligator Lake, located at the end of a short spur trail about an hour and

Loop Trail junction. Turn south here and continue toward Bear Lake and Henrys Fork Lake. There are several signs in this area indicating that you are now on the Highline Trail, but these signs are in error. The real Highline Trail (Forest Service Trail #25) is still many miles to the south. You won't reach it until you have crossed the Uinta Divide at Gunsight Pass.

Five minutes after leaving the junction between the North Slope Trail and the West Side Loop Trail you should see the calm waters of Bear Lake flickering through the trees on your left. There is no trail to the lake, but it is only 100 yards off the trail. There are many good campsites around Bear Lake and it is a fine place to stop for the day. You can also visit Sawmill Lake, a slightly smaller lake 200 yards farther down the drainage from the east end of Bear Lake.

Day 2 (6.8 miles)

Between Bear Lake and the bottom of Gunsight Pass you will pass by several more picturesque lakes, the largest of which is Henrys Fork Lake. 0.3 mile after leaving Henrys Fork Lake the trail passes by a tiny cabin that has been used for many years as a sheep herders' bivouac. Henrys Fork Basin is heavily grazed during the summer months and you will almost certainly see sheep while you are there. Many hikers are offended by the sights and sounds of domestic animals in this high wilderness valley. They do contaminate the water sources and destroy the wildflowers, but for me the sounds of their bells and their baa-a-a-as drifting through the alpine valley seem to add a certain tranquility to the pastoral scene.

Finally, 3.8 miles from Bear Lake, the West Side Loop Trail crosses Henrys Fork Basin to end at Henrys Fork Trail. The elevation at this point is 11,000 feet, just above timber line, and there are few trees. A mile to the southeast you can see Gunsight Pass, a deep notch in the Uinta Divide where the trail crosses to the South Slope. And south, above the basin you can see Anderson Pass and Kings Peak. Your route to the summit will be along the ridge south of Anderson Pass.

The trail climbs slowly up the east side of Henrys Fork Basin until it reaches the top of Gunsight Pass. If it is late in the day you might want to establish a camp on the northern side of Gunsight Pass rather than continuing into Painter Basin. There is a flat grassy area beside a small pond just below the northern side of the pass. The elevation here is 11,460 feet, about 430 feet below the top of the pass. If time permits, however, I suggest you continue another 2.0 miles across the pass and into Painter Basin where you will find a

Camping below the north side of Kings Peak

View from Gunsight Pass into Painter Basin

Soon you will cross a small drainage, and not long afterward you will intersect the Highline Trail. From there it is only 1.7 miles up the Highline to the top of Anderson Pass.

At Anderson Pass you must leave the trail and start picking your way up the ridge to the top of the peak. There are cliffs on the west side of the ridge, but the slopes are more gradual on the east side. You will see occasional cairns, but they really don't do much good. It is pretty obvious where you are going, and there is really no easy way. It is just a matter of making your way slowly upward over the jumble of jagged boulders, and if you are persistent the goal will be reached in about an hour.

One of the most astonishing features of the view from Kings Peak is the vastness of the panorama. Other than a few threadlike trails in the basins below there are virtually no signs of human activity. The nearest road is ten miles away and the nearest town is twice that distance. Another striking feature is the number of lakes that can be seen. More than a dozen large lakes in Garfield, Henrys Fork, Atwood, and Painter Basins are visible. But probably the most notable characteristic is the amount of land that is above timberline (about 11,000 ft.) and devoid of trees. In fact the Uintas have more square miles of land in the Arctic-Alpine Tundra Life Zone than any other mountain range, outside Alaska, in the United States.

The descent from Kings Peak back to Anderson Pass is even more tricky than the assent, so be careful. There are many loose rocks, and I can't think of a worse place to break a leg. Once you reach the pass,

better place to camp.

About 0.6 mile below the south side of Gunsight Pass you will see a less distinct trail veering off to the right along the foot of the cliffs. The main trail continues southeast across Painter Basin for 1.0 mile before doubling back to the west, so you can save a lot of time by taking the less distinct shortcut south through the basin below the bottom of the cliffs. This shortcut trail eventually fades and disappears, but that isn't a problem. Just continue due south in the grassy meadow along the base of the talus slope. About 0.7 mile after leaving the main trail you will see a fresh water spring flowing out of the rocks at the edge of the meadow. This area is an excellent place to stop and make camp for the night.

Day 3 (10.1 miles)

Painter Basin is only 2.9 miles from the top of Kings Peak, but you still have a 2,120-foot elevation gain to deal with as well as some off-trail scrambling. There is no trail for the last 0.8 mile. Also, remember you can't walk as fast at the high altitude. Leave your packs at your camp and get an early start so you will have plenty of time for a leisurely lunch at the top.

From the spring continue walking south along the western side of Painter Basin.

however, it is a very pleasant walk back to Painter Basin. Some people spend a second night at the Painter Basin campsite, but if you want to complete the trip in the allotted four days you should pack your belongings and walk down to Dollar Lake for the third night.

Dollar Lake is probably the most beautiful of all the lakes in Henrys Fork Basin. Unfortunately it is heavily used by campers, and many other hiking books encourage you to camp elsewhere. But if you can find a site it really is an exquisite place to spend the night. The lake is surrounded by a grove of tall Engelmann spruce, and there is a marvelous afternoon view of Kings Peak from its southern shore.

The lake is not visible from the trail and there is no established trail leading to it; consequently it is easy to miss. When you reach the trail junction below Gunsight Pass where the West Side Loop Trail departs, make a note of the time and continue straight ahead on the Henrys Fork Trail. After about 15 minutes you will leave the meadow and enter into a large grove of spruce. Within ten minutes after entering the trees you should see one or two small cairns on the right side of the trail. Leave the trail at this point and walk due east for 200 yards and you will run into the lake. The main trail continues north for another 300 yards before entering the meadow again. If you come to the point where the trail leaves the trees it means you have gone too far.

Day 4 (7.6 miles)

From Dollar Lake back to the trailhead is only 7.6 miles and it is downhill all the way. There are no more lakes to explore, but there is plenty of otherwise fine scenery. The first 2.0 miles follow the east side of the meadow to Elkhorn Crossing. This is prime moose habitat and you probably have at least a fifty-fifty chance of seeing one if you are observant. At Elkhorn Crossing the trail crosses to the west side of Henrys Fork. Look for the footbridge about 100 yards downstream from the point where the main trail fords the creek. Once you are back on the west side of Henrys Fork you can simply retrace your original footsteps back to the trailhead.

Dollar Lake (Kings Peak in the distance)

Red Castle Lakes

★★★★

Distance:	25.0 miles (round trip)
Walking time:	day 1: $7^3/_4$ hours day 2: $3^3/_4$ hours day 3: $6^1/_4$ hours
Elevations:	3,010 ft. gain/loss Cache Trailhead (start): 9,340 ft. Bald Mountain Ridge: 11,530 ft. Lower Red Castle Lake: 10,760 ft. Red Castle Lake: 11,300 ft.
Trail:	The trail is generally well marked and easy to follow.
Season:	Midsummer to mid-fall. The trails around the Red Castle Lakes are usually covered with snow from mid-November until July.
Vicinity:	North slope of the High Uintas Wilderness Area, near Evanston, Wyoming
Maps:	Lyman Lake, Mount Powell *(USGS)* High Uintas Wilderness *(Trails Illustrated, #711)*
Information:	http://www.utahtrails.com/redcastle.html *(Utah Trails)* http://www.fs.usda.gov/uwcnf/ *(Uinta-Wasatch-Cache Nat. Forest)* phone: (307) 789-3194 *(Evanston Ranger District)*

Drive east from Kamas on the Mirror Lake Highway (Highway 150) toward Evanston, Wyoming. After driving 47 miles you will pass the Bear River Ranger Station on your right, and another 2.2 miles will bring you to a well marked gravel road leading to Lyman Lake and the Blacks Fork River. This is Forest Road No. 58, popularly known as the North Slope Road. Turn right here and *stay on Road No. 58 for the next 18.6 miles, following the signs to East Fork Blacks Fork. The road is used by logging trucks and is badly washboarded in a few places, but it is still suitable for ordinary cars. After 18.6 miles you will see another road branching off to the right (Road No. 65) with a sign that says "East Fork Blacks Fork Trailhead, 6 miles". Turn right here and drive for 4.9 miles to another sign that says "Bear River-Smiths Fork Trail". This trail crossing, sometimes called the Cache Trailhead, is where the hike begins. The small dirt road on the left leads to a convenient parking area near a gravel pit about*

100 yards from the main road. The trail runs about 150 feet to the south of the gravel pit.

Hikers planning a trip to the scenic Red Castle Lakes on the north slope of the High Uintas generally have two different trails to choose from: the East Fork Smiths Fork Trail or the Bald Mountain Trail. The first route, beginning at China Meadows and following the East Fork Smiths Fork all the way to its source, is the most popular route. The East Fork Smiths Fork Trail is very well maintained and has a total elevation gain (to Lower Red Castle Lake) of only about 1,280 feet. The Bald Mountain Route, on the other hand, is much more strenuous. It begins at East Fork Blacks Fork and climbs over Bald Mountain Ridge before reaching the lower lake, achieving an elevation gain of 2,190 feet. Both trails are within a quarter-mile of the same length.

I have chosen here to describe the Bald Mountain route to the Red Castle Lakes, primarily because it is the more scenic of the two. The additional 900 feet of elevation gain is compensated for by the fine views that can be had from Bald Mountain Ridge. The trail follows the grassy, treeless ridge at an elevation of 11,500 feet for almost two miles before dropping down to the East Fork Smiths Fork drainage, and Red Castle Peak occupies a prominent place on the skyline for almost the entire distance.

The most interesting way to see the Red Castle Lakes is to hike in on the Bald Mountain Trail and hike out on the East Fork Smiths Fork Trail to China Meadows. Not many people do this, however, because the two trailheads are 50 miles apart. (See pages 48-49 for instructions on how to get to China Meadows.)

Day 1 (9.2 miles)

From Cache Trailhead the Bear River-Smiths Fork Trail heads east and, after about 200 yards, crosses the East Fork Blacks Fork Creek. It will be necessary to get your feet wet here, as there is no bridge and no stepping stones crossing the creek.

Red Castle Peak, as viewed from Bald Mountain Ridge

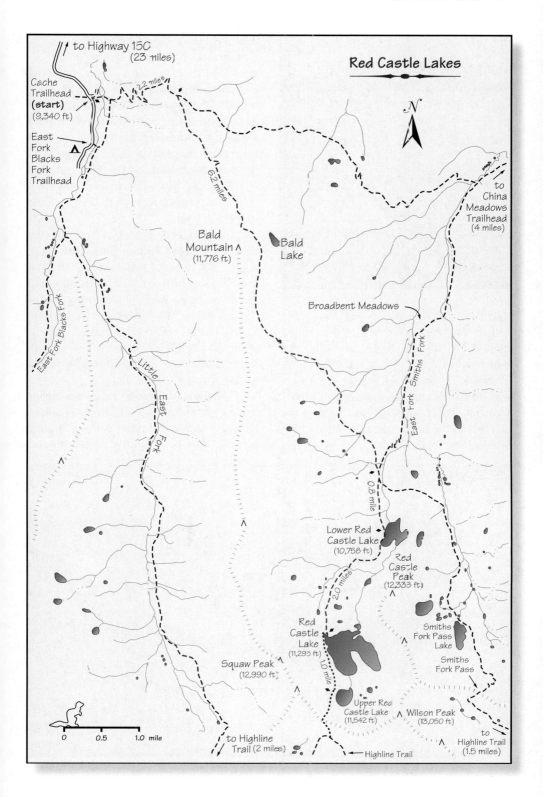

Red Castle Lakes

to Highway 150
(23 miles)

Cache
Trailhead
(start)
(9,340 ft)

2.2 miles

East
Fork
Blacks
Fork
Trailhead

6.2 miles

to
China
Meadows
Trailhead
(4 miles)

Bald
Mountain ∧
(11,776 ft)

Bald
Lake

Broadbent Meadows

East Fork Blacks Fork

East Fork Smiths Fork

Little East Fork

0.8 mile

Lower Red
Castle Lake
(10,758 ft)

Red
Castle
Peak
(12,333 ft)

2.0 miles

Red
Castle
Lake
(11,295 ft)

Smiths
Fork Pass
Lake

Smiths
Fork Pass

Squaw Peak
(12,990 ft)

1.0 mile

Upper Red
Castle Lake
(11,542 ft)

Wilson Peak
(13,050 ft)

to
Highline Trail
(1.5 miles)

0   0.5   1.0 mile

to Highline
Trail (2 miles)

Highline Trail

Trail below Bald Mountain

Normally the water is only ankle deep, but if there has been a lot of rain you might want to consider beginning your hike 0.6 mile farther down the road at the East Fork Blacks Fork Trailhead, where the Forest Service has constructed a bridge. There is a convenient connecting trail joining the east side of the bridge with the Bear River-Smiths Fork Trail. Of course, if you do this the hike will be 0.6 miles longer.

Once it crosses the river the trail almost immediately starts upward, gaining a little over a thousand feet in the next two miles. After reaching the top of the ridge it temporarily levels out and meets the Bald Mountain Trail junction. Bear to the right here, as indicated by the sign. Soon the path begins to climb again and within a mile you will be above timberline. Bald Mountain (11,776 ft.) is the large, gently sloping dome in front of you.

At its highest point the trail passes within 0.3 mile of the top of Bald Mountain. If you want to make a detour to the summit it is an easy off-trail walk with only 250 feet of elevation gain. On the other side of the trail, about 300 yards to the east is Bald Lake. The lake is so close it almost seems as though you could hit it from the trail with a stone, but because it is 450 feet lower it is seldom visited.

From Bald Mountain the trail continues to meander along the top of Bald Mountain Ridge for another 1.3 miles before dropping into the East Fork Smiths Fork drainage.

Bald Lake

The Red Castle

The remaining three miles to Lower Red Castle Lake is a beautiful walk through scattered forest and meadow land, with lots of water and good camping spots. If you got off to a late start you won't have any problem finding a place to spend the night. This is also a summer grazing area for sheep ranchers, and you will probably see signs of sheep if not the sheep themselves.

Finally, a mile after the trail reaches East Fork Smiths Fork, you will come to Lower Red Castle Lake. There are several good camping spots near the trail on the

Sheep herder above Lower Red Castle Lake

west side of the lake, and the views of Red Castle Peak are fabulous, After supper you will probably want to spend an hour beside the lake watching the reflections while the last rays of sunset transform the Castle into a glowing ember of red. But please note that campfires are prohibited in this area.

Day 2 (6.0 miles)

From Lower Red Castle Lake it is a pleasant 6-mile round trip hike to the two upper Red Castle Lakes. The scenery is excellent, but there are no good camping spots at Red Castle or Upper Red Castle Lake, so leave your camp at the lower lake. The trail continues up the west side of Lower Red Castle Lake, then bends around the west side of the Castle, finally reaching Red Castle Lake on its northern shore. Red Castle Lake is 537 feet higher than Lower Red Castle which places it well above timberline. Consequently, there are no trees whatsoever around the higher lake.

From this vantage point you can see that Red Castle Peak is actually the end of a short ridge that extends northward from Wilson Peak on the Uinta Crest. The formation seems oddly out of place because although the Uinta Crest is composed almost entirely of gray colored Precambrian quartzite the Red Castle is composed primarily of sandstone and shale based material. As a result the castle-shaped peak is not only a different color than the other surrounding peaks, but it has eroded into an entirely different form. Because of the contrast, this rugged peak is probably the most picturesque summit in the entire range.

On the northwestern corner of Red Castle Lake you will find a well cairned trail leading up the talus slope toward Upper Red Castle Lake. The route is not difficult, and the elevation gain to Upper Red Castle is only 247 feet. Upper Red Castle Lake is a small, rocky pond about 200 yards in diameter. It is fed entirely from the melting snows on the higher slopes of Red Castle Basin and it is not very deep; hence its size varies a great deal from year to year.

The primitive trail from Red Castle Lake does not stop at Upper Red Castle Lake, but continues upward to a small pass on the ridge 628 feet above Upper Red Castle. The extensive Highline Trail is only 0.2 mile south of this low point on the ridge; hence there are many possibilities for extended backpacking trips from Upper Red Castle Lake. Squaw Pass, for instance, is 3.5 miles west along the Highline Trail, and from there it is possible to walk back along the Little East Fork Trail to Cache Trailhead where the hike began. Another possibility: Kings Peak, the highest point in Utah, is only ten miles further east along the Highline Trail.

Day 3 (9.2 miles)

The hike back to Cache Trailhead from Lower Red Castle Lake is just the reverse of Day 1. The return is much less tiring, however, since the elevation gain required to get back on Bald Mountain Ridge is only 770 feet, and from there the hike is all downhill.

Red Castle Lake

Amethyst Lake

★★★

Distance:	13.0 miles (round trip)
Walking time:	day 1: 4¼ hours day 2: 4 hours
Elevations:	1,950 ft. gain/loss Christmas Meadows Trailhead (start): 8,790 ft. Amethyst Meadow: 10,360 ft. Amethyst Lake: 10,740 ft.
Trail:	Reasonably good trail most of the way, but very rocky in places. Can also be muddy in spots, especially in early summer before all of the snow has melted. A compass is useful for finding Ostler Lake.
Season:	Midsummer through mid-fall. The higher parts of the trail are usually covered with snow from November until mid-July.
Vicinity:	High Uintas Wilderness Area, near Evanston, Wyoming
Maps:	Christmas Meadows (*USGS*) High Uintas Wilderness (*Trails Illustrated, #711*)
Information:	http://www.utahtrails.com/amethystlake.html (*Utah Trails*) http://www.fs.usda.gov/uwcnf/ (*Uinta-Wasatch-Cache Nat. Forest*) phone: (307) 789-3194 (*Evanston Ranger District*)

Drive east from Kamas on Highway 150 toward Evanston, Wyoming. 6 miles from Kamas you will pass a Forest Service booth where you must purchase a recreation pass to hike in the area ($3.00/day for each vehicle). You will pass the Mirror Lake turnoff about 31.5 miles from Kamas. Continue on past this turnoff for another 14.3 miles to a small bridge where Highway 150 crosses *the Bear River. 0.4 mile beyond the bridge, on the right, you will see the road to Christmas Meadows Campground. (Do not be confused by the turnout to Stillwater Campground, nearer the bridge.) Take the Christmas Meadows road and drive 4.3 miles to the end of the road, where you will see the Christmas Meadows (Stillwater) Trailhead and parking area.*

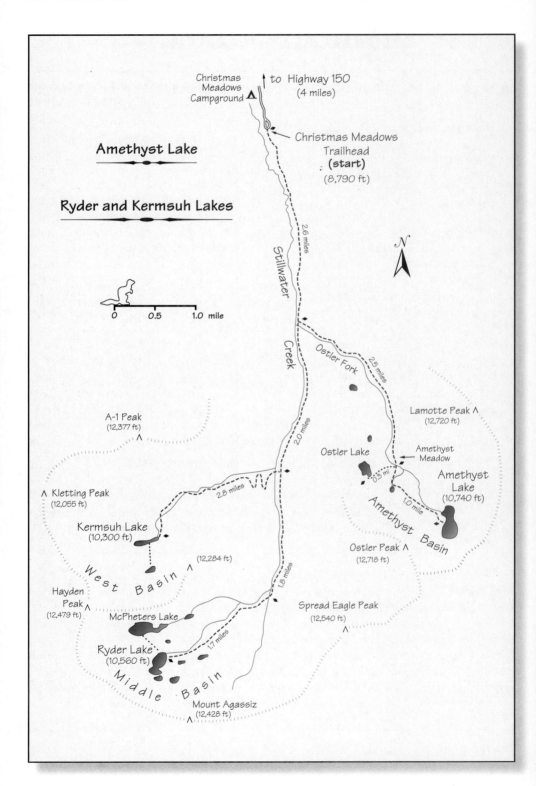

Christmas
Meadows
Campground △

to Highway 150
(4 miles)

Christmas Meadows
Trailhead
(start)
(8,790 ft)

Amethyst Lake

Ryder and Kermsuh Lakes

0   0.5   1.0   mile

2.6 miles

Stillwater

Ostler Fork

2.5 miles

Creek

Lamotte Peak ∧
(12,720 ft)

A-1 Peak
(12,377 ft)
∧

2.0 miles

Ostler Lake

Amethyst
Meadow

∧ Kletting Peak
(12,055 ft)

Amethyst
Lake
(10,740 ft)

0.3 mi

2.8 miles

Amethyst

1.0 mile

Kermsuh Lake
(10,300 ft)

Basin

(12,284 ft)

Ostler Peak ∧
(12,718 ft)

W e s t   B a s i n ∧

Hayden
Peak ∧
(12,479 ft)

McPheters Lake

1.8 miles

Spread Eagle Peak
(12,540 ft)
∧

Ryder Lake
(10,560 ft)

1.7 miles

M i d d l e   B a s i n

Mount Agassiz
(12,428 ft)
∧

N

Easily accessible from Salt Lake City, the hike to Amethyst Lake is one of the most popular hikes into the rugged, north-slope drainages of the High Uintas. The Uinta Mountains are bisected by a long, winding spine of Precambrian rock that runs for a hundred miles in an east-west direction across northeastern Utah. The north and south facing slopes of this ridge are punctuated by two dozen glacier-carved valleys that all end abruptly against the quartzite cliffs of the cordillera. Amethyst Lake is located in the back of one of these alpine valleys at the headwaters of the Stillwater Drainage.

Day 1 (5.9 miles)

For the first two miles the trail to Amethyst Lake meanders along the east side of Christmas Meadows, a pleasant, open grassland surrounding Stillwater Creek. This is a popular fishing area, and there are usually a few fly fishermen along the creek. The meadow is also favored by grazing animals, and it is not uncommon to see deer and moose grazing nearby. So many people visit Christmas Meadows now that in the last 20 years the moose have become almost tame.

Shortly after leaving Christmas Meadows you will encounter a forest service sign informing you that you are entering the High Uintas Wilderness Area, and five minutes later the trail forks. A smaller sign has been nailed to a tree at the junction instructing hikers that they should take the left fork,

leading away from Stillwater Creek, to reach Amethyst Lake.

Soon after leaving Stillwater Creek the trail abruptly becomes much steeper, gaining 600 feet in the first half mile. The route is also very rocky here, and hikers carrying a backpack should take care not to twist an ankle. The monotony of the tiring climb is broken by several picturesque cascades along Ostler Creek only a few feet from the trail. After the first half mile the grade decreases, and the trail settles down to a more gradual but steady climb upward. Occasionally the path breaks briefly out of the trees to give hikers fine views of Ostler and LaMotte Peaks, which lie just above the lake. Then, 2.5 miles after leaving Stillwater Creek, the trail enters Amethyst Meadow, a picture-book wetland with a stunning view of Ostler Peak on its south side.

Amethyst Meadow is an ideal place to make camp, and I suggest you pitch your tent here. Although Amethyst Lake is only another mile up the trail it is much harder to find good camp sites along its rocky shores. In consideration of others, however, please pitch your tent at least a few hundred feet from the trail and away from the water.

You will probably have a little time left

Ostler Lake

for some afternoon exploring after you have set up camp, but I suggest you save Amethyst Lake for the morning and check out Ostler Lake. At the edge of Amethyst Meadow, just beyond the point where the trail crosses Ostler Creek, you will see a sign that says "Ostler Lake, ¹/₂ mile". Unfortunately there is no reliable trail to Ostler Lake, but it isn't too hard to find if you have a compass. From the sign, head straight into the woods along a compass bearing of about 240 degrees (slightly south of magnetic west). After walking 0.3 mile and gaining 250 feet of elevation you will cross a rocky ridge and be greeted by Ostler Lake.

The lake is roughly circular in shape, about 700 feet in diameter. If you can arrange to be on the north shore of the lake an hour before the sun goes down, and if the wind is calm, you will see an unforgettable reflected view of Ostler Peak in the shaded water.

Day 2 (7.1 miles)

Before returning to the trailhead you will want to visit Amethyst Lake, the highlight of the trip. After the trail crosses Ostler Creek it continues south for about 0.2 mile along the west side of a smaller stream. Don't cross the stream until you arrive at the unnamed lake from which the stream flows. This small but scenic lake (400 feet in diameter) is also a good place to camp if you prefer to spend the night next to a lake.

Upon reaching the unnamed lake the trail crosses the stream and heads east into the basin. Amethyst Lake is about 0.8 mile further. The trail may be hard to follow in the early summer when snow covers parts of it, but don't worry too much about staying on the trail. Just proceed into the basin, keeping the talus slopes of Mount Ostler on your right, and as the valley gets narrower you will soon run into the lake. Amethyst Lake lies in the extreme southern corner of Amethyst Basin at an elevation of 10,740 feet. The lake is quite large – 850 feet across and a half mile long, and is enclosed on three sides by the rocky slopes of the 12,000-foot Ostler-LaMotte ridge.

Amethyst Lake

Ryder and Kermsuh Lakes

 ★★★★

Distance:	22.6 miles (round trip)
Walking time:	day 1: 6¹/₂ hours day 2: 5 hours day 3: 4 hours
Elevations:	1,770 ft. gain/loss Christmas Meadows Trailhead (start): 8,790 ft. Ryder Lake: 10,560 ft. Kermsuh Lake: 10,300 ft.
Trail:	Good trail, but very rocky in places. Can also be muddy in spots, especially in the early summer before all of the snow has melted. A compass is useful for finding McPheters Lake.
Season:	Midsummer through mid-fall. The higher parts of the trail are usually covered with snow from November through mid-July.
Vicinity:	High Uintas Wilderness Area, near Evanston, Wyoming
Maps:	Christmas Meadows, Hayden Peak *(USGS)* High Uintas Wilderness *(Trails Illustrated, #711)*
Information:	http://www.utahtrails.com/ryder.html *(Utah Trails)* http://www.fs.usda.gov/uwcnf/ *(Uinta-Wasatch-Cache Nat. Forest)* phone: (307) 789-3194 *(Evanston Ranger District)*

Drive east from Kamas on Highway 150 toward Evanston, Wyoming. 6 miles from Kamas you will pass a Forest Service booth where you must purchase a recreation pass to hike in the area ($3.00/day for each vehicle). You will pass the Mirror Lake turnoff about 31.5 miles from Kamas. Continue on past this turnoff for another 14.3 miles to a small bridge where Highway 150 *crosses the Bear River. 0.4 mile beyond the bridge, on the right, you will see the road to Christmas Meadows Campground. (Do not be confused by the turnout to Stillwater Campground, nearer the bridge.) Take the Christmas Meadows road and drive 4.3 miles to the end of the road, where you will see the Christmas Meadows (Stillwater) Trailhead and parking area.*

Ryder and Kermsuh Lakes are the other two major lakes, besides Amethyst Lake, that lie within the Stillwater Drainage of the High Uintas Wilderness Area. When ancient glaciers were carving the glove-shaped valley during the past ice age three large fingers were gouged out of its southern flanks. Today we call these depressions Amethyst Basin, West Basin, and Middle Basin. These high mountain basins became natural places for the formation of tarns when the glaciers melted; hence the presence of Ryder, Kermsuh, and Amethyst lakes. Amethyst Lake, of course, is located in Amethyst see map page 62 Basin. Kermsuh Lake is in West Basin and Ryder is in Middle Basin. All are surrounded almost entirely by the billion-year-old Precambrian quartzite cliffs that define the Uinta Crest.

Day 1 (8.1 miles)

For the first 2.6 miles the trail to Kermsuh and Ryder Lakes is the same as the trail to Amethyst Lake (page 61). The path winds lazily along the eastern side of Christmas Meadows. Moose are common in this area, and if you gaze out into the meadow from time to time there is a good chance of seeing at least a moose cow or young bull. Don't count on seeing an older bull, however, as they are much more reclusive than the younger males. There are also a lot of beaver in the meadow as evidenced by the fallen aspen along the way. Beaver seem to prefer aspen to the other trees—probably because the wood is softer and less resinous.

After about two miles Christmas Meadows and most of the quaking aspen are left behind; the canyon floor narrows, and the creek begins to run a little faster. At this point the forest is predominantly lodgepole pine, with some scattered Engelmann spruce. Soon you will encounter a Forest Service sign informing you that you have crossed the northern boundary of the High Uintas Wilderness Area, and a few minutes later you will see the trail to Amethyst Lake leaving on the left. Keep to the right here, continuing to follow along the left bank of the Stillwater Creek.

The trail continues on for another 2.0 miles, climbing very gradually along the canyon floor until it comes to the next trail junction. As you walk you will begin to see glimpses of A-1 Peak through the trees on your right and Mount Agassiz straight ahead. These rocky peaks, reaching 3,000 feet above Stillwater Creek, are a preview of what lies ahead. Finally, at a point that is directly magnetic east of A-1 Peak, the trail forks again and a small sign on a tree indicates the way to Kermsuh Lake on the right. You should make a mental note of this trail junction because you will be

Unnamed lake in Middle Basin below Hayden Peak

taking the Kermsuh Lake trail on the return from Ryder, and it is easy to miss the sign when walking in the opposite direction. For now, however, continue straight ahead along the creek.

The trail continues for another 1.8 miles beyond the Kermsuh Lake trail junction before leaving Stillwater Creek. Finally, at an elevation of 9,870 feet, the path crosses the creek and begins climbing for the last 1.7 miles into the Middle Basin. But when you reach this point you will probably want to pause for a while before continuing because the scenery is delightful. A clearing in the forest presents you with an marvelous view of Mount Agassiz across a grassy meadow.

McPheters Lake

If it is late summer the meadow will be filled with wildflowers.

From Stillwater Creek the trail climbs rather steeply for 0.5 mile, then levels out for another beautiful, gentle walk through the high alpine meadows toward the back of the basin. It is a stunning approach to the lake. For almost 360 degrees around you can see the rocky cliffs that surround Middle Basin, and as you progress westward you will see Hayden Peak rising up on your right. Finally, after passing several ponds, you will cross a small rise in the land to see the large lake in front of you. Ryder Lake is some 600 feet wide and a third off a mile long. It is surrounded by Engelmann spruce, and there are some very nice camping sites on the eastern side. Frequently there are no other people camping at the lake, and if you are there on one of those days it will feel as if you own the entire Middle Basin.

Day 2 (7.1 miles)

If you have time after breaking camp, you should take a short side hike to McPheters Lake, only 0.4 mile northwest of Ryder. If you have a compass, select a heading

Ryder Lake

due northwest of Ryder. If you don't have a compass just head for the lowest point in the ridge east of Hayden Peak. You should see the lake after a fifteen-minute walk and an elevation gain of 240 feet. McPheters, about the same size as Ryder, is reputed to be deeper and there are said to be some large fish in the bottom of the Lake. There are not many trees around the lake, however, and the camping is far nicer at Ryder.

From the Middle Basin you must backtrack to Stillwater Creek and down to the Kermsuh Lake Trail that you passed on the way to Ryder Lake. Again, the trail to Kermsuh Lake rises rather steeply for about 0.5 mile after leaving Stillwater, but soon settles down to a very pleasant walk through a series of meadows to the back of West Basin. Finally, 2.8 miles from Stillwater Creek and 920 feet higher in elevation, you will come to Kermsuh Lake.

Kermsuh is somewhat smaller than either Ryder or McPheters Lakes—about 400 feet wide and 500 yards long—and, although the scenery is quite dramatic, the camp sites are not as nice as those at Ryder. Most people camp on the south end of the lake, but unfortunately the water is to shallow on that side for good fishing. The best fishing opportunities are on the north side of Kermsuh where the water is deeper.

The summit of Hayden Peak lies less than a mile southwest of Kermsuh, and the mountain's steep talus slopes seem so close that there couldn't possibly be any other nearby lakes in that direction. But, surprisingly, there is another lake. If you walk 0.3 mile due south from Kermsuh, gaining 170 feet in elevation, you will come to another small tear drop-shaped lake about 500 feet long. This tiny unnamed lake is too shallow to support fish, but the view from its rocky shore beneath Hayden Peak is breathtaking.

Day 3 (7.4 miles)

From Kermsuh Lake it is an easy downhill walk back to Stillwater Creek and on through Christmas Meadows to the trailhead. The total distance is 7.4 miles, and the elevation loss is 1,510 feet.

West Basin

Brown Duck Mountain Loop

★★

High Uintas Wilderness Area
bicycle useful
4-day hike

Distance:	34.0 miles (loop)
Walking time:	day 1: 5³/₄ hours
	day 2: 4³/₄ hours
	day 3: 6¹/₄ hours
	day 4: 6¹/₂ hours
Elevations:	4,320 ft. gain/loss
	Lake Fork Trailhead (start): 8,200 ft.
	Atwine Lake: 10,160 ft.
	Cleveland Pass: 11,200 ft.
	Tworoose Pass: 10,660 ft.
Trail:	The trails are generally well maintained and well marked.
Season:	Midsummer to mid-fall. Because of the high elevations, the trails are usually covered with snow from mid-November until early July.
Vicinity:	High Uintas Wilderness Area, near Duchesne
Maps:	Kidney Lake, Tworoose Pass, Explorer Peak, Oweep Creek *(USGS)*
	High Uintas Wilderness *(Trails Illustrated, #711)*
Information:	http://www.utahtrails.com/brownduck.html *(Utah Trails)*
	http://www.fs.fed.us/r4/ashley/ *(Ashley National Forest)*
	phone: (435) 722-5018 *(Roosevelt Ranger District)*

Take Highway 40 east of Heber for 70 miles (or Highway 191 north of Helper for 44 miles) until you reach the town of Duchesne. From Duchesne take Highway 87 north for 16 miles, then turn left on the paved road leading to Mountain Home and Moon Lake. The road ends at the Moon Lake Campground 34 miles from Duchesne.

The Brown Duck Trail leaves Lake Fork Trail just outside the Moon Lake Campground, and ideally the Lake Fork Trailhead would also be located adjacent to the campground. But because of the large number of horseback riders using the trails the Forest Service has established a separate trailhead and parking area 0.8 mile back down the road from the camping area. Long term car parking is not allowed in the camping area, but if you have

a bicycle you can save a few extra steps by riding it to a point nearer the Brown Duck Trail. The best place to lock up your bicycle for a few days is at the lake shore access parking area. From there a short connecting trail follows the shoreline for 0.2 mile to the well marked junction where the Brown Duck Trail begins.

This hike is perfect for fishing enthusiasts looking for an extended trip into a high alpine wilderness area. The trail passes by no fewer than nine good fishing lakes, with short side trips leading to at least ten more. The route circles Brown Duck Mountain (11,866 ft.), passing through Brown Duck Basin, East Basin and Squaw Basin, and it features many fine views of the mountain's rocky peaks and cold, clear lakes. Most of the lakes lie at elevations of around 10,400 feet. The highest point is at the top of Cleveland Pass where the trail climbs out of East Basin and drops down into Squaw Basin. Cleveland Lake, frozen most of the year, lies near the top of the pass at an elevation of 11,172 feet.

Brown Duck Mountain is a favorite des-tination for horseback riders, so if you are put off by piles of horse manure along the trail and in the meadows then this is not the best hike for you. The most popular location for campers with pack animals is East Basin (day 2), a lush, green area with gorgeous meadows and a half-dozen small lakes. It is not unusual to see twenty or thirty horses and mules grazing in the meadows beside the East Basin lakes. Fortunately there are other off-trail places to camp in the basin that are just as pretty but without the livestock.

Day 1 (6.8 miles)

As explained earlier, the easiest place to begin this hike is the lake shore access parking area adjacent to the Moon Lake Campground. From there a small trail leads

Unnamed lake in the East Basin

Brown Duck Mountain

west along the side of the lake for 0.2 mile to the Lake Fork Trail. Soon after you reach the Lake Fork Trail you will see a small sign marking the beginning of the Brown Duck Trail on the left.

If you are starting from the official Lake Fork Trailhead, 0.8 mile down the road from the campground, you will see another sign directing you along an old jeep road that eventually meets the Brown Duck Trail higher up the mountain. Don't take this route. Instead, follow the Lake Fork Trail in a direction parallel to the road for 0.8 mile, then turn left onto the Brown Duck Trail when you reach the trail junction just described. The hike along the jeep road is 0.2 mile further and the scenery is much less interesting.

The first 0.5 mile of the Brown Duck Trail, from where it leaves the shore of Moon Lake, is the steepest part of this entire hike. After making two long switch backs and climbing about 400 feet above the lake the trail settles down to a gradual incline that will continue for most of the first day. Initially the

trail is immersed in a forest of lodgepole pine, but as you gain elevation you will see the trees gradually replaced with Engelmann spruce and subalpine fir, which seem to do better above 9,000 feet.

After 1.0 mile the trail merges with the old jeep road that originated at the Lake Fork Trailhead and follows it for another 1.3 miles. Then, almost immediately, the road ends and a foot path begins. If you are observant you will see the tell-tale signs of mining activity above the end of the road—an indication of what the road was originally built for. Thank goodness the High Uintas are now a protected wilderness area, and prospecting is no longer allowed.

Just beyond the end of the jeep road

Trail north of Clements Lake

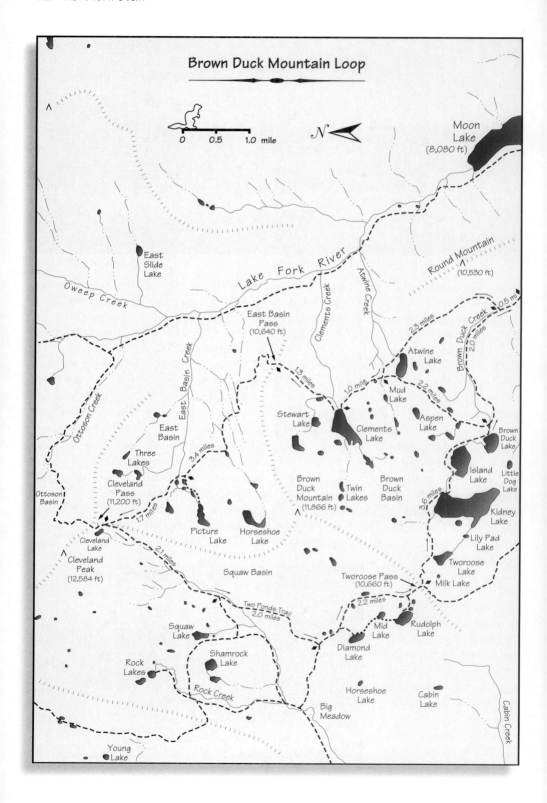

Brown Duck Mountain Loop

0   0.5   1.0 mile

N

Moon Lake (8,080 ft)

East Slide Lake

Oweep Creek

Lake Fork River

Atwine Creek

Round Mountain (10,530 ft)

Brown Duck Creek

0.5 mi

East Basin Pass (10,640 ft)

East Basin Creek

Clements Creek

2.3 miles

2.0 miles

1.3 miles

Atwine Lake

1.0 mile

2.2 miles

Ottoson Creek

East Basin

Three Lakes

3.4 miles

Stewart Lake

Mud Lake

Clements Lake

Aspen Lake

Brown Duck Lake

Cleveland Pass (11,200 ft)

Ottoson Basin

1.7 miles

Picture Lake

Horseshoe Lake

Brown Duck Mountain (11,866 ft)

Twin Lakes

Brown Duck Basin

Island Lake

Little Dog Lake

3.6 miles

Kidney Lake

Cleveland Lake

Cleveland Peak (12,584 ft)

2.1 miles

Squaw Basin

Lily Pad Lake

Tworoose Lake

Milk Lake

Tworoose Pass (10,660 ft)

2.2 miles

Two Ponds Trail 2.0 miles

Squaw Lake

Shamrock Lake

Mid Lake

Rudolph Lake

Rock Lakes

Diamond Lake

Rock Creek

Big Meadow

Horseshoe Lake

Cabin Lake

Cabin Creek

Young Lake

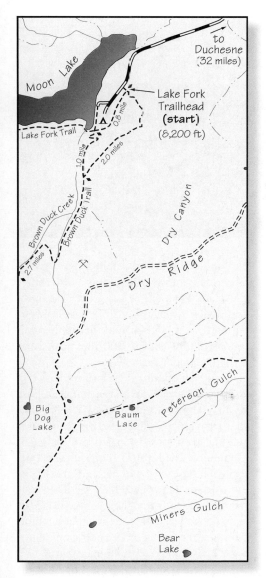

the trail swings north to cross Slate Creek, and soon afterward it crosses the official boundary of the High Uintas Wilderness Area. From that point on the Brown Duck Trail never strays far from the south shore of Brown Duck Creek.

About a half hour after leaving the wilderness boundary you should see a trail junction marked by a small wooden sign nailed to a tree on the right. This is the beginning of the trail to Atwine Lake, and you must leave the Brown Duck Trail here. You will have to cross the river at this point—the only place on the entire hike where you must get your feet wet. Be sure to find a good strong stick to help with the river crossing. The current is often strong, but it is seldom more than knee deep.

The Atwine Lake Trail is not nearly as well frequented as the Brown Duck Trail; consequently it may be difficult to follow in places. Basically it heads uphill for a half mile until it reaches the rocky base of Round Mountain, and then it turns northwest along more level terrain toward the lake. The trail passes by the north side of two small meadows before reaching the lake. Try not to make noise as you approach the meadows and you may be lucky enough to see an elk, deer, or moose. If there are any large grazing animals in the meadows they will usually be found along the perimeter near the edge of the forest.

The trail first reaches Atwine Lake on its northeastern shore, which is also the best place to make camp. If there are any other campers at Atwine they will probably be on the west side, near the better used East Basin Trail. Atwine is a large, relatively undisturbed lake with heavy timber growing right to the water's edge. The lake has never been dammed and it appears to be in pristine condition. Furthermore, since there are no good pastures around the lake it is seldom used by campers with pack animals. Most visitors prefer to make camp at the better known Kidney, Island, Brown Duck, or Clements Lakes, but in my opinion Atwine Lake is the prettiest, by far, of the basin's five major lakes.

Day 2 (7.0 miles)

From the trail junction on the north side of Atwine Lake continue northward toward East Basin. After only a half hour you will come to Clements Lake, a large lake about twice the size of Atwine with an earthen dam across its eastern side. Clements is a popular fishing lake, well stocked with cutthroat and brook trout, but it is not a particularly scenic lake. Like all dammed lakes its water level fluctuates with the seasons and the shoreline is marred by dead trees and mud flats.

East Basin Lake

Nearly all of the lakes surrounding Brown Duck Mountain eventually drain into Moon Lake Reservoir, an important reservoir used by the farmers of Duchesne County, and most of the lakes have been dammed in order to increase the water storage capacity of the watershed. It is now illegal to build dams in a designated wilderness area, but these dams were built long before the 1984 creation of the High Uintas Wilderness Area.

1.3 miles beyond Clements Lake the trail climbs out of Brown Duck Basin, crosses East Basin Pass (10,630 ft.), and drops down into the East Basin. The climb to the top of the pass is so gradual you will scarcely know you are going uphill. As you start down the other side, however, the trail gets much steeper and more rocky. Then, when you break out of the trees you will suddenly

be confronted with a marvelous view of fifty square miles of Uintas wilderness. Cleveland Peak (12,584 ft.), the next day's destination, is clearly visible four miles to the northwest, and beyond that is the long line of 12,000- and 13,000-foot peaks that form the Uinta Crest.

From the bottom of East Basin Pass it is an easy 3.4-mile walk to the center of East Basin. Along the way you will pass by a small meadow wedged between the trail and the steep rocky slopes of Brown Duck Mountain. The last time I was on this trail I saw a moose cow and her calf grazing in this meadow—they must have felt a sense of security knowing that their habitat was protected on at least one side by the mountain. I am sure the young moose calf would have made a tasty meal for a mountain lion.

Before starting up the slope toward Cleveland Pass the trail passes by the east side of an exceptionally pretty group of small lakes surrounded by the lush green East Basin Meadows. This area is a fine place to stop for the night, but unless you are very lucky you will probably find the meadows filled with pack horses and the best camp sites already occupied by their owners. As mentioned earlier, the East Basin area is an extremely popular destination among

East Basin

campers with pack animals.

If you crave solitude, don't despair. Just 0.8 mile off the trail is a seldom visited lake that may be the prettiest spot in the entire Brown Duck Mountain loop. It is called Picture Lake, and it is well named because it lies in a setting that is truly picture perfect. The lake is surrounded by timber with a small, wooded island in the center, and it lies just below an 11,789-foot peak of Brown Duck Mountain. There is usually snow on the mountain until late in the summer, sometimes extending down the slopes almost to the water. Best of all, horses cannot easily get to the lake, and since it is not on the main trail you are likely to have the lake all to yourself.

Although there is no path leading to Picture Lake, it is only a twenty-minute walk from the main trail. Just follow the drainage uphill from the southwest side of the lower group of lakes. After skirting around the last meadow and climbing 130 feet you will cross a low ridge, just beyond which is the lake. Picture Lake is about 150 yards wide by 500 yards long, and it lies at an elevation of 10,731 feet. There are a few small but pleasant campsites along its northern shore.

If you want to spend more time exploring the area there is another lake of similar size and elevation called Horseshoe Lake about 0.8 mile south of Picture Lake along the base of Brown Duck Mountain. I have never visited this lake, but it must also be very scenic. It lies directly north of the highest peak on Brown Duck Mountain. On the map it looks like an interesting cross-country hike would be to walk south from Picture Lake to Horseshoe lake, and then follow the drainage from the southern side of the lake back to the East Basin Trail.

Day 3 (9.0 miles)

From East Basin Meadows the trail climbs north for another 1.5 miles to the top of Cleveland Pass, the highest point on the hike. There is a small lake near the summit of the pass, but the most notable point

Picture Lake

Squaw Basin

should see another sign where the Two Ponds Trail joins Squaw Basin Trail. If you want to make a side trip to Squaw Lake or do some exploring elsewhere in Squaw Basin you should keep to the right at this point and continue walking down the Squaw Basin Trail. Otherwise turn left at the junction onto the Two Ponds Trail. The Two Ponds Trail is basically a shortcut to Brown Duck Basin. It is a relatively new trail and is not shown on most of the older maps, but it cuts about 2.2 miles off the total distance to Brown Duck Basin.

The Two Ponds Trail is about 2.0 miles long, ending when it reaches the trail to Tworoose Pass and Brown Duck Basin. Turn left when you reach the junction and proceed toward the pass, 2.2 miles away. Over the next 5.8 miles the Tworoose Pass Trail passes by no fewer than 6 lakes, so this is a good time to start thinking about where you plan to pitch camp for the night. In my opinion the best choices for a small group of backpackers are the first two lakes: Diamond and Rudolph. The short spur trail to Diamond Lake is 0.6 mile from the Two Ponds Trail junction. The trail is easy to see, but unfortunately there is no sign marking it. Just proceed along the Tworoose Pass

of interest is Cleveland Peak, just north of the pass.

When you descend from Cleveland Pass you will be following the Squaw Basin Trail which follows Squaw Basin Creek down the west side of the mountain. It is also possible to make another loop hike back to Moon Lake by continuing north from Cleveland Pass on the Ottoson Basin Trail. That trail eventually runs into the Lake Fork Trail which follows Lake Fork River back to Moon Lake. The hike described here is much more scenic, though. Once you drop into Lake Fork Canyon there isn't much to see except tall trees.

2.1 miles after leaving Cleveland Pass you

Rudolph Lake

Island Lake

easily visible from the trail and there is no spur trail leading to it, but it isn't difficult to reach. Just walk down the trail from the top of the pass for 15 minutes, then turn south and walk downhill through the woods for another 150 yards. From there you should be able to see Tworoose Lake.

The next lake the trail passes is Kidney Lake, quickly followed by Island Lake and Brown Duck Lake. All three of these lakes have been dammed and made into reservoirs; hence they are not as scenic as some of the other lakes on this hike. Like Clements Lake, the fluctuating water levels have left their shores marred with dead trees and lifeless piles of bleached white rocks. Nevertheless, the lakes are well stocked with game fish and are very popular with campers.

Upon leaving Brown Duck Lake the trail follows the south side of Brown Duck Creek for 6.4 miles to Moon Lake, and then turns south for the final 15 minutes to the trailhead.

Trail for about fifteen minutes and then start watching the right side of the path for the trail junction. The spur trail is about 0.3 mile long, and there are some small campsites near the north end of the lake. The trail to Rudolph Lake is 1.9 miles from the Two Ponds Trail junction, or 0.2 mile before you reach the top of Tworoose Pass. This short trail is marked by a small sign at the junction, but it is easy to miss so keep your eyes open. The trail to Rudolph Lake is 0.4 mile long.

Day 4 (11.2 miles)

From Rudolph Lake to the Lake Fork Trailhead and the end of the hike is 11.2 miles, but it is nearly all downhill and should be easy walking. Almost the only part that is uphill is the 200-foot climb to get from Rudolph Lake to the top of Tworoose Pass.

Beyond Tworoose Pass the trail gradually descends into Brown Duck Basin, soon passing by Tworoose Lake. Tworoose Lake is not

Brown Duck Creek, near Island Lake

Grandaddy Basin

★★★★

Distance: 16.1 miles (loop)

Walking time: day 1: 5³/₄ hours
day 2: 5 hours

Elevations: 940 ft. gain/loss
Grandview Trailhead (start): 9,700 ft.
Hades Pass: 10,640 ft.
Grandaddy Lake: 10,300 ft.
Governor Dern Lake: 9,980 ft.

Trail: The trails in Grandaddy Basin are extremely popular. Most are well maintained and well marked with signs.

Season: Midsummer to mid-fall. Because of the high elevations, the trails are usually covered with snow from mid-November until July.

Vicinity: High Uintas Wilderness Area, between Heber and Duchesne

Maps: Grandaddy Lake, Hayden Peak *(USGS)*
High Uintas Wilderness *(Trails Illustrated, #711)*

Information: http://www.utahtrails.com/grandaddy.html *(Utah Trails)*
http://www.fs.fed.us/r4/ashley/ *(Ashley National Forest)*
phone: (435) 738-2482 *(Duchesne Ranger District)*

Take Highway 40 east of Heber for 52 miles (or west of Duchesne for 17 miles) to the intersection with Highway 208. Turn onto Highway 208 and drive north for 10.3 miles to Highway 35. When you arrive at Highway 35 turn left (west) and drive for another 12.9 miles, through the towns of Tabiona and Hanna, until you reach a clearly marked paved road on the *right leading up the North Fork of the Duchesne River to Grandaddy Basin. Turn here and proceed north. After 4.2 miles the pavement ends and becomes a graded gravel road. After 6.5 miles you will encounter a fork in the road with a sign pointing the way to Grandview Trailhead on the right (road 315). The road dead ends at the trailhead, 5.8 miles beyond the fork.*

The High Uintas Wilderness Area is a paradise for sport fishermen. More than a thousand lakes lie within the boundaries of the wilderness area, and according to Utah's Department of Wildlife Resources some 650 of them contain significant populations of game fish. The 170-acre Grandaddy Lake is the largest natural lake in the Uintas, and also one of the most popular. It is very scenic, easy to get to, and generally well stocked with cutthroat and brook trout.

Unfortunately, there are usually so many campers around Grandaddy Lake it is not possible to enjoy a real wilderness experience there. But there are many other lakes nearby that are not so well visited. There are over twenty lakes within a two-hour walk of Grandaddy. The fishing is good in most of them, and excellent campsites are easy to find.

There are also numerous other trails in Grandaddy Basin, and many variations of this hike are possible. The route outlined here is a loop tour of nine of the better known lakes. The minimum recommended time for the trip is two days, but one could easily spend a week in the basin–especially if catching fish is on the agenda. If you have more time to spare I suggest you establish a camp at one of the lakes and explore the other lakes on day trips.

Day 1 (8.4 miles)

From Grandview Trailhead the trail climbs gently upward through the lodgepole pine and Engelmann spruce forest for 2.2 miles before reaching Hades Pass, the entryway into Grandaddy Basin. At 10,640 feet above sea level–940 feet above the trailhead–Hades Pass is the highest point on the hike. The slope on either side of the pass is so gradual, however, that you will scarcely know you have reached the summit.

Just beyond the pass Heart Lake comes into view at the foot of East Grandaddy Mountain, and soon afterward you will reach Grandaddy Lake. Don't be discouraged at the number of hikers you encounter between

Grandaddy Lake

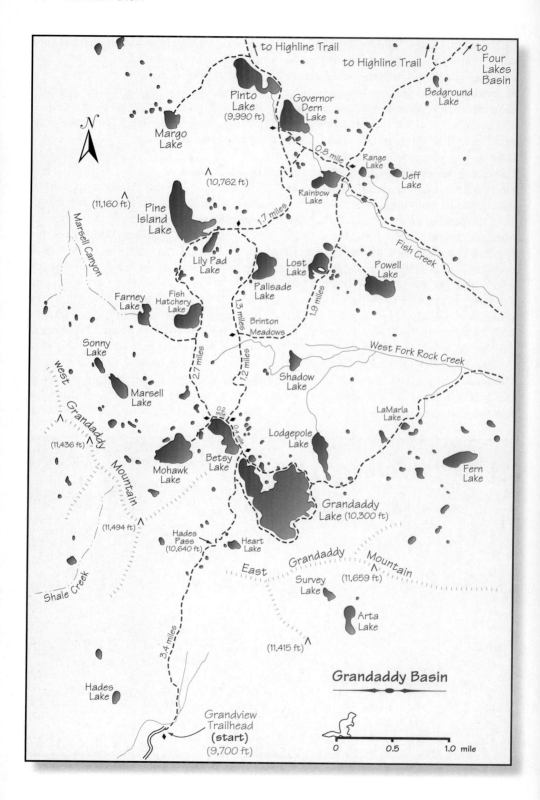

to Highline Trail

to Highline Trail

to Four Lakes Basin

Pinto Lake (9,990 ft)

Governor Dern Lake

Bedground Lake

Margo Lake

∧ (10,762 ft)

0.8 mile

Range Lake

Jeff Lake

∧ (11,160 ft)

Pine Island Lake

Rainbow Lake

Marsell Canyon

1.7 miles

Fish Creek

Lily Pad Lake

Lost Lake

Powell Lake

Farney Lake

Fish Hatchery Lake

Palisade Lake

Sonny Lake

1.3 miles

Brinton Meadows

1.9 miles

West Fork Rock Creek

2.7 miles

1.2 miles

Shadow Lake

Marsell Lake

west

Grandaddy

LaMarla Lake

∧ (11,436 ft)

0.2 mile

Mountain

∧

0.4 mile

Lodgepole Lake

Fern Lake

Mohawk Lake

Betsy Lake

Grandaddy Lake (10,300 ft)

∧ (11,494 ft)

Hades Pass (10,640 ft)

Heart Lake

East   Grandaddy   Mountain

Shale Creek

∧ (11,659 ft)

Survey Lake

Arta Lake

3.4 miles

∧ (11,415 ft)

Grandaddy Basin

Hades Lake

Grandview Trailhead **(start)** (9,700 ft)

0   0.5   1.0 mile

the trailhead and Grandaddy Lake. On some summer weekends there may literally be hundreds of hikers on this trail, but the great majority of them never go beyond Grandaddy Lake, 3.4 miles from the trailhead.

On the northwestern side of Grandaddy the trail splits with the right fork going to LaMarla Lake and beyond and the left fork continuing north into Grandaddy Basin. Bear to the left here and continue northward along the eastern shore of Betsy Lake. Then after 0.4 mile you will reach another junction. This is the beginning of the loop trail to Governor Dern Lake. The direction in which you walk the loop doesn't matter much, but for the sake of discussion I will assume that you turn left here onto the Pine Island Lake Trail.

Notice the side trail going to Mohawk Lake as the main trail leaves the north end of Betsy Lake. Mohawk is a little larger than Betsy, but still only about a third the size of Grandaddy. The spur trail is only 0.4 mile long over level ground, and there are some

nice campsites near the lake. It is a good alternative if you are looking for a secluded spot near Grandaddy Lake.

From Betsy Lake, the main trail continues north for 1.1 miles to Fish Hatchery Lake. The abundance of grass along the shore of Fish Hatchery is a good indication of the reduced number of campers here as compared to Betsy and Grandaddy. Just before you reach Fish Hatchery you will also see another spur trail leading to Farney Lake, 0.6 mile away. There are some fine camping sites around Farney Lake, but unfortunately it is too shallow for fish to survive the winter. Two other small lakes, Sonny Lake and Marsell Lake can also be reached by walking from Farney Lake through the timber for about 20 minutes along a bearing slightly west of magnetic south. The forest floor is quite level here and quite open, so the lakes are easy to find. They are both nestled against the north side of a low ridge that runs along the northeast side of West Grandaddy Mountain.

Pine Island Lake

Grandaddy Basin

Back on the Pine Island Lake Trail, the route next passes between Pine Island Lake and Lily Pad Lake. Again, Lily Pad is too shallow for good fishing, but that is not the case with Pine Island Lake. Pine Island (80 acres in area) is the second largest lake in the basin and the fishing is good. Unfortunately Pine Island Lake is a favorite destination for groups with pack animals, and the best camping area on the southern end of the lake is littered with horse manure.

0.3 miles after leaving Pine Island Lake you will come to the Palisade Lake Trail that heads south to Palisade Lake and Brinton Meadows. This trail offers a shorter return loop for those not wishing to continue to Governor Dern Lake. Palisade Lake, located 0.4 mile from the main trail is a very pretty lake with some good camping sites.

1.4 miles farther north from the junction with the Palisade Lake Trail is another shortcut trail leading to Rainbow Lake. Don't even consider taking this trail, because if you do you will miss Governor Dern Lake, which in my opinion is the prettiest of all the Grandaddy Basin Lakes. Governor Dern is much more open than most of the other lakes, with fine views of Mount Agassiz on the main ridge of the Uintas four miles further north. The lake is also completely surrounded with grass and has many fine campsites. Unfortunately Governor Dern Lake is rather shallow, and the fishing is not as good as at Pine Island and some of the other lakes in the vicinity.

Day 2 (7.7 miles)

There are a number of nice day hikes in the vicinity of Governor Dern Lake if you have the time to spend a few nights there. Pinto Lake is only 0.4 mile north, and the Highline Trail is only 2.5 miles farther along the Pinto Lake Trail.

One particularly interesting day hike from Governor Dern involves walking around a loop, past Pinto Lake, Margo Lake, Pine Island Lake, and back to Governor Dern Lake. A primitive trail leads to Margo Lake from the north side of Pinto. After you reach Margo, work your way around to the south side of the lake and then walk cross country for about 0.4 mile along a heading slightly east of magnetic south until you reach the top of a wide saddle. Pine Island Lake is located 0.2 mile below the south side of the saddle. Once you reach Pine Island, it is an easy walk around its eastern side back to the Pine Island Lake Trail and on to Governor Dern Lake. The total distance of this loop is 5.5 miles.

Another nice day hike from Governor Dern Lake is along the trail to the Four Lakes Basin (see map on page 89). The trail

Grandaddy Basin

leaves from Rainbow Lake, 0.8 miles south of Governor Dern, and proceeds along a gentle uphill slope for 2.5 miles to Jean Lake (10,753 ft.) and its three companion lakes: Daynes, Dale, and Dean. Nestled against the southern side of the Uintas ridge amidst scattered stands of Engelmann spruce, these glacial lakes are very picturesque. The fishing is also good and there are plenty of good campsites in the basin, but it is difficult for most people to get a good night's sleep at this altitude. If you don't want to return the same way you can go north another 1.2 miles to the Highline Trail, then west to the Pinto Lake Trail, and south again, past Pinto Lake, to Governor Dern Lake. Total distance: 8.7 miles.

When you leave Governor Dern Lake you will be walking back to Grandaddy Lake via Rainbow Lake, Lost Lake, and Brinton Meadows. Bear right at the two major trail junctions near Rainbow Lake and head due south on the Hades Trail towards Lost Lake. Just before reaching Lost Lake you will notice another spur trail leading to Powell Lake about 0.6 mile away–another possible side trip.

1.2 miles after passing Lost Lake you will arrive at Brinton Meadows and the Palisade Lake Trail junction. For twenty years the Forest Service maintained a guard station at Brinton Meadows, but under pressure from the Sierra Club they were forced to remove the station in 1995. The law forbids permanent dwellings within a designated wilderness area, so, although the guard station was little more than a tent with a wooden floor, it had to go. This is a shame because rangers staffing the guard station during the summer months provided a valuable service in cleaning up camp sites, monitoring and controlling damage to the ecosystem, and providing emergency assistance. Grandaddy Basin is so heavily impacted by backpackers and pack horses that the absence of the Brinton Meadows Guard Station is now sorely missed.

From Brinton Meadows it is another 1.2 miles back to Betsy Lake, from where you can retrace your steps past Grandaddy lake, over Hades Pass, and back to your car at the Grandview Trailhead.

Governor Dern Lake, Grandaddy Basin

Naturalist Basin

★★★★

Distance:	19.0 miles (round trip)
Walking time:	day 1: 5 hours day 2: 5³/₄ hours
Elevations:	1,370 ft. gain/loss Highline Trailhead (start): 10,350 ft. Packard Lake: 9,980 ft. Jordan Lake: 10,630 ft. Faxon Lake: 10,980 ft.
Trail:	Naturalist Basin is a very popular destination, and the trails to the lower part of the basin are well maintained. A small portion of this hike, however, is in the upper part of the basin where there are no trails. The upper basin is all above timber line and the route is easy, but you should carry a compass.
Season:	Midsummer to mid-fall. Because of its high elevation, Naturalist Basin is usually covered with snow from mid-November until July.
Vicinity:	The High Uintas Wilderness Area, near Kamas
Maps:	Hayden Peak *(USGS)* High Uintas Wilderness *(Trails Illustrated, #711)*
Information:	http://www.utahtrails.com/naturalist.html *(Utah Trails)* http://www.fs.usda.gov/uwcnf/ *(Uinta-Wasatch-Cache Nat. Forest)* phone: (435) 783-4338 *(Kamas Ranger District)*

To get to the trailhead drive east from Kamas on Highway 150 toward Mirror Lake. 6 miles from Kamas you will pass a Forest Service booth where you must purchase a recreation pass to hike in the area ($3.00/day for each vehicle). 35 miles from Kamas, or 3.0 miles after passing the Mirror Lake turnoff, you will see a well marked road on the right side of the highway leading to the Highline Trailhead.

The High Uintas are famous for their gorgeous alpine basins, but none of them can beat the memorable scenery of Naturalist Basin. In my opinion, this small collection of lakes and meadows, nestled together against the southern slopes of Mount Agassiz and Spread Eagle Peak, is the crown jewel of the High Uintas Wilderness Area. Unfortunately Naturalist Basin is also one of the most popular backpacking destinations in the High Uintas, so if you are looking for solitude you had better choose another hike. Most hikers tend to congregate around Jordan Lake and the Morat Lakes, where the best fishing can be found, so if you are willing to camp elsewhere it is still possible to enjoy a measure of privacy.

Few hikers venture onto the upper plateau of Naturalist Basin, where 2.5 miles of this hike are located. Five icy lakes cling tenaciously to the talus slopes in the top of the basin just below the 11,000-foot contour line and just above timberline. Hiking across the stark, sparsely vegetated terrain that separates the small lakes can be an almost otherworldly experience. It is an environment where most life ceases to exist during the wintertime, but during the two or three months of summer a few dormant species suddenly burst forth to quickly mature and reproduce before the arctic cold again forces them into submission. By the end of July, after most of the snow has melted, the thin, rocky soil is usually covered with a colorful carpet of tiny blossoms as the hardy plants begin another cycle of their precarious existence.

Day 1 (8.6 miles)

From the Highline Trailhead the trail meanders gradually downhill through a forest of Engelmann spruce and lodgepole pine. At the higher elevations the forest is almost entirely spruce, but more and more lodgepole pine begin to appear as elevation is lost. After walking for an hour you will see your first lake, Scudder Lake, glinting through the trees. This lake is popular with

Naturalist Basin

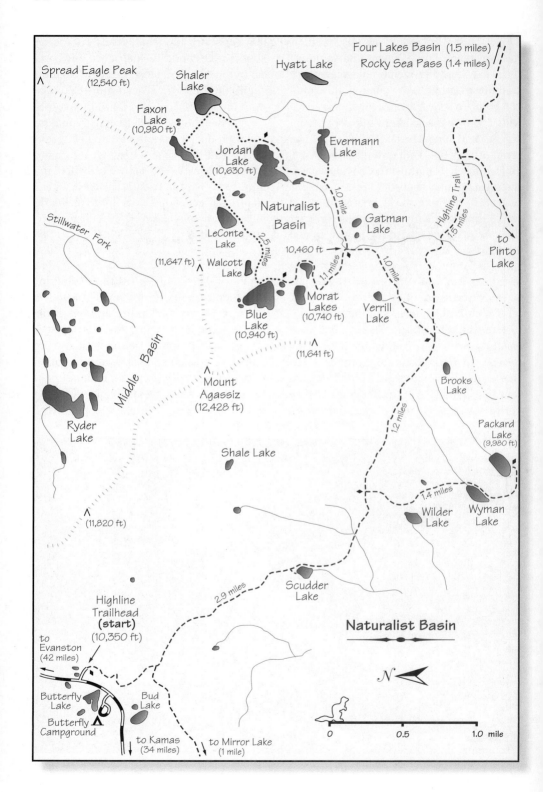

Four Lakes Basin (1.5 miles)
Rocky Sea Pass (1.4 miles)

Spread Eagle Peak
(12,540 ft)
^

Hyatt Lake

Shaler
Lake

Faxon
Lake
(10,980 ft)

Jordan
Lake
(10,630 ft)

Evermann
Lake

Naturalist
Basin

Highline Trail

1.0 mile

Stillwater Fork

LeConte
Lake

Gatman
Lake

to
Pinto
Lake

2.5 miles

1.5 miles

(11,647 ft) ^   Walcott
Lake

10,460 ft

1.1 miles

1.0 mile

Morat
Lakes
(10,740 ft)

Verrill
Lake

Blue
Lake
(10,940 ft)

^
(11,641 ft)

Middle Basin

Brooks
Lake

^
Mount
Agassiz
(12,428 ft)

1.2 miles

Packard
Lake
(9,980 ft)

Ryder
Lake

Shale Lake

1.4 miles

Wyman
Lake

Wilder
Lake

^
(11,820 ft)

Naturalist Basin

Scudder
Lake

Highline
Trailhead
(start)
(10,350 ft)

2.9 miles

N

to
Evanston
(42 miles)

Butterfly
Lake

Bud
Lake

Butterfly
Campground △

to Kamas
(34 miles)

to Mirror Lake
(1 mile)

0   0.5   1.0 mile

day hikers, although it is too shallow for good fishing. It can be accessed over a short spur that branches off to the right of the main trail.

From Scudder Lake it is another half hour walk to the Packard Lake trail junction. Once you reach this junction you are only 2.2 miles from Naturalist Basin, so unless you got off to a late start you will probably want to take a short side trip to see Wilder, Wyman, and Packard Lakes. They are all on the 1.4-mile-long Packard Lake Trail. There is also a nice view of the Uintas near the end of the trail. Packard Lake is situated only a hundred yards north of the rim of a 600-foot-deep canyon, in the bottom of which runs the East Fork of the Duchesne River.

When you return to the Highline Trail continue walking east, and after 1.2 miles you will see a sign directing you to Naturalist Basin. Turn left here and proceed north. The path climbs very gradually for about a mile before emerging from the trees on the

Wyman Lake, just off the Highline Trail

edge of a wide green meadow with the picturesque cliffs of the Uinta Crest behind it. From the scene in front of you, it should be immediately obvious that you are entering a very special place.

As you enter Naturalist Basin turn right, across the stream, and start looking for a camp site. If you want to camp by a lake you can try Jordan Lake, about 0.9 mile from the entrance. Jordan is the largest lake, but it is also the most popular. If there are no spaces available at Jordan, or if you want more pri-

Jordan Lake

vacy, then Evermann Lake is your best bet.

Evermann Lake is a beautiful place to camp, but it is slightly off the main trail and many people don't even know of its existence. To get there proceed eastward from the entrance of the basin, along the edge of the meadow, for about 0.5 mile until you reach a point where the trail crosses a small drainage, turns north, and starts climbing up to Jordan Lake. Leave the main trail here and continue east along the drainage. You will run into Evermann Lake within 0.2 mile. When setting up camp please be advised that because of heavy visitation the Forest Service has now permanently banned open campfires in Naturalist Basin.

Day 2 (10.4 miles)

Before leaving this beautiful spot be sure to visit the lakes in the upper part of the basin. The 4.6 mile tour around the basin's eight major lakes takes only 2¹/₂ hours, and since it is a loop you can leave your backpack in camp. The route is easy, but there is no trail so you should have a compass.

Continue on the path along the southern side of Jordan Lake until it disappears at the eastern end of the lake. From there you will have to do some minor scrambling to get to the top of the plateau above the lake.

After you have gained about 200 feet in elevation the terrain levels off and the walking is easy. If you walk along a bearing of 25 degrees east of magnetic north (slightly east of Spread Eagle Peak) for about fifteen minutes you will run right into Shaler Lake. There are very few trees at this elevation and your view is relatively unobstructed, so you can't miss the lake.

Next, Faxon Lake is almost due west of magnetic north from Shaler Lake, just to the left of a saddle on the ridge between Spread Eagle Peak and Mount Agassiz. It is only 0.3 mile away, so you should be there in ten minutes. From Faxon it is easy to find LeConte, Walcott, and Blue Lake. They are all situated at about the same elevation along a line at the base of the Uinta crest, so just follow the base of the ridge in an easterly direction toward Mount Agassiz and you will run into them in succession. Again, they are all less than 0.3 mile apart, so you don't have to walk long.

There are at least some fish in all of the upper lakes of Naturalist Basin, with the possible exception of Walcott Lake. There isn't much to eat in these high lakes, however, so they cannot sustain a very large population of fish. It never ceases to amaze me how much difference a few hundred feet at these altitudes can make to an ecosystem. The difference in elevation between the upper and lower parts of Naturalist Basin is only 350 feet, yet their ecologies are worlds apart.

From the south side of Blue Lake a primitive trail leads down to the twin Morat Lakes. The trail is vague at first, but soon becomes

Faxon Lake

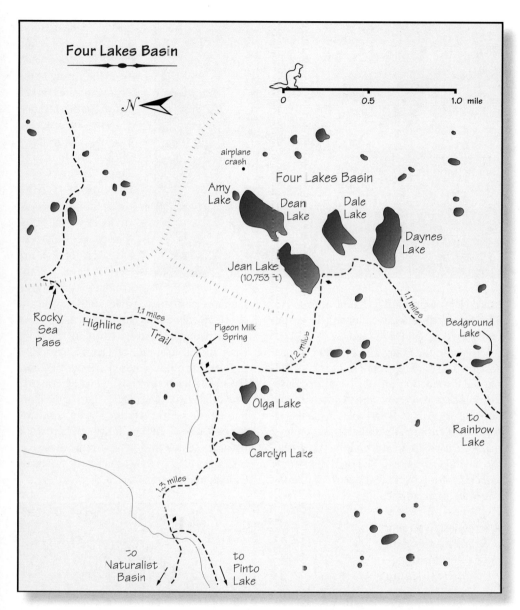

Four Lakes Basin

0   0.5   1.0 mile

N

airplane
crash

Four Lakes Basin

Amy
Lake

Dean
Lake

Dale
Lake

Daynes
Lake

Jean Lake
(10,753 ft)

Rocky
Sea
Pass

Highline

1.1 miles

Trail

Pigeon Milk
Spring

1.1 miles

Bedground
Lake

1.2 miles

Olga Lake

to
Rainbow
Lake

Carolyn Lake

1.3 miles

to
Naturalist
Basin

to
Pinto
Lake

more distinct as it begins to descend into the lower basin. As you make the short descent you will be treated to a nice view of the two Morat Lakes, with the wide expanse of the Uintas below them. Thank goodness this magnificent land is now protected as a wilderness area. From Morat Lakes a good trail will take you the remaining 0.6 mile back to the bottom of the lower meadow, and from there you can easily retrieve your backpack for the walk back to the Highline Trailhead.

Four Lakes Basin

For those who want to get farther away from civilization than Naturalist Basin and still enjoy the serenity of a beautiful alpine basin on the south slopes of the Uintas, Four

Jean Lake

spring on the extreme northern end of Dean, but it is a long walk from the spring to the best campsites on the lake's southern shore.

The water is deeper along the northern shores of Jean and Dean Lakes, where they abut a high quartzite ridge south of Rocky Sea Pass. The chances of hooking a larger fish are better there, but the fishing is also good on the more easily accessible southern shores.

Lakes Basin provides a good alternative. The fishing is also excellent there – especially at Jean and Dean Lakes.

To get to the Four Lakes Basin continue eastward on the Highline Trail for 2.8 miles beyond the junction with the Naturalist Basin Trail. There you will come to another junction with the trail to Four Lakes departing on the right. Turn south, and after another 1.2 miles you will arrive at Jean Lake, the first of the basin's four lakes. The total distance to Jean Lake from Naturalist Basin is 5.0 miles, one way, or from the Highline Trailhead it is 8.1 miles. The route is clearly marked with Forest Service signs.

The best camp sites are at Dean Lake. There is no proper trail to Dean, but it is easy to find. Just walk along the southern shore of Jean Lake to its eastern side, and a few hundred feet more will bring you to Dean Lake. There is a good fresh-water

If you feel like exploring, there is an old airplane crash a short way up the slope from the eastern end of Dean Lake. The unfortunate pilot was only about 500 feet too low to clear the ridge when he crashed. The other two lakes, Dale and Daynes, are another 0.5 mile south of Jean Lake on the east side of the main trail. There are a number of good camp sites around those two lakes as well, but they aren't quite as scenic as Jean and Dean.

Dean Lake

Lofty Lake Loop

★★★

Distance:	7.9 miles (loop, to all points of interest)
Walking time:	5½ hours
Elevations:	1,820 ft. gain/loss
	Pass Lake Trailhead (start): 10,160 ft.
	Cuberant Lake: 10,410 ft.
	Lofty lake: 10,830 ft.
	Ruth Lake: 10,375 ft.
Trail:	Generally well marked and easy to follow
Season:	Midsummer to mid-fall. Much of the trail is usually covered with snow from mid November until July.
Vicinity:	West of the High Uintas Wilderness Area, near Kamas
Maps:	Mirror Lake (*USGS*)
	High Uintas Wilderness Area (*Trails Illustrated, Map #711*)
Information:	http://www.utahtrails.com/loftylake.html (*Utah Trails*)
	http://www.fs.usda.gov/uwcnf/ (*Uinta-Wasatch-Cache Nat. Forest*)
	phone: (435) 783-4338 (*Kamas Ranger District*)

Drive east from Salt Lake City on I-80 for 30 miles to Wanship; then turn south onto Highway 32 and drive for another 17 miles to Kamas. When you reach Kamas proceed to the center of town and turn east onto Highway 150 (the Mirror Lake Highway). After 6 miles you will pass a Forest Service booth where you must purchase a recreation pass ($3.00/vehicle for one day, or $6.00 for a week). 32.5 miles after leaving Kamas, or 0.8 mile beyond the Mirror Lake turnoff, you will see a well marked gravel road on the left leading to the Pass Lake Trailhead. Turn here and drive the last 200 yards to the trailhead and parking area. The hike begins on the Cuberant Lake Trail, located on the west side of the parking lot. Don't confuse the Cuberant Lake Trail with the Scout Lake Trail which departs on the right side of the parking lot, 150 feet east of the beginning trailhead. The return portion of the hike will be along the Scout Lake Trail.

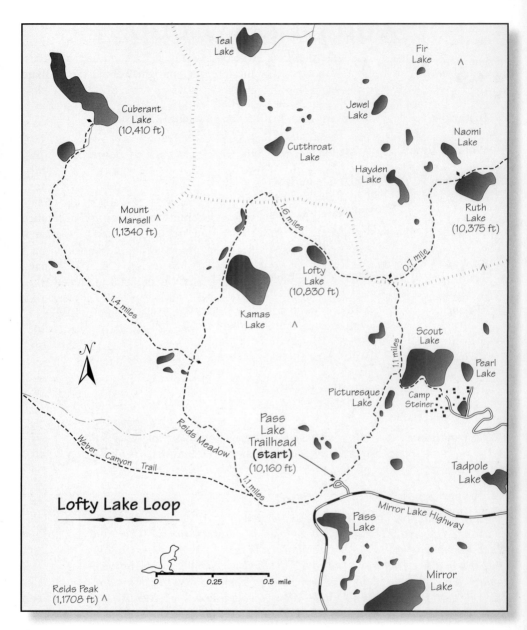

Teal
Lake

Fir
Lake ∧

Cuberant
Lake
(10,410 ft)

Jewel
Lake

Naomi
Lake

Cutthroat
Lake

Hayden
Lake

Ruth
Lake
(10,375 ft)

Mount
Marsell ∧
(1,1340 ft)

1.6 miles

∧

0.7 mile

∧

Lofty
Lake
(10,830 ft)

1.4 miles

Kamas
Lake ∧

Scout
Lake

1.1 miles

Pearl
Lake

Picturesque
Lake

Camp
Steiner

N

Reids Meadow

Pass
Lake
Trailhead
(start)
(10,160 ft)

Tadpole
Lake

Weber Canyon Trail

1.1 miles

Mirror Lake Highway

Pass
Lake

Lofty Lake Loop

0   0.25   0.5 mile

Mirror
Lake

Reids Peak
(1,1708 ft) ∧

This hike provides a fine sampling of the extraordinary landscape in the high country of northeast Utah. Although the trail lies just outside the boundaries of the adjacent High Uintas Wilderness Area it is every bit as pristine and scenic. The trail passes six named lakes and several un-named ones as it threads its way around the quartzite cliffs of Mount Marsell and briefly crosses the east/west crest of the Uinta Mountains for some spectacular views to the north. If you are looking for a shorter loop the total mileage of this hike can be halved by excluding the spur trails to Cuberant Lake and Ruth Lake. Doing so will also reduce the total elevation gain to a very manageable 920 feet, making this an excellent hike for the whole family. Unfortunately, however, the shortened hike also misses Ruth Lake, which in my opinion is one of the most beautiful lakes in the Uintas.

From the parking area the trail begins by making its way through a towering forest of Engelmann spruce and subalpine fir. As you walk across the rocky but relatively level terrain you will occasionally catch tantalizing glimpses of a picturesque mountain called Reids Peak that rises abruptly to a height of 11,708 feet just one mile west of the trailhead. At first the trail heads directly toward the peak, but it soon begins a long, sweeping turn to the north. Then, after 20 minutes of walking, the trail breaks out of the trees and begins skirting the northeastern side of a large open area called Reids Meadow. The treeless meadow provides an uninterrupted view of Reids Peak, now 0.8

mile away, and if you are there early in the morning you will be in for a special treat. The steep, symmetrical mountain, bathed in the morning sunlight, behind the brilliant green due-covered grass of Reids Meadow is truly a sight to behold.

A quarter-mile after leaving Reids Meadow the trail comes to a signed junction where the Cuberant Lake Trail departs on the left. Unless you have opted for the shorter hike around the Lofty Lake Loop you must turn left here to begin the 2.8-mile round trip side trip to Cuberant Lake. Soon you will notice that the spur trail is not as well traveled and, hence, not as well maintained as the main trail. That, however, is the very reason many people prefer Cuberant to the other lakes on this hike. It is especially attractive for fishermen—not only is it the least visited of the lakes featured on this hike, but it is also the largest.

From the junction the trail to Cuberant Lake continues in a northwesterly direction with very little change in elevation for

Reids Peak above Reids Meadow

Cuberant Lake

0.6 mile, but then it breaks out of the trees and begins climbing up the rocky slopes of Mount Marsell. After gaining 250 feet it drops down onto the west side of the mountain before beginning the last moderate climb to the southern shore of the lake. Just 0.2 mile before reaching Cuberant the trail passes the east side of another smaller lake that many hikers mistakenly believe is Cuberant. The crude trail seems to disappear at that point, but don't give up. The real Cuberant Lake is connected to the lower lake by a small creek that runs into the east side of the lower lake. Continue northward along the shore of the lower lake until you come to the inlet drainage, and 150 feet from the lakeshore you will see where the trail to the upper lake crosses the drainage. From there the trail continues up the west side of a small ravine for another 300 yards and 60 feet of elevation gain to the upper lake. There you will see a wooden sign nailed to the trunk of a large spruce that says "Cuberant Lake".

Back on the main trail, it is an uneventful 0.4 mile climb from the Cuberant Lake trail junction to Kamas Lake, a somewhat smaller lake sandwiched into a narrow basin on the southeast side of Mount Marsell. From there the trail continues to climb northward for another 15 minutes until it finally reaches the top of the ridge above Kamas Lake. At this point you are on the long east/west summit ridge of the Uinta Mountains, and the view looking north into the Hayden Fork Drainage and the headwaters of the Bear River is quite spectacular. The trail follows the summit ridge briefly before again turning south onto a high alpine bench where Lofty Lake is located. Lofty Lake lies just below timber line and the area is nearly devoid of trees. The lake is scarcely 100 yards in diameter and doesn't appear to be deep enough to avoid freezing solid in the winter. I would be surprised if it could sustain a population of fish.

Upon leaving Lofty Lake the loop trail begins a long, unbroken descent of 670 feet over 1.4 miles back to the Pass Lake Trail-

Trail above Kamas Lake

ite slickrock that was polished smooth by the glacier that carved out Ruth Lake a hundred thousand years ago.

It should be said that there is another way to get to Ruth Lake. If you continue north on the Mirror Lake Highway from the Pass Lake Trailhead for another 2.9 miles you will come to the well-marked Ruth Lake Trailhead and parking area on the left side of the road. From there it is only a 0.8-mile walk to the lake with 250 feet of elevation gain. This easy hike is great for kids; consequently there are often families with children camping at Ruth Lake.

Back on the main trail, it is an easy downhill walk from the Ruth Lake trail junction back to the Pass Lake Trailhead. Along the way the trail passes the east side of Scout Lake, which is heavily used by the boy scouts at nearby Camp Steiner during the summer, and Picturesque Lake, which is probably the least picturesque lake on this hike. You should arrive at the trailhead after about 30 minutes.

head. But after just 0.3 mile you will come to another junction where the spur trail to Ruth Lake begins. The Forest Service has not placed a sign at the junction, but it is well marked with a large stone monument. If you have opted for the shorter hike you should continue straight at this point, but if you wish to include Ruth Lake in your itinerary you must turn left at the junction. A round trip visit to Ruth Lake will add 1.3 miles onto the distance of the shorter hike and 330 feet of additional elevation gain, but in my opinion the reward is well worth the extra effort.

Ruth Lake is one of the most beautiful lakes in the Uintas, and the afternoon view from the east side of the lake with Mount Hayden standing prominently above the western shore is an outstanding spectacle. The trail down to the lake is quite interesting as well. It passes over a long stretch of quartz-

Ruth Lake

Notch Mountain Trail

★★★

shuttle car or bicycle required
day hike

Distance:	10.5 miles (plus 4.1 miles by car or bicycle)
Walking time:	6¹/₂ hours
Elevations:	1,130 ft. gain, 2,070 ft. loss Bald Mountain Trailhead (start): 10,760 ft. Meadow Lake: 9,820 ft. The Notch: 10,590 ft. Trial Lake Trailhead: 9,820 ft.
Trail:	Well marked, well maintained trail
Season:	Midsummer through mid-fall. The trail is generally covered with snow from mid-November until July.
Vicinity:	Near Heber and the High Uintas Wilderness Area
Maps:	Mirror Lake *(USGS)* High Uintas Wilderness *(Trails Illustrated, #711)*
Information:	http://www.utahtrails.com/notchmountain.html *(Utah Trails)* http://www.fs.usda.gov/uwcnf/ *(Uinta-Wasatch-Cache Nat. Forest)* phone: (435) 783-4338 *(Kamas Ranger District)*

Drive east from Salt Lake City on I-80 for 30 miles to Wanship and the junction with Highway 32; then turn south on Highway 32 and drive for another 17 miles to Kamas. Turn left in the center of Kamas and drive east on Highway 150 (the Mirror Lake Highway). After 6 miles you will pass a Forest Service booth where you must purchase a recreation pass ($3.00/vehicle for one day, or $6.00 for a week). 26 miles from Kamas there is a well-marked gravel road on the left leading to Trial Lake. Take this turn and follow the signs for 0.3 mile to the fisherman's parking area near the Trial Lake Dam. This is where the hike will end and where you should leave your shuttle car.

To reach the Bald Mountain Trailhead where the hike begins return to Highway 150 and continue driving east for 3.8 miles to the top of the Bald Mountain Pass. At the summit of the pass you will see a sign directing you to the Bald Mountain Trailhead. Turn left here and drive the final 0.1 mile to the trailhead and parking area.

The Notch Mountain Trail is a delightful path on the western side of the Uinta Mountains that winds lazily through the subalpine forest west of Bald Mountain and eventually returns to the Mirror Lake Highway through the notch in Notch Mountain. It is an area strewn with lakes and talus covered mountain peaks—all shaped and sculpted by the glaciers of the last Ice Age. A hundred thousand years ago this area was a sea of ice, broken only by the island peaks of Bald Mountain, Notch Mountain, Mount Watson, Haystack, and a few other nearby summits. At least four separate glaciers came together on the slopes of Bald Mountain, with long fingers extending for up to twenty miles down the north and south slopes of the Uintas. As the glaciers moved they gouged deep pockets into the earth, and today the result is a landscape punctuated by scores of picturesque lakes.

The trail begins on the south side of Bald Mountain and proceeds westward along its rocky base. A hundred yards from the trailhead you will come to a junction where the 1.7-mile trail to the summit of Bald Mountain takes off on the right. Bearing left, the Notch Mountain Trail continues along the southern slopes of the peak for another 0.6 mile and then turns northwest toward Notch Mountain.

After about 45 minutes the trail passes by the western side of Clegg Lake.

Clegg is one of the smaller lakes you will see on this hike, but none can beat it for scenic beauty. Unlike many of the Uinta lakes, it was never dammed, and it is still in a pristine state. The setting is exquisite, with Bald Mountain to the east and Trial Peak to the west. On calm, clear days the reflections of these two peaks on the mirror smooth water of Clegg Lake are unforgettable: Trial Peak in the morning and Bald Mountain in the late afternoon.

Soon after leaving Clegg Lake the trail crosses between Bald Mountain and Notch Mountain, leaving the Provo River Drain-

Bench Lake

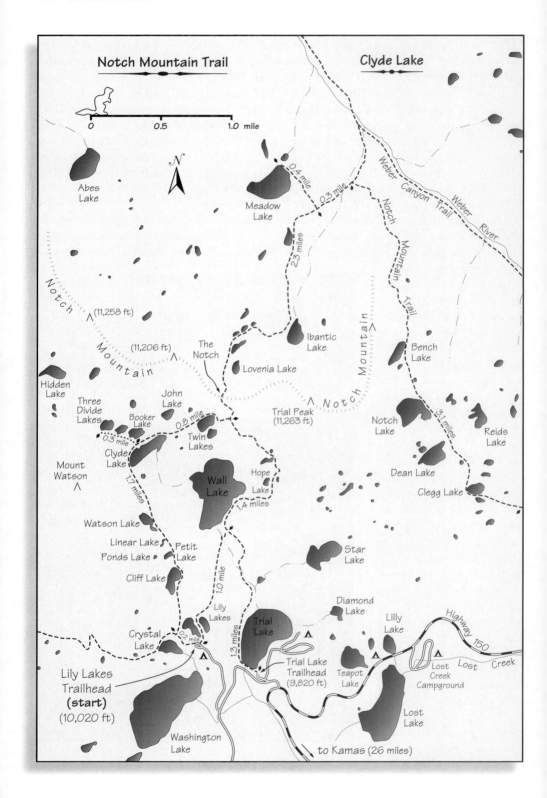

Notch Mountain Trail

Clyde Lake

0   0.5   1.0 mile

N

Abes Lake

Meadow Lake

0.4 mile

0.3 mile

2.3 miles

Weber Canyon Trail

Weber River

Notch Mountain Trail

(11,258 ft)

(11,206 ft)

The Notch

Ibantic Lake

Bench Lake

3.1 miles

Notch Mountain

Notch Mountain

Lovenia Lake

Hidden Lake

Three Divide Lakes

Booker Lake

John Lake

0.8 mile

Trial Peak (11,263 ft)

Notch Mountain

Notch Lake

Reids Lake

0.3 mile

Clyde Lake

Twin Lakes

Mount Watson

Wall Lake

Hope Lake

Dean Lake

Clegg Lake

1.7 miles

1.4 miles

Watson Lake

Linear Lake
Ponds Lake

Petit Lake

Star Lake

Cliff Lake

1.0 mile

Lily Lakes

Diamond Lake

Lilly Lake

Highway 150

Crystal Lake

0.2 mile

Trial Lake

1.3 miles

Trial Lake Trailhead (9,820 ft)

Teapot Lake

Lost Creek Campground

Lost Creek

Lily Lakes Trailhead **(start)** (10,020 ft)

Washington Lake

Lost Lake

to Kamas (26 miles)

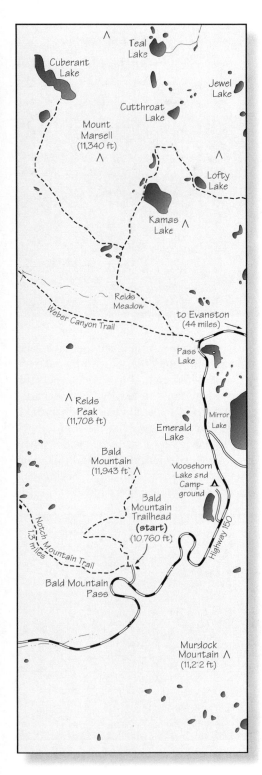

age and entering the Weber River Drainage. Within the next mile three more lakes will come into view along the eastern slopes of Notch Mountain: Dean Lake, Notch Lake, and Bench Lake. Of these three, Notch Lake is the biggest and the most popular among fishermen, but I really can't say much for its scenic attraction. It has an active dam, and when the water level is low at the end of summer about half of the lake's surface area is replaced by lifeless, sun-bleached shoreline. Bench Lake, on the other hand, is a scenic gem with huge Engelmann spruce growing right to the water's edge.

The trail continues downhill from Bench Lake for another 1.5 miles, then crosses a small creek and begins a gentle uphill climb. Ten minutes later you should see the spur trail to Meadow Lake leaving on the right. The junction is marked by a small sign nailed to a spruce tree, but if you aren't paying attention you can easily miss it. Meadow Lake is 0.4 mile off the main trail. It is the second largest off-road lake you will see on this hike, and it is a popular overnight stop with scout groups. Unfortunately, however, the lake has suffered from the same fate that has befallen so many other lakes in the High Uintas. It has an active dam on its north side, and the resulting fluctuations in the water level often expose large ugly swathes of lifeless wasteland along its shores. But I am told that the fishing is good; Meadow Lake contains a large population of cutthroat trout.

The second half of this hike, from Meadow Lake to Trial Lake, is perhaps the most interesting. The trail meanders gently uphill for 2.0 miles, past Ibantic Lake and Lovenia Lake, then crosses through the Notch of Notch Mountain and drops down again into the Provo River watershed. There is a fine view of Lovenia Lake from the Notch, and to the south Wall Lake, the largest lake along this trail, glints through the forest.

Clegg Lake

Wall Lake was "under construction" when I last stood in the Notch in the summer of 1999. The sounds of heavy equipment drifted up from far below, and I could see from the denuded land on the south side of the lake that a major earth moving project was well underway. Although Wall Lake was no longer used for water storage, its ancient dam had for years been in need of repair. Many environmentalists suggested that the dam should be breached and the lake allowed to return to its natural size. The lake is very popular with fishermen, however, and for that reason the Forest Service decided to reconstruct the dam and maintain the lake at its current size.

From the Notch, the trail descends across two narrow benches before com-

ing to the southeast shore of Wall Lake. The route then follows the shore of the lake for 0.2 mile before coming to a junction near the dam where the trail to Lily Lakes departs. Bear left here for Trial Lake. Soon the lake will come into view, with the trail following closely along its western side. When you reach the south end of Trial Lake you can walk across the dam to the parking area where your shuttle car is parked.

Trial Lake

Clyde Lake Loop

★★

Distance:	5.7 miles (loop)
Walking time:	3 hours
Elevations:	420 ft. gain/loss
	Lily Lakes Trailhead (start): 10,020 ft.
	Clyde Lake: 10,420 ft.
Trail:	Easy walk, but the trail can be confusing. In some places it seems briefly to disappear, and in other places there is more than one trail. A compass is useful.
Season:	Midsummer to mid-fall. Parts of the trail are usually covered with snow from mid-November until July.
Vicinity:	West of the High Uintas Wilderness Area, near Kamas
Maps:	Mirror Lake *(USGS)*
	High Uintas Wilderness *(Trails Illustrated, #711)*
Information:	http://www.utahtrails.com/clydelake.html *(Utah Trails)*
	http://www.fs.usda.gov/uwcnf/ *(Uinta-Wasatch-Cache Nat. Forest)*
	phone: (435) 783-4338 *(Kamas Ranger District)*

To get to the trailhead drive east from Kamas on Highway 150 toward Mirror Lake. 6 miles from Kamas you will pass a Forest Service booth where you must purchase a recreation pass to hike in the area ($3.00/day for each vehicle). 26 miles from Kamas, or 6 miles before reaching Mirror Lake, there is a well marked road on the left leading to Trial Lake. Take this turn and follow the signs to Crystal Lake Trailhead 1.2 miles from the highway. You will come to two junctions before the road reaches Crystal Lake Trailhead, but there are good signs marking the way at each junction. As you enter the trailhead parking area look for a large horse loading ramp made of logs on the right side of the road. The trail to Wall Lake and Clyde Lake begins at this ramp.

There are literally thousands of mountain lakes in and around the High Uintas. On the 55-square-mile Mirror Lake Quad-rangle map alone there are 72 named lakes and several hundred unnamed ones. It is a fisherman's paradise, although most of the lakes are so high they are frozen much of the year. The area surrounding Clyde Lake is particularly well endowed with lakes. The loop trail described here, though only 5.7 miles long, passes by no fewer than fifteen of them.

Shortly after leaving the parking area the trail passes between the two Lily Lakes, each about 200 yards long and 100 yards wide, and then continues northward along an almost level grade for another 0.7 mile to Wall Lake. Because of the presence of an earthen dam on its southern side, Wall Lake is one of the largest lakes in the area; it is over a half mile long.

From Wall Lake the well-worn trail veers east and then north, passing Hope Lake and several other tiny unnamed lakes along the way. Just beyond Hope Lake the grade increases sharply as the forest opens up to a fine view of Mount Watson, a dome-shaped peak 1.5 miles to the west. The second half of this hike will take you down the opposite side of Wall Lake, past Clyde Lake, Watson Lake and several other small lakes that lie near the base of Mount Watson.

From this view point the trail continues on toward Notch Mountain for 0.5 mile, past another unnamed lake, before finally coming to the Clyde Lake trail junction. To complete the loop past Clyde and Watson Lakes and back to the trailhead you must turn left here, but care is needed since the vague Clyde Lake trail is unmarked and can easily be missed. The junction is located in the middle of a large flat clearing,

see map
page 98

about two hundred feet wide, that runs along the base of Notch Mountain in an east-west direction. The most clearly defined path continues northward and soon starts climbing up into the Notch of Notch Mountain. The fainter Clyde Lake Trail leaves to the west and begins a very gradual descent to Twin Lakes, just 200 yards away. Don't worry if you have difficulty following the trail; it gets better. Just walk due west along the base of Notch Mountain, neither climbing nor descending, and you should run right into the Twin Lakes.

The larger Twin Lake is about 500 feet in diameter, and the smaller Twin on the southern side is about half that size. Although there is only a thin stretch of land between the two, the larger lake cannot be seen from its smaller twin. If you run into the smaller lake first turn north to find the larger one. The trail, more distinct now, runs around the northern shore of the larger Twin Lake. After leaving the Twin Lakes the trail continues in a westerly direction for another 0.2 mile before reaching the northeastern corner of Clyde Lake.

Clyde is a long narrow lake, about 500 feet wide and 0.3 mile long. At 10,420 feet above sea level, it is close to the highest point and roughly midway through the hike.

Hope Lake below Mount Watson

If you want to do some fishing and have time for an overnight stay, there is a fine camping site on the northeastern corner of the lake.

Before leaving Clyde Lake, you should take a short side trip to the Three Divide Lakes, located in the saddle between West Notch Mountain and Mount Watson. There is no trail to these lakes, but they are very close to Clyde and little climbing is involved. Simply turn north near the west end of Clyde Lake and walk away from the trail for about 300 feet. You should run right into Booker Lake, the first of the Three Divide Lakes. Turn west from Booker and you will soon see the other two. These lakes are all about 600 feet in diameter. They lie along an east-west line with only about 200 feet of land separating them from each other. The total distance from Clyde Lake to the last of the Three Divide Lakes is 0.3 mile.

From Clyde Lake the trail turns southward along the base of Mount Watson to reach Watson Lake, 0.4 mile away. Watson Lake, which is about 500 feet in diameter, is the first of several small lakes that lie like a string of beads along the downhill path leading back to the Crystal Lake Trailhead. The path passes by Watson Lake, tiny Linear Lake, slightly larger Petit Lake, and finally Cliff Lake, all within a half mile of each other. Cliff Lake, about twice the size of Watson, is, in my opinion, the prettiest of the four. The route passes along the eastern shores of these lakes, so hikers coming down from Clyde Lake should bear to the left.

After leaving the southern corner of Cliff Lake the trail heads south into the woods again, loosing 240 feet of elevation and arriving at West Lily Lake after another 0.2 mile. Here the path intersects the Crystal Lake Trail, and in order to return to the

Near Twin Lakes, east of Clyde Lake

parking area you must turn left. If you are in the mood for one more lake, however, Crystal Lake is just a five minute walk to the right from the junction.

The Notch and Meadow Lake

As mentioned earlier, the Notch of Notch Mountain is only 0.2 mile from the point where the Clyde Lake Trail leaves the main trail. Before making the turn to Clyde Lake some hikers may want to climb into the Notch. At an elevation of 10,580 feet it is only 120 feet higher than the trail junction, and the view is well worth the climb. If you drop down on the other side of the Notch for another 0.2 mile you will come to Lovenia Lake, about 300 feet across. From there the trail continues past Ibantic Lake and eventually ends at Meadow Lake. Meadow Lake, another dammed lake, is nearly as large as Wall Lake. It is located 2.5 miles north of the Notch. (See *Notch Mountain Trail*, page 96).

Lake Country

★★★

Distance:	8.0 miles (loop)
Walking time:	4¾ hours
Elevations:	690 ft. gain/loss Crystal Lake Trailhead (start): 10,020 ft. Island Lake: 10,160 ft. Duck Lake: 9,790 ft.
Trail:	Easy, well marked trail
Season:	Midsummer through mid-fall. The trail is generally covered with snow from mid-November through late June.
Vicinity:	Near Heber and the High Uintas Wilderness Area
Maps:	Mirror Lake, Erickson Basin *(USGS)* High Uintas Wilderness *(Trails Illustrated, #711)*
Information:	http://www.utahtrails.com/lakecountry.html *(Utah Trails)* http://www.fs.usda.gov/uwcnf/ *(Uinta-Wasatch-Cache Nat. Forest)* phone: (435) 783-4338 *(Kamas Ranger District)*

Drive east of Salt Lake City on I-80 for 30 miles to Wanship and the junction with Highway 32. Then turn south on Highway 32 and drive for another 17 miles to Kamas. Turn left in the center of Kamas and drive east on Highway 150 (the Mirror Lake Highway). After 6 miles you will pass a Forest Service booth where you must purchase a recreation pass ($3.00/vehicle for one day, or $6.00 for a week). 26 miles from Kamas there is a well-marked road on the left leading to Trial Lake. Take this turn and follow the signs for the next 1.2 miles to the Crystal Lake Trailhead. There are two trailheads at the end of the road. The one next to the packhorse loading ramp is not the one you want. The Crystal Lake Trailhead is 100 feet west of the loading ramp.

Two miles west of Trial Lake, on the western side of the Uinta Mountains, lies a high alpine bench that the Forest Service is fond of calling Lake Country. The bench lies at the headwaters of the Weber River drainage (to the north) and the Provo River drainage (to the south), and there are dozens of lakes in the area. Needless to say it is a

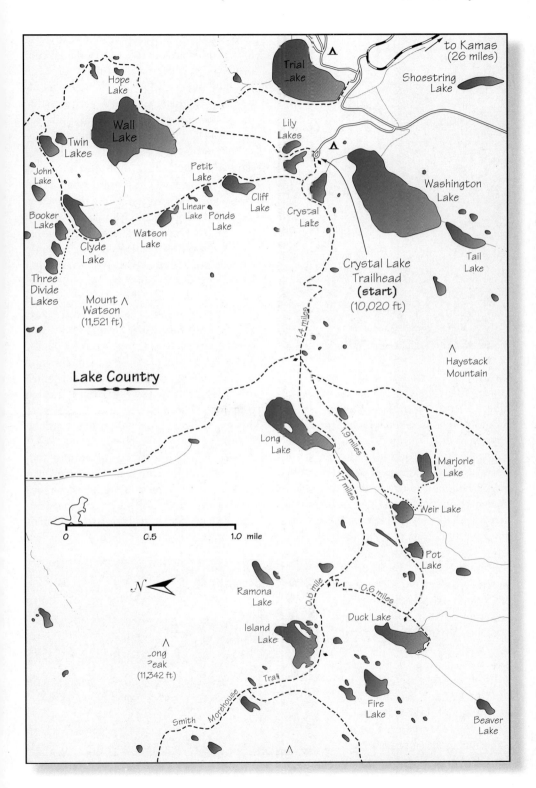

to Kamas
(26 miles)

Shoestring
Lake

Trial
Lake

Hope
Lake

Wall
Lake

Twin
Lakes

John
Lake

Booker
Lake

Clyde
Lake

Three
Divide
Lakes

Mount ʌ
Watson
(11,521 ft)

Lake Country

Petit
Lake

Cliff
Lake

Linear
Lake Ponds
Lake

Watson
Lake

Lily
Lakes

Crystal
Lake

Washington
Lake

Tail
Lake

Crystal Lake
Trailhead
(start)
(10,020 ft)

1.4 miles

ʌ
Haystack
Mountain

Long
Lake

1.9 miles

1.7 miles

Marjorie
Lake

Weir Lake

0 C.5 1.0 mile

N ◀

Pot
Lake

0.6 mile 0.6 miles

Ramona
Lake

Duck Lake

Island
Lake

ʌ
Long
Peak
(11,342 ft)

Trail

Smith Morehouse

Fire
Lake

Beaver
Lake

ʌ

Crystal Lake

favorite area for backcountry anglers, and you are likely to see many fishermen on this hike. Access into Lake Country is on the Smith Morehouse Trail which begins at the Crystal Lake Trailhead. The route described below is an easy day hike that passes by three large lakes and a half-dozen smaller ones. For more adventurous backpackers interested in getting off the "beaten path" there are also several interesting off-trail lakes within a mile of the main trail.

The trail begins by winding westward toward the north shore of Crystal Lake. For the first few hundred yards it follows what was once a road to the lake, but soon the road narrows down to a footpath. After 0.2 mile you will see the trail to Cliff Lake and Clyde Lake branching off to the right, and shortly afterward the crystal blue water of Crystal Lake makes its appearance on the left. Few hikers bother to

stop at Crystal Lake because it is so close to the trailhead, but it is one of the prettier lakes you will see on this hike. Although it is dammed its water level is no longer allowed to fluctuate; hence it is more pristine than many of the others, with grass and trees growing right to the water's edge.

After leaving Crystal Lake the trail climbs 250 feet to the top of a low pass between Haystack Mountain and Mount Watson and then back down to the junction with North Fork Trail. Mount Watson is a particularly prominent landmark along this part of the walk. Its talus slopes rise gently to the top of a barren, dome-shaped summit a mile north and 1,300 feet above the trail.

When you reach the North Fork Trail junction, 40 minutes from Crystal Lake, turn right toward Long Lake. This is the beginning of a loop through Lake Country that will take you past five named lakes and several smaller unnamed ones. Your return route will be along the North Fork Trail on your left. There is also a third trail near this junction that branches north toward the Middle Fork of the Weber River, but its departure point is unmarked and hard to find.

Another fifteen minutes will bring you to Long Lake, the largest of the lakes encountered on this hike. The trail crosses the dam on the south side of the lake, and then turns left along the west side of the drainage below

Duck Lake

Smith Morehouse Trail

an active reservoir and there is usually a lot of bleached barren land exposed around the shoreline. Nevertheless, it is very popular with fishermen.

Watch for a fork in the trail about midway along the east side of Duck Lake, where you should bear left for Weir Lake. There are no signs at the junction, but the trail is well trodden and easy to spot. From Duck Lake the trail passes Pot Lake and two smaller unnamed ponds before arriving on the north side of Weir Lake.

Long Lake. In the next mile you will pass by two more unnamed lakes before arriving at the junction where the Duck Lake Trail begins. Later you will have to turn south at this junction to complete the Lake Country loop, but not before you have seen Island Lake. Like Crystal Lake, the water level in Island Lake does not fluctuate, and ,in my opinion, it is the most scenic lake you will see on this hike.

To reach Island Lake just continue west on the Smith Morehouse Trail for another 0.5 mile. After gaining 200 feet in elevation the trail levels out on the south side of the lake. If you are looking for a place to spend the night, Island is a good choice. There are some good campsites on its west side, and this lake does not seem to be as heavily impacted as the other large lakes in the area. Beyond Island Lake there are no other major lakes on the Smith Morehouse Trail.

The trail to Duck Lake departs from the Smith Morehouse Trail at the junction mentioned above, and arrives at the north end of the lake after a short 10-minute downhill walk. Duck Lake is

Soon after leaving Weir Lake the trail passes another more primitive path near a sign that says "Route to Marjorie Lake". If you take this path you will reach Marjorie in about 15 minutes. Marjorie Lake is slightly larger and deeper than Weir, and some people claim that the fishing opportunities are better at Marjorie than any of the other lakes in the vicinity. The Forest Service regularly stocks both Marjorie and Weir with grayling trout.

Connecting trails have been built from both Weir Lake and Marjorie Lake to the North Fork Trail, and when you reach the North Fork Trail you must turn left to get back to the Smith Morehouse Trail. From there it is an easy 40-minute walk back to the Crystal Lake Trailhead.

Weir Lake

Fish Lake Loop

★

Distance:	9.4 miles (loop)
Walking time:	6½ hours
Elevations:	2,400 ft. gain/loss Fish Lake Trailhead (start): 8,000 ft. Fish Lake: 10,180 ft. highest point: 10,400 ft.
Trail:	The first part of the trail is well used and easy to follow. The return portion of the loop from Fish Lake back to the road is sometimes vague, but the route is so well defined that a good trail is not really necessary.
Season:	Midsummer through mid-fall. The higher parts of the trail are usually covered with snow from mid-November until July.
Vicinity:	40 miles northeast of Heber, near Oakley
Maps:	Whitney Reservoir *(USGS)* High Uintas Wilderness *(Trails Illustrated, #711)*
Information:	http://www.utahtrails.com/fishlake.html *(Utah Trails)* http://www.fs.usda.gov/uwcnf/ *(Uinta-Wasatch-Cache Nat. Forest)* phone: (435) 783-4338 *(Kamas Ranger District)*

Drive east from Salt Lake City on I-80 for about 31 miles to Wanship and the junction with Highway 32. Turn south on Highway 32, towards Kamas, and drive for another 10 miles until you reach the farming community of Oakley. In the center of Oakley, just before you reach a Sinclair gas station, you will see a large sign directing you to "Smith and Morehouse" and "Weber Canyon". Turn left here onto the Weber Canyon Road. After 12 miles the Weber Canyon Road forks and the pavement ends. Make a note of your odometer reading here, and continue driving straight ahead into the privately owned Thousand Peaks Ranch. From this point on you will see dozens of signs warning you not to leave the road. If you feel unwelcome it is probably because you are. But, although the land is privately owned, the road itself is a public right-of-way that extends for 8.5 miles to the Forest Service boundary. 6.8 miles after entering the Thousand Peaks Ranch you will pass the entrance to the Holiday Park Subdivision. 0.2 miles later the road crosses Dry Fork Creek, and after another 0.2 miles

you will see a small parking area on the left, next to a sign marking the trailhead.

Fish Lake is a perfect example of why it is so imperative that we preserve the best of Utah's wild lands while we still can. Cut off from the High Uintas Wilderness Area by the Mirror Lake Highway, Fish Lake is located just above the beautiful Weber River Drainage on the western side of the Uintas. Conservationists have long pleaded that this region should be given wilderness protection too, but it is probably too late now for Fish Lake to be included. There are currently active housing developments within four miles of the lake, and the pressure to use the area's resources is unrelenting. Fish Lake is being used as a reservoir by the nearby inhabitants, and its shores are marred by the presence of dead trees, killed by fluctuating water levels. Also, ATV trails now climb the ridge west of the lake, and before too many more years they will almost certainly reach the lake itself.

From the parking area the trail heads east through the aspen trees for 0.2 mile before reaching Dry Fork. In spite of the name, Dry Fork is seldom dry and must be forded (usually not a problem). The trail then climbs a few hundred feet above the north side of the creek for the next 1.3 miles, finally dropping back down to the stream in the middle of a small clearing for another crossing. Don't be confused at this point by the presence of another primitive trail that continues along the north side of Dry Fork. The trail up to the lakes lies on the south side of the creek.

After crossing Dry Fork, the trail leaves the water and begins a long slow ascent for the next 2.1 miles to Round Lake, the smallest of the three lakes you will pass on this hike. At 9,950 feet, Round Lake is 230 feet lower than Fish Lake and well below timberline. It is situated in a grassy meadow, surrounded by lodgepole pine and spruce, with a nice camping area on its northern shore.

From Round Lake the trail continues climbing to Sand Lake (larger, but not as pretty), and finally, after 1.2 miles, to Fish Lake. Fish Lake is situated at the headwaters of Dry Fork, and there is a small dam on its

Dry Fork

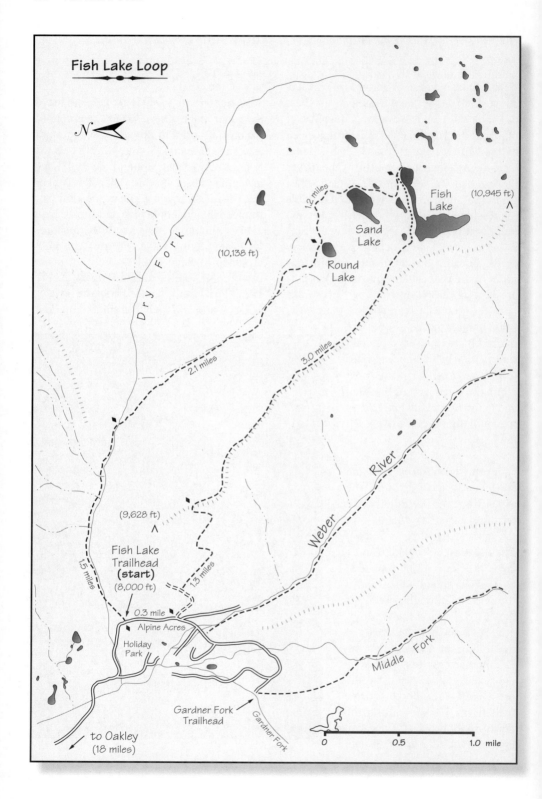

Fish Lake Loop

N

Dry Fork

(10,945 ft) ∧

Fish
Lake

Sand
Lake

Round
Lake

(10,138 ft) ∧

1.2 miles

2.1 miles

3.0 miles

Weber   River

(9,628 ft) ∧

Fish Lake
Trailhead
(start)
(8,000 ft)

1.5 miles

1.3 miles

0.3 mile

Alpine Acres

Holiday
Park

Middle   Fork

Gardner Fork
Trailhead

Gardner Fork

to Oakley
(18 miles)

0   0.5   1.0   mile

eastern side where the trail meets the lake. The flow through the dam is regulated to assure that there is always water running down the Dry Fork drainage when it is needed below. The L-shaped lake is scenically situated at the base of a rocky ridge with one side of the L parallel to the ridge. The shores are also very rocky, but there are a few good camp sites on the northern side. Round, Sand, and Fish Lakes are all well stocked with Arctic grayling, and the fishing is usually good in all three lakes. (The biggest ones are in Fish Lake!)

The trail seems to end at the dam, but if you proceed along the northern shore to the western end of the lake you will see another obvious trail starting up the ridge in a westerly direction from the corner of the L. The trail climbs 200 feet to the top of the ridge and then follows the crest back toward the road. The upper part of the trail is not well used and may occasionally seem to disappear. But don't be concerned if you have trouble following the trail. Just continue along the top of the ridge. Walking is very easy through the open forest, and as long as you stay on the ridge you can't really get lost. After 3.0 miles you will come to a saddle where the trail drops off the ridge's western side. Beyond the saddle the ridge heads abruptly upward to the top of a small peak. But the trail is very distinct as you approach the saddle, so you really don't have to worry about missing the route down.

The last 1.3 miles of trail, from the ridge to the road below, have been seriously degraded by ATVs driving up and down the mountain. The trail is occasionally completely obliterated by the ATV roads. About 0.5 mile before reaching the bottom you will encounter a steep, narrow gravel road that is part of the Alpine Acres housing development. Just follow this road downhill until it reaches the main access road near the Weber River. When you reach the main road turn right and walk the last 0.3 mile back to your car.

Round Lake

Row Bench

Distance:	5.2 miles (plus 14.8 miles by car)
Walking time:	3¹⁄₄ hours
Elevations:	960 ft. gain, 2,520 ft. loss Row Bench Trailhead (start): 8,240 ft. highest point: 9,200 ft. Center Canyon Trailhead: 6,720 ft.
Trail:	Little used, but not too difficult to follow. Numerous sheep trails in the area can cause some confusion. A compass is useful.
Season:	Summer through mid-fall. The road to Row Bench Trailhead may be closed from mid-November through May, and snow can be expected on the trail until mid-June.
Vicinity:	Daniels Canyon, near Heber
Maps:	Twin Peaks, Co-op Creek *(USGS)* Wasatch Front *(Trails Illustrated, #709)*
Information:	http://www.utahtrails.com/rowbench.html *(Utah Trails)* http://www.fs.usda.gov/uwcnf/ *(Uinta-Wasatch-Cache Nat. Forest)* phone: (435) 654-0470 *(Heber Ranger District)*

Drive south from Heber on Highway 40 toward Strawberry Reservoir for 11 miles until you see a small sign on the left side of the road marking the turnout to Center Canyon. Turn left here onto a small road that drops down to a parking area beside Daniels Creek. This parking area marks the end of the hike, and the shuttle car should be parked here.

To get to the beginning of the hike return to Highway 40 from Center Canyon and drive south for another 8.8 miles. You will come to a gravel road on the left side of the highway that heads north through a wide, flat valley along the east side of the Strawberry River. Take this road (Forest Road #49) and drive north for 5.9 miles to Mill B Flat. There you will see a large livestock corral on the left side of the road. Park your car near the corral and walk about 200 yards farther down the road, across a cattle guard and a small bridge, where you will see a sign marking the Row Bench Trailhead.

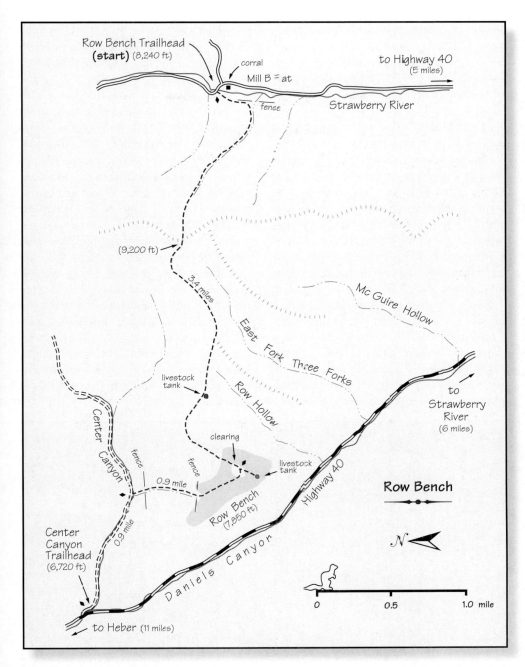

Row Bench Trailhead **(start)** (8,240 ft)

corral

to Highway 40 (5 miles)

Mill B = at

Strawberry River

fence

(9,200 ft)

3.4 miles

Mc Guire Hollow

East Fork Three Forks

livestock tank

Row Hollow

to Strawberry River (6 miles)

clearing

livestock tank

Center Canyon

fence

fence

Highway 40

0.9 mile

Row Bench

0.9 mile

Row Bench (7,850 ft)

Center Canyon Trailhead (6,720 ft)

Daniels Canyon

N

0   0.5   1.0 mile

to Heber (11 miles)

The Row Bench Trail is a little-used hiking trail that connects the upper part of Strawberry Valley to Daniels Canyon, southeast of Heber. Most of the walk is through dense quaking aspen with some Douglas fir. It is very pretty-especially in September when the aspen are changing color. During the second half of the hike, as you begin to drop down from the ridge that separates Strawberry Valley from Daniels Canyon, the forest opens up to some breathtaking views of Daniels Canyon and the mountains beyond. The area is open rangeland, so you may see some sheep. There is also a large population of deer in the area.

From Mill B Flat the trail rises gently in a southerly direction up the side of Strawberry Valley for about 0.2 mile before turning west to follow a dry wash toward the ridge above. You will see a barbed wire fence running below and parallel to the trail for about 0.1 mile before the path turns up the wash. After turning west the trail climbs up the bottom of the dry wash for about 1.0 mile, then levels out near the top of the ridge above Strawberry Valley.

Soon after reaching this ridge, the trail crosses to a second ridge separating Center Creek and East Fork Three Forks. It then winds pleasantly along the crest for another 1.5 miles before descending abruptly onto Row Bench. Row Bench is a relatively flat plateau on the side of the mountain, running parallel to and about 900 feet above the Daniels Canyon road. If you listen carefully you may hear the traffic on the road below at this point.

After you reach Row Bench the trail becomes somewhat confusing because sheep grazing on the bench have created other trails, and it is sometimes difficult to tell which trail is which. The correct trail continues in a southwesterly direction to a large clearing near the southern end of the bench, and then turns 90 degrees to a northwest heading. If you are on the correct trail you should see occasional blaze marks on some of the larger aspen trees. About 0.3 mile from the clearing the trail passes through a log fence and begins descending sharply through another small wash toward the bottom of Center Canyon. Finally, 0.5 mile after leaving the bench you will intersect a jeep road at the bottom of Center Canyon. Turn left and follow this jeep road for 0.9 mile to Highway 40 where your shuttle car is parked.

Row Bench Trail

Grandeur Peak

★ **day hike**

Distance:	5.2 miles (round trip)
Walking time:	4 hours
Elevations:	2,340 ft. gain/loss Grandeur Peak Trailhead (start): 5,960 ft. Grandeur Peak: 8,299 ft.
Trail:	Well marked and well maintained
Season:	Summer through fall. The upper parts of the trail are usually covered with snow from late November through early June.
Vicinity:	On the east side of Salt Lake City
Maps:	Mount Aire, Sugar House *(USGS)* Wasatch Front *(Trails Illustrated, #709)*
Information:	http://www.utahtrails.com/grandeur.html *(Utah Trails)* http://www.fs.usda.gov/uwcnf/ *(Uinta-Wasatch-Cache Nat. Forest)* phone: (801) 236-3400 *(Salt Lake Ranger District)*

Drive south from of Salt Lake City on I-215 and take the 3900 South exit; then turn east on 3900 South and drive under the freeway to Wasatch Boulevard. Drive one block north on Wasatch Boulevard to 3800 South and turn east again. 3800 South is the main road into Mill Creek Canyon. As you enter the canyon you will come to a toll booth where you will be charged an entrance *fee of $3.00 per vehicle. Continue into the canyon for 2.3 miles beyond the toll booth, then turn left into the Church Fork Picnic Area. The trailhead is on the north side of the picnic area, 0.3 mile from Mill Creek Canyon Road.*

There is only enough room for 8 cars at the trailhead, so unless you arrive early you may have to park on the main road outside the picnic area. This will add an additional 0.6 mile round trip to the hike, but the walk up Church Fork is very pretty– even from the road. (Note: the road through the picnic area is closed at 10:00 each night, so if you are planning a moonlight hike you had better park on the main road.)

Grandeur Peak is a favorite among residents of Salt Lake City simply because of its commanding position above the city. It is the last peak on the ridge separating Mill

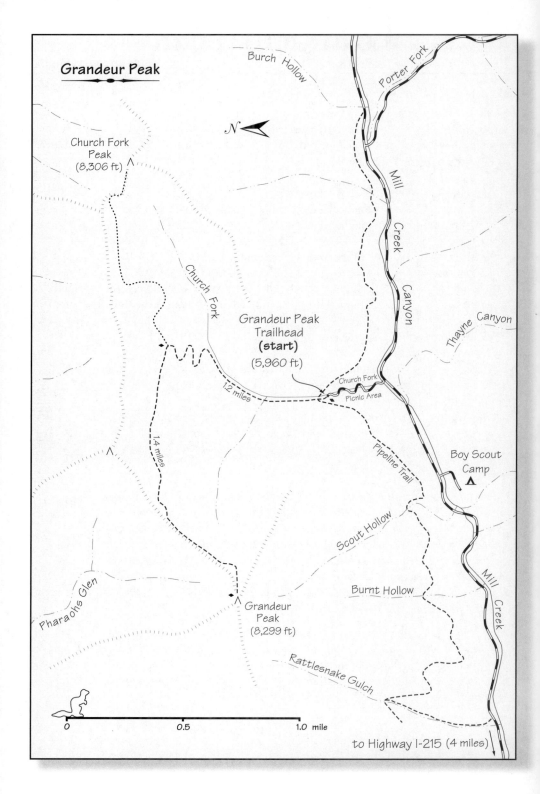

Grandeur Peak

Burch Hollow

Porter Fork

Mill Creek Canyon

N

Church Fork
Peak
(8,306 ft)

Church Fork

Grandeur Peak
Trailhead
(start)
(5,960 ft)

12 miles

14 miles

Church Fork
Picnic Area

Thayne Canyon

Pipeline Trail

Boy Scout
Camp

Scout Hollow

Pharaohs Glen

Grandeur
Peak
(8,299 ft)

Burnt Hollow

Mill Creek

Rattlesnake Gulch

0   0.5   1.0 mile

to Highway I-215 (4 miles)

Creek Canyon from Parleys Canyon, and it seems to stand like a sentinel over South Salt Lake watching every move in the city below. At 8,299 feet above sea level the peak is not particularly high, but from the ground it looks very imposing and many a resident of southeast Salt Lake has felt compelled to climb Grandeur just for the opportunity to view his neighborhood from the air.

The summit of Grandeur Peak is an especially fun place to be at sunset on a night with a full moon. As the sun sheds its last light on the valley the lights of the city slowly start to flicker on until eventually the entire valley is aglow with the beacons of human activity. The moonlit descent down the upper portion of the trail is easy, but you will need a flashlight for the last 0.7 mile through the darker recesses of Church Fork Canyon.

For the first 0.7 mile the trail winds upward through the bottom of the heavily forested Church Fork drainage. The trail is shaded by numerous bigtooth maples that turn fiery red in the Autumn, and the gurgling sounds of Church Fork are never far from the path. This pleasant part of the trail only lasts for 15-20 minutes though. Soon the small canyon veers east toward Church Fork Peak, and the trail begins a series of switchbacks up the north side of the canyon. Water becomes a more precious commodity as you leave the drainage, and the stately maple trees soon give way to a bushier cover of Gambel oak,

After leaving Church Fork the trail climbs steeply northward up the side of Mill Creek Ridge for 0.5 mile, and then turns west for a more gradual assent to the top of the ridge. At the point where the trail finishes its last switchback and turns west toward Grandeur Peak you will see a more primitive trail departing on the right. This secondary, unmaintained trail leads to the top of Church Fork Peak, 1.2 miles away at the top of the Church Fork drainage.

Twenty minutes after leaving the primitive Church Fork Peak Trail you should arrive at the top of the Mill Creek Ridge, and from there it is an easy 0.6 mile walk to the summit of Grandeur. As you approach Grandeur Peak the entire Salt Lake Valley will open up under you. To the north are the high buildings surrounding Temple Square, and to the south are the more suburban towns of Murray and Midvale. Behind you is Church Fork Peak with Mount Aire rising directly behind it. Further south the Twin Peaks, Lone Peak, and a dozen other peaks are prominently displayed above the Wasatch Front.

Grandeur Peak

Mount Olympus

Distance: 6.4 miles (round trip)

Walking time: 6 hours

Elevations: 4,200 ft. gain/loss
Mount Olympus Trailhead (start): 4,830 ft.
Mount Olympus: 9,026 ft.

Trail: This is a very popular hike. The trail is well used and generally easy to follow. The last 0.1 mile below the summit, however, is very steep and rocky and some scrambling is necessary.

Season: Summer through mid-fall. The upper parts of the trail are usually covered with snow from mid-November to early June.

Vicinity: Near Murray and Salt Lake City

Maps: Sugar House *(USGS)*
Wasatch Front *(Trails Illustrated, #709)*

Information: http://www.utahtrails.com/mountolympus.html *(Utah Trails)*
http://www.fs.usda.gov/uwcnf/ *(Uinta-Wasatch-Cache Nat. Forest)*
phone: (801) 236-3400 *(Salt Lake Ranger District)*

This hike begins southeast of Salt Lake City, just east of I-215 on Wasatch Boulevard. Drive south on I-215 and take the 3900 South exit; then turn east and drive under the freeway to Wasatch Boulevard. Turn right on Wasatch and drive south for another 2.3 miles. There you will see a paved parking lot on the east side of the road near a sign that says "Mt. Olympus Trailhead".

Mount Olympus, the peak for which the Mount Olympus Wilderness Area was named, forms a very prominent part of the Murray skyline, and it has been a favorite hike of the nearby residents for almost as long as Murray has been a city. It is not unusual on weekends to see fifty hikers relaxing together on the rocky summit.

The climb described here leads to the south summit of Mount Olympus, but there is also a north summit. The two are about 300 yards apart, separated by the upper reaches of Tolcats Canyon. The south summit is higher than the north summit by 67 feet. It is also the only one with a good trail leading to it and the one most frequently

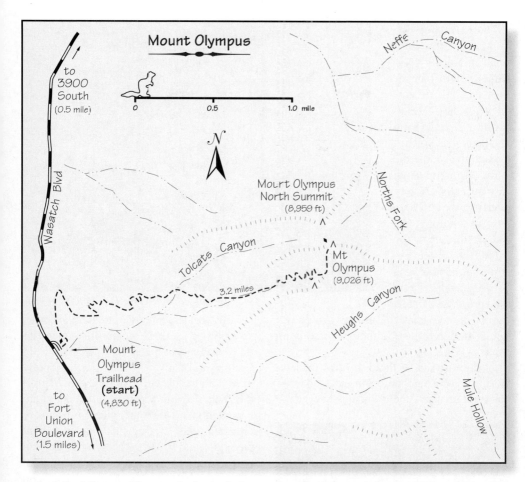

Mount Olympus

to
3900
South
(0.5 mile)

0   0.5   1.0 mile

N

Neffe Canyon

Mount Olympus
North Summit
(8,959 ft)

Norths Fork

Wasatch Blvd

Tolcats Canyon

^

^
Mt
Olympus
(9,026 ft)

3.2 miles

^

Heughs Canyon

Mule Hollow

← Mount
Olympus
Trailhead
(start)
(4,830 ft)

to
Fort
Union
Boulevard
(1.5 miles)

visited by hikers. The north face of the north summit, however, is a favorite among more serious mountain climbers. Although it looks foreboding, there is actually a route up the north face that requires little or no technical rock climbing skill. (See *Hiking the Wasatch*, by John Veranth.[2])

As you start up the trail to Mount Olympus you can look down and be thankful that in 1984, after a long and difficult fight by concerned citizens, most of it was included in the Mount Olympus Wilderness Area. The first half mile of the trail, however, crosses private land, and there is a real

danger that some day it will be obliterated by real estate developers. Hopefully when this land is developed public access to the trail will be preserved.

Initially this is a desert hike. The trail winds upward from the parking area on Wasatch Boulevard through the dry grass lands that dominate the foothills, finally coming to the first juniper trees after a climb of about 500 feet. Then, as the trail enters Tolcats Canyon, the dominant vegetation turns to Gambel oak. The path crosses the bottom of Tolcats Canyon 1.7 miles from the trailhead, but, except in early spring, there is seldom water in the canyon.

---

[2] John Veranth, *Hiking the Wasatch*, Wasatch Publishers, Salt Lake City, 1991.

Continuing upward along the south side of Tolcats Canyon, the trail never stops climbing until it reaches a small saddle 0.2 mile from the peak. As you approach the saddle the conditions change dramatically. A very pretty grove of Douglas fir occupies the ridge, and, for the first time since beginning the hike, you are on level ground. The presence of a few

Looking west from the summit of Mount Olympus

campsites indicates that hikers sometimes spend the night here, although there is no water.

From the saddle the trail turns directly north and soon encounters the rocky base of the summit. From there you must ascend the

Just below the summit of Mount Olympus

last 500 feet in scarcely more than 0.1 mile, scrambling up the Precambrian quartzite that caps most of the mountains around Big Cottonwood Canyon. You will occasionally need both hands, but if you stick to the trail the danger of injury from a fall is not great. Pay attention to the route. There is basically only one easy way up this side of Mount Olympus, and if you take a wrong turn you will soon be confronted with a much more difficult climb. If that happens just stop and look around, and you will probably find the trail just a few feet away. The greatest danger is from falling rocks, so as you climb be careful not to dislodge loose rocks onto other climbers below.

The summit is little more than a giant's rock pile of jagged boulders, but the views are great. Much of Salt Lake City lies below, and the full expanse of the Wasatch Mountains stretches to the east. Lone Peak, Twin Peaks, and Dromedary Peak are clearly visible to the south across the Cottonwood Canyons. To the north the summit drops off sharply into the upper reaches of Tolcats Canyon, beyond which, less than 300 yards away, is the north summit of Mount Olympus.

Gobblers Knob-Alexander Basin

 ★★★★

Mount Olympus Wilderness Area
shuttle car or bicycle useful
day hike

Distance:	7.0 miles (loop)
	(plus 3.4 miles by car or bicycle)
Walking time:	6¼ hours
Elevations:	4,030 ft. gain, 3,110 ft. loss
	Bowman Trailhead (start): 6,220 ft.
	Baker Pass: 9,340 ft.
	Gobblers Knob: 10,246 ft.
	Alexander Basin Trailhead: 7,140 ft.
Trail:	The trail to the top of Gobblers Knob is mostly well maintained and easy to follow, but for 0.7 mile from Gobblers Knob down into the upper part of Alexander Basin there is no trail. The descent is very steep and rocky but not technically difficult.
Season:	Midsummer to mid-fall. Alexander Basin is usually filled with snow each year until July. Also, the road to the Alexander Basin Trailhead is closed each year until July 1.
Vicinity:	Mill Creek Canyon, 10 miles east of Salt Lake City
Maps:	Mount Aire *(USGS)*
	Wasatch Front *(Trails Illustrated, #709)*
Information:	http://www.utahtrails.com/gobblers.html *(Utah Trails)*
	http://www.fs.usda.gov/uwcnf/ *(Uinta-Wasatch-Cache Nat. Forest)*
	phone: (801) 236-3400 *(Salt Lake Ranger District)*

Drive south of Salt Lake City on I-215, take the 3900 South exit and turn east. After driving under the freeway turn left onto Wasatch Boulevard, drive one block north, and then east again onto 3800 South. 3800 South is the main road into Mill Creek Canyon. As you enter the canyon you will come to a toll booth where you will be charged an entrance fee of $3.00 per vehicle. Continue into the canyon for 3.9 miles beyond the toll booth, then turn right into the Terrace Campground. The Bowman Trailhead is near a parking area in the back of the campground 0.2 mile from the main road. This is where the hike begins.

To get to the Alexander Basin Trailhead, where the hike ends, return to the Mill Creek Canyon Road and drive 3.2 miles further up the canyon. Just beyond "The Firs" summer

homes area you will see a small sign marking the Alexander Basin Trailhead on the right.

Note: Before July 1 of each year a locked gate on the Mill Creek Canyon Road prevents cars from driving the last 2.4 miles to the Alexander Basin Trailhead. The Forest Service closes the gate ostensibly because of winter snow conditions, but I suspect there are other reasons as well. The snow in Mill Creek Canyon is usually gone well before mid-June.

The relative ease with which Gobblers Knob can be climbed makes it one of the most popular summit destinations in the Wasatch Mountains. It is the highest point on the ridge separating Mill Creek Canyon from Big Cottonwood Canyon, and the view from the top is exceptional. It lies on the boundary of the Mount Olympus Wilderness Area just above the north-facing bowl of picturesque Alexander Basin. Gobblers Knob's proximity to Alexander Basin is in large part why it is such a delightful place, but, regrettably, it was also this proximity that prevented it, in 1984, from being wholly included in the Mount Olympus Wilderness Area. As a result there is now a very real possibility that some day the view from the peak will be marred by the presence of ski lifts on its northern slopes.

Alexander Basin is one of those alpine gems for which the future is very uncertain. A fierce political battle was fought in the early 1980s over the boundaries of the proposed Mount Olympus Wilderness Area. Protection of Alexander Basin was a high priority among Utah's environmentalists, but since the basin is used by helicopter skiers they were opposed by the state's skiing industry. In the end the skiers won, and the scenic glacial cirque was excluded. The boundaries of the Mount Olympus Wilderness Area are now distorted by a huge gouge on the eastern side where Alexander Basin lies. Not only is the basin still

Bowman Fork Trail

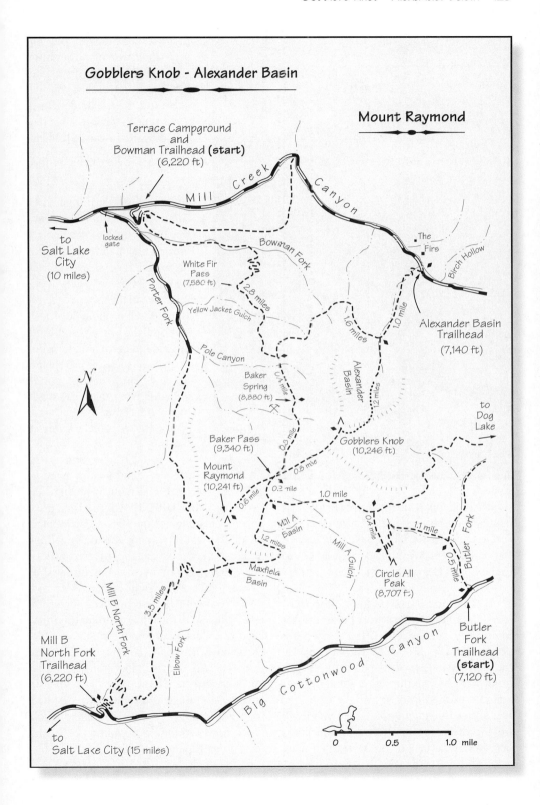

Gobblers Knob - Alexander Basin

Mount Raymond

Terrace Campground
and
Bowman Trailhead **(start)**
(6,220 ft)

Mill Creek Canyon

to
Salt Lake
City
(10 miles)

locked
gate

Porter Fork

White Fir
Pass
(7,580 ft)

Bowman Fork

2.8 miles

Yellow Jacket Gulch

Pole Canyon

Baker
Spring
(8,880 ft)

0.4 mile

1.6 miles

1.0 mile

The
Firs

Birch Hollow

Alexander Basin
Trailhead
(7,140 ft)

Alexander
Basin

1.2 miles

N

Baker Pass
(9,340 ft)

0.9 mile

Gobblers Knob
(10,246 ft)

to
Dog
Lake

Mount
Raymond
(10,241 ft)

0.8 mile

0.2 mile

1.0 mile

0.6 mile

Mill A
Basin

Mill A Gulch

0.4 mile

1.1 mile

Butler Fork

0.5 mile

1.2 miles

Maxfield
Basin

Circle All
Peak
(8,707 ft)

Mill B North Fork

3.5 miles

Elbow Fork

Mill B
North Fork
Trailhead
(6,220 ft)

Big Cottonwood Canyon

Butler
Fork
Trailhead
(start)
(7,120 ft)

to
Salt Lake City (15 miles)

0   0.5   1.0 mile

Looking north from Baker Pass

gradual climb. Soon you will see Mount Raymond looming through the quaking aspen, and shortly after that you will see a trail to Alexander Basin departing on the left. Continuing upward toward Gobblers Knob, the next point of interest is Baker Spring.

Baker Spring was once the site of an old mining camp. There was a cabin here until the 1980s, but unfortunately it burned down and now there is no trace left of it. If you look around, however, you will see remnants of the mining activity. Baker Mine is about 300 yards south of the spring, and there are remains of a smaller mine just above the trail. Gobblers Knob is said to have gotten its name from the noise made by a flock of turkeys that were once kept by miners living in the area.

Beyond Baker Spring the scenery continues to become more and more inspiring. As you pass the 9,000 foot level the forest opens up to some fine views of Gobblers Knob, Mount Raymond, and the Great Salt Lake. When you reach the summit of Baker Pass, 0.8 mile later, you will be greeted by a panorama of the Twin Peaks Wilderness Area south of Big Cottonwood Canyon. To the right and to the left are Mount Raymond and Gobblers Knob, both rising about 900 feet above the saddle. Also at the crest of the pass you will see two other trails taking off in either direction along the ridge to the two nearby summits. You should turn east here for the climb to the top of Gobblers Knob. (See page 126 for a description of the trail up Mount Raymond.)

used by helicopter skiers, but, even worse, it could easily become part of a future ski resort in upper Mill Creek Canyon. Proposals for such a resort have already been submitted to the Forest Service.

For the first 1.1 miles the trail to Gobblers Knob follows Bowman Fork, a small, pleasantly shaded creek that originates north of the peak. All too soon, however, the path leaves the water and begins a series of switchbacks up through a stand of large conifers to the top of White Fir Pass, 600 feet above Bowman Fork. Once you reach the top of he pass the forest becomes less dense, and the trail settles down to a more

Summit of Gobblers Knob

The trail up Gobblers Knob is not maintained, but it is well used and easy to follow. Except for the fact that it is all uphill, it is a fairly easy walk. The only downside is that there are several false summits along the route, and it is discouraging to see another heart-pounding climb in front of you after reaching what you thought was the top. Nevertheless, 45 minutes of determined walking should get you to the summit. The views are similar to the views from Baker Pass, but from this vantage point you can look down on Mount Raymond (5 feet lower).

Alexander Basin is the large bowl immediately northeast of Gobblers Knob. There is no trail from the top of the Knob into Alexander Basin, but it is not too difficult to drop off the summit and pick your way down through the basin to the trail below. The best way is to circle around the south side of Gobblers Knob to a saddle that lies about 400 yards east of the summit. The slope is very steep, but it is not too difficult to walk or slide down the north side of the saddle into Alexander Basin. Try to stay on the east side of the bowl as you make your descent,

and after you have lost about 800 feet you will run into the trail coming up from the Alexander Basin Trailhead. From there it is an easy 1.3 miles of downhill walking to the Mill Creek Canyon Road.

Mount Raymond, seen from Gobblers Knob

Mount Raymond

Mount Olympus Wilderness Area
shuttle car or bicycle useful
day hike

Distance:	9.3 miles (plus 3.9 miles by car or bicycle)
Walking time:	7 hours
Elevations:	3,120 ft. gain, 4,020 ft. loss Butler Fork Trailhead (start): 7,120 ft. Baker Pass: 9,340 ft. Mount Raymond: 10,241 ft. Mill B North Fork Trailhead: 6,220 ft.
Trail:	The trail is generally well used and easy to follow, except for the last two hundred yards below the summit of Mount Raymond. Here the path vanishes, and some scrambling is needed for the final ascent up a rocky ridge to the top.
Season:	Midsummer to mid-fall. The higher parts of the trail are usually covered with snow each year until late June.
Vicinity:	Big Cottonwood Canyon, east of Salt Lake City
Maps:	Mount Aire *(USGS)* Wasatch Front *(Trails Illustrated, #709)*
Information:	http://www.utahtrails.com/raymond.html *(Utah Trails)* http://www.fs.usda.gov/uwcnf/ *(Uinta-Wasatch-Cache Nat. Forest)* phone: (801) 236-3400 *(Salt Lake Ranger District)*

Drive south from Salt Lake City on I-215 and take the 6200 South exit. After exiting turn left under the highway overpass, and drive southeast for about 1.8 miles. The road soon becomes Wasatch Boulevard, and shortly afterward you will come to a stop light at Fort Union Boulevard. Turn left on Fort Union and proceed into Big Cottonwood Canyon. About 4.3 miles up the canyon the *road enters a big "S" curve. Half way through the "S" there is a turn to the right into a parking area at the Mill B North Fork Trailhead. This is where the hike ends, and where you should leave your shuttle car or bicycle.*

To get to the Butler Fork Trailhead, where the hike begins, continue up Big Cottonwood Canyon for another 3.9 miles. There you will see a smaller parking area on the left side of the road next to a sign marking the trailhead.

Mount Raymond is slightly lower than its popular neighbor, Gobblers Knob, but it is more fun to climb. The angular peak rises from the apex of three weathered limestone ridges that come together at roughly equal angles on the eastern side of the Mount Olympus Wilderness Area. The assent route described here follows one of the ridges up from Baker Pass. It is an easy walk most of the way, but the last few hundred yards involve just enough scrambling to make the climb interesting. At the top you will be treated to an exhilarating view of Dromedary Peak and Twin Peaks on the other side of Big Cottonwood Canyon and Gobblers Knob east of Baker Pass.

see map
page 123

The hike begins near the mouth of Butler Fork, an especially pretty tributary of Big Cottonwood Canyon. The path follows the streambed through a forest of aspen and Douglas fir for about 0.5 mile. Then it turns left onto another trail that climbs out of the canyon to the top of the ridge separating Butler Fork from Mill A Basin. A Forest Service sign clearly marks the trail junction where you must bear left. From the canyon floor the trail climbs steadily to the west, beginning a series of switchbacks just before it reaches the crest of the ridge.

When you reach level ground at the top of the ridge you should stop for a moment and look both ways. The main trail turns north to begin a long traverse around Mill A Basin, but another fainter trail turns south. This is the trail to Circle-All Peak. Circle-All Peak is 0.2 mile away with an elevation gain of only 150 feet, so it would be a shame to miss it. The five-minute walk south along the ridge to Circle-All Peak will reward you with nice views of Big Cottonwood Canyon as well as Mount Raymond, your destination.

Continuing north on the main trail for 0.4 mile will bring you to another trail junction. If you turn right here you will end up at Dog Lake, but to get to Baker Pass and Mount Raymond you must turn left. Again, the junction is clearly marked with a Forest Service sign.

The next 1.2 miles across Mill A Basin to the top of Baker Pass is one of the most pleasant parts of this hike. The forest is more open here with only an occasional grove of quaking aspen blocking the view, and Mount Raymond is clearly in sight. Note the ridge on the northeast side of Mount Raymond that connects the mountain to Baker Pass. Your final assent route to the summit will be along this ridge. Notice the outcroppings of limestone on the ridge as it nears the top

Butler Fork

of the mountain. Some minor scrambling will be necessary when you reach this point.

Five minutes before arriving at Baker Pass you will come to an unmarked junction where a less-used trail departs on the left. This is the Mill B North Fork Trail that you will be following on your way down the mountain. The main trail continues upward, reaching the top of the pass after another 0.2 mile.

From Baker Pass it is a short but steep climb to the top of Mount Raymond. You still have about 900 feet of elevation gain ahead of you at this point. Two small trails depart from the main trail at the top of the pass, one leading to Gobblers Knob and one leading to Mount Raymond. Turn left here for Mount Raymond. (See page 121 for a discussion of the trail to Gobblers Knob.)

The trail to Mount Raymond climbs steadily up the grassy slope for 0.5 mile, but then seems to disappear at the base of a badly fractured knife-edge outcropping of limestone. Proceed straight up the crest of the ridge. Although you will need both hands, the climb along the 30-foot-long knife-edge is not nearly as bad as it looks. Furthermore, this is the worst part of the climb. Beyond the knife-edge there is more minor scrambling, with bits and pieces of the trail visible. Stay right on the crest of the ridge, and within another five or ten minutes you should be on the summit.

While you are on the top of Mount Raymond be sure to study the descent route from Baker Pass south and east on the Mill B North Fork Trail. The first part of the trail is clearly visible on the south side of the peak. Also, you might want to study the ridge connecting Baker Pass to Gobblers Knob, just in case you want to do that hike on another day.

When you are ready to return, retrace your steps to the point about 0.2 mile below Baker Pass where you earlier passed the Mill B North Fork Trail junction. Turn right here and continue walking in a southerly direction. The Mill B North Fork Trail winds around the south side of Mount Raymond for 1.2 miles, then comes to another junction with the Porter Fork Trail. Bear to the left at this point toward Big Cottonwood Canyon. For the next 3.5 miles the trail meanders down the southwest side of Mount Raymond, cutting through two small canyons and a grove of huge Douglas fir trees before reaching the Mill B North Fork Trailhead.

Finally, if you have time and energy left, you might want to double back up the bottom of Mill B North Fork Canyon to see the Hidden Falls before you leave. The falls are only 0.1 mile from the trailhead.

Mount Raymond, viewed from Gobblers Knob

Dog Lake

★

Mount Olympus Wilderness Area
shuttle car or bicycle useful
day hike

Distance: 5.2 miles (loop)
(plus 0.8 mile by car, bicycle, or foot)

Walking time: 3³/₄ hours

Elevations: 1,680 ft. gain, 1,540 ft. loss
Butler Fork Trailhead (start): 7,120 ft.
Dog Lake: 8,740 ft.
Mill D Trailhead: 7,260 ft.

Trail: Popular, well maintained trail

Season: Summer through mid-fall. The higher parts of the trail are usually covered with snow until early June.

Vicinity: Big Cottonwood Canyon, near Salt Lake City

Maps: Mount Aire (*USGS*)
Wasatch Front (*Trails Illustrated, #709*)

Information: http://www.utahtrails.com/doglake.html (*Utah Trails*)
http://www.fs.usda.gov/uwcnf/ (*Uinta-Wasatch-Cache Nat. Forest*)
phone: (801) 236-3400 (*Salt Lake Ranger District*)

Drive south from Salt Lake City on I-215 and take the 6200 South exit. Turn east on 6200 South (which soon becomes Wasatch Boulevard) and drive for two miles to the stop light at Fort Union Boulevard. Turn left on Fort Union, note your odometer reading, and proceed into Big Cottonwood Canyon. You will see the Mill D Trailhead and parking area on the left side of the road 9.1 miles up the canyon. This trailhead marks the end of the hike.

To get to Butler Fork Trailhead, where the hike begins, drive a short distance from Mill D Trailhead back down Big Cottonwood Canyon toward Salt Lake City. After 0.8 mile you will see another parking area on the north side of the road and a small sign marking the Butler Fork Trailhead.

The prettiest part of the Dog Lake loop is probably the first two miles of trail along Butler Fork. For the first hour you will be following the picturesque creek northward through a narrow canyon filled with dense groves of quaking aspen. Then as the trail

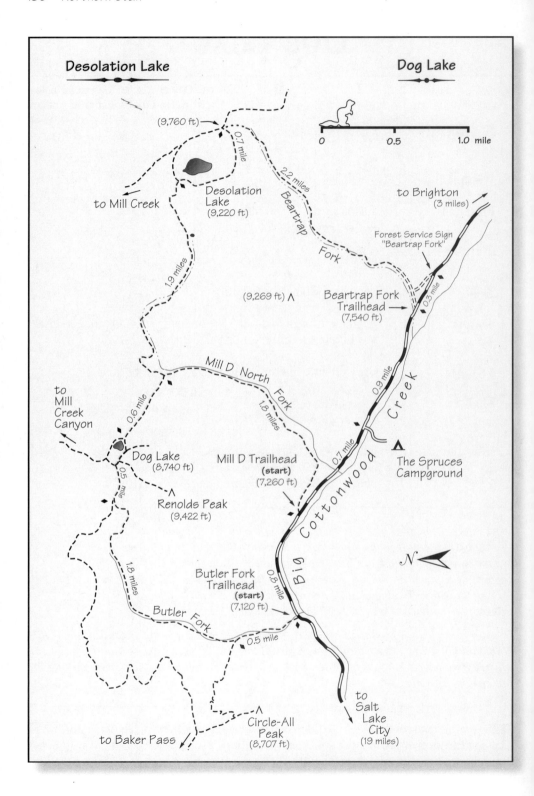

Desolation Lake

Dog Lake

(9,760 ft)

0.7 mile

to Mill Creek

Desolation Lake
(9,220 ft)

Beartrap Fork

2.2 miles

0   0.5   1.0 mile

to Brighton
(3 miles)

Forest Service Sign
"Beartrap Fork"

Beartrap Fork
Trailhead
(7,540 ft)

0.5 mile

0.9 mile

(9,269 ft) ∧

1.9 miles

Mill D North Fork

1.8 miles

to
Mill
Creek
Canyon

0.6 mile

Big Cottonwood Creek

0.7 mile

The Spruces
Campground

Dog Lake
(8,740 ft)

0.5 mile

Mill D Trailhead
(start)
(7,260 ft)

∧
Renolds Peak
(9,422 ft)

1.8 miles

0.8 mile

N

Butler Fork
Trailhead
(start)
(7,120 ft)

Butler Fork

0.5 mile

to
Salt
Lake
City
(19 miles)

∧
Circle-All
Peak
(8,707 ft)

to Baker Pass

approaches the creek's headwaters it climbs into the more open forest of Engelmann spruce and Douglas fir that surrounds the ridge above Mill Creek Canyon. Although Dog Lake itself lies outside the wilderness boundary, Butler Fork is part of the Mount Olympus Wilderness Area, and it is not uncommon to see moose here. Look for their hoof tracks along the path—similar to deer tracks, but two or three times larger.

Dog Lake is located in a shallow, heavily forested basin just south of the ridge that separates Mill Creek Canyon from Big Cottonwood Canyon. It is aptly named, since it is very popular among hikers with dogs. If you want to take a dog to Dog Lake, however, you will have to use the Big Water Trail which begins in Mill Creek Canyon. The Big Cottonwood Creek watershed area is a source of culinary water for Salt Lake City; hence dogs are prohibited along the route described here.

About 0.5 mile from the Butler Fork Trailhead you will come to a trail junction with the better used left fork leading to Mill A Basin. Take the right fork for Dog Lake. The trail climbs steadily for another 1.8 miles, finally coming to another junction about 1,680 feet above the trailhead at the top of the ridge. Again, bear right along the crest of the ridge. As you near Dog Lake, about 0.5 mile further east along the ridge, you may be confused by a number of trails that branch off to the north and south. Pay attention

to the map, and remember that Dog Lake is just a short way below the south side of the ridge. If you start climbing abruptly to the south you are probably headed for Renolds Peak. If you start descending abruptly to the north you are probably headed down into Mill Creek Canyon. Look for Dog Lake just a few hundred feet after the trail begins descending to the south.

From the southeast corner of Dog Lake a well used mountain bike trail descends for 0.6 mile to another trail junction. Here you will see a sign directing you to either Desolation Lake (left) or Mill D Trailhead (right). Take the right fork to the Mill D Trailhead. There are more hikers on this side of the loop than along Butler Fork. There are also some summer homes along the east side of Mill D North Fork, and you may catch glimpses of a lower trail that follows the east side of the creek. Finally, you should arrive at Big Cottonwood Canyon and the Mill D Trailhead about an hour after leaving Dog Lake.

Dog Lake

Desolation Lake

shuttle car or bicycle useful
day hike

Distance:	6.6 miles (loop)
	(plus 1.6 miles by car, bicycle, or foot)
Walking time:	5 hours
Elevations:	2,500 ft. gain, 2,220 ft. loss
	Mill D Trailhead (start): 7,260 ft.
	Desolation Lake: 9,220 ft.
	Desolation Lake Overlook: 9,760 ft.
	Beartrap Fork Trailhead: 7,540 ft.
Trail:	Most of the trail is well maintained and easy to follow, but some parts of the Beartrap Fork section can be confusing.
Season:	Summer through mid-fall. The higher parts of the trail are usually covered with snow until early June.
Vicinity:	Big Cottonwood Canyon, near Salt Lake City
Maps:	Mount Aire, Park City West *(USGS)*
	Wasatch Front *(Trails Illustrated, #709)*
Information:	http://www.utahtrails.com/desolation.html *(Utah Trails)*
	http://www.fs.usda.gov/uwcnf/ *(Uinta-Wasatch-Cache Nat. Forest)*
	phone: (801) 236-3400 *(Salt Lake Ranger District)*

Drive south from Salt Lake City on I-215 and take the 6200 South exit. Turn east on 6200 South (which soon becomes Wasatch Boulevard) and drive for two miles to the stop light at Fort Union Boulevard. Turn left on Fort Union Boulevard, note your odometer reading, and proceed into Big Cottonwood Canyon. You will see the Mill D Trailhead and parking area on the left side of the road 9.1 miles up the canyon. This trailhead marks the beginning of the hike.

To get to Beartrap Fork Trailhead, where the hike ends, continue up the canyon for another 1.6 miles until you see a locked gate on the left side of the road with the words "Beartrap Fork Gate No. 1" painted on it. This is where the hike will end, and this is where you should leave your shuttle car or bicycle. Don't be confused by a Forest Service sign 0.3 mile further up the highway that says "Beartrap Fork". If you park your shuttle at the Forest Service sign you will have that much farther to walk along the road.

Desolation Lake is a popular destination for mountain bikers, so you are bound to see a few of them on this hike. But don't expect all of them to be riding—there is a 2,000-foot elevation gain from the trailhead to the lake, and riding a bike uphill is much harder than walking.

The lake itself is located at the bottom of what, at first glance, looks like an old volcanic crater. The 550-foot-deep crater is actually a large bowl that was scooped out at the head of Mill D North Fork Canyon by a glacier during the last ice age. The view from the crater rim can be quite spectacular, especially in early September when the aspen trees on the northwest side of the lake are displaying their fall colors. On weekends one can often see fifteen or twenty mountain bikers parked on the trail above the lake, pausing to enjoy the view before their long downhill ride back into Big Cottonwood Canyon.

From Mill D Trailhead the trail winds up through the aspens along the north side of Mill D North Fork for 1.8 miles to the intersection with Desolation Trail. If you want to see Dog Lake before continuing on, bear left here for 0.6 mile. Otherwise, turn right for Desolation Lake.

Up to this point the hike has been an almost unbroken uphill climb. There is still more uphill walking to come, but for the last 1.9 miles before Desolation Lake there is also a fair amount of level ground. It is a beautiful walk through occasional meadows with fine views of the surrounding peaks. Finally, with almost no warning, the trail runs into the lake.

To reach the rim above Desolation Lake, bikers normally take the better used trail that goes up the northern side of the crater. But if you want to connect with Beartrap Fork, as I suggest, you should bear right and go up the lesser used path that climbs the crater's southern flank. Once you have negotiated the 550-foot climb to the top, follow the south rim trail around in an easterly direc-

see map
page 130

Mill D North Fork Trail

tion until it meets the trail coming from the north. At the point where the trails meet, above the southeastern side of the lake, you will see Beartrap Fork Canyon directly below you to the south. This is the route that will take you back to the highway in Big Cottonwood Canyon.

Unfortunately, the first few hundred feet of the Beartrap Fork Trail are so vague you probably won't believe you are on a trail at all. But don't worry, the track soon becomes evident. As you descend from the top of the ridge into Beartrap Fork you will first see an occasional cairn. Then you will see faint trample marks in the grass, and by the time you reach the trees, 100 yards from the rim, you will be on a proper hiking trail. Initially the trail tends to follow the right side of the creek bed, which is on the left side of the canyon.

There are few switchbacks on the Beartrap Fork Trail, and for the first mile the path is quite steep. But soon the canyon

Desolation Trail

floor levels out in a dense grove of quaking aspen, where you will begin to appreciate the beauty of the little-used route. Finally, about 0.5 mile from the highway, the trail turns into a jeep road. Some confusion may occur as you near the end because the jeep road is intersected by other primitive roads. Just remember to always take the road that heads downhill, and you should intersect the highway exactly at the point where you parked your shuttle.

Desolation Lake

Lake Blanche

★★★

Twin Peaks Wilderness Area
day hike

Distance:	5.6 miles (round trip)
Walking time:	4¹/₂ hours
Elevations:	2,580 ft. gain/loss Lake Blanche Trailhead (start): 6,320 ft. Lake Blanche: 8,900 ft.
Trail:	Popular, well maintained trail
Season:	Summer through mid-fall. Snow can be expected on the upper parts of the trail from mid-November through mid-June.
Vicinity:	Big Cottonwood Canyon, near Salt Lake City
Maps:	Mount Aire, Dromedary Peak *(USGS)* Wasatch Front *(Trails Illustrated, #709)*
Information:	http://www.utahtrails.com/blanche.html *(Utah Trails)* http://www.fs.usda.gov/uwcnf/ *(Uinta-Wasatch-Cache Nat. Forest)* phone: (801) 236-3400 *(Salt Lake Ranger District)*

Drive south from Salt Lake City on I-215 and take the 6200 South exit. After exiting turn left, under the highway overpass, and drive southeast for about 1.8 miles. The road soon becomes Wasatch Boulevard, and shortly afterward you will come to a stop light at Fort Union Boulevard. Turn left on Fort Union and proceed into Big Cottonwood Canyon. About 4.3 miles up the canyon the road enters a big "S" curve. Just as the "S" begins you will notice a smaller road branching off to the right. Take this road for 0.2 mile and look for the Lake Blanche Trailhead near a Forest Service toilet on the right.

Lake Blanche is one of the most popular hikes in the Salt Lake City area, not only because the walk is relatively short and the trailhead easy to get to, but because of the scenic beauty and the geologic attractions within the Lake Blanche Basin. Blanche and its two sister lakes, Florence and Lillian,

sit in a high alpine basin that was dug out by a glacier during the last ice age. Long straight scratch marks and deep polished grooves, etched out by the glacier, are still clearly visible on the stone surrounding the lakes. Picturesque Sundial Peak (10,320 ft.), which the Wasatch Mountain Club uses as

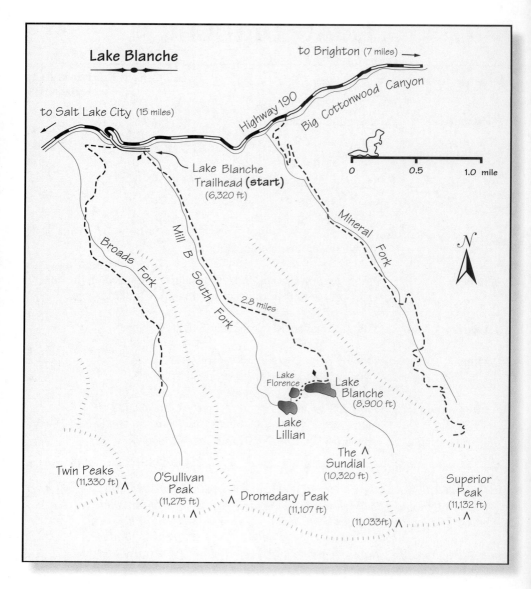

its emblem, rises abruptly from the south shore of Lake Blanche, and Dromedary Peak (11,170 ft.) is only a mile to the southwest. Blanche, its two sister lakes, Dromedary Peak, and the Sundial are all part of Utah's 11,300-acre Twin Peaks Wilderness Area.

From the trailhead the path begins climbing immediately, and continues to climb at a fairly steady grade of about a thousand feet per mile all the way to the lake. The trail crosses Mill B South Fork once, after 0.3 mile, and then stays on the east side of the canyon for the rest of the hike. About half way to the lake the trail leaves the stream and veers to the east in order to avoid some cliffs at the head of the canyon. Also at about this time you will leave the quaking aspen and enter into a conifer forest.

As you climb toward the lake you will

see frequent evidence of winter and spring avalanches, and in at least one area a rock slide has obliterated the trail. When you reach this part of the path just proceed across the slide area and look for the trail continuing on the other side. Such gaps in the track are never very long, but they do serve to warn hikers of the potential dangers of hiking the Wasatch in the early spring.

Glacier scratches near Lake Blanche

When you are near the top you will begin to see the Sundial rising behind the pass at the head of the canyon. The trail gets steeper here, but you can take heart in the fact that you are almost at the end. Lake Blanche is just on the other side of the pass. As you approach the lake be sure to look for the long scratches in the polished red rock, scraped out by the glacier that carved Lake Blanche Basin in the last million years.

Most hikers don't bother to visit Lake Florence and Lake Lillian. The two smaller lakes can't actually be seen from Lake Blanche, but they are only a short walk away and shouldn't be missed. Walk to the old dam at the west end of Blanche and you will be able to look down on Florence and Lillian, about 120 feet lower and 200 yards away. The view of the Sundial isn't quite as spectacular from Florence and Lillian, but if you enjoy solitude either one is a much more peaceful place to eat your lunch than Blanche. Also you are more likely to see deer and other wildlife there.

Sundial Peak above a frozen Lake Blanche

Red Pine Lake

Distance:	7.0 miles (round trip)
Walking time:	5 hours
Elevations:	2,040 ft. gain/loss White Pine Trailhead (start): 7,580 ft. Red Pine Lake: 9,620 ft.
Trail:	Popular, well maintained trail
Season:	Summer through mid-fall. The upper parts of the trail are usually covered with snow from late November through late June.
Vicinity:	Little Cottonwood Canyon, near Salt Lake City
Maps:	Dromedary Peak *(USGS)* Wasatch Front *(Trails Illustrated, #709)*
Information:	http://www.utahtrails.com/redpine.html *(Utah Trails)* http://www.fs.usda.gov/uwcnf/ *(Uinta-Wasatch-Cache Nat. Forest)* phone: (801) 236-3400 *(Salt Lake Ranger District)*

Drive south from Salt Lake City on I-215 and take the 6200 South exit. After exiting turn left, under the highway overpass, and drive southeast onto Wasatch Boulevard. The road soon passes the entrance to Big Cottonwood Canyon at Fort Union Boulevard and, after another four miles, arrives at the entrance to Little Cottonwood Canyon. Here you should turn left toward the Snowbird and Alta skiing areas. Five miles up from the mouth of Little Cottonwood Canyon, or 1.2 miles past the Tanner Flats Campground, you will come to a paved parking lot on the right side of the highway where you will find the White Pine Trailhead. This is also the trailhead for Red Pine Lake.

Located in the heart of Utah's Lone Peak Wilderness Area, Red Pine Lake definitely ranks among the prettiest of the Wasatch Mountains' high alpine lakes. It is a popular day or overnight hike and you are bound to meet many other trekkers along the way. But if you are looking for more solitude there are also several possible side trips off the main trail that receive far fewer visitors.

From the parking area the trail winds down a short distance to Little Cottonwood

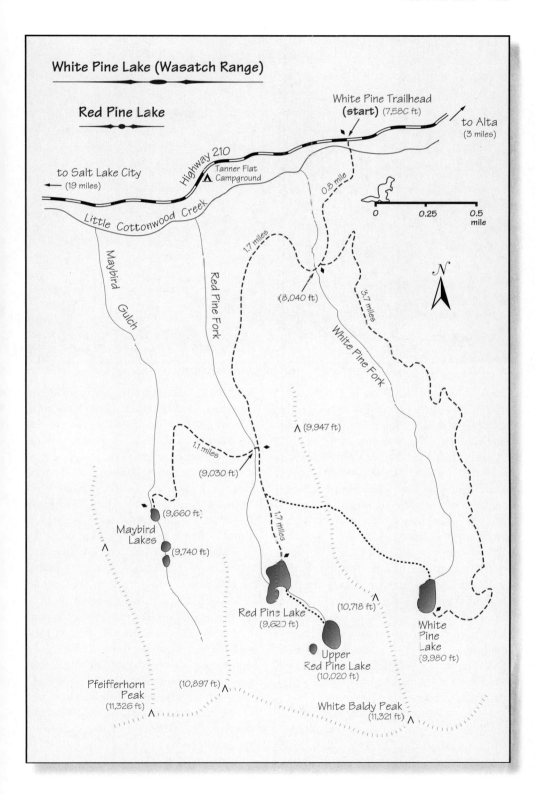

White Pine Lake (Wasatch Range)

Red Pine Lake

White Pine Trailhead
(start) (7,580 ft)

to Alta
(3 miles)

Highway 210

Tanner Flat
Campground

to Salt Lake City
(19 miles)

Little Cottonwood Creek

0.8 mile

0   0.25   0.5
mile

1.7 miles

(8,040 ft)

3.7 miles

Maybird   Gulch

Red Pine Fork

White Pine Fork

N

(9,947 ft)

1.1 miles

(9,030 ft)

(9,660 ft)

1.7 miles

Maybird
Lakes

(9,740 ft)

Red Pine Lake
(9,620 ft)

(10,718 ft)

White
Pine
Lake
(9,980 ft)

Upper
Red Pine Lake
(10,020 ft)

Pfeifferhorn
Peak
(11,326 ft)

(10,897 ft)

White Baldy Peak
(11,321 ft)

Junction where the Red Pine Lake Trail departs from the White Pine Lake Trail

Creek, which it crosses on a wooden foot bridge, and then proceeds over a gentle upward grade along the east side of White Pine Canyon. The first part of the trail is actually an old jeep road that was once used by miners to access their claims in upper White Pine Canyon. The mining activity long ago proved uneconomical, however, and today few signs of this piece of White Pine Canyon's history are evident. Vehicles are no longer allowed on the trail.

About a mile from the parking lot the trail breaks out of the aspen trees to meet the shore of White Pine Fork, and at this point the Red Pine Lake trail branches off to the right. Red Pine hikers must cross another foot bridge and follow the smaller westward trail. The elevation at this junction is about 8,040 feet, or 460 feet higher than the trailhead parking lot.

Half a mile after leaving the junction the Red Pine Lake trail rounds the ridge separating Red Pine Canyon from White Pine Canyon and again bends to the south. At one

point the terrain drops off precipitously on the right, opening up a panorama of Little Cottonwood Canyon. Tiny cars can be seen meandering up from the canyon mouth on a gray thread of asphalt two thousand feet below, but after a few hundred feet the trail ducks back again into the trees and the brief contact with civilization is lost. The grade then becomes somewhat steeper as the path climbs deeper into Red Pine Canyon.

Finally, at an elevation of 9,030 feet and a distance of 2.5 miles from the trailhead, the trail reaches the creek in the bottom Red Pine Canyon. At this point there is another junction in the trail, with the path to Maybird Lakes crossing Red Pine Creek on the right. Red Pine Lake hikers should continue straight ahead on the east side of the creek, but not before pausing to appreciate the beauty of this spot. The forest now has turned from aspen to conifer, and there is an abundance of wildflowers along the grassy river bank—perfect for a short break.

Large patches of snow often lie across

the last mile of the trail, sometimes until late July. This section of the canyon is well shaded on all sides except the north, and the snow seems to last forever. The path also gets noticeably steeper near the top of the canyon. Finally, at an elevation of 9,600 feet, the trail abruptly levels off, and another five minutes of easy walking will bring you to the lake.

The setting of Red Pine Lake is exquisite. The rugged crest that separates Little Cottonwood and American Fork Canyons, as well as the Wasatch and Uinta National Forests, lies just beyond the lake. White Baldy Peak (11,321 ft.) juts out prominently a mile to the southeast, and to the north, across Little Cottonwood Canyon, Dromedary Peak (11,107 ft.) and Superior Peak (11,132 ft.) are clearly visible. The lake itself is about 600 feet across, with a smaller bay protruding on the south end where the forest comes right to the water's edge.

Upper Red Pine Lake

Upper Red Pine Lake is situated 0.4 mile above the southeast side of the lower lake. There is no developed trail to Upper Red Pine and very little vegetation exists around the lake, but the setting is spectacularly wild and rugged. The upper lake, which is about the same size as its lower twin, lies directly beneath the dramatic White Baldy summit ridge. The best way to get there is along a primitive hiker-made trail that begins near the small stream connecting the upper lake to the southeast side of the lower lake. The route involves some scrambling with 400 feet of elevation again, but is not technically difficult.

Maybird Lakes

As mentioned earlier, the trail to Maybird Lakes leaves the Red Pine Trail about 2.5 miles from the highway, or about one mile down from Red Pine

Lake. The Maybird Lakes Trail branches to the west, crossing Red Pine Fork on a narrow wooden bridge just after Red Pine Trail first meets the creek. It then follows a fairly level route for about 0.5 mile in a westerly direction before turning south again for the assent through Maybird Gulch to the three tiny Maybird Lakes.

The first lake is about 1.3 miles from the Red Pine trail junction at an elevation of 9,660 feet, and the second and third lakes are situated a quarter of a mile further up the gulch. The lakes are all small, only 100 to 150 feet across, and the trees surrounding them are stunted. The gulch is filled with the breakdown of the nearby cliffs, and there is not enough soil to support a more luxuriant forest. But the lack of vegetation does afford a fine view of Pfeifferhorn Peak, a popular summit that cannot be seen from the Red Pine Lakes.

Red Pine Lake (early June)

White Pine Lake (Wasatch Range)

★ day hike

Distance:	9.0 miles (round trip)
Walking time:	6½ hours
Elevations:	2,540 ft. gain/loss White Pine Trailhead (start): 7,580 ft. White Pine Lake: 9,980 ft.
Trail:	Well maintained, easy to follow trail
Season:	Summer through mid-fall. Upper parts of trail are usually covered with snow from mid-November through mid-June.
Vicinity:	Little Cottonwood Canyon, near Salt Lake City
Maps:	Dromedary Peak *(USGS)* Wasatch Front *(Trails Illustrated, #709)*
Information:	http://www.utahtrails.com/whitepine.html *(Utah Trails)* http://www.fs.usda.gov/uwcnf/ *(Uinta-Wasatch-Cache Nat. Forest)* phone: (801) 236-3400 *(Salt Lake Ranger District)*

Drive south from Salt Lake City on I-215 and take the 6200 South exit. After exiting turn left, under the highway overpass, and drive southeast onto Wasatch Boulevard. The road soon passes the entrance to Big Cottonwood Canyon at Fort Union Boulevard and, after another four miles, arrives at the entrance to Little Cottonwood Canyon. Here you should turn left toward the Snowbird and Alta skiing areas. Five miles up from the mouth of Little Cottonwood Canyon, or 1.2 miles past the Tanner Flats Campground, you will come to a paved parking lot on the right side of the highway where you will find the White Pine Trailhead.

Like Alexander Basin, ten miles to the north, the area around White Pine Lake has long been the subject of intense controversy between Utah's environmentalists and ski resort owners. The original boundaries of Lone Peak Wilderness Area, created in 1977, were meant to include White Pine Lake, but lobbyists representing the nearby Snowbird Ski Resort succeeded in having White Pine Canyon excluded. Snowbird's Gad Valley ski lifts are only one mile from White Pine Fork, yet in spite of the nearness of civilization the pristine

see map page 139

alpine lake still has that wild feeling of remoteness. What a shame it would be to open it up to commercial activity.

The trail to White Pine Lake actually follows an old jeep road that was built in the early 1900s to service small-claim mines in the canyon. The mining activity proved uneconomical, however, and it has been many years since the road was used. Now the Forest Service no longer allows motor vehicles in the area, and the vegetation has been so successful in reclaiming the track that few hikers will recognize that they are following an old road. Because the trail was originally a road it is not as steep as it would otherwise be. But, by the same token, the winding route is much longer than necessary.

From the parking area the White Pine Trail first crosses Little Cottonwood Creek on a small wooden foot bridge and

White Pine Trail

then begins its long gentle assent up White Pine Canyon. After 0.8 mile it breaks out of the quaking aspen to meet White Pine Fork, then it abruptly swerves to the east away from the water. Near the water's edge the path splits, with the trail to Red Pine Lake departing to the right. If you cross the creek you are on the wrong trail.

After a long switch-back the trail again turns south and continues its meandering course toward the lake. The path never returns to the stream again, but it passes through several very attractive meadows. If you have sharp eyes you may spot the tailings of a few abandoned mines along the way, but time and nature have already healed

most of the canyon's scars and the forgotten mines are no longer obvious.

As you approach the end of the trail the route makes a few large switchbacks up the east side of White Pine Cirque and then traverses westward along the talus slopes. Finally the trail drops 120 feet into a small basin on the west side of the cirque, wherein is located the lake. White Pine Lake is about 300 feet wide and 600 feet long, about the same size as Red Pine Lake. The altitude is too high for lush vegetation, but there are some fair-sized spruce trees near the water's edge and a few good camping sites on the south shore. The elevation of the lake is just short of 10,000 feet.

White Pine Trail

138). The traverse is not technically difficult, but be prepared for some scrambling across the bolder-strewn ridge. There is no established trail between the two lakes.

Begin by following the contour of the land from the northern shore of White Pine Lake in a general westerly direction for 0.5 mile to the crest of the ridge. From there Red Pine Lake is visible below, and it is just a matter of picking your way down the slope to intersect the Red Pine Trail a short distance north of the lake. The traverse can also be done in the opposite direction, but it is less tiring to start from White Pine Lake which is about 360 feet higher than Red Pine.

Traversing to Red Pine Lake

Some experienced trekkers might want to add a little off-trail adventure to this hike by crossing the ridge that separates White Pine Lake from Red Pine Lake and returning to the trailhead via the Red Pine Trail (page

White Pine Lake

Lake Mary - Grizzly Gulch

 ★★★

shuttle car or bicycle useful
day hike

Distance:	6.4 miles (plus 2.5 miles by car or bicycle)
Walking time:	4¼ hours
Elevations:	1,370 ft. gain, 2,030 ft. loss Catherine Pass Trailhead (start): 9,400 ft. Catherine Pass: 10,220 ft. Lake Mary: 9,520 ft. Twin Lakes Pass Trailhead: 8,740 ft.
Trail:	Easy to follow, but numerous jeep roads and ski runs in the area create some confusion.
Season:	Midsummer through mid-fall. The higher parts of the trail are usually covered with snow until July.
Vicinity:	Alta ski area near Salt Lake City
Maps:	Brighton, Dromedary Peak *(USGS)* Wasatch Front *(Trails Illustrated, #709)*
Information:	http://www.utahtrails.com/lakemary.html *(Utah Trails)* http://www.fs.usda.gov/uwcnf/ *(Uinta-Wasatch-Cache Nat. Forest)* phone: (801) 236-3400 *(Salt Lake Ranger District)*

Drive south from Salt Lake City on I-215 and take the 6200 South exit. After exiting turn left, under the highway overpass, and drive southeast onto Wasatch Boulevard. The road soon passes the entrance to Big Cottonwood Canyon at Fort Union Boulevard and, after another four miles, arrives at the entrance to Little Cottonwood Canyon. Here you should turn left toward the Snowbird and Alta skiing areas. Eight miles up Little Cottonwood Canyon you will enter the town of Alta, and after another 0.5 mile the pavement ends. Just before the pavement ends you will see a large parking lot on the right side of the highway overlooking two ski lifts that run up the side of Albion Basin. On the left side of the highway, directly across from the parking lot, a small sign marks the trail that leads up Grizzly Gulch to Twin Lakes Pass. This is where your hike will end, and where you should leave your shuttle car.

To get to Catherine Pass Trailhead, where the hike begins, continue up the highway for another 2.5 miles toward the Albion Basin Campground. About 0.2 mile before reaching the

campground you will come to a short, 100-yard-long road departing on the left. Catherine Pass Trailhead, also called Lake Mary Trailhead, is at the end of this road.

This hike is located between the ends of Big and Little Cottonwood Canyons, in the midst of the Brighton and Alta ski areas. It is a very pretty area with many alpine lakes and green meadows, but unfortunately the presence of so much commercial activity has inevitably degraded the area's hiking potential. Especially around Brighton, at the end of Big Cottonwood Canyon, the mountains have been extensively bulldozed to fill the ever growing need for more ski runs and their associated service roads.

Grizzly Gulch, the return leg of this hike, is an open museum of the mining activity in Utah at the turn of the last century. There are dozens of abandoned mines in the steep canyon along with old boilers, pipes and other relics of days gone by. Like most history lessons, this one also contains a message for the present. Looking at the heaps of mine tailings that now fill Grizzly

Gulch, one can't help but wonder what the once pristine canyon was like before man's arrival, and how many other beautiful areas are being destroyed, even now, by unregulated mining activity.

From Catherine Pass Trailhead the trail immediately starts up a series of switchbacks. It continues to climb for about 820 feet, finally reaching the summit of Catherine Pass after a distance of 1.0 mile. Catherine Pass, with Catherine Lake immediately below it, is the most impressive viewpoint on this hike. The trail forks here, with the main trail dropping down to Catherine Lake on the left. If you enjoy panoramic views, however, you might want to turn right and climb to the top of Sunset Peak before continuing. Sunset Peak is the highest point on the ridge above Catherine Lake. The trail to the summit is 0.6 mile

Catherine Pass

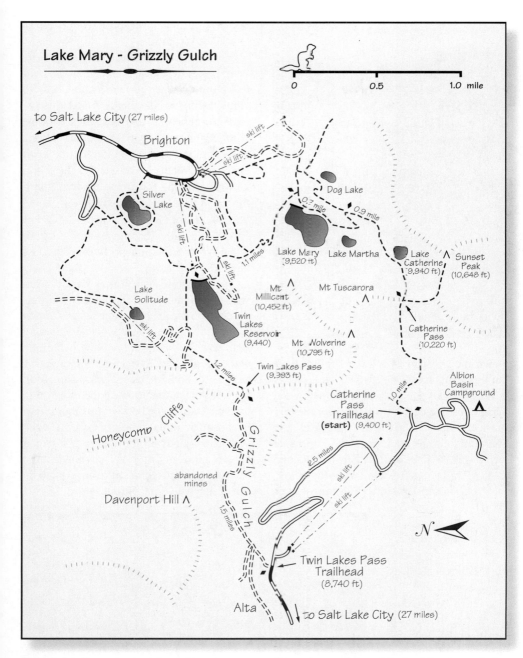

Lake Mary - Grizzly Gulch

0   0.5   1.0 mile

to Salt Lake City (27 miles)

Brighton

Silver Lake

Dog Lake

ski lift

0.7 mile   0.9 mile

Lake Mary (9,520 ft)   Lake Martha   Lake Catherine (9,940 ft)   ∧ Sunset Peak (10,648 ft)

1.1 miles

Lake Solitude

Mt Millicent (10,452 ft)   ∧   Mt Tuscarora   ∧

Twin Lakes Reservoir (9,440)   Mt Wolverine (10,795 ft)   ∧   Catherine Pass (10,220 ft)

.2 miles   Twin Lakes Pass (9,393 ft)

Honeycomb Cliffs

Catherine Pass Trailhead (start) (9,400 ft)   1.0 mile   Albion Basin Campground ∧

abandoned mines

Grizzly Gulch

Davenport Hill ∧   1.5 miles   2.5 miles   ski lift

N

ski lift

Twin Lakes Pass Trailhead (8,740 ft)

Alta   to Salt Lake City (27 miles)

long (1.2 miles round trip), and involves an additional climb of 430 feet.

After passing Catherine Lake the next point of interest is Lake Martha, a small but very pretty lake at the base of the cliffs below Mount Tuscarora. Finally, only a few minutes beyond Lake Martha is Lake Mary. Lake Mary, actually a reservoir, is quite large (about 1,500 by 800 feet) and deep. It is also very scenic when full. But since it is used as part of Salt Lake City's water supply its size varies considerably, and

Trail below Catherine Pass

on a jeep road that was built from Brighton to service the dam.

Once you are on the north side of the Twin Lakes Reservoir start following a trail that climbs in a westerly direction, roughly parallel with the lake shore. Follow this trail until it intersects a ski run, then continue climbing on the ski run for another 0.2 mile or so until you see the trail departing again on the left. When this trail leaves the ski run it climbs steeply for a few hundred feet to the top of the ridge, from where you can see the Twin Lakes Reservoir again far below. From there the trail traverses across the top of the Wolverine Cirque to Twin Lakes Pass, about 0.4 mile away.

To get from Twin Lakes Pass to Alta, where your shuttle car is parked, you must descend on the trail through Grizzly Gulch. This part of the trail is actually an old wagon road that was originally built by miners working the canyon over a century ago. It is very rocky and, in places, very steep. Judging from the remnants of all the mine shafts that scar the canyon bottom, there must have been a thriving community here. Grizzly Gulch may soon become the site of still more construction activity; it is now the location of another proposed ski lift from Alta to the top of the Wolverine Cirque.

when the water level is low its shores have an ugly barren look. After the trail passes Lake Mary Dam it starts descending toward Brighton. Watch carefully here for another trail that leads off to the left, just below the dam, and climbs back up to the north side of the lake. This trail, called the Granite Lakes Trail, goes to Twin Lakes Reservoir.

You should follow the Granite Lakes Trail for 1.1 miles until it arrives at Twin Lakes Reservoir, crossing under the Millicent Ski Lift along the way. When you reach Twin Lakes Dam you must once again walk below and around the dam to the north side of the lake where you will find the trail that goes to Twin Lakes Pass. For a short distance below the dam you will be

Twin Lakes, from Twin Lakes Pass

Silver and Silver Glance Lakes

★★★

Distance:	5.6 miles (round trip)
Walking time:	4¼ hours
Elevations:	2,430 ft. gain/loss
	Silver Lake Trailhead (start): 7,470 ft.
	Silver Lake: 8,960 ft.
	Silver Glance Lake: 9,900 ft.
Trail:	Excellent, well maintained trail as far as Silver Lake. There is no trail for the last 0.7 mile from Silver Lake to Silver Glance Lake, but the route is not difficult to follow.
Season:	Midsummer through mid-fall. There is usually snow around Silver Glance Lake until mid-July. The best time to do this hike is during the last three weeks of July when most of the snow has melted but the lakes are still full of water. The water levels drop significantly in August after the winter snow pack has melted, but if you go before the end of June the snow might prevent you from reaching the upper lake.
Vicinity:	Near Lehi
Maps:	Dromedary Peak *(USGS)*
	Uinta National Forest *(Trails Illustrated, #701)*
Information:	http://www.utahtrails.com/silverglancelake.html *(Utah Trails)*
	http://www.fs.usda.gov/uwcnf/ *(Uinta-Wasatch-Cache Nat. Forest)*
	phone: (801) 785-3563 *(Pleasant Grove Ranger District)*

Drive north from Lehi on I-15 for 4.0 miles to exit 287. Turn east at exit 287 and drive toward the mountains on Highway 92. After 7.3 miles the road enters American Fork Canyon, where you will be required to buy a Forest Service recreation pass ($6.00 per vehicle). 2.5 miles from the mouth of the canyon the road passes Timpanogos Cave National Monument, and 2.6 miles later *you will come to the junction with North Fork Road. Turn left here and follow North Fork Road for 3.3 miles, past Tibble Fork Reservoir, to Granite Flat Campground. Just before the entrance to the campground you will see a gravel road departing on the right. This is the Silver Lake Flat Road. Drive north on this road for the last 3.2 miles to the parking area* *and trailhead on the north side of Silver Lake Flat Reservoir. (The Silver Lake Flat Road is not well maintained, but with care it is usually passable for most high-clearance cars.)*

Before starting this hike you might want to pause for a few minutes to enjoy the spectacular scenery at Silver Lake Flat. Silver Lake Flat Reservoir is surrounded by a mixture of conifers and quaking aspen with the Wasatch peaks rising prominently on all sides. The trailhead is located on the northern shore of the reservoir, and the view to the south includes a marvelous panorama of Mount Timpanogos and the adjacent peaks. Silver Lake Flat is a popular destination for fishermen, and the reservoir is stalked with rainbow trout throughout the summer, but unfortunately overnight camping is not permitted within a half mile of the water. The nearest campground is at Granite Flat, three miles below the reservoir.

The hike from Silver Lake Flat to Silver Lake is a relatively easy 2.1-mile climb up the southern slopes of Lone Peak Wilderness to a small bench below the Little Matterhorn/Twin Peaks summit ridge. That is as far as most people get, but if you still have energy to spare it is not too difficult to continue upward from Silver Lake for another 0.7 mile to Silver Glance Lake, a somewhat smaller tarn located 940 feet higher in elevation. Silver Glance is

very different from the lower lake in a wild and remote sort of way. It is situated in a tiny basin just 900 feet below the summit ridge, and the setting is pristine. Although the lake is on the south-facing side of the ridge it is usually at least partially frozen and surrounded by snow well into July. Occasionally an adventurous hiker will continue beyond Silver Glance, scrambling the last

Silver Lake

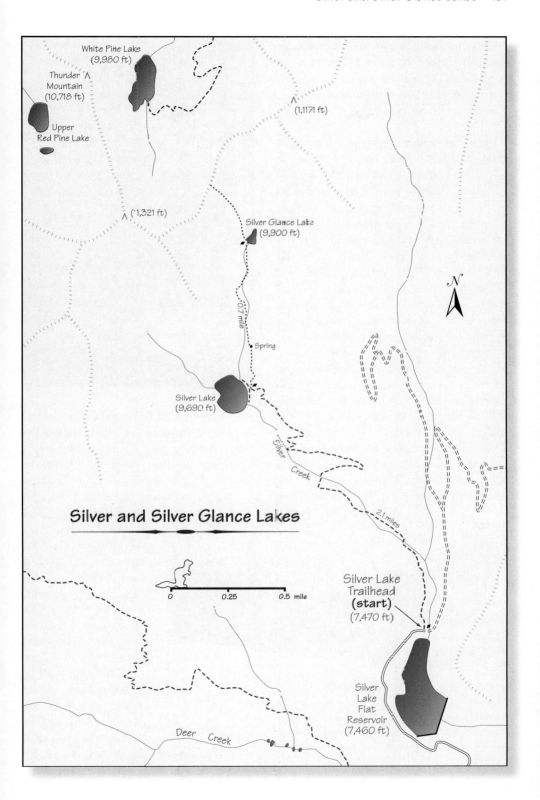

White Pine Lake
(9,980 ft)

Thunder Λ
Mountain
(10,718 ft)

Upper
Red Pine Lake

Λ (1,1171 ft)

Λ (1,321 ft)

Silver Glance Lake
(9,900 ft)

0.7 mile

Spring

Silver Lake
(9,690 ft)

Silver Creek

2.1 miles

Silver and Silver Glance Lakes

0   0.25   0.5 mile

Silver Lake
Trailhead
(start)
(7,470 ft)

Silver
Lake
Flat
Reservoir
(7,460 ft)

Deer Creek

N

760 feet to a low point on the ridge to peer down into Little Cottonwood Canyon on the north side of the wilderness area. The reward is an unforgettable view of White Pine Lake, 0.5 mile north and 680 feet below the saddle.

The trail begins as a very pleasant walk through a grove of aspen trees along the left side of Silver Creek. Unfortunately the creek is mostly heard rather than seen, but you may notice a few short spurs where hiker-made trails depart from the main path for better views of the cascades. After 0.4 mile the trail approaches the creek for the first time and crosses on a log to the east side of the stream. From that point the trail continues at a somewhat steeper grade along the right side of the stream, crossing once again to the left side after another 0.2 mile.

Shortly after the second stream crossing the trail leaves most of the aspen trees behind and enters into an open forest of scattered spruce and subalpine fir. Also at about this time the trail doubles back across the stream to begin a series of long switchbacks up the side of the mountain. Silver Lake Flat Reservoir is clearly visible in the canyon below, and Mount Timpanogos stands out in the distance. The Timpanogos Glacier is

Trail to Silver Lake

also clearly visible from this vantage point. Studying the route ahead you can see that the trail is heading toward a relatively flat area higher up the slope. That bench is where Silver Lake is located.

The trail below the lake is littered with granite boulders, and at one point it crosses the tailings of an old mine – one of many in these mountains. Finally, as the trail comes to within 250 feet of the east side of Silver Lake you will see many hiker-made secondary trails branching off in both directions. Some of the trails head for the southern side of the lake and some head for the eastern shore.

Trail to Silver Glance Lake (early July)

Silver Lake is directly above you at this point, and it doesn't matter much which path you take. They all lead to the same place. However, if you are looking for the trail to Silver Glance Lake you should bear right at each of the forks as you approach the lower lake. If you do this you will soon come to the east side of Silver Lake, and at the point where the lake first comes into view you will notice a faint hiker-made trail turning to the right to continue up the slope. This is the beginning of the unmarked trail to Silver Glance Lake.

The trail to Silver Glance Lake begins about 300 feet southeast of the inlet to Silver Lake. Although the route is somewhat steep, there is little ground cover in this area and the walking is relatively easy. After 0.2 mile you will pass a small fast-running natural spring where you can enjoy a drink of cool, clean water, and beyond the spring the trail pretty much disappears. Just pick a route that continues upward with as few obstacles as possible and you will be fine. The best route gradually angles to the left, toward the drainage that connects the two lakes. After you have walked 0.4 mile from the lower lake you should be in or near the bottom of the drainage, and from there you can just follow the depression the rest of the way to Silver Glance. Don't stray too much to the east. Keep to the west along the base of the ridge and soon you will run into the upper lake.

Silver Glance is considerably smaller than Silver Lake, but in my opinion it is much prettier. Unlike the lower lake, Silver Glance is well shaded by some good sized trees. Also, the smaller lake is dramatically situated below the slopes of the Little Matterhorn/Twin Peaks summit ridge, and it is easy to imagine that some of the huge granite boulders near its shore rolled down from the peaks only yesterday. I doubt, however, that the lake has much of a fish population. It probably freezes solid in the winter.

Silver Glance Lake (early July)

Mount Timpanogos

★★★★★

Mount Timpanogos Wilderness Area
shuttle car required
overnight hike

Distance: 17.3 miles
(plus 5.3 miles by car or bicycle)

Walking time: day 1: 8½ hours
day 2: 6½ hours

Elevations: 5,730 ft. gain, 5,280 ft. loss
Aspen Grove Trailhead (start): 6,910 ft.
Emerald Lake: 10,380 ft.
Mount Timpanogos: 11,749 ft.
Timpooneke Trailhead: 7,360 ft.

Trail: Popular, well maintained trail

Season: Midsummer through mid-fall. The higher parts of the trail are usually covered with snow from mid-November until July.

Vicinity: Near Sundance Ski Resort, above Provo and Orem

Maps: Timpanogos Cave, Aspen Grove *(USGS)*
Uinta National Forest *(Trails Illustrated, #701)*

Information: http://www.utahtrails.com/timpanogos.html *(Utah Trails)*
http://www.fs.usda.gov/uwcnf/ *(Uinta-Wasatch-Cache Nat. Forest)*
phone: (801) 785-3563 *(Pleasant Grove Ranger District)*

Drive north through Provo on Highway 189 (University Avenue), or east through Orem on Highway 52 (800 North), until you reach the mouth of Provo Canyon. Continue east into the canyon on Highway 189 for 6.8 miles to the junction with Highway 92. Turn north here and drive for another 4.9 miles, past the Sundance Ski Resort, until you see a Forest Service sign on the left  *marking the Theater in the Pines Picnic Area. The Aspen Grove Trailhead, where the hike begins, is located just west of the Theater in the Pines parking area. (Note: Just before you reach the picnic area you will pass a Forest Service booth where you must purchase a $6.00/day recreation pass to park and hike in the area.)*

To get to the Timpooneke Trailhead, where the hike ends, continue north on Highway 92 for another 5.0 miles to the entrance of Timpooneke Campground. Turn into the campground and drive the last 0.3 mile to the Timpooneke Trailhead and parking area. (Note: parking is limited at both trailheads, so be sure to arrive early!)

Timpanogos Trail, upper Primrose Cirque

Mount Timpanogos has, for most of this century, been the most popular mountain climbing destination in Utah. The majestic mountain, second highest in the Wasatch Range, seems to have everything—an alpine lake just below the summit, a small glacier, waterfalls along the trail, and high alpine meadows that in late summer are filled with wildflowers. A herd of mountain goats can frequently be seen at the higher elevations, and history buffs can visit the remains of an old World War Two bomber that crashed north of the summit in the winter of 1955.

Timpanogos was popularized in the early 1900s by a local folk hero named Eugene "Timp" Roberts. Roberts was raised in Provo, and later became the athletic director at Brigham Young University. As a young man he enjoyed exploring the mountains along the Wasatch Front, and while he was working at the university he began taking small groups of students up Mount Timpanogos. (In those days the trail began in Provo Canyon, and getting to the summit and back was a three-day trip.) The excursions gradually grew in popularity, and by 1913 Roberts' hikes to the top of Timpanogos had become a university tradition.

Soon other enthusiasts from outside the university were clamoring to join the outings, and the annual event took on a life of its own. All-night parties were held in Aspen Grove, commemorative badges were handed out on the summit, special walking sticks were presented to dignitaries, sandwiches were sold at Emerald Lake, buses were chartered to carry hikers to the trailhead, and people showed up by the thousands. The event continued for the next 59 years.

In 1961 over 2,000 people reached the summit in a single day, and the Forest Service began to worry openly about the impact that so many hikers were having on

Waterfall in Primrose Cirque

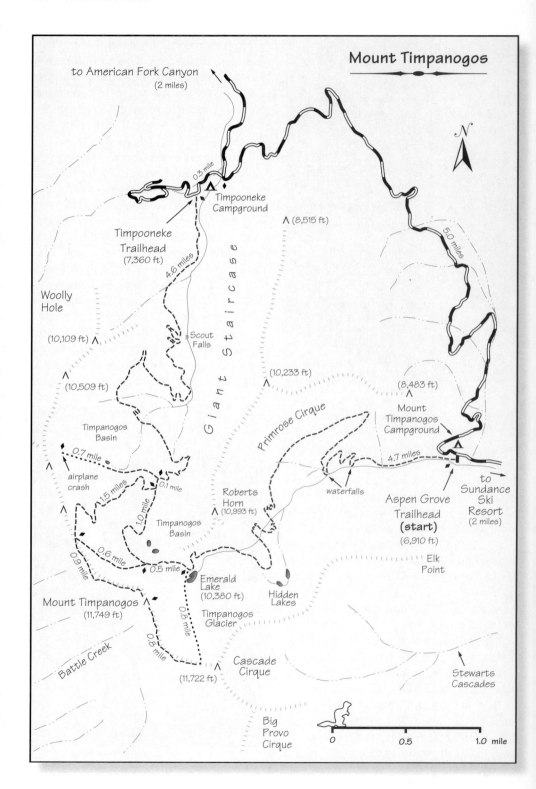

Mount Timpanogos

to American Fork Canyon
(2 miles)

N

0.3 mile

Λ Timpooneke
Campground

Timpooneke
Trailhead
(7,360 ft)

4.6 miles

Λ (8,515 ft)

Woolly
Hole

(10,109 ft) Λ ‡ Scout
Falls

Λ (10,509 ft)

Giant Staircase

5.0 miles

Timpanogos
Basin

Λ (10,233 ft)

Primrose Cirque

(8,483 ft)
Λ

Mount
Timpanogos
Campground

0.7 mile

airplane
crash

1.5 miles

0.1 mile

1.0 mile

Roberts
Horn
Λ (10,993 ft)

waterfalls

4.7 miles

Λ

Aspen Grove
Trailhead
(start)
(6,910 ft)

to
Sundance
Ski
Resort
(2 miles)

Timpanogos
Basin

0.6 mile

0.9 mile

0.5 mile

Emerald
Lake
(10,380 ft)

Hidden
Lakes

Elk
Point

Mount Timpanogos Λ
(11,749 ft)

Timpanogos
Glacier

0.8 mile

Battle Creek

0.8 mile

Λ
(11,722 ft)

Cascade
Cirque

Stewarts
Cascades

Big
Provo
Cirque

0   0.5   1.0 mile

Timpanogos Trail, above Primrose Cirque

the environment. In 1970 over 7,000 people participated in the "Timp Hike" with 3,500 of them reaching the summit. The pressure of so many hikers on the mountain in one day proved to be an unmitigated environmental disaster, and reluctantly the Forest Service ended the popular event.

Although the Timp Hike is no longer an organized annual event the mountain is still very popular, and thousands of people continue to climb to its summit every summer. Now, however, the trails are much better maintained and the number of visitors is more evenly distributed throughout the summer. Also the trails are now patrolled during summer weekends and holidays by a volunteer organization known as the Timpanogos Emergency Response Team (TERT). The primary purpose of the TERT volunteers is to provide emergency medical assistance, but they also help protect the mountain by reporting illegal fires and other environmentally destructive activities to the Forest Service.

Day 1 (7.5 miles)

From the Aspen Grove Trailhead the route heads west along a small unnamed creek that drains Primrose Cirque. Initially the grade is very gradual, but that soon changes. After 0.9 mile the trail reaches the base of a small waterfall, where it makes an abrupt right turn and begins climbing through a series of switchbacks. In another 0.5 mile the path passes a second waterfall, and then it enters a long switchback as it continues its assent up the north side of the cirque.

Finally, after a distance of 3.8 miles and an elevation gain of 2,930 feet from the trailhead, the well-worn path reaches the top of Primrose Cirque and passes into a flat open area south of Roberts Horn. If you got off to a late start you will see a delightful camping spot in a small grove of Engelmann spruce at the edge of the meadow; the site is about 100 yards south of the main trail at the end of a short spur. From this point it is another 1.0 miles to Emerald Lake, the first major attraction of this hike.

Emerald Lake is one of the gems that make the Timpanogos hike so special. The tiny lake lies just on the edge of timberline at an elevation of 10,380 feet. To the south is Roberts Horn, and to the west, only 550 horizontal yards away, is the summit of Mount Timpanogos. The lake is frozen most

Emerald Lake below Timpanogos Glacier

of the year, but even when it is not covered with ice its temperature hovers near freezing. It is fed by a permanent snowfield that descends from the summit ridge to the south end of the lake. Although this snowfield is hardly a glacier it has been affectionately referred to as the Timpanogos Glacier at least since 1916.

The small valley around Emerald Lake

also seems to be a favorite late-summer hangout for the mountain goats that live in the wilderness area, so be sure to look for them while you are there. The shaggy, majestic creatures have thrived since their introduction in 1981. Occasionally they venture to within a hundred feet of campers by the lake, but more often you will need a pair of binoculars to study them in detail.

Many backpackers camp at Emerald Lake on their way up Mount Timpanogos, especially if they plan to return to the Aspen Grove Trailhead. If you didn't bring a tent it is possible to sleep in a stone shelter that was built there in 1959 during the days of the Timp Hike. You will probably be more comfortable in a tent, though, as the stone shelter is very dark and dingy inside and has a cold cement floor. If you plan to finish the hike at the Timpooneke Trailhead, as I describe, I suggest you continue for another 1.8 miles into the Timpanogos Basin before making camp.

From Emerald Lake the trail continues west for 0.5 mile, and then loses 200 feet as it contours around the southwest side of Timpanogos Basin. 1.5 miles after leaving the lake you will come to a junction where the summit trail takes off to the left. Bear right at the summit trail junction, and within

photo by Kris Lander

Mountain goats above Emerald Lake

Emerald Lake, viewed from summit

is almost exactly magnetic west of the Forest Service toilet.

The airplane that crashed was a World War Two B-25. Both engines are still intact, as are the main landing gear and some sections of the wings and tail. The airplane did not ignite on impact, although the Forest Service later burned the wreckage in an attempt to dispose of it. You may notice a peculiar chemical smell near the crash site; perhaps it is a remnant of the aviation fuel that was dumped on the ground when the plane crashed.

Day 2 (9.8 miles)

In order to climb to the top of Mount Timpanogos you must backtrack to the summit trail, which departs from the main trail 0.1 mile south of the Timpanogos Basin trail. You will be coming back the same way, so you can leave your backpack in Timpanogos Basin and

200 yards you should see another trail leaving on the left near a sign that says "toilet". Turn left here and walk west into the upper part of Timpanogos Basin. You will pass the Forest Service toilet after 100 yards, and another 150 yards will bring you to an excellent camping area with running water nearby.

If you have time after making camp you will probably want to see the remains of the bomber that crashed in the back of Timpanogos Basin in 1955. It is only 0.5 mile from your campsite; in fact if you know what to look for you can see it from your camp. Look west, high into the back of the basin, and find the long line of cliffs that begin about 200 feet below the summit ridge. Just below the cliffs is a steep bench, and for a few hundred yards on the south side of the basin the bench is covered with talus from the cliffs above. The airplane crash is near the middle of this talus slope, about 400 feet above the bottom of the basin. It is an easy climb up to the crash. You should head in a direction that

Airplane crash in Timpanogos Basin

Looking northwest from the summit of Mount Timpanogos

retrieve it on the way down.

The summit trail immediately starts winding upward toward a saddle on the ridge north of the peak. The saddle is about 900 feet higher than the basin and well above timberline, so be ready for some marvelous views. Provo, Orem, and Utah Lake are prominently displayed below the west side of the ridge, while Timpanogos Peak holds a commanding position above the ridge 0.6 mile to the south.

The trail crosses the ridge and goes into a series of short, rocky switchbacks on the west side of the mountain, then, after a half-hour, it ends at the small metal shelter that marks the summit. The steel structure was originally built by surveyors who, before the days of aerial mapping, used the peak as a triangulation point for their measurements.

Mount Timpanogos is situated directly on the geological boundary that separates the Rocky Mountain Province from the Great Basin Province. To the east, as far as the eye can see, is nothing but mountains; while to the west the Great Basin Desert stretches endlessly across western Utah, Nevada, and into California. Three other wilderness

areas lie to the north within twenty miles of Timpanogos, and many other popular peaks such as Lone Peak and Twin Peaks are clearly visible. Mount Nebo, the highest mountain in the Wasatch Range, is 35 miles to the south.

The 4.6-mile walk down from Timpanogos Basin to the Timpooneke Trailhead provides another interesting lesson in geology. The route descends through a steep, glaciated valley that looses about 3,000 feet over a distance of two miles, but the grade is far from uniform. The valley descends over a series of five flat benches that are collectively known as the "Giant Staircase". It is interesting to speculate how these stair steps were formed. The structural characteristics of the various horizontal layers of rock that make up the mountain are undoubtedly an important factor; the Timpanogos massif is composed primarily of limestone, quartzite, and sandstone, and I noticed that the tops of at least two of the benches are made up of smooth, unfractured limestone. Another factor could be that the valley was not carved by a single glacier, but by several glaciers of varying sizes and thicknesses. Over the past 2.5 million years the mountain has been subjected to the forces of glaciation on at least five different occasions.

One-day hike

If you are planning this hike as a one-day outing I suggest you begin at the Aspen Grove Trailhead and return the same way, mostly because this route will give you the opportunity to visit Emerald Lake. The total distance to the summit and back from Aspen Grove is 13.4 miles and the elevation gain is 4,840 feet.

There is a shortcut trail near Emerald Lake that allows hikers to climb to the summit ridge without walking all the way into Timpanogos Basin. The shorter trail leaves the main trail 0.5 mile west of the lake near the bottom of a talus slope. You may have trouble finding the trail, since the talus is very unstable and subject to occasional landslides. If the shortcut trail has been obliterated just angle up the side of the slope in a northwesterly direction for a few hundred yards until you run into the well-marked summit trail just below the top of the ridge.

The normal return to Emerald Lake is along the same trails used for the assent; however more adventurous hikers might want to attempt an alternative route down the Timpanogos Glacier. A faint trail continues along the summit ridge for another 0.6 mile beyond the top of Mount Timpanogos to the top of the glacier that feeds the lake. It is only a fifteen-minute slide from the ridge to the lake, but be aware that under some conditions the descent down the glacier can be dangerous. Many injuries have been sustained by people sliding into rocks on the glacier, especially late in the summer when buried boulders are often exposed by the melting snow. There have also been cases of people breaking legs after falling through snow bridges, and even falling into the freezing lake at the bottom of the glacier. In my opinion, however, the degree of danger is not great for a person with some experience on snow and some common sense. The grade is very steep for the first few hundred feet, but after that one can easily walk down the snow. An ice axe is useful but thousands of hikers make the descent every summer without one. A short, strong stick can also be a great help in steering and braking on the snow, but don't expect to find any sticks above Emerald Lake.

Trail below Timpanogos Basin (early July)

Grove Creek – Battle Creek

 ★★★

shuttle car or bicycle useful
day hike

Distance:	6.1 miles (plus 1.8 miles by car or bicycle)
Walking time:	4³/₄ hours
Elevations:	2,580 ft. gain, 2,370 ft. loss Grove Creek Trailhead (start): 5,140 ft. Grove Creek Spring: 7,460 ft. Battle Creek Trailhead: 5,340 ft.
Trail:	Excellent, well marked trail
Season:	Summer through Fall: The higher parts of the trail are usually covered with snow from late November until early June.
Vicinity:	Near Provo
Maps:	Timpanogos Cave, Orem *(USGS)* Uinta National Forest *(Trails Illustrated, #701)*
Information:	http://www.utahtrails.com/grovebattlecreek.html *(Utah Trails)* http://www.fs.usda.gov/uwcnf/ *(Uinta-Wasatch-Cache Nat. Forest)* phone: (801) 785-3563 *(Pleasant Grove Ranger District)*

Drive East from the town of Pleasant Grove on Battle Creek Drive (200 South). The road dead ends at the mouth of Battle Creek Canyon near the entrance to Kiwanis Park. The Battle Creek trailhead is located on the east side of the parking lot, just to the right of the park entrance. This is where the hike will end and where you should leave your shuttle car or bicycle.

To get to the Grove Creek trailhead where the hike begins you must drive back down Battle Creek Drive a distance of 0.5 mile to 1300 East Street. Turn right here and proceed north on 1300 East and Dalton Drive for another 0.8 mile to Grove Creek Drive. Turn north on Grove Creek Drive and continue the last 0.2 mile to the Grove Creek trailhead and parking area at the end of the road.

The western slopes of Mount Timpanogos contain some great hiking opportunities for people living in Provo and the adjacent towns. The lower part of the mountain is serrated by a series of deep canyons that drain the snow fields above, and

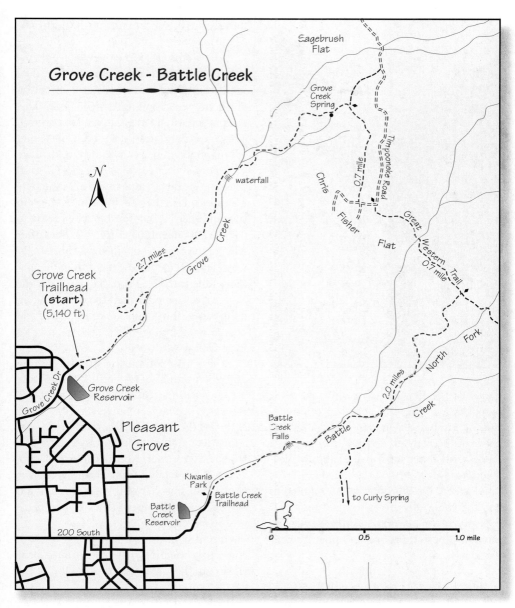

Grove Creek - Battle Creek

Sagebrush Flat

Grove Creek Spring

Timpooneke Road

0.7 mile

waterfall

Chris

Fisher

Flat

Great Western Trail

0.7 mile

2.7 miles

Grove Creek

Grove Creek Trailhead
(start)
(5,140 ft)

Grove Creek Dr.

Grove Creek Reservoir

North Fork

2.0 miles

Creek

Pleasant Grove

Battle Creek Falls

Battle Creek

Kiwanis Park

Battle Creek Trailhead

Battle Creek Reservoir

to Curly Spring

200 South

0   0.5   1.0 mile

N

---

nearly all of the canyons contain developed trails. Three particularly interesting trails climb upward from the towns of Lindon and Pleasant Grove, through Dry Canyon, Battle Creek Canyon, and Grove Canyon, to a high plateau on the west side of the Timpanogos summit ridge. The three trails are all connected at the top by a segment of the Great Western Trail; hence several loop hikes are possible.

The hike I will describe here goes up Grove Creek to its headwaters, then crosses Fisher Flat on the Great Western Trail, and finally descends through Battle Creek Canyon to the town of Pleasant Grove. Along the way you will pass two major waterfalls and several smaller ones, and the views of Mount Timpanogos rising above the gor-

Grove Creek Trail

the creek to begin climbing up the north side of the canyon.

After some 400 feet of elevation gain the trail doubles back and resumes a gradual uphill climb in a northeasterly direction about 400 feet above the canyon floor. This is a particularly interesting part of the trail. There are gorgeous views both of Mount Timpanogos and Utah Valley with little vegetation to impede the scenery. The trail crosses the talus slopes below Mahogany Mountain, further to the north, and in several places dynamite has been used to carve a path out of the cliffs. 1.2 miles after leaving the creek you will see a spectacular waterfall 160 feet below the trail in the bottom of the canyon. Then, 0.1 mile later the trail arrives once again at the canyon floor, it crosses to the south side of the creek and begins climbing again through a grove of huge Douglas fir trees.

The trail continues to climb, gaining 720 feet over the next 0.8 mile before finally arriving at Grove Creek Spring. The spring is located in a large, relatively flat open area at the southern end of Sagebrush Flat. It is a favorite camping area for boy scouts, and is sometimes referred to as Indian Camp. The water bubbling up from the ground is cool, clean, and refreshing, and even if you don't intend to camp it makes a great place to stop for lunch.

Just 100 yards past the spring you will come to a junction, where you must bear right onto the Great Western Trail. For the next 0.2 mile the trail passes over a series of horizontal terraces, or ditches, that were dug into the side of the mountain by the Forest Service in the early 1960s. These terraces were constructed as a means of controlling erosion on land that had been severely overgrazed by local sheep and cattle ranchers. Thankfully grazing in the area is now carefully controlled by the Forest Service; the land has recovered nicely and erosion is

geous Fisher Flat Meadow will take your breath away. The very best time to do this hike is around the first of June, after the snow in the canyons has melted but while there is still ample snow on the summit ridge. Then, for a few weeks, the meadows are a vivid green, the wild flowers are in bloom, and the waterfalls are running at their full capacity. Don't expect too much solitude, though. These trails are very popular with the locals.

For the first 0.2 mile you will be following an old, unused jeep road that proceeds along the north side of Grove Creek. Soon, however, it dips to the right and ends at the water's edge. Bear left at this point and follow the footpath as it veers away from the road and continues climbing along the left side of the stream. Then, 0.5 mile from the trailhead, you will come to a switchback where the trail makes a sharp turn away from no longer a serious problem.

After gaining 200 feet in elevation the Great Western Trail levels out onto the vast, grass-covered meadow that defines Fisher Flat. Then, after a 20-minute walk across the meadow you will arrive at the Timpooneke Road, a 4WD track coming in from the north side of the mountain. Here you must turn left and walk east along the road for 150 yards to an obvious trail that departs from the right side of the road. This is the Baldy Trail, a connector trail that crosses Battle Creek and eventually arrives at the head of Dry Canyon. Big Baldy Mountain is the dome-shaped mountain that lies 4.6 miles southeast of the Timpooneke Road.

A 2.4-mile downhill stroll along the Baldy Trail will bring you to a signed junction at the start of the Battle Creek Trail. All of the climbing is behind you now, and the 2.2-mile walk down Battle Creek Canyon to the ending trailhead is pure pleasure. The trail meets the creek 0.6 mile after leaving the junction, and then proceeds to follow fairly closely along the stream for the rest of the distance. 1.0 mile after leaving the junction you will come to another sign marking the Curly Spring Trail on the left, another route that eventually leads to Dry Canyon. (See page 166.) 0.7 mile beyond the Curley Spring trail junction the Battle Creek Trail arrives at Battle Creek Falls, an 80-foot drop that is said to be the highest waterfall on Timpanogos Mountain. A short spur trail descends from the main trail to the base of the Battle Creek Falls, and it is a popular stopping point. It is only a half-mile walk from the lower Battle Creek Trailhead to the falls, and there is usually a crowd of people there in the summertime cooling off in the spray.

Five minutes after leaving Battle Creek Falls you will again be back on an old jeep road that was built many years ago to access a water collection point for the city of Pleasant Grove. Finally, another ten-minute walk will bring you to the end of the hike at the Kiwanis Park parking area.

Fisher Flat

Dry Canyon Loop

★★

Distance:	8.2 miles (loop)
Walking time:	6³/₄ hours
Elevations:	3,400 ft. gain/loss
	Dry Canyon Trailhead (start): 5,497 ft.
	Baldy Pass: 8,336 ft.
	Curly Spring: 6,269 ft.
Trail:	well marked and well maintained
Season:	Midsummer through mid Fall. The upper part of the trail is generally covered with snow from late November through mid-June
Vicinity:	Near Provo
Maps:	Orem, Timpanogos Cave *(USGS)*
	Uinta National Forest *(Trails Illustrated, Map #701)*
Information:	http://www.utahtrails.com/drycanyon.html (Utah Trails)
	http://www.fs.usda.gov/uwcnf/ *(Uinta-Wasatch-Cache Nat. Forest)*
	phone: (801) 785-3563 *(Pleasant Grove Ranger District)*

Drive east toward the mountains on 2000 North Street in Orem. (This road marks the boundary between Orem and Lindon, where it is called 200 South Street.) As the road nears the mountains it begins to make a long, sweeping turn from east to south. At the point where the turn begins you will see a smaller road on the left called Dry Canyon Road. Turn left here and follow Dry Canyon Road uphill for the last 0.6 mile to the Dry Canyon Trailhead and parking lot. The hike begins on the northeast side of the parking area.

As noted in the previous chapter, Dry Canyon is one of three major canyons north of Provo where hikers can follow well established trails up the Wasatch Front to the meadows above. These trails have been in use for over a hundred and fifty years, first by the early Mormon settlers who were grazing their sheep in the upper meadows as early as the 1850s, then by the residents of Linden and Pleasant Grove who built reservoirs and pipe lines in the canyons to channel water to their farms, and finally by hunters and other outdoor recreationists.

Sheep ranching was a huge industry in Utah's early history, and by the early 1900s over 100,000 sheep could be seen grazing in the summertime in the lush grasslands above Dry Creek, Battle Creek, and Grove Creek Canyons. The environmental damage from overgrazing was tremendous, but it wasn't until the late 1950s that extensive remedial action was taken to correct the problem. The number of grazing permits issued by the Forest Service was greatly reduced, and a network of contour trenches or terraces were laboriously constructed on the slopes above the three canyons in an effort to prevent further erosion. Fifty years later, it has to be said that the massive federal assistance program of the 1950s and '60s to revegetate the western slopes of Mount Timpanogos and restore the watershed above Lindon and Pleasant Grove was an enormous success. Flooding is no longer a problem and the once barren meadows along this trail, for example, are now covered with grasses that are often shoulder high.

The first half of this hike is the hardest. The trail begins climbing immediately after leaving the Dry Canyon parking lot, gaining 2,840 feet over the next 2.6 miles before reaching the highest point at the summit of Baldy Pass. For the first 100 yards you will be climbing a series of knee-busting steps constructed by the Forest Service from old railroad ties, then the grade diminishes slightly as you enter a shaded forest composed mainly of Gambel oak and Rocky Mountain maple. As you walk you may notice bits and pieces of an old unused iron pipeline that was built sometime before World War Two. It was replaced in the 1940s by a newer pipeline buried underneath the first part of the trail that carries water to an aqueduct at the base of mountains. If you listen carefully you can occasionally hear water gurgling beneath the path.

The trail works its way up the left side of Dry Canyon, and after 0.5 mile it passes between two picturesque limestone cliffs known locally as the Great Blue Gate. Beyond the Gate the forest opens into a small

Dry Canyon Trail

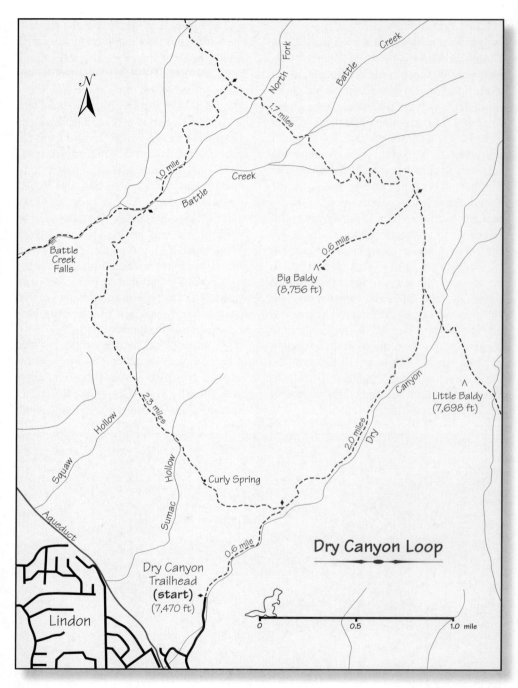

N

North Fork

Battle   Creek

1.7 miles

1.0 mile

Battle   Creek

Battle
Creek
Falls

0.6 mile

Big Baldy
(8,756 ft)

2.3 miles

Canyon

Little Baldy
(7,698 ft)

Hollow

2.0 miles   Dry

Squaw

Sumac   Hollow

Curly Spring

Aqueduct

0.6 mile

Dry Canyon Loop

Dry Canyon
Trailhead
(start)
(7,470 ft)

Lindon

0   0.5   1.0 mile

but very scenic meadow where you will be treated to a brief stretch of level ground and a fine view of Mount Timpanogos. Soon you will come to a signed trail junction where the trail to Curly Spring and Battle Creek branches off to the left. This will be your return trail, but for now you must continue straight ahead toward Baldy Pass.

Just 150 feet beyond the Curly Spring trail junction you will come to another unsigned junction where forest trail #51 branches off to the right. Bear left at this point onto trail #49 which you will be following all the way to Baldy Pass. Beyond the junction the trail begins climbing again in earnest, and you can expect very little additional level ground until you reach the top of the pass. The good news is that there is a great deal of shade along the way, which makes the climb more bearable.

1.5 miles from the Curly Spring Trail junction, at an elevation of 7,600 feet, the forest again opens up to some nice views of the mountains that surround you. At this point you are in a scattered forest of quaking aspen, and although there is very little shade along this section of trail it is, for me, much more enjoyable than being immersed in the dense tangle of Gambel oak.

Dry Canyon Trail

Next you will pass another signed trail junction where the Little Baldy Trail departs to the right, and ten minutes later you will arrive at the top of Baldy Pass, the highest point on this hike. There is an obvious hiker-made trail leading from the top of Baldy Pass to the summit of Big Baldy Peak, and if you are inclined to add some additional mileage to this hike you might want to make a side trip to the top of the mountain. Big Baldy is a prominent peak overlooking Utah Valley, and from the top you will be treated to a rare bird's eye view of the metropolis below. The view includes the entirety of Utah Lake, extending all the way from Lehi to the Goshen Valley. The spur trail to the summit of Big Baldy is 0.6 mile long, with 420 feet of additional elevation gain. There is also a good camping spot at the top of the pass, which suggests to me the possibility of an enjoyable overnighter. Watching the sunset across Utah Lake from the summit of Big Baldy Peak, 3,800 feet above Utah Valley, would surely be a memorable experience.

From Baldy Pass the trail plunges downward through a series of switchbacks into the Battle Creek watershed. The character of the forest changes once again as you descend along the north-facing side of Big Baldy, and soon you will enter a grove of stately Douglas fir trees. 1.0 mile below the pass the trail crosses the South Fork of Battle Creek, a tributary that is usually dry, and 0.2

Curly Spring Trail

mile later it crosses Battle Creek itself. Ten minutes after crossing Battle Creek, which is also normally dry after midsummer, the trail crosses the North Fork of Battle Creek, which almost always has water. If you are hiking in late summer the North Fork of Battle Creek will probably be the first running water you see on this hike. Finally, 0.2 mile after fording the North Fork you will come to a signed junction where you must turn left onto the Battle Creek Trail.

It is a pleasant 1.0-mile downhill walk on the Battle Creek Trail to the Curly Spring Trail junction. When you reach the junction you are actually only 1.2 miles from the Battle Creek Trailhead, so it is possible to shorten this hike by 1.7 miles if you decide to end there instead of completing the loop and ending at the Dry Canyon Trailhead. (See page 162 for more information about the Battle Creek Trail.) A small sign on the north side of Battle Creek marks the point where you must leave Battle Creek Trail for Curly Spring and Dry Canyon. There is no bridge, however, and Curly Spring is on the opposite side of the creek, so prepare to get

your feet wet. The creek is normally about 15 feet wide and 10 inches deep.

Once you are on the south side of Battle Creek you will see the continuation of the trail following downstream along the shore of the creek for 200 feet before veering away to begin a gentle climb out of the canyon. (Another trail heads directly away from the water's edge and immediately begins climbing steeply into the forest. This is the wrong trail!) Soon after leaving Battle Creek the trail begins a long gradual climb through a shaded forest of Gambel oak and Rocky Mountain maple. Then, after realizing an elevation gain of about 400 feet over a distance of 0.7 mile the forest opens up again to an expansive view of the city below, and the trail begins its gradual descent into Dry Canyon. 1.8 miles after leaving Battle Creek the trail passes by Curly Spring, a tiny spring said to have been named after an Indian the white settlers called Curly who camped there sometime in the 1870s or '80s. Today Curly Spring is little more than a small pipe beside the trail out of which trickles a tiny stream of water. The water is cool and refreshing, however, and it runs throughout the summer. Most hikers are happy to stop for a taste of mountain spring water as they pass by.

The Curly Spring Trail ends in Dry Canyon 0.5 mile beyond the spring. From there it is an easy walk down the last 0.6 mile, through the Great Blue Gate to the Dry Canyon Trailhead where your car is parked.

Curly Spring

Hot Pots

★★★   **day hike**

Distance:	4.4 miles (round trip)
Walking time:	2.5 hours
Elevations:	650 ft. gain/loss Three Forks Trailhead (start): 5,550 ft. Hot Pots: 6,200 ft. Fifth Water Trailhead: 6,880 ft.
Trail:	Unmarked but otherwise excellent, well maintained trail
Season:	The Hot Pots receive many hikers throughout the summer; however the best time for a visit is in early June, when the snow is melted but there is still plenty of water in the creek. The trail is generally covered with snow from mid-November through mid-May.
Vicinity:	Near Spanish Fork
Maps:	Rays Valley *(USGS)*
Information:	http://www.utahtrails.com/hotpots.html *(Utah Trails)* http://www.fs.usda.gov/uwcnf/ *(Uinta-Wasatch-Cache Nat. Forest)* phone: (801) 798-3571 *(Spanish Fork Ranger District)*

Exit Highway I-15 at Spanish Fork (exit 258) and drive east on Highway 6 into Spanish Fork Canyon. 11 miles after leaving I-15, or 5.5 miles from the mouth of the canyon, you will see a sign marking the Diamond Fork Road on the left. Turn here and continue on this paved road for another 9.9 miles, past Diamond Campground and Red Ledges Picnic Area, until you see a turnout on the right near a small sign that says "Three Forks Trailhead". Turn here and proceed the last 200 feet to the parking area and trailhead on the southeast side of Diamond Fork.

As explained below, people sometimes prefer to access the Hot Pots from the Fifth Water Trailhead on Sheep Creek Road. To get there you must continue up Spanish Fork Canyon on Highway 6 for another 10.9 miles beyond the Diamond Fork turnoff. There you will see another paved road, the Sheep Creek Road (County Road 51), where you must turn left. The Fifth Water Trailhead is located 14.1 miles from Highway 6 on the left side of the Sheep Creek Road. Unfortunately the trailhead is not well marked, but if you watch your odometer you should be able to find it. Look for a short wooden fence 100 feet from the left side of the road just after the point where the road dips down to cross the headwaters of Fifth Water Creek. There is a small sign on the trail beside the fence that says "Forest Service Trail 015".

This hike is not well known outside Utah County. It almost seems like the Forest Service doesn't want outsiders to know about it, but it has long been a favorite of the locals. The Hot Pots of Diamond Fork are probably the best undeveloped hot springs in the state, and, as a bonus, they are located in a beautiful canyon with several scenic waterfalls nearby. The hike to the springs in only 2.2 miles long, and every summer hikers from Spanish Fork, Provo, and the surrounding towns flock to the Hot Pots to picnic, enjoy nature, and soak up the therapeutic warmth of the pools.

There have been numerous accounts of lewd behavior at the Hot Pots over the years, including stories of indiscrete nude bathers (mostly old men), and nighttime beer parties staged by local unrestrained university and high school students. Such stories are most likely a reason why the Forest Service is not eager to publicize the Hot Pots. Another nearby hot spring, Castilla Springs, was destroyed by the authorities of Utah County sometime in the 1980s because they "had trouble controlling the visitors". The Castilla Springs were located in the bottom of Spanish Fork Canyon about 8 miles northeast of Spanish Fork

I have personally visited the Hot Pots on several occasions over the past 15 years, and although I have occasionally seen nude bathers soaking in the pools they have always been discrete and I have never been particularly offended by them. Spending the night there is not something I would relish, but I wouldn't hesitate to take my children there on a day hike.

Finally, I should mention that the flow rate of Fifth Water Creek, where the Hot Pots are located, varies a great deal throughout the year, and it is best to visit the area during the spring and early summer when there is

Hot Pots, lower pools

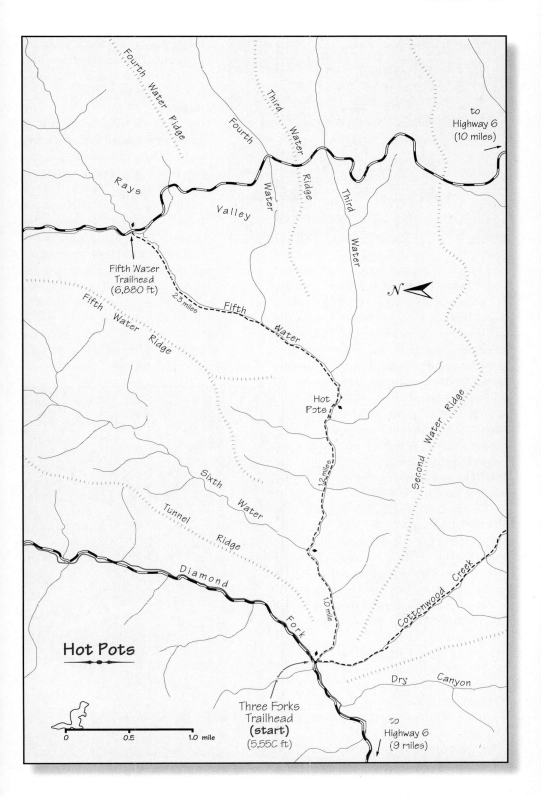

Fourth Water Ridge

Third Water Ridge

Fourth Water

Third Water

to
Highway 6
(10 miles)

Rays

Water Valley

Fifth Water
Trailhead
(6,880 ft)

N

2.3 miles

Fifth

Water

Fifth Water Ridge

Hot
Pots

Second Water Ridge

Sixth Water

1.2 miles

Tunnel Ridge

Diamond

Fork

1.0 mile

Cottonwood Creek

Hot Pots

Three Forks
Trailhead
(start)
(5,550 ft)

Dry Canyon

to
Highway 6
(9 miles)

0   0.5   1.0 mile

Hot Pots Trail

bridge and heads south along the shore of Cottonwood Creek. Don't take this trail, but rather bear to the left and continue walking along the north shore of Fifth Water. This section of the hike is a beautiful riparian area, shaded by lots of maple and boxelder trees, with a noisy, fast running stream usually less than 50 feet from the path. If you are observant you will also notice a fair amount of poison ivy near the stream. The trail is excellent and well maintained, but there are no signs directing you to your destination. If the lack of signs is part of the Forest Service's effort to keep the Hot Pots a secret their efforts have failed miserably, for the trail is obviously well used. If you are hiking in the early summer you will probably even see a few bicycles along the way, although to my

more water. The main pools are located just below the first waterfall, and although there is generally water in the pools throughout the year, the volume of water coming over the fall is often reduced to a mere trickle in late summer. This, of course, renders the area less picturesque, but another problem is that the temperature in the pools goes up when this happens. The volume of hot water seeping out of the ground below the fall is more or less constant throughout the year, and when the cool water from the creek ceases to flow into the pools some of them can become uncomfortably hot.

Occasionally people also visit the Hot Pots in winter, but the trail can be very icy and even dangerous at that time if you don't have crampons on your shoes. I have never been there in the wintertime, but soaking in the warm water in the midst of the snow covered hills must be a memorable experience.

The path starts out in a southeasterly direction from the Three Forks Trailhead, following closely along the north side of Fifth Water Creek. After walking just 50 feet you will come to a junction where another trail veers off to the right across an iron foot

Fifth Water, near the confluence with Diamond Fork

Hot Pots, upper pool

mind the trail is not really good enough for a comfortable bicycle ride. On one of my trips I even saw a couple pushing a jogging stroller over the rocks and roots.

After 1.0 mile the trail turns abruptly to the right to cross another iron bridge at the confluence of Sixth Water Creek. It then settles into a long, gradual climb up the canyon, again following closely along the left side of Fifth Water. After you have walked about 0.8 mile from the Sixth Water crossing you may begin to notice the faint smell of hydrogen sulfide in the air–a sure sign that you are approaching a geothermal area. Then, 0.3 mile further, you will come to the first two of the Hot Pots bathing pools.

Pause to admire the rock work around these two well constructed pools. Two carefully arranged rings of stones have been carefully cemented in place above a delightful cascade on the north side of the creek. The work even includes steps made from flat stones that descend into one of the 2-foot-deep pools. Most visitors assume the Forest Service is responsible for these improvements, but rangers from the Spanish Fork District Office have told me that all of the improvements at the Hot Pots were done by hikers.

Continuing upstream for another 200 feet will bring you to the next two bathing pools, just beyond which is the picturesque Hot Pots Waterfall. The pool closest to the fall is particularly interesting. There are three separate springs on the left side of this pool where hot water bubbles up out of the ground and flows into the tub. This is the hottest of the pools–too hot for my taste even in the early summer when the creek is full. Most of the thermal activity in this area is just below the waterfall; consequently the lower pools are not as hot. My favorites are the first two pools, located about 250 feet below the fall, where the temperature is usually just about right for a long refreshing soak.

The Hot Pots Waterfall also has an interesting feature. Fifth Water is heavily mineralized, and over the years an accumulation of calcium deposits has formed a cave-like travertine shield behind the waterfall. As a result, it is now possible to climb up a narrow ledge behind the fall to a point where one can look out through a small opening behind the torrent.

The Hot Pots via Rays Valley

From the Hot Pots the trail continues upward, following the left side of Fifth Water for another 2.2 miles before ending in Rays Valley at Sheep Creek Road. Consequently hikers sometime access the area from Rays Valley rather than Diamond Fork. Sheep Creek Road is almost exactly the same distance from the Hot Pots as the Three Forks Trailhead, but the elevation change is 150 greater. Nevertheless, some people prefer this approach–especially in winter when the Diamond Fork Road may be closed. There are also two more waterfalls along the trail to Rays Valley.

Continuing up the trail from the Hot Pots for just a few hundred feet will bring you to a fork where another spur branches off and descends to the creek below. At the end of this short trail are two more pools that were built years ago by a legendary Payson resident named Ross Lundgren. Lundgren often visited the Pots by bicycle in the summer and with skis in the winter. He built the pools in this secluded place above the first fall, so he could enjoy a more private bath. Today these pools are still much more hidden that the lower pools, and even when there are crowds below the waterfall it is still usually possible to find an element of solitude at Lundgren's pools.

Continuing on the trail above Lundgren's pools the second and highest waterfall on Fifth Water soon comes into view. Here, off the right hand side of the trail the creek plunges down for about 40 feet, and then almost immediately makes another 40-foot drop. The trail provides a marvelous, unimpeded view of the fall just 200 feet away.

Beyond that point the trail continues along a gentle upward grade, climbing just 700 feet over the next 2.2 miles. In general this part of the trail strays further from the water's edge than the lower trail to the Hot Pots, although it does pass by another nice waterfall about a mile above the second fall. Finally, as you approach the Sheep Creek Road the path levels out in a large nearly treeless meadow. Watch for deer in this area.

Waterfall near the upper pools

Santaquin Peak

★★

Distance:	11.4 miles (round trip)
Walking time:	8 hours
Elevations:	3,195 ft. gain/loss Loafer Mountain Trailhead (start): 7,490 ft. Santaquin Peak: 10,685 ft.
Trail:	Well used and easy to follow
Season:	Summer through mid-fall. The upper parts of the trail are usually covered with snow from mid-November through late June.
Vicinity:	Near Spanish Fork and Payson
Maps:	Payson Lakes, Birdseye *(USGS)* Uinta National Forest *(Trails Illustrated, #701)*
Information:	http://www.utahtrails.com/santaquin.html *(Utah Trails)* http://www.fs.usda.gov/uwcnf/ *(Uinta-Wasatch-Cache Nat. Forest)* phone: (801) 798-3571 *(Spanish Fork Ranger District)*

Leave I-15 at exit 250 and drive one mile south into the town of Payson. Once you are in Payson make your way to the corner of 100 North and 600 East and turn south onto 600 East. This is the beginning of the Mount Nebo Scenic Loop Drive. 12.2 miles from the beginning of the scenic loop drive, or 0.1 mile before reaching the turnoff to Payson Lakes, you will see a small parking area on the left next to a sign marking the Loafer Mountain Trailhead.

Although many peaks along the Wasatch Front are considerably higher than Santaquin Peak, few of the area's hikes are more scenic than this one. The trail is especially beautiful in the fall, as it passes through numerous groves of maple and aspen on its way to Loafer Ridge. Although the elevation gain is over 3,000 feet, the gain is fairly well distributed along the 5.7-mile length of the hike; hence the climb is not excessively strenuous. You should carry a pair of binoculars to the top since there is a lot to see. Splendid views of Mount Nebo and the Payson Lakes can be seen to the south, while Mount Timpanogos and Utah Lake provide a backdrop for Provo, Payson, and other nearby towns in the north.

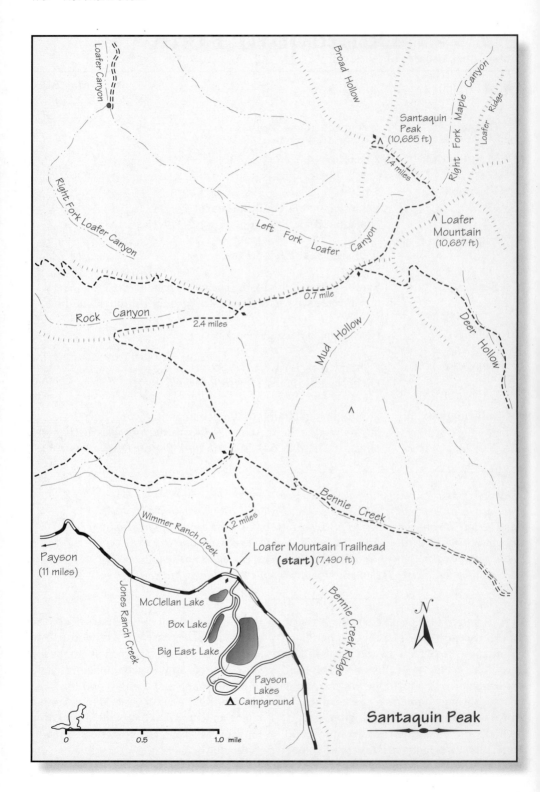

Loafer Canyon

Broad Hollow

Right Fork Maple Canyon

Loafer Ridge

Santaquin
Peak
(10,685 ft)

1.4 miles

Right Fork Loafer Canyon

Left Fork Loafer Canyon

^ Loafer
Mountain
(10,687 ft)

0.7 mile

Rock   Canyon

2.4 miles

Mud Hollow

Deer Hollow

^

^

Bennie   Creek

Wimmer Ranch Creek

1.2 miles

Loafer Mountain Trailhead
(start) (7,490 ft)

Payson
(11 miles)

Jones Ranch Creek

McClellan Lake

Box Lake

Big East Lake

Bennie Creek Ridge

N

Payson
Lakes
△ Campground

0   0.5   1.0 mile

Santaquin Peak

From the trailhead the path winds through the woods for 1.1 miles, gaining about 350 feet in elevation before coming to a trail sign and junction near an old coral. Turn left here in order to stay on the Loafer Mountain Trail. (You will be on the Loafer Mountain Trail for the first 4.3 miles of this hike.) The trail continues east for only 0.1 mile before coming to another junction where you must turn right. Again, there is a Forest Service sign at the junction. You should stay on the Loafer Mountain Trail, No. 98.

The trail now settles down to a long, gradual climb of 2,000 feet over the next 2.4 miles to the top of the Loafer Mountain Ridge. Once you reach the ridge you will be out of the trees and you can start enjoying the views. Payson Lakes are directly below you, and Mount Nebo (11,928 ft.) is the pyramid-shaped peak above the horizon 12 miles to

Maple tree on Loafer Mountain Trail

the south. Santaquin Peak, your destination, will also come into view in front of you as

Loafer Mountain Trail

you climb onto the ridge. Santaquin is the most prominent peak on the left.

After another 0.7 mile the ridge reaches a shallow saddle, where a faint trail branches off to the right. The lesser used trail is the continuation of the Loafer Mountain Trail, which swings to the east at this point and eventually descends down the mountain through Deer Hollow. To reach Santaquin Peak you must bear left at this saddle, staying on the better trail. There shouldn't be any confusion because the other trail is so vague you might not even see it. Furthermore, your goal, Santaquin Peak, is directly in front of you now and it is quite obvious which direction you should go.

Before continuing, pause for a moment at the saddle to study the two peaks in front of you, Santaquin on the left and Loafer on the right. They are about 0.7 mile apart and are separated by a deep notch. From this prospective Santaquin appears to be the higher of the two, but it is actually two feet

Looking north from Santaquin Peak

lower. Nevertheless, Santaquin is a much more interesting climb. Loafer is not really a peak at all, but rather just the highest point on a long, unappealing ridge. Also, it is hard to see Utah Valley from Loafer Peak because the view is obstructed by Santaquin. But if you insist on scaling the higher of the two peaks it isn't too difficult to make your way from the saddle up the ridge to the top of Loafer. The climb will require about 880 feet of elevation gain. There is no trail but there are no serious obstacles either, and the route is quite straightforward.

The trail from the saddle to the top of Santaquin Peak contours around the west side of the Loafer Mountain Ridge until it reaches the bottom of the notch separating the two peaks. It then ascends toward the top of Santaquin, traversing around the south side of the summit and reaching the peak 0.6 mile later. The elevation gain from the bottom of the notch is about 430 feet.

Loafer Mountain Trail

Mount Nebo, south summit

★

Distance:	13.2 miles (round trip)
Walking time:	day 1: 5 hours day 2: 7 hours
Elevations:	5,400 ft. gain/loss Nebo Bench Trailhead (start): 6,480 ft. suggested campsite: 9,440 ft. Mt. Nebo (south summit): 11,877 ft.
Trail:	The trail is generally easy to follow, however it is very steep in places and has no reliable water.
Season:	Midsummer through mid-fall. The upper parts of the trail are usually covered with snow from mid-November until late July.
Vicinity:	Mount Nebo Wilderness Area, near Nephi
Maps:	Nebo Basin, Mona (USGS) Uinta National Forest (Trails Illustrated, #701)
Information:	http://www.utahtrails.com/nebosouth.html (Utah Trails) http://www.fs.usda.gov/uwcnf/ (Uinta-Wasatch-Cache Nat. Forest) phone: (801) 798-3571 (Spanish Fork Ranger District)

Take Exit 225 off I-15 near Nephi and proceed east on Highway 132 towards Moroni. After you have driven 5.0 miles from I-15 you will see a sign direct-ing you to the Mount Nebo Scenic Loop Road on the left. Turn here and drive north for 3.3 miles until you see another paved road on the left going to Pon-derosa Campground. Turn left again and drive for 1.3 miles, past Ponderosa Campground, until you see a small parking area on the left where there is a trail register and a sign marking the Nebo Bench Trailhead.

This trail was constructed sometime before the 1970s when it was believed that the south summit of Mount Nebo was the highest peak in the Wasatch Mountains. Nebo contains three major summits, and a few years after the south summit trail was finished a new survey revealed that the northern peak is actually 51 feet higher. Nevertheless, many more people have climbed the south summit than its northern

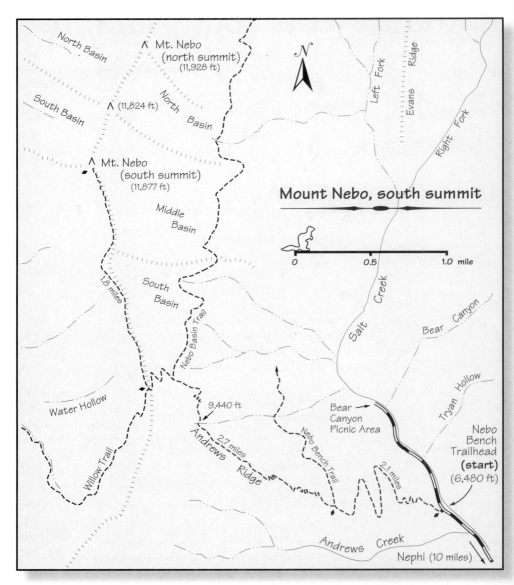

Mount Nebo, south summit

neighbor. Before 2000 an ascent up the north summit of Mount Nebo required 2,600 feet of grueling scrambling up steep talus slopes with no established trail. Ten years ago a new trail was constructed, but even now the arduous scramble up the last 1,330 feet to the top of the northern peak remains more than most people want to attempt. Consequently many hikers still opt for the less difficult trail to the south summit.

That is not to say that the hike to Nebo's south summit is an easy hike. Although there is a good trail all the way to the top, it is a long, tiring walk with over a mile of elevation gain. Many people do it as an overnighter, camping near the top of Andrews Ridge, but there really are no good campsites along the way. Water is also a problem–there are no reliable sources of water on this trail. Personally, I prefer to climb

Nebo's south summit as an overnighter, but because of the lack of good campsites most people prefer to walk the 13.2-mile round trip distance as a long day hike.

Occasionally hikers who have climbed to the south summit will attempt the traverse across the summit ridge that separates the north and south summits. Locally known as the "triple", this traverse also allows them to ascend the middle summit (11,824 ft.) along the way. However, I would not recommend this traverse unless you really know what you are doing. It is not technically difficult but it involves a lot of scrambling, and there is some exposure in the middle of the traverse. The 0.9-mile scramble from the south summit to the north summit includes 550 feet of elevation gain and 500 feet of loss. It takes over an hour each way, and the time and energy required are beyond the limits of most people.

Andrews Ridge

Day 1 (3.8 miles)

From the trailhead the Nebo Bench Trail begins by ascending in a westerly direction through the dense conifer forest. Then, after about 0.5 mile, it swings to the north to begin the first of four wide, altitude-gaining switchbacks up to Andrews Ridge. This section of the trail was improved and relocated in the early 1990s, probably for the benefit of the many pack horses that use the Nebo Bench Trail. After 2.0 miles the trail finally breaks out of the forest into a relatively clear area of wildflowers, sage brush, and scattered shrub oak. This clearing represents the beginning of Andrews Ridge, up which the Nebo Peak Trail runs for the next 1.5 miles.

The Nebo Peak Trail departs from the Nebo Bench Trail just above the point where it first reaches Andrews Ridge. Watch carefully as you leave the clearing, and after about 200 yards you should see a smaller trail leaving the main trail on the left. The summit trail is unmarked and, worse, it is obscured by a dense undergrowth of Gamble

oak, but if you are attentive you should be able to spot it. The main trail continues climbing gradually in a northerly direction, while the trail up Mount Nebo rises more steeply to the west.

Beyond the trail junction the Nebo summit trail makes its way westward along Andrews Ridge for a distance of 1.4 miles before finally dropping off the north side of the ridge. I suggest you establish a camp here at the top of the ridge. At this point you are 3.1 miles from the south summit of Mount Nebo, and the elevation is 9,450 feet. There are also some nice camp sites on the summit ridge, 1,100 feet higher, but you will sleep much better at the lower altitude. Furthermore, carrying a backpack above 10,000 feet is very tiring.

Day 2 (9.4 miles)

From the top of Andrews Ridge the trail bears north for 0.9 mile, crossing into South Nebo Basin, and then turns west again for the climb up to the top of the summit ridge. Don't be confused by another less well used trail that continues north across South Nebo Basin. This is the old route of the Nebo Bench Trail. Finally, 1.3 miles after leaving Andrews Ridge the trail climbs into a shallow saddle on the summit ridge. An old wooden sign indicates that this is also the point where Willow Creek Trail reaches the ridge. The Willow Creek Trail is another route to the top of Mount Nebo that begins east of the town of Mona.

The next 1.3 miles along the summit ridge, toward the base of Mount Nebo's south summit, is probably the most pleasant part of the hike. The views are outstanding. On the west side of the ridge is the farming community of Mona, surrounded by fields of grain and alfalfa, with I-15 snaking past on its way up the Utah Valley. To the east, as far as the eye can see, are mountains and forests – Uinta National Forest, Manti-La Sal National Forest, and beyond that, Ashley National Forest. Even in mid-July the ridge is often accented with patches of white snow, and the prevailing west winds frequently pile the snow into long graceful cornices along the eastern side. The trail avoids the cornices by staying slightly below the western side of the ridge.

Just before reaching the south summit the trail crosses a small flat bench before it climbs the last 500 feet to the top. When you reach the summit your reward will be a spectacular view to the north along the Nebo summit ridge, where the three peaks of Mount Nebo, each one more rugged than the last, cling tenuously to the knife-edge ridge of uplifted limestone as they reach for the open sky above.

The trail ends at the south summit, and this is as far as most people go. The north summit, 0.9 mile further on, is 51 feet higher, but, as noted earlier, getting there and back is a strenuous, time consuming scramble and there are a few places where a fall could be disastrous. The north summit is best reached as a separate hike (see page 185).

The middle and north summits of Mount Nebo, as seen from the south summit

Mount Nebo, north summit

Mount Nebo Wilderness Area
day hike

Distance:	8.6 miles (round trip)
Walking time:	9 hours
Elevations:	3,270 ft. gain/loss
	Mona Pole Trailhead (start): 9,260 ft.
	Wolf Pass: 10,600 ft.
	false summit: 11,450 ft.
	Mount Nebo north summit: 11,928 ft.
Trail:	Good trail as far as Wolf Pass. The last mile involves a steep scramble up a rocky ridge with 1,375 feet of total elevation gain.
Season:	Midsummer through mid-fall. The upper parts of the trail are usually covered with snow from mid-November until August.
Vicinity:	Mount Nebo Wilderness Area, near Nephi
Maps:	Nebo Basin, Mona (*USGS*)
	Uinta National Forest (*Trails Illustrated, #701*)
Information:	http://www.utahtrails.com/nebonorth.html (*Utah Trails*)
	http://www.fs.usda.gov/uwcnf/ (*Uinta-Wasatch-Cache Nat. Forest*)
	phone: (801) 798-3571 (*Spanish Fork Ranger District*)

Leave I-15 at exit 250 and drive one mile south into the town of Payson. Once you are in Payson make your way to the corner of 100 North and 600 East and turn south onto 600 East. This is the beginning of the Mount Nebo Scenic Loop Drive. 23 miles from the beginning of the scenic loop drive you will come to a large sign on the right marking the turnout to the Monument Trailhead. Turn here, and just 50 feet after leaving the highway you will see another narrow unpaved road, the Mona Pole Road, where you must again turn right. Drive north on the Mona Pole Road for 0.3 mile to where the road crosses a cattle guard. The trailhead is on the northwest side of the cattle guard near a Forest Service sign that says "Trail 089".

As noted in the previous chapter, Mount Nebo consists of three major summits with separate trails leading to the south sum-mit and the north summit. Before the 1970s it was believed that the south summit was the highest, and the southern trail was the

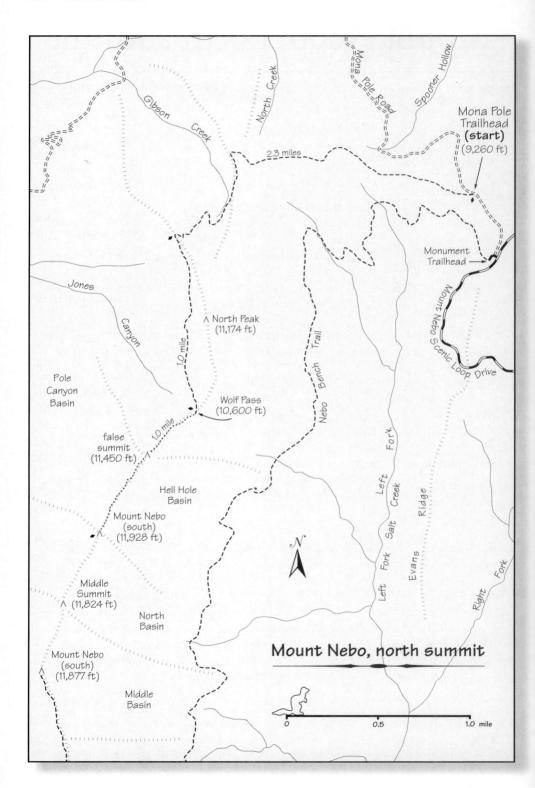

Mount Nebo, north summit

Mount Nebo north summit trail

the top of the northern summit. Still, I consider this trail to be a great hike, quite different from most of the other mountain trails in Utah. You probably won't see any other people along the way, the scenery is magnificent, and your destination is the highest point in the Wasatch Mountains.

first one to be built. A later survey, however, revealed that the northern summit is slightly higher, and ten years ago the trail described here was constructed up the northern side of the mountain.

Before the year 2000 the climb to the highest summit of Nebo usually involved a strenuous 1,300-foot scramble up to Wolf Pass, a 10,600-foot saddle on the north side of the peak. The new trail provides relatively easy access to Wolf Pass—a great improvement from the past—but getting from the pass on up to the top of the mountain still involves grueling scramble with 1,375 feet of elevation gain. Consequently, even with the new trail, this hike is still extremely strenuous.

Although the round trip distance to the north summit is four miles shorter than the south summit trail and the total elevation gain is 2,100 feet lower there is nothing on the south summit trail that can compare with the demanding scramble from Wolf Pass to

From the trailhead the path begins climbing immediately at a moderate grade, closely following a barbed wire fence on the south side of the trail. After 0.2 mile the fence and the trail reach the top of a small knoll, then for the next 0.3 mile the path drops slightly through a very pleasant meadow filled with sagebrush and wildflowers. Initially you will be able to see Mount Nebo, your destination, peeking out from behind North Peak, but as the trail continues westward the higher peak is soon hidden from view and the vista is completely dominated by North Peak. On the south side of the fence the terrain drops off precipitously to the Nebo Bench below,

Mount Nebo north summit trail

North Peak on the left, with the north summit of Mount Nebo on the right

and if you have very sharp eyes you may be able to spot the Nebo Bench Trail winding through the lower meadows.

About 25 minutes into the hike the trail climbs up the side of a 200-foot ridge that forms the boundary between Utah County from Juab County. It then turns away from the fence and begins following the ridge westward toward the headwaters of Gibson Creek. Soon the path crosses into the Gibson Creek watershed to begin a 950-foot climb over the next mile to the crest of the north ridge of North Peak.

The trail finally reaches the top of the ridge at an elevation of 10,500 feet and then turns south to follow the ridge toward the summit of North Peak. Soon, however, it leaves the ridge and begins traversing around the west side of the peak. After reaching an elevation of 10,800 feet,

just 370 feet lower than the summit of North Peak, the trail starts descending again toward Wolf Pass.

The first part of this hike, from the Mona Pole Trailhead to Wolf Pass, is a very pleasant walk of 3.3 miles over a good trail with an elevation gain of only 1,900 feet. However, that is about to change. From Wolf Pass the route continues up Nebo's brutally steep summit ridge for another 850 feet of elevation gain to the top of an intermediate false summit. The false summit is only 0.36

Climbing from Wolf Pass the false summit on the north side of Nebo

mile from Wolf Pass, but the 850-foot elevation gain translates to an exhausting angle of assent of 25 degrees. There is a primitive trail, and if you stay on it the climb will be a little easier. Unfortunately the trail has been badly degraded by the shifting talus on the steep slope and it is often difficult to follow. Also, parts of the trail may remain covered with snow that often clings to the mountain even into early August.

When you reach the false summit stop to rest for a few minutes, because the final scramble to the top of Mount Nebo is even more grueling. The "trail" drops about 50 feet, then continues along the ridge for 300 yards before beginning another arduous 525-foot climb up the rocky north slope of the final summit. Long, narrow outcroppings of jagged, broken limestone make the scramble much more difficult than it would otherwise be. The sharp, pointy shards of stone are uncomfortable to walk on, let alone climb over. Finding the best route up the ridge is challenging, but it appears that the easiest way up the lower part of the assent is on the right side of the ridge. Then, as you near the end of the climb you will come to another outcropping that is best avoided by going to the left side of the ridge.

The top of Mount Nebo, the highest point in the Wasatch Mountains, is a glorious place to pause and relish your accomplishment. The tiny cars on I-15, nearly 7,000 feet below, look like ants creeping across the valley floor. West of the highway is Mona, and beyond that the Great Basin. To the east the scene is an unbroken panorama of the Wasatch Mountains. The south summit of Mount Nebo rises a mile away on the south side of the mountain, with the middle summit about half way between the two higher peaks. Parts of a hiker-made trail are visible below the south side of Nebo, made by previous hikers who occasionally follow the summit ridge between the north and south summits to ascend all three of the Nebo peaks in sequence. This, however, is considerably more difficult than climbing the north and south summits separately from Wolf Pass and Andrews Ridge.

The south summit of Mount Nebo, as seen from the north summit

Fish Creek

★

Distance:	9.9 miles (plus 38 miles by car)
Walking time:	5 1/2 hours
Elevations:	1,080 ft. loss Upper Fish Creek Trailhead (start): 8,780 ft. Lower Fish Creek Trailhead: 7,700 ft.
Trail:	This trail has been designated as a National Recreation Trail. It is a gentle, downhill walk along a small mountain stream, usually well maintained and easy to follow.
Season:	Summer through mid-fall. The road to the upper trailhead is generally closed each year from the end of November until mid-June, and the upper reaches of the trail are very muddy until the end of June.
Vicinity:	Fifty miles southeast of Spanish Fork, near Scofield
Maps:	C Canyon, Scofield Reservoir *(USGS)*
Information:	http://www.utahtrails.com/fishcreek.html *(Utah Trails)* http://www.fs.usda.gov/mantilasal/ *(Manti-LaSal Nat. Forest)* phone: (435) 637-2817 *(Price Ranger District)*

Turn off I-15 at exit 258 (near Spanish Fork) and drive east on Highway 6 toward Price for 44 miles until you reach the junction with Highway 96. Turn right here and drive south for another 16.7 miles to the town of Scofield. On the west side of Scofield you will find a small paved road that heads north along the west side of the Scofield Reservoir. Drive north on this road. After 3.6 *miles the pavement ends, and 0.3 mile farther the road splits. Bear to the left here, away from the lake, and within 1.6 miles you will arrive at Fish Creek Campground where the lower Fish Creek Trailhead is located. This is where the hike ends, and where you should leave your shuttle car.*

To get to the upper trailhead, where the hike begins, drive back to Scofield and continue south on Highway 96. After three miles you will encounter a junction where Highway 264 begins. You should bear to the right here onto Highway 264. Finally, 18.5 miles from

Scofield, you will come to a stop sign at the junction where Highway 264 meets Highway 31. Two hundred yards before you reach the stop sign you will see a gravel road, North Skyline Drive, leaving on the right. Turn onto North Skyline (forest road 150) and continue for 13.7 miles until you see a small Forest Service sign that says "Fish Creek Trail". The actual trailhead is about 200 yards down a jeep road that begins near this sign.

Note: You can get back to Highway 6 by continuing north on Skyline Drive for another 14.7 miles beyond the trailhead.

Fish Creek runs down a wide, gently sloping canyon from a point near Skyline Drive to the Scofield Reservoir. The canyon is popular with hunters because of the abundance of deer and elk in the area. Deer are everywhere, but the elk seem to prefer grazing in the large open meadows high above the south bank of the creek. Take along a pair of binoculars and stop occasionally to scan these grassy meadows. If you are attentive you are almost certain to see at least a few of the magnificent animals.

The creek runs from west to east, and you will notice a tremendous difference in vegetation between the north and south facing sides of the canyon. The north facing side is covered with aspens and conifers, interspaced with lush green meadows. The south facing side, on the other hand, is sagebrush country with scarcely a tree to be found. Unfortunately the trail spends most of its time on the shadeless south facing side of the canyon.

From Upper Fish Creek Trailhead the path winds down Straight Fork a distance of 1.9 miles before reaching the confluence with Fish Creek. Occasionally you may see other faint trails coming into the canyon,

including one where Straight Fork joins Fish Creek. If you are confused just take the path that follows closest to the creek; the route never strays far from the bottom of the valley. Over the length of the hike the path crosses the creek four times, but for the most part it stays on the north side

Fish Creek

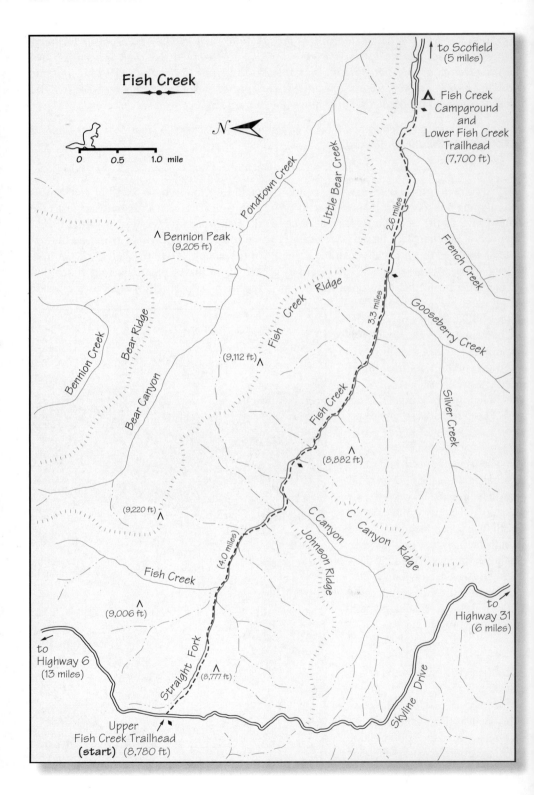

Fish Creek

N

0   0.5   1.0 mile

to Scofield
(5 miles)

Fish Creek
Campground
and
Lower Fish Creek
Trailhead
(7,700 ft)

Pondtown Creek

Little Bear Creek

French Creek

2.6 miles

^ Bennion Peak
(9,205 ft)

Fish Creek Ridge

3.3 miles

Gooseberry Creek

Bear Ridge

Bennion Creek

Bear Canyon

(9,112 ft) ^

Fish Creek

Silver Creek

(8,882 ft) ^

(9,220 ft) ^

C Canyon

C Canyon Ridge

Johnson Ridge

4.0 miles

Fish Creek

^
(9,006 ft)

to
Highway 31
(6 miles)

to
Highway 6
(13 miles)

Straight Fork

^
(8,777 ft)

Skyline Drive

Upper
Fish Creek Trailhead
(start) (8,780 ft)

of the streambed.

After walking 4.0 miles you will encounter the first of three Forest Service signs: a sign marking the bottom of C Canyon Ridge. C Canyon Ridge is also a popular access route into Fish Creek Canyon, and it was once possible to get to within a mile of the creek on a jeep road that follows the ridge. For several reasons, however, including the fact that Fish Creek is an important part of Scofield Reservoir's watershed area, the road is now closed.

As you continue down the canyon the volume of water in Fish Creek gradually increases, but for most of its length the stream isn't deep enough for good fishing. There would be more fish if the canyon's beaver population could make more permanent ponds in the streambed. The trail passes by numerous beaver dams, but virtually all of them have been breached. The dams rarely survive the spring floods. Only after Gooseberry Creek joins Fish Creek, 2.6 miles above the campground, does fishing really become feasible.

Fish Creek Trailhead

At French Creek, 0.7 miles from the end, the trail finally crosses to the shady south side of the canyon. Then, fifteen minutes later, it emerges from the forest at the lower trailhead in Fish Creek Campground.

Fish Creek Trail

Candland Mountain Loop

★★

shuttle car or bike required
day hike

Distance:	9.1 miles
	(plus 4.4 miles by car or bicycle)
Walking time:	6¼ hours
Elevations:	2,125 ft. gain, 2,505 ft. loss
	Mill Canyon Trailhead (start): 8,080 ft.
	Candland Mountain: 10,205 ft.
	Left Fork Huntington Creek Trailhead: 7,700 ft.
Trail:	Most of the trail is well maintained and easy to follow, but there are a few confusing junctions near the crest of the mountain.
Season:	Summer through mid-fall. Upper parts of trail are usually covered with snow from mid-November through mid-June.
Vicinity:	Huntington Canyon, near Price
Maps:	Candland Mountain *(USGS)*
Information:	http://www.utahtrails.com/candland.html *(Utah Trails)*
	http://www.fs.usda.gov/mantilasal/ *(Manti-LaSal Nat. Forest)*
	phone: (435) 637-2817 *(Price Ranger District)*

Drive south from Price on Highway 10 for 20 miles to the town of Huntington. At Huntington turn north on Highway 31 toward Huntington Canyon and Cleveland Reservoir. After 18 miles you will see a sign marking the turnoff to the Forks of Huntington Campground on your left. The Left Fork Huntington Creek Trailhead is at the back of the Forks of Huntington Campground, *0.3 mile from the highway. This trailhead marks the end of the hike, and a shuttle car or bicycle should be left here.*

To get to the Mill Canyon Trailhead where the hike begins return to Highway 31 and note the mileage on your odometer at the entrance to the Campground. Drive north for exactly 4.1 miles, where you will see a small meadow on the west side of the road at the mouth of Mill Canyon. There is a small parking area beside the stream on the shoulder of the highway at the north end of the meadow, and if you look carefully across the stream you will see a small sign marking the beginning of Mill Canyon Trail. If you can't find the sign, don't worry. Just proceed across the meadow toward the mouth of the small canyon and within a few hundred feet you should stumble onto the trail.

The Candland Mountain Loop offers a fine combination of mountain and canyon hiking, with just enough elevation gain to let you know that you have been on a hike and not just a Sunday afternoon stroll. The final 4.2 miles of the hike are down the Left Fork of Huntington Creek, an exceptionally pretty stream, on a designated National Recreation Trail.

From the mouth of Mill Canyon the trail begins its assent almost immediately, gaining about a thousand feet per mile for the next 2.1 miles. When you reach the top

of the ridge you will intersect an old pack trail that starts farther north and follows the long summit ridge of Candland Mountain. You could continue straight across the pack trail at this point, but if you do so you will miss the marvelous views along the ridge. Instead, turn left and follow the pack trail along the ridge in a southerly direction.

After a five-minute climb up the old Candland Mountain pack trail you will reach a local summit (10,205 ft.) where the forest opens up in the west for a wonderful view of Miller Flat and Hog Flat below. Bald Mountain is clearly visible along the

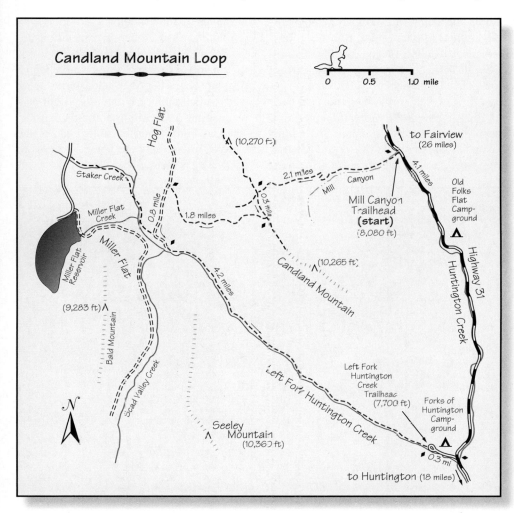

western boundary of Miller Flat, and Seeley Peak lies about 2.5 miles to the south. In between Candland Mountain and Seeley Peak is the 2,000-foot-deep Left Fork Huntington Canyon, which will be your return route. The two mountains were once connected, before the erosive powers of the Left Fork of Huntington Creek carved the deep gouge between them millions of years ago. Continuing southward on the pack trail for 10 minutes more will bring you to another junction where a trail drops off to the right. You should leave the ridge at this point and begin your descent to Hog Flat.

After walking 1.8 miles and dropping 1,600 feet below the Candland Mountain ridge, the trail intersects a jeep road. Turn left and walk along the jeep road for another 0.8 mile to the mouth of Left Fork Huntington Canyon where the road ends and a new trail begins. The trail follows the Left Fork of Huntington Creek westward, entering a deep gorge in the mountains, and within just a few hundred feet the terrain changes completely from a sage-covered flat to a tree-lined canyon. This canyon will be your route through the mountains back to Highway 31—a much easier walk that the climb over Candland Mountain was!

All that remains of the hike now is to walk down the Left Fork of Huntington Creek for the final 4.2 miles to the Forks of Huntington Campground. This is the segment that follows the National Recreation Trail, and it is very pretty. Huge conifers grow right to the water's edge on the south side of the stream with bands of quaking aspen higher up the canyon walls. There are several excellent camping areas farther downstream where many people stay to take advantage of the fishing.

Note the difference in vegetation between the north and south facing sides of the canyon. The forest is much more alpine in nature on the heavily shaded north-facing side, while sage brush and other semi-arid plants grow on the sunny south-facing side. The trail runs along the sunny side of the canyon, where there are fewer obstacles to impede its progress.

Left Fork Huntington Creek

San Rafael River Gorge

★★★

shuttle car required
overnight hike

Distance:	16.4 miles (plus 18.3 miles by car)
Walking time:	day 1: 4 hours day 2: 5 hours
Elevations:	160 ft. loss Fuller Bottom (start): 5,250 ft. San Rafael Campground: 5,090 ft.
Trail:	There is a good horse trail most of the way along the river. The trail crosses the river fifteen times, so be sure to wear wettable shoes.
Season:	Summer, fall. The most important factor to consider in planning this hike is the amount of water in the San Rafael River. The water level is highest in the spring between early May and mid-June, and fording the river with a backpack may be difficult or impossible at that time. Before driving to the trailhead I strongly suggest that you go to the USGS website listed below or call the BLM in Price to find out the river's current flow rate. If it is higher that 120 cfs (cubic feet per second) you may have difficulty. When the flow rate reaches 180 cfs the deepest ford will be about 3 feet. If the rate is greater than 150 cfs you might want to consider floating down the river in a small rubber raft or canoe. Floating the San Rafael can be a delightful experience.
Vicinity:	Near Price
Maps:	Sids Mountain, Bottleneck Peak *(USGS)* San Rafael Swell *(Trails Illustrated, #712)*
Information:	http://www.utahtrails.com/sanrafael.html *(Utah Trails)* http://www.blm.gov/utah/price/ *(BLM, Price)* http://waterdata.usgs gov/nwis/uv?09328500 *(USGS water data)* phone: (435) 636-3600 *(BLM, Price Field Office)*

Take Exit 241 off Highway 6 in Price, and drive south on Highway 10 towards Castledale. After you have driven 11.4 miles you will come to the junction with Highway 155. Turn left here and follow the signs to Cleveland. Continue driving south through Cleveland until you come to a T junction 1.5 miles from the town center. Turn east here and begin following the signs to Buckhorn Wash and San Rafael Campground. There are many roads in this area, but the junctions are all clearly marked with BLM signs. It is 26.4 miles from Cleveland to the bottom of Buckhorn Wash where the San Rafael Campground is located. Only the first two miles are paved.

You can also get to the San Rafael Campground from Interstate Highway 70. Take exit 129 31 miles west of Green River and follow the signs north for 20 miles to the bottom of Buckhorn Wash.

The San Rafael Campground is where this hike ends and where you should leave your shuttle car. To get to Fuller Bottom where the hike begins drive back up Buckhorn Wash towards Cleveland for 12.3 miles until you come to a 4-way junction, then turn left toward the Wedge Overlook. Just 0.5 mile from the 4-way junction you will see a smaller dirt road departing on the right for Fuller Bottom. This road deadends after 5.4 miles at the San Rafael River in Fuller Bottom, where the hike begins. The road is sandy in places, but with care an ordinary car can usually make it.

This hike provides an opportunity to follow a small desert river along a meandering course that cuts directly through one of Utah's most interesting geologic formations: the San Rafael Swell. The San Rafael Swell is a huge elliptical-shaped bubble in the Colorado Plateau that formed some 65 million years ago during a time of great mountain building activity in the American West (known to geologists as the Laramide Orogeny event). The uplift, or anticline, is some 70 miles long and 35 miles wide, with the San Rafael River flowing through its northern half. About half way between Fuller Bottom and Buckhorn Wash the river flows through a particularly scenic section of the gorge known as the Little Grand Canyon. Here the canyon walls rise abruptly over a thousand feet above the river as it meanders around a fin-like obstacle below the Wedge Plateau.

In addition to the hike through the San Rafael River Gorge there are several other points of interest in this area that you may want to see before or after your hike. The Cleveland Lloyd Dinosaur Quarry is located

San Rafael River Trail

Buckhorn Wash pictographs

at the end of a gravel road about ten miles east of Cleveland. This is one of the world's most prolific dinosaur fossil sources, having yielded more than 30 complete dinosaur skeletons since excavations first began in 1929. Also one of the best prehistoric Indian pictograph panels in Utah is located beside the road in Buckhorn Wash four miles above the San Rafael Campground. Finally, if time permits you should drive to the Wedge Overlook, 6.2 miles off the road to Fuller Bottom. The Wedge Overlook offers a fine view of the San Rafael Gorge from a vantage point directly above the Little Grand Canyon.

Day 1 (7.0 miles)

The best way to begin this hike is to cross the river at Fuller Bottom and follow a jeep road downstream along the south shore of the river for 30 minutes. But

before you start find yourself a strong stick at least 7 or 8 feet long to help with the river crossings. As you walk place the stick on the river bottom, tilted at a 45 degree angle on the downstream side, and use it like a third leg. The extra support is a tremendous help, especially if the current is strong.

After walking 1.2 miles along the jeep road you will see another short jeep road that branches off to the left (east) and ends 200 yards later. At the end of this spur there is a trail that winds 130 feet down to the bottom of the canyon and begins following along the south side of the San Rafael. This is the trail that you will be following for the duration of this hike.

After leaving the jeep road the trail stays on the south side of the river for 0.6 miles before crossing again to to the north side. This is the second of 15 fords that will be necessary between Fuller Bottom and Cane Wash, so don't discard your stick yet. About ten minutes after the river crossing to the

Petroglyphs near Sorrel Mule Mine

map continues on bottom of next page

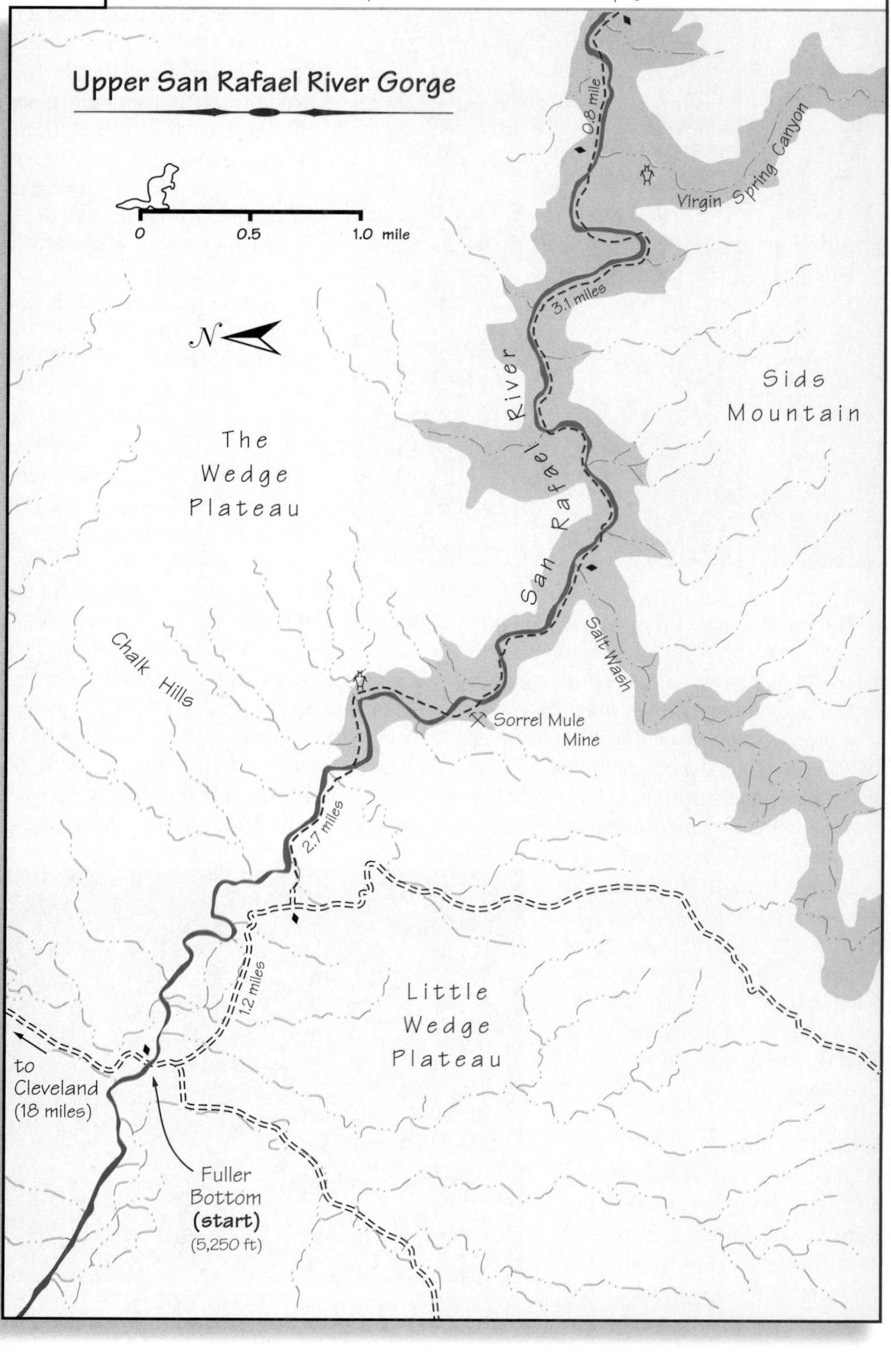

Upper San Rafael River Gorge

0   0.5   1.0 mile

N

The
Wedge
Plateau

Chalk Hills

0.8 mile

Virgin Spring Canyon

3.1 miles

Sids
Mountain

San Rafael River

Salt Wash

Sorrel Mule
Mine

2.7 miles

1.2 miles

Little
Wedge
Plateau

to
Cleveland
(18 miles)

Fuller
Bottom
(start)
(5,250 ft)

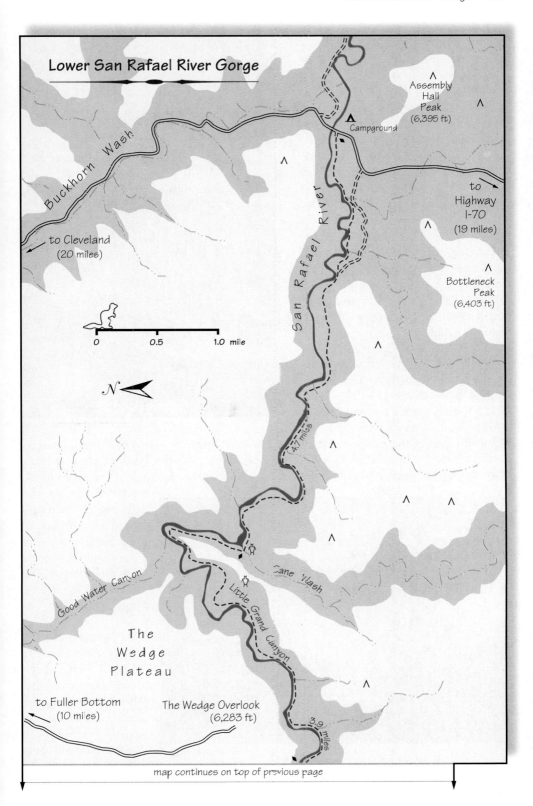

Lower San Rafael River Gorge

Buckhorn Wash

Assembly Hall Peak (6,395 ft)

Campground

San Rafael River

to Cleveland (20 miles)

to Highway I-70 (19 miles)

Bottleneck Peak (6,403 ft)

0   0.5   1.0 mile

N

(4.7 miles)

Cane Wash

Good Water Canyon

Little Grand Canyon

The Wedge Plateau

3.9 miles

to Fuller Bottom (10 miles)

The Wedge Overlook (6,283 ft)

map continues on top of previous page

north shore the trail passes below a small petroglyph panel at the base of the south facing cliffs on the left. Watch carefully as it is easy to miss. Then, after another ten minutes, you will come to the next river crossing.

The next item of interest is easy to spot: the Sorrel Mule Mine. It is situated about 60 feet above the west side of the river, at the top of a large pile of yellowish tailings just 200 yards beyond the third river ford. A close look at the area will reveal the rotting timbers of an old log cabin near the mine as well as dozens of rusted tin cans. Copper was briefly extracted from the Sorrel Mule Mine in 1898. Amazingly, the small shaft penetrates some 2000 feet into the mountain.

A mile below the Sorrel Mule Mine you will cross Salt Wash, a wide, sandy bottomed dry wash that enters the San Rafael River Gorge from the south, and 3.1 miles farther you will come to Virgin Spring Canyon. Virgin Spring Canyon is easily the prettiest side canyon in the gorge. It is one of the few canyons that isn't heavily grazed by cattle, and there

San Rafael River

is a reliable spring not too far from its entrance. It is an excellent place to make camp for the night and, if time permits, do a little exploring. Unfortunately the trail is on the wrong side of the gorge as it passes the mouth of Virgin Spring Canyon, but the river is an easy ford at this point.

Day 2 (9.4 miles)

Before leaving Virgin Spring Canyon take some time to check out the pictographs. The Virgin Spring pictograph panel is located about

San Rafael River

a quarter of a mile from the mouth of the canyon on its west side. It is high on the canyon wall, about 15 feet from the ground. The spring is located about 150 yards further upcanyon from the pictographs at the head of the Virgin Spring Box.

From the mouth of Virgin Spring Canyon the trail continues down the San Rafael River for a mile or so before coming to the next point of interest: the Little Grand Canyon. This is the deepest part of the gorge, a three-mile stretch of river that lies just below the Wedge Overlook. There is also another interesting panel of pictographs near the end of the Little Grand Canyon that you may want to see before continuing.

About 3.0 miles from the mouth of Virgin Spring Canyon the river swings north in order to get around a large fin-like protrusion in the streambed. The pictographs lie on the west side of this fin, just below its highest point. Look for a clearly visible window in the sandstone fin high above the trail. The pictograph panel is to the right of the window at the bottom of the Wingate Sandstone cliffs.

Beyond the pictographs the trail continues north for 0.5 mile and then swings south toward the mouth of Cane Wash, where there are still more pictographs to be seen. The Cane Wash Pictographs are about 100 yards from the river on the east side of the wash. Look for them in the back of a small alcove just above the sandy canyon floor.

From Cane Wash to the campground the trail is well used by day hikers. You will be on the south side of the river for the remainder of the hike; hence no more crossings are necessary. After about 3 more miles the valley widens and the vegetation is dominated by tamarisk trees. 1.5 miles from the end you will encounter another jeep road which you can take if you prefer, although the trail along the river is more interesting. The jeep road joins Buckhorn Wash Road 0.4 mile south of the San Rafael Campground.

San Rafael River

Lower Black Box of the San Rafael

Distance: 15.3 miles (round trip)

Walking time: day 1: 2¹/₂ hours
day 2: 7 hours
day 3: 3 hours

Elevations: 1,250 ft. loss/gain
2WD car park (start): 5,550 ft.
beginning of Lower Black Box: 4,400 ft.
Sulphur Spring: 4,300 ft.

Trail: There is no trail through the Lower Black Box. In many places the canyon floor is filled with water and swimming or floating is necessary. In other places it is necessary to scramble over rock falls. Do not attempt this hike without adequate preparation.

Season: Midsummer to mid-fall. The success of this hike requires good weather, warm temperatures, and low river flow rates; consequently there are only a few weeks during the year when it should be attempted. The best all around time is usually between early July and mid-August. Some important points:
(1) Always make sure you have a good weather forecast before entering into the Black Box, but be especially careful during the rainy season in late summer and early fall.
(2) Water temperatures in the Black Box are too cold for travel in the winter or early spring.
(3) There is generally too much water flowing in the San Rafael River to attempt the Black Box in late spring or early summer. Whatever date you choose, you should go to the USGS website listed below or call the BLM in Price to find out the river's current flow rate. If it is higher that 50 cfs (cubic feet per second) don't go.

Vicinity: Near Green River

Maps: Spotted Wolf Canyon *(USGS)*
San Rafael Swell *(Trails Illustrated, #712)*

Information: http://www.utahtrails.com/blackbox.html (Utah Trails)
http://www.blm.gov/utah/price/ *(BLM, Price)*

http://waterdata.usgs.gov/r_wis/uv?09328500 *(USGS water data)*
phone: (435) 636-3600 *(BLM, Price Field Office)*
phone: (801) 539-1311 *(river flow rates recording, updated daily)*

Drive west of Green River on I-70 for 30 miles and take Exit 131. After you leave I-70 drive east along the gravel frontage road on the north side of the highway toward Buckhorn Wash. The frontage road parallels the highway for 3.3 miles and then veers to the north. After you have driven 5.6 miles on this road you will come to a sign marking a smaller road on the right that leads to Sinkhole Flat and Jackass Benches. Make a note of your odometer reading and turn east onto this road. After 1.7 miles you will come to a junction where you must bear left. At 4.4 miles you will encounter the road to Sulphur Springs. Again, turn left. At 7.3 miles you will see the road to Drowned Hole Draw on your left; bear right here. At 8.9 miles, another road on the right that leads to Sulphur Springs; bear left towards Swasey's Leap. At 10.1 miles you will come to a small pullout. At this point you are still 4.5 miles from the San Rafael River, but this is about as far a you can go without a 4WD vehicle. If you are in a 4WD vehicle continue driving on this road for another 2.4 miles to the boundary of the Mexican Mountain Wilderness Study Area. Park your car at the gate and walk the last 2.1 miles to the view point above Swasey's Leap and the San Rafael River.

Note: Some people prefer to start at Sulphur Springs and walk along the canyon rim to Swasey's Leap before floating the river instead of the other way around. If you choose to do this, however, you should have a 4WD vehicle. To get to Sulphur Springs turn right at the last junction (1.2 miles before the 2WD pullout on the Swasey's Leap road). Drive 1.1 miles on this road to the next junction, then turn left onto the Sulphur Springs Road. After another 2.6 miles You will come to a barrier at the boundary of the Mexican Mountain Wilderness Study Area, where you must park your car and walk the last 1.2 miles to Sulphur Springs.

The Lower Black Box is a deep, narrow canyon of the San Rafael River located on the eastern edge of the San Rafael Swell. This hike involves floating 3.7 miles down the river through the Lower Black Box, and then walking back 2.6 miles along the eastern side of the gorge to the starting point. The trip is an exciting one with a lot to see, but it requires careful planning and it isn't suitable for everyone.

First, the trip through the Lower Black Box shouldn't be attempted by anyone who doesn't know how to swim. It is also important that everyone

Northern end of the Lower Black Box

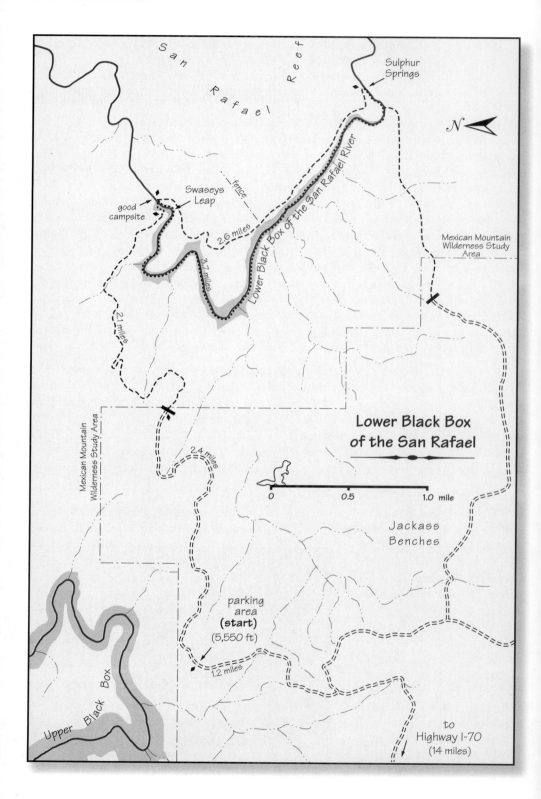

San Rafael Reef

Sulphur Springs

N

Swaseys Leap

fence

good campsite

2.6 miles

Lower Black Box of the San Rafael River

Mexican Mountain Wilderness Study Area

3.7 miles

2.1 miles

Mexican Mountain Wilderness Study Area

Lower Black Box of the San Rafael

2.4 miles

0   0.5   1.0 mile

Jackass Benches

parking area **(start)** (5,550 ft)

1.2 miles

Upper Black Box

to Highway I-70 (14 miles)

in the group have an inflated inner tube to float through the long, deep pools. I have done this trip with a small rubber raft, but I don't recommend it. There are a number of places in the canyon where scrambling is necessary to get around rock falls, and getting a rubber raft across these obstacles is difficult.

Second, don't try to carry anything more than your inner tube, a small floatable day pack, and a walking stick when you go through the Black Box. Both of your hands must be free when you are scrambling over the rock falls and fighting your way through the canyon narrows. You should include a 50-foot length of rope in your pack for emergency use and for lowering down backpacks. As for clothing: shorts, a shirt, and wettable boots are best. You will be walking over submerged rocks much of the time, so be sure you have good footwear. Also, forget about trying to keep your things dry. Everything you take with you will be soaking wet when you finish with this trip.

Third, timing is important. Once you enter the Black Box it is difficult to turn around. It isn't the sort of place you want to get caught in after dark, so be sure to allow plenty of time for the trip. The season is also important. You don't want to do this trip unless the weather is good, the temperature is warm, and there isn't too much water in the canyon.

Day 1 (4.5 miles)

From the car parking area to the San Rafael River and the Lower Black Box is only a 2½ hour walk, but since it is best to get an early start when you go through the Box you should plan on going only as far as the river on the first day. There are several

Lower Black Box of the San Rafael River

good campsites on the river just above the entrance to the Lower Black Box.

From the 2WD parking area just continue walking east along the jeep road towards Swasey's Leap. The road/trail ends after 4.5 miles at a view point above the river overlooking Swasey's Leap. If you have a 4WD vehicle you can shorten the walk by driving another 2.4 miles down the road. In the past it was possible to drive a 4WD vehicle all the way to the river, but the area is now part of the Mexican Mountain Wilderness Study Area and the last 2.1 miles of the road have been closed by the BLM.

From the view point at the end of the road it is an easy fifteen-minute scramble down the last 280 feet to the river. The best route is down a small rock-filled drainage on the north side of the view point. Once you

Swasey's Leap (1995)

reach the river you will find a good campsite about a hundred yards upstream near the tamarisk trees.

Swasey's Leap is the name given to the narrowest part of the canyon just below the overlook point. According to local legend a cowboy named Sid Swasey once won a bet from his brother, Joe, by jumping the ten-foot gap on his horse. A few years later, probably just after the turn of the last century, two sheep ranchers named Paul Hanson and Hyrum Seeley built a log bridge across Swasey's Leap for the purpose of getting their sheep across the flooded river. The crude structure remained intact for almost a hundred years, but in 1997 the last remnants of the span finally tumbled into the river.

Day 2 (6.3 miles)

Getting through the Lower Black Box and back is the goal of the second day. Going through the Box can be an exciting and interesting experience, but, once again, make sure you are prepared and that the weather is good before you start out. Although the

Lower Black Box is only 3.7 miles long, you should allow 7 hours for the round trip, including 2 hours for the walk back from the bottom of the Box.

The first point of interest is Swasey's Leap. You will float under it just a few minutes after leaving your campsite. Looking up at the narrow opening where the bridge was will probably make you wonder how many sheep Hanson and Seeley lost getting their herd across the canyon.

The first few hundred yards of the journey through the Box are a very pleasant float, but soon after passing under Swasey's Leap you will begin to encounter a series of obstacles. There are about six or eight places in the upper half of the canyon where large rock falls will force you to climb out of the stream to scramble over the sandstone boulders. Although the conditions change from year to year, the rock falls are generally not difficult to get around—just tiring and time consuming. But be sure you have a rope in

Lower Black Box of the San Rafael River

case you encounter something unexpected. Usually you will be back in the water again floating comfortably on your inner tube after ten minutes of scrambling.

In many areas it is possible to walk on a sandy bank near the canyon wall, but if the ground is too wet you will soon discover that quicksand is a problem. It is usually easier to stay in the water.

After the first two miles the canyon starts getting easier to negotiate, and soon you will pass the last serious rock fall. The last rock fall is located in the middle of a long straight section of river that runs almost due southeast for a full mile. As you near the end of this straight section of river you will begin to see water seeping out of the porous sandstone of the canyon walls. The seeps become more and more prodigious as you progress downstream. Also, you will notice that the height of the canyon walls is decreasing.

Eventually the river makes a sharp bend to the southwest, and then bends lazily around again to a northeasterly course. Pay attention to where the sun is. If it is shining in your face when you look downstream and if it is about the middle of the day, then the river has turned south and you are near the end of your float. When the river's course swings to the northeast start looking for a large spring that flows down the right bank. This is Sulphur Spring, and it isn't hard to see why it is called that. You can smell the sulphur and see the twigs and branches on the south side of the river encased in a yellowish crust. Needless to say, this water is not drinkable.

When you reach Sulphur Spring it is time to climb back out of the water and begin your trek back to camp along the east side of the San Rafael. Soon you should see a hiker-made trail that follows the bench above the river. The walk is an easy one with only a little up and down, the scenery is excellent, and the warm desert sun is welcome. There are also a number of impressive views down into the Lower Black Box on the way back. Stopping occasionally to enjoy the scenery, you should get back to your camp near Swasey's Leap after about two hours.

Day 3 (5.0 miles)

All that remains of the hike now is the walk back to your car. It will take about 2.5 hours if you parked at the 2WD area, or less if you drove a 4WD vehicle to the wilderness study area boundary.

Lower Black Box near Sulphur Spring

Devils Garden

★★★★★

Distance: 8.1 miles, including side trips to all points of interest

Walking time: 4½ hours

Elevations: 280 ft. gain/loss
Devils Garden Trailhead (start): 5,180 ft.
Landscape Arch: 5,320 ft.
Dark Angel: 5,460 ft.

Trail: Generally easy, well used trail

Season: Spring, summer, fall, winter. The trail is quite hot in summer, so carry plenty of water.

Vicinity: Arches National Park, near Moab

Maps: Mollie Hogans, Klondike Bluffs *(USGS)*
Arches National Park *(Trails Illustrated, #211)*

Information: http://www.utahtrails.com/devils.html *(Utah Trails)*
http://www.nps.gov/arch/ *(Arches National Park)*
phone: (435) 719-2299 *(Visitor Center)*

Drive north from the Arches National Park Visitor Center along the scenic park road for a distance of 19 miles. Devils Garden Trailhead is at the end of the road just beyond the campground. (Note: If you plan to stay at the campground you had better arrive early. It is very popular.)

If the strange and wonderful rock formations of Southern Utah interest you you will love this hike. Devils Garden contains no fewer than nine sandstone arches, including the magnificent Landscape Arch, the park's longest span. The area is a particularly good place to study the life cycle of natural arches. You will see many spans of different ages as you wander through the jumbled canyons of stone as well as the

Devils Garden Trail

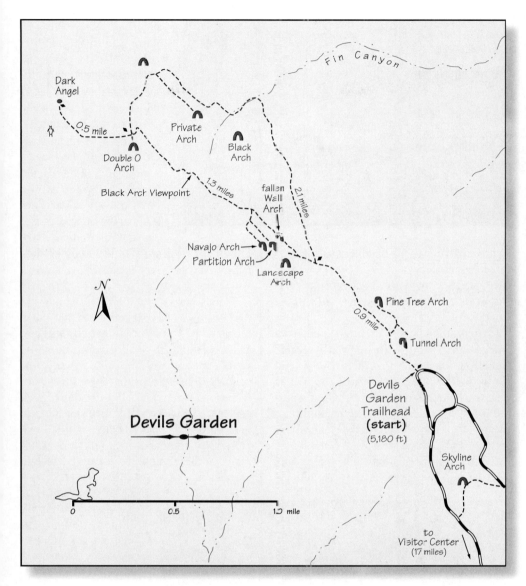

Dark
Angel

Fin Canyon

0.5 mile

Private
Arch

Double O
Arch

Black
Arch

Black Arch Viewpoint

1.3 miles

fallen
Wall
Arch

2.1 miles

Navajo Arch
Partition Arch

Landscape
Arch

Pine Tree Arch

0.9 mile

Tunnel Arch

Devils
Garden
Trailhead
(start)
(5,180 ft)

Skyline
Arch

N

Devils Garden

0   0.5   1.0 mile

to
Visitor Center
(17 miles)

remains of one large arch that finally fell down just four years ago.

On the return portion of the hike along the Primitive Loop Trail you will pass through a giant maze of long vertical sandstone fins, all parallel to one another with narrow canyons between. These fins are the raw materials from which future arches are being made. In another million years, when all of the present arches are gone, there

will be many new ones in these canyons to replace them. Some of the new arches might even be more spectacular than the present ones. Nature is continually modifying and replacing her artwork.

From the trailhead the path goes for only 0.3 mile before another spur trail leaves on the right to Pine Tree Arch and Tunnel Arch. Both Pine Tree and Tunnel are young arches

Tunnel Arch

physics. At its thinnest point Landscape Arch is only 6 feet thick, yet the ribbon of stone rises 77 feet above the sandy desert floor and extends for some 290 feet from base to base. According to recent calculations it is the longest natural arch in the United States, although Kolob Arch in Zion National Park is about the same size. Because of its immense size

with relatively small openings surrounded by large masses of rock. The 15-minute detour to see them serves as a nice prelude to the next arch—the oldest one you will see on this hike.

Continuing northward on the main trail for another 0.5 mile will bring you to another junction where the Primitive Loop Trail joins the Devils Garden Trail. You will be returning on the path to the right, so for now bear left for a short distance to the Landscape Arch. For many people Landscape Arch is the high point of this hike

This arch is so improbably long and slender its span seems to defy the laws of

Landscape Arch is difficult to photograph, but if you want to try make sure you have a wide angle lens.

Landscape is a very old arch, definitely in the last stages of its existence, but how much longer it will endure is anybody's guess. Maybe another decade, maybe a hundred years but certainly not more that a few centuries. In 1991 visitors were shocked to witness a 60-foot long, 180-ton slab of rock peel away from the arch's right side and fall to the ground. Then, in June of 1995, two more large chunks of rock fell from Landscape Arch, prompting the Park Service to permanently close the trail beneath it.

As if to remind us of Landscape Arch's limited lifespan, another nearby arch collapsed in 2008. 200 yards north of Landscape the trail passes the remains of Wall Arch, a 71-foot span of rock that collapsed sometime before the morning of August 4, 2008. Wall was the 12th largest arch in the national park.

Beyond Landscape and Wall Arch-

Landscape Arch

Devils Garden Trail

Partition Arch, so named because of a vertical column of stone that divides it into two separate arches, can also be seen from the trail near Landscape Arch. Navajo Arch, smaller than the others, is located in a cool, sheltered area with lots of shade – great place for a break. Also, the path to Navajo Arch passes a wall of interesting eroded sandstone etchings that look almost as if they were carved by a artist.

Continuing on from the Navajo Arch junction, the main trail skirts the southwest side of an amazing collection of sandstone fins. After 0.7 mile the path begins following along the top of one of the fins with a terrific view to the north into the upper reaches of Fin Canyon. At the north end of the fin there is a viewpoint from which you can see the Black Arch, about 500 yards northeast of the trail.

es the trail is less well developed, and as you leave the fallen rubble of Wall Arch some minor scrambling is briefly required. Then, after about 5 minutes, you will see a Park Service sign marking another spur trail that leads to Partition Arch. 0.2 mile away, and Navajo Arch, 0.3 mile from the main trail.

The next arch you will encounter on this hike is the Double O Arch, 0.4 mile beyond the Black Arch viewpoint at the end of the Devils Garden Trail. Double O, one of my favorites, consists of a huge O-shaped opening with a smaller O directly below it. You can also see the Dark Angel 0.4 mile west

Double O Arch

of Double O, and there is a great vantage point on the south side of Double O for photographing both of the landmarks.

Just a few yards before the Devils Garden trail ends at the Double O Arch you will pass a sign that marks the beginning of the Dark Angel Trail and the Primitive Loop Trail. The Dark Angel Trail heads west for 0.5 mile to end at the foot of an impressive 150-foot sandstone monolith that stands prominently on the edge of a long narrow bench overlooking Salt Valley and the Klondike Bluffs on the western edge of the national park. There are also several interesting panels of petroglyphs 150 yards from the trail on the south side of the Dark Angel.

The Primitive Loop Trail will be your return route to the Devils Garden Trailhead. This trail is not as well maintained, but it is well cairned and quite easy to follow. In my opinion it is the most interesting part of this hike, but be advised that this route does require a bit of scrambling over the slickrock in a few places. The trail wonders through an intriguing collection of thin sandstone fins, all aligned in a northwest-southeast direction. The fins were formed millions of years ago when the ground rose beneath a solid block of Entrada Sandstone, causing it to fracture and separate into long, parallel vertical sheets. The existence of these large fins is the primary reason why so many arches have been formed in Arches National Park.

0.4 mile after leaving the Double O Arch on the Primitive Loop Trail you will see a park service sign marking the beginning of a secondary trail that leads to Private Arch. This delightful trail winds through the sandstone fins for 0.3 mile before finally arriving at the end of one of the fins where the secluded arch is located.

Back on the Primitive Loop Trail again, the path continues to wind through the rugged backcountry for another 0.5 mile before dropping into a sandy wash on the floor of Fin Canyon. It follows the wash for ten minutes, then climbs out onto the eastern side of Devils Garden for the last 1.0 mile back to the trail junction east of Landscape Arch. From there it is an easy 0.8-mile walk back to the Devils Garden Trailhead.

Devils Garden Trail

Delicate Arch

★★

Distance:	3.0 miles (round trip)
Walking time:	2 hours
Elevations:	530 ft. gain/loss Delicate Arch Trailhead (start): 4,300 ft. Delicate Arch: 4,830 ft.
Trail:	Easy, well used trail
Season:	Spring, summer, fall, winter.
Vicinity:	Arches National Park, near Moab
Maps:	The Windows Section, Big Bend *(USGS)* Arches National Park *(Trails Illustrated, #211)*
Information:	http://www.utahtrails.com/delicatearch.html *(Utah Trails)* http://www.nps.gov/arch/ *(Arches National Park)* phone: (435) 719-2299 *(Visitor Center)*

From the Arches National Park Visitor Center you must drive 12.7 miles into the park following the signs to the Wolfe Ranch and Delicate Arch Trailhead. After 9.0 miles you will pass the turnoff to The Windows where you must bear left. Another 2.4 miles will bring you to the Wolfe Ranch Road, where you must turn right and continue the last 1.2 miles to the trailhead parking area.

Of all the arches in Utah's Arches National Park, the best known is the Delicate Arch. Although it is only 52 feet tall, it has a certain rugged grace that seems to set it apart from all the others. Isolated on the edge of a high escarpment above Winter Camp Wash, it stands alone against the backdrop of the La Sal Mountains, symbolizing the rugged beauty of the Utah landscape and personifying the proud, independent spirit of the state's people. Images of the famous landmark have appeared over the years on postage stamps, license plates, government letterheads and publicity pamphlets. Its fame has grown accordingly, so that now if you do this hike on a summer afternoon you will see hundreds of visitors gathering near the arch, waiting to photograph its red sunset glow. The group always includes visitors from all over the world, and for many this is the only hike they will do in Utah.

The Delicate Arch was given its present

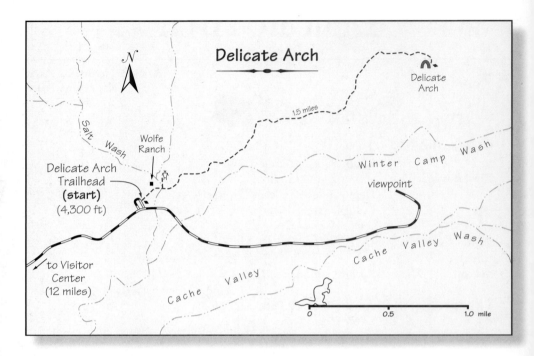

name by Frank Beckwith, who led the Arches National Monument Scientific Expedition into the area in the early 1930s. But before then the local cowboys had long known it as "The Schoolmarm's Bloomers". Many visitors see in the arch an almost irresistible challenge to climb to the top, but there has been only one documented ascent. A man named Dean Potter made a free solo assent of the Delicate Arch with no ropes or other protection in May of 2006. Potter's ascent created a great deal of controversy, however, and shortly afterward the Park Service disallowed future climbs on any named arch within the park.

Just 250 feet from the parking lot the trail passes a corral and an old log cabin that was, a hundred years ago, the center of life on the Wolfe Ranch. John Wesley Wolfe, a disabled veteran of the Civil War, and his son, Fred, came here from Ohio in the late 1800s looking for a place to begin life anew. They were attracted to the grass filled pastures that then filled Salt Wash Valley and the reliable source of water in the wash, so they decided to settle and start a small ranching operation. Life was good for a few years. In addition to raising cattle, they dammed Salt Wash and raised a variety of vegetables and melons that they traded with the local Indians and sold in Moab. But eventually the land was degraded by the detrimental effects of overgrazing, and the bounty of the land declined.

In 1906 Wolf's daughter, Flora, came from Ohio with her husband and two children to join her father on their ranch. They stayed only two years before moving on to Moab, but it was during that time that the present cabin was built. John and Fred remained on the ranch for another two years, but in the spring of 1910 they too moved to Moab. Soon afterward the ranch was sold and the entire family moved back to Ohio.

100 yards after leaving the Wolfe cabin the trail crosses a footbridge that spans Salt Wash, and as you leave the bridge you will

Delicate Arch

see a sign directing you to a small panel of Indian petroglyphs 150 yards north of the main trail. Indians have always been present in Salt Wash Valley. There is no evidence of any permanent settlements, but they often camped nearby and frequently bartered with the Wolfes for melons, jerky, and other items. The petroglyphs near the ranch feature etchings of bighorn sheep as well as three men on horseback. It is notoriously difficult to date rock art, but the presence of horses in the panel indicates that it could not be more than 350 years old.

The trail continues to meander across the desert for another 0.6 mile before coming to the base of a long sloping ramp of slickrock that rises to the top of the Navajo Sandstone formation. The climb up the slickrock lasts for the next 0.4 mile, over which your elevation gain will be about 300 feet.

The last 0.3 mile of trail is across a gently undulating sea of slickrock sandstone with one particular interesting section that climbs along a narrow elevated path high on the side of a sandstone ridge. Finally, with no warning, the trail bends around the east side ridge to reveal a large amphitheater with the Delicate Arch poised majestically above Winter Camp Wash on the southern side of the bowl.

Trail to the Delicate Arch

Lower Courthouse Wash

★★

Arches National Park
shuttle car required
day hike

Distance:	6.2 miles (plus 6.7 miles by car)
Walking time:	3¹/₂ hours
Elevations:	130 ft. loss Courthouse Wash Trailhead (start): 4,110 ft. Highway 191: 3,980 ft.
Trail:	No trail, but very easy walking along the bottom of a sandy wash. Some wading is necessary, so wear wettable shoes.
Season:	Spring, summer, fall, winter.
Vicinity:	Arches National Park, near Moab
Maps:	The Windows Section, Moab *(USGS)* Arches National Park *(Trails Illustrated, #211)*
Information:	http://www.utahtrails.com/courthouse.html *(Utah Trails)* http://www.nps.gov/arch/ *(Arches National Park)* phone: (435) 719-2299 *(Visitor Center)*

Drive north from the Visitor Center along the road into Arches National Park for a distance of 4.6 miles to the point where the road crosses Courthouse Wash. The wash is clearly marked by a road sign. There is a small parking area about 100 yards beyond the wash on the west side of the road. The hike begins in the wash on the east side of the bridge.

Before beginning the hike you will have to leave a shuttle car or bicycle where Courthouse Wash crosses Highway 191. Drive east on Highway 191, toward Moab, for a distance of 1.8 miles from the entrance of Arches National Park. Here, just before the highway crosses Courthouse Wash, you will see a small Park Service parking lot on the left where you can leave your shuttle.

Courthouse Wash is a short, but very pretty canyon near the entrance to Arches National Park. You won't see any arches in Courthouse but it is, nevertheless, a pleasant half-day walk. The canyon almost always has at least some water in it; consequently it is filled with cottonwoods and willows. The easiest place to walk is usually in the stream

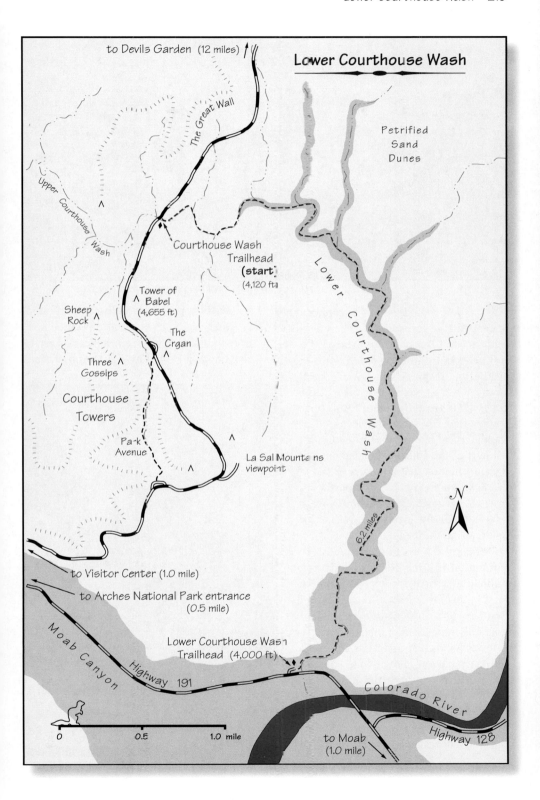

Lower Courthouse Wash

to Devils Garden (12 miles)

The Great Wall

Petrified
Sand
Dunes

Upper Courthouse Wash

Courthouse Wash
Trailhead
(start)
(4,120 ft)

Tower of
Babel
(4,655 ft)

Sheep
Rock

The
Organ

Three
Gossips

Courthouse
Towers

Park
Avenue

La Sal Mountains
viewpoint

Lower Courthouse Wash

6.2 miles

N

to Visitor Center (1.0 mile)

to Arches National Park entrance
(0.5 mile)

Lower Courthouse Wash
Trailhead (4,000 ft)

Moab Canyon

Highway 191

Colorado River

to Moab
(1.0 mile)

Highway 128

0   0.5   1.0 mile

Looking south from the Lower Courthouse Wash Trailhead

bed, so you should wear sneakers or other shoes suitable for wading. There are deer and raccoon tracks in the canyon, but the animal you are sure to see a lot of is frogs.

Before dropping into lower Courthouse Wash to begin your hike, pause for a while to study the red sandstone towers that rise from the surrounding valley. These photogenic formations are all part of the Entrada Sandstone geologic formation that dominates most of Arches National Park. The Courthouse Towers, after which Courthouse Wash was named, are located about a mile south of the trailhead.

Underneath the Entrada Sandstone Formation lies the Navajo Sandstone, a thick layer of light-colored rock that is very prominent in the canyons of Southern Utah. Navajo Sandstone is generally much whiter than the reddish Entrada Sandstone, and it tends to erode into deep narrow canyons and smooth-walled cliffs with little fracturing. Entrada Sandstone, on the other hand, has an interesting tendency to erode into unlikely looking pillars and arches of the kind that have made Arches National Park famous.

The hike begins very close to the boundary that separates the Entrada Sandstone from the older Navajo Sandstone. At first the canyon is very shallow, but as you proceed

Lower Courthouse Wash

Lower Courthouse Wash

Highway 191 at the top of upper Courthouse Wash. The upper part of the wash begins on the east side of Highway 191, 5.7 miles north of the park entrance or about 0.2 mile south of the road leading to Dead Horse Point. This route first passes through a narrow canyon in the Entrada Sandstone, and then, after about 2.5 miles, emerges into a wide valley at the bottom of the Entrada. There is usually water in the streambed after the first 2.3 miles. Finally, after 7.8 miles, the wash reaches the national park road, where the hike through Lower Courthouse Wash begins.

downstream the gorge cuts deeper into the Navajo Sandstone and the canyon walls soon become much higher.

You will be following the bottom of Courthouse Wash all the way to the point where Highway 191 crosses it near the Colorado River. The canyon starts out in a general easterly direction, then gradually swings around to the south. Four smaller side canyons join the wash before it reaches the Colorado, all coming in from the northeast, but in each case it is obvious which canyon is the main one. The smaller canyons all lead to an area in the park known as the Petrified Sand Dunes.

Sand, of course, is a by-product of the erosion that carved Courthouse Wash, and the floor of the canyon is filled with a thick layer of it. Walking on the dry, loose sand is tiring, but there is usually a lot of water in the streambed and it is easier to walk in or along the edge of water. Many people take their shoes off and walk barefoot most of the way.

Upper Courthouse Wash

If you want a longer walk you can begin your hike farther north on

Lower Courthouse Wash

Mill Creek Canyon

★★★

Distance:	5.5 miles (round trip)
Walking time:	3 hours
Elevations:	500 ft. gain/loss Mill Creek Trailhead (start): 4,250 ft. Upper Trailhead: 4,690 ft.
Trail:	Generally easy to follow, although multiple hiker-made trails can sometimes be confusing.
Season:	All year round
Vicinity:	Near Moab
Maps:	Moab, Mill Creek *(USGS)*
Information:	http://www.utahtrails.com/millcreek.html *(Utah Trails)* http://www.blm.gov/utah/moab/ *(BLM, Moab)* phone: (435) 259-2100 *(BLM, Moab Field Office)*

Drive east of Center Street in Moab on Highway 191 for a distance of 2.4 miles to Mill Creek Drive. Turn left on Mill Creek Drive and proceed north for another 0.9 mile to Powerhouse Road. Turn right on Powerhouse Road and continue for the last 0.6 mile to the trailhead and parking area at the end of the road.

This delightful hike will take you into a scenic desert canyon that cuts its way through the pinkish domes and bluffs of the Navajo Sandstone formation south of Arches National Park. Best of all there is a picturesque creek in the bottom of the canyon that runs throughout the year, and the water-filled pools and slides in the slickrock streambed are a great place to cool off during the hot summer months. Mill Creek Canyon is a favorite summer afternoon destination of the

Mill Creek

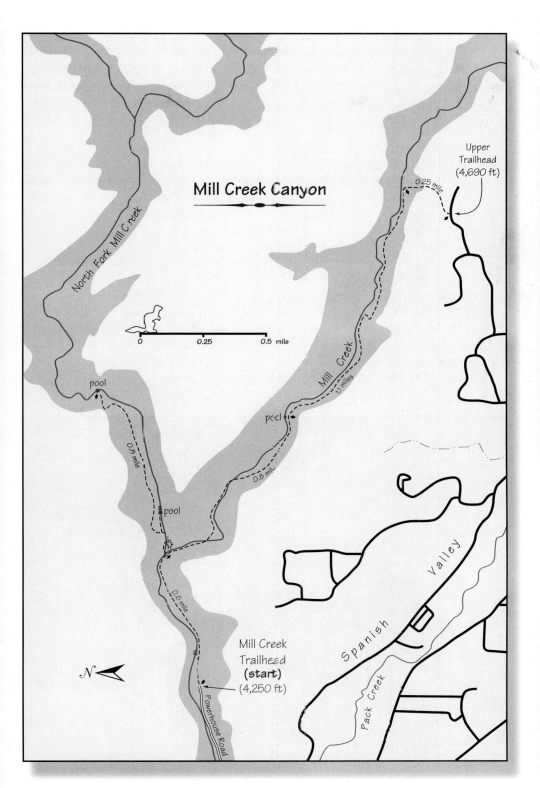

Mill Creek Canyon

North Fork Mill Creek

Upper
Trailhead
(4,690 ft)

0.25 mile

Mill Creek

1.1 miles

pool

0.8 mile

pool

pool

0.8 mile

pool

0.6 mile

Mill Creek
Trailhead
(start)
(4,250 ft)

Spanish   Valley

Pack Creek

Powerhouse Road

N

0   0.25   0.5 mile

residents of nearby Moab, so if you are looking for solitude this is the wrong hike. But the great majority of visitors never venture beyond the first few pools near the trailhead, so it is usually possible to find a measure of seclusion further up the canyon.

The trail leaves the east side of the parking lot and proceeds up the south side of the creek where, within a few hundred feet, you will pass the canyon's first swimming hole. This pool is usually filled with swimmers, but don't despair: the crowds thin out very quickly as you continue upstream. Within a minute or two you will pass the south side of a 20-foot waterfall that is also a favorite destination of the locals. Teenage daredevils seem to delight in jumping from a point halfway up the opposite side of the fall into the pool below, but the water is not really deep enough to do this safely.

This waterfall and the concrete dam above it are the remnants of a small hydro-electric generating station that was built across Mill Creek by the Moab Light and Power Company in 1919. The facility provided electrical power for the residents of Moab until Utah Power and Light completed a high voltage transmission line from Price to Moab in 1945.

If you are observant you may notice a few weathered Indian petroglyphs on the rocks just beyond the waterfall on the right side of the trail. Mill Creek was well known to the Native Americans long before the arrival of white men, and their ancient art work can still be seen on numerous rocks and cliff faces throughout the canyon.

0.6 mile from the trailhead the canyon splits, with the North Fork of Mill Creek coming in from the east. The most obvious trail veers to the right at this point, staying on the south side of the water as it continues into Mill Creek Canyon. You may not even notice the junction in the river, but there is another trail that crosses the water near

Mill Creek Canyon

the confluence and proceeds into the North Fork of the canyon. More on the North Fork Trail later.

Continuing south from the North Fork confluence into the main canyon the trail stays close to the water for the next 200 yards, then crosses the stream and climbs out to a sandy bench above the north side of the creek. If you miss this turn you will soon find yourself mired in the tangle of vegetation that surrounds Mill Creek. The path stays above the north side of the creek for the next 0.2 mile before again returning to the canyon floor and crossing to the south side of the stream where it stays for the remainder of the hike.

There are many great swimming holes in Mill Creek Canyon, but the best one, in my opinion, is the one you will pass 0.8 mile from the North Fork confluence. The trail at this point is about 50 feet beyond the right side of the creek. It passes through an opening that was once a gate in an old fence, and just beyond the gate you will see a short spur trail departing toward the pool. This delightful pocket of water lies at the bottom of a short waterslide that empties into its deepest end, and it is surrounded by shelves of slickrock that are perfect for sunbathing. Furthermore, few people care to walk this far up the trail, so there are usually few if any other swimmers present.

The trail continues up the canyon for another 1.2 miles, passing several more water slides and pools along the way, before making a sharp right turn to begin climbing out of the canyon. The trail finally ends 0.2 mile later in a gated community south of Moab. Even if you do not intend to terminate your hike here it is worthwhile climbing partway up this last segment of the trail for

the view back into the gorge. The domes of Navajo Sandstone that surround the north rim are a gorgeous backdrop for this beautiful canyon.

The upper trailhead of Mill Creek Canyon is not well marked and there is no place to park beside the narrow road, so most people simply return to the public trailhead at the mouth of the canyon. Another option, however, is to have someone drop you off at the upper trailhead. To get there you must drive south from Center Street in Moab on Highway 191 for 4.2 miles to the Spanish Trail Road. Turn left and drive north on Spanish Trail for 1.0 mile to Murphy Lane. Drive west on Murphy Lane for 0.1 mile to Desert Hill Drive. Turn right on Desert Hill Drive and continue north for 0.5 mile to E. George White Road. Turn right on E. George White Road and drive east for 0.3 mile to Red Rock Road. Turn right on Red Rock Road and drive into the Navajo Ridge gated community for the last 0.2 mile to the trailhead. The only marker you will see at the trailhead is a 4x4 post on the left side of the road with the words "Mill Creek" inscribed on it.

Flying Men Petroglyphs

North Fork of Mill Creek Canyon

As mentioned earlier, there is another trail that leaves Mill Creek Canyon to follow the North Fork of the Canyon just 0.6 mile from the trailhead. When you come to the point where the two canyons split you must leave the main trail and wade across both of the two creeks to get to the north side of the North Fork. There you will find another hiker-made trail that proceeds in an easterly direction into North Fork Canyon.

Look to your left as you walk, and there, near the canyon wall on the south side of the water, just 150 feet upstream from the confluence, you will see two large boulders that are covered with petroglyphs. The ancient artwork contains many familiar features—a desert bighorn sheep, a hand print, some snakelike spirals—but the thing that makes the artwork unique is the presence of dozen or so human figures that appear to have feathers sprouting from their heads and arms. Some people imagine the drawings to be humans with wings instead of arms; hence their name: the "Flying Men Petroglyphs".

The trail crosses the water two more times in the next 200 feet before finally settling on the south side of the creek. Five minutes after leaving the petroglyphs you will come to a large pool that effectively blocks further progress up the canyon. The pond makes a perfect swimming hole for summer hikers, and previous visitors have constructed a crude rock dam across the creek to enlarge and deepen it. As a bonus, the pool even has a pic-turesque 15-foot waterfall pouring into it on the upstream side. The only downside is that the basin is completely enclosed by the steep canyon walls, and the only way in or out is across the hiker-made dam.

Further progress up North Fork Canyon appears to be blocked by the waterfall, but if you will backtrack down the trail for 100 yards you will find another less obvious trail that climbs to the top of a bench 20 feet above the south side of the creek, thus providing a route around the fall.

From there the trail stays high above the canyon floor for the next 0.6 mile, winding through the desert vegetation below the towering cliffs of Navajo Sandstone before finally returning to the water at the end of the trail. When you reach the end your reward will be another tempting desert swimming pool surrounded by cottonwoods with a small stream of water pouring in across the slickrock on the upstream side. This pool is perfect for children: relatively shallow with a clean sandy beach and plenty of shade.

North Fork Mill Creek Canyon

Negro Bill Canyon

★★

Distance:	4.4 miles (round trip)
Walking time:	2¾ hours
Elevations:	400 ft. gain/loss Negro Bill Canyon Trailhead (start): 3,980 ft. Morning Glory Natural Bridge: 4,380 ft.
Trail:	Moderately popular, easy to follow trail
Season:	Spring, summer, fall, winter. There is occasionally snow in the canyon during the winter months.
Vicinity:	Near Moab and Arches National Park
Maps:	Moab *(USGS)* Arches National Park *(Trails Illustrated, #211)*
Information:	http://www.utahtrails.com/negrobill.html *(Utah Trails)* http://www.blm.gov/utah/moab/ *(BLM, Moab)* phone: (435) 259-2100 *(BLM, Moab Field Office)*

Drive north from Moab for two miles on Highway 191, then turn east onto Highway 128 and continue along the southeast shore of the Colorado River. 3.2 miles after turning onto Highway 128 you will see a paved parking area on the right near a BLM sign marking the mouth of Negro Bill Canyon. The trailhead is on the northeast side of the parking lot.

Negro Bill Canyon was named after William Granstaff, an African American prospector and rancher who grazed his cattle here during the late 1800s. It is a lovely canyon, cut into the Navajo Sandstone by a small, perennial stream that begins about six miles above the eastern shore of the Colorado River. The trail winds along the stream through an oasis of boxelder and willow trees, cut off from the desert above by towering sandstone cliffs. Like all good hikes, this one also has a reward at the end; Morning Glory Natural Bridge spans the head of one of Negro Bill's side canyons at the end of the trail. According to Bureau of Land Management statistics, Morning Glory is the sixth largest natural bridge in the United States. It's span is 243 feet.

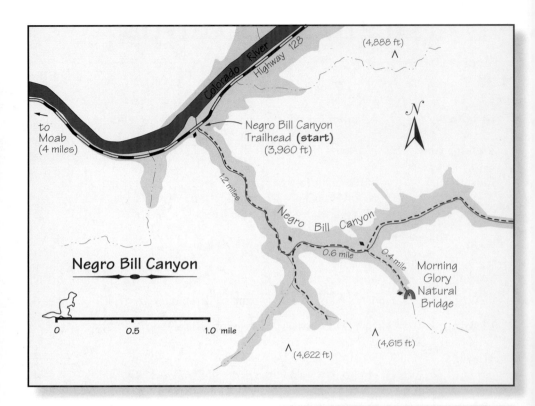

In 1979 Negro Bill Canyon gained a great deal of notoriety over an action of the so called "Sagebrush Rebellion". The Bureau of Land Management, wanting to study the canyon as a possible wilderness area, placed a barrier at its entrance to keep out recreational vehicles. This infuriated a group of local anti-wilderness activists who, with the help of the Grand County commissioners, bulldozed down the barrier. The county commissioners then publicly declared that the county, not the federal government, owned the canyon, and when another barrier was erected it was again bulldozed down. The conflict was resolved only after a lawsuit was filed against Grand County in the U.S. district court.

Today the canyon is still a wilderness study area and may some day become part of a Negro Bill Canyon Wilderness Area. Many residents of Grand County are still against the idea, but fortunately tempers are

Negro Bill Canyon

no longer as hot as they once were. Four-wheel-drive vehicles are not now using the beautiful canyon, and although there are still some faintly visible signs of the old jeep roads time has erased most of the mess. With each passing year the old, unsightly scars are becoming less noticeable.

From the mouth of Negro Bill Canyon the trail begins by winding its way up the left side of the stream. Wildlife is abundant along the watery canyon floor, and you can often see hawks soaring over the pink sandstone cliffs searching for prey. After a hundred yards the path drops down into the willows and birch trees that grow beside the water, where it remains for most of the hike. Watch for poison ivy as you proceed; there are many large patches of it on the canyon floor.

After 1.0 mile the trail crosses to the right side of the creek. The water is seldom more than ankle deep, but don't bother taking off your shoes and socks because you will encounter six more crossings over the next mile. Hopefully you are wearing wet-table shoes.

0.2 mile (and three more creek crossings) after first fording the creek the trail passes the mouth of a large side canyon that joins Negro Bill from the south. Years ago there was a jeep road turning into this tributary, but now the mouth of the canyon is so well disguised by new vegetation that you may not even notice its presence.

Continuing up the main canyon for another 0.6 mile will bring you to the next major side canyon, again intersecting Negro Bill Canyon from the south. Here the path crosses the water for the seventh time, leaving Negro Bill Canyon and turning south into the new canyon. This is the canyon in which Morning Glory Natural Bridge, your final destination, is located. The bridge lies at the extreme end of the side canyon, 0.4 mile from its confluence with Negro Bill.

Morning Glory Natural Bridge is unique because it was carved in front of a waterfall rather than across an open stream as most natural bridges are. The space between the bridge and the cliff over which the water once plunged is extremely narrow, only about 15 feet wide, but the span of the bridge is awesome. What a spectacle the waterfall behind the sandstone bridge must have been when the water was flowing in full force.

Water seldom flows in the dry river bed now, but there is a permanent spring near the base of the bridge's eastern leg and a small pool of water beneath the bridge on the floor of the canyon. Again, be careful not to touch the poison ivy that grows in the back of the canyon near the bridge! It is the plant with the dark green leaves arranged in clusters of three, often with small clusters of white berries.

Morning Glory Natural Bridge

Fisher Towers

★★★   **day hike**

Distance:	4.2 miles (round trip)
Walking time:	2¹/₂ hours
Elevations:	650 ft. gain/loss Fisher Towers Trailhead (start): 4,740 ft. viewpoint: 5,390 ft.
Trail:	Popular, easy to follow trail
Season:	Spring, summer, fall, winter. There may be some snow on the trail during the winter months. This area is very hot in the summer months and there is no water, so be sure to carry some.
Vicinity:	Near Moab
Maps:	Fisher Towers *(USGS)* Moab North *(Trails Illustrated, #500)*
Information:	http://www.utahtrails.com/fishertowers.html *(Utah Trails)* http://www.blm.gov/utah/moab/ *(BLM, Moab)* phone: (435) 259-2100 *(BLM, Moab Field Office)*

Drive north from Moab for two miles on Highway 191, then turn east on Highway 128 and continue along the southeast shore of the Colorado River. Exactly 21 miles after turning onto Highway 128 (just a few feet from milepost 21) you will see a gravel road leaving to the right with a small sign that says "Fisher Towers". (Do not confuse this road with the road to Fisher Valley Ranch nearer milepost 20.) Turn here and drive for 2.2 miles to the small Fisher Towers Campground, where the trail starts.

Few of natures geologic creations are more bizarre to look at than Utah's Fisher Towers. About a dozen of the strange monoliths stand near the Colorado River east of Moab, grouped together like petrified skyscrapers from some prehistoric city. The brick-red sandstone skyscrapers rise abrupt-ly from the desert floor, while a network of gullies and canyons form the city's avenues and boulevards below. The residents of this weird metropolis are an endless collection of goblins and gargoyles frozen in the canyon walls beneath the towers.

    The Fisher Towers first appeared on the

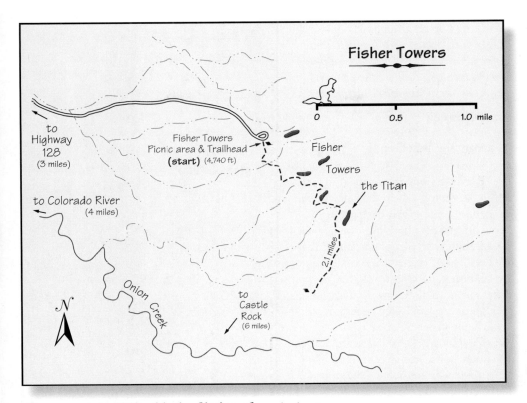

silver screen in 1949 with the filming of John Ford's popular western, *Wagon Master*. Hollywood immediately recognized the area's potential, and over the next decade ten more movies were filmed here. To date 27 movies have featured scenes taken of the Fisher Towers.

The towers have also held a long fascination for rock climbers, and on holidays and weekends you are likely to see a few of the human spiders along this trail. The path passes by a half dozen of the sandstone monoliths, including the 900-foot Titan, and finally ends on the crest of a ridge that commands a spectacular view of the towers. Try to be at the viewpoint about half an hour before sunset when the low western sun inflames the spires' reddish hue and striates them with deep shadows.

The Titan, largest of the Fisher Towers, remained unclimbed until 1962 when a team of three Colorado climbers, sponsored by the National Geographic Society, made an assent to the top. On his impressions at the top of the 900-foot pinnacle, team member Huntley Ingalls wrote:

Fisher Towers Trail

It was a strange, awesomely isolated place, a flat, rough area of bare orange sandstone about 70 feet long and 40 feet wide. Its boundary was the free air. It overhung the body of the tower below it, which plunged in rippling bulges and converging fluted ribs to the distant desert floor.[3]

From the campground the trail first drops down to cross a small dry wash and then winds its way back to the towers. For the next hour it proceeds in a general southerly direction along the towers' bases, meandering in and out of a succession of arroyos, but never straying far from the towers. The entire length of the trail is decorated with an enormous variety of rock art, sculpted by the wind and the rain from the soft red sandstone, and it is in large part this spectacle that makes the hike so delightful.

The last major tower on the route is the Titan, which the trail passes after about 1.5 miles. After passing the Titan the path veers southwest onto a long ridge from which you will be rewarded with a majestic view of the towers. The most common assent route up the Titan is on the south side—the side nearest to the viewpoint.

The ridge at the end of the trail also offers a fine view of Castle Rock and the Priest and Nuns, about six miles to the southwest. Confusingly, there is also another formation which the USGS Fisher Tower map calls Titan Tower 1.2 miles northeast of the viewpoint. The tower that most locals know as the Titan, however, and the one scaled by the National Geographic team is the one near the trail.

Climbing the Titan

---

[3] Huntley Ingalls, We Climbed Utah's Skyscraper Rock, National Geographic Magazine, November, 1962.

Mount Tukuhnikivatz

★

Distance:	4.8 miles (round trip)
Walking time:	4½ hours
Elevations:	2,362 ft. gain/loss La Sal Pass (start):　10,120 ft. Mount Tukuhnikivatz: 12,482 ft.
Trail:	There is a vague hiker-made trail most of the way to the top of Tukuhnikivatz, but don't worry if you never see it. It is fairly easy to trace the route up the mountain. The terrain is relatively open with few obstacles to impede your progress, but the climb is very steep.
Season:	Midsummer through mid-fall. The road to La Sal Pass is usually closed from mid-November until the end of June.
Vicinity:	Near Moab
Maps:	Mount Tukuhnikivatz, Mount Peale (*USGS*)
Information:	http://www.utahtrails.com/tukuhnikivatz.html (*Utah Trails*) http://www.fs.usda.gov/mantilasal/ (*Manti-LaSal Nat. Forest*) phone: (435) 259-7155 (*Moab Ranger District*)

Drive south from Moab on Highway 191 for 23 miles to the La Sal Junction. *Turn left here and drive east on Highway 46 for another 9 miles to the town of La Sal. Continue past La Sal for 3.7 miles to the Canopy Gap Road, a gravel road, where you must turn left. Another 2.0 miles will bring you to San Juan County Road 123 (La Sal Pass Road), where you must again turn left. After driving 2.1 miles on Road 123 you will come to La Sal Creek. This small creek has to be forded, but under normal conditions most cars shouldn't have a problem getting across. The creek is only 10 feet wide and seldom more than 10 inches deep. It can be a problem, however, after a heavy rain. Continuing on Road 123 beyond the creek for 5.3 miles will bring you to the top of La Sal Pass and the trailhead. You will know you have reached La Sal Pass when you see a sign identifying Mount Peale near a short log fence on the right side of the road 0.3 mile beyond the turnoff to Medicine Lake.*

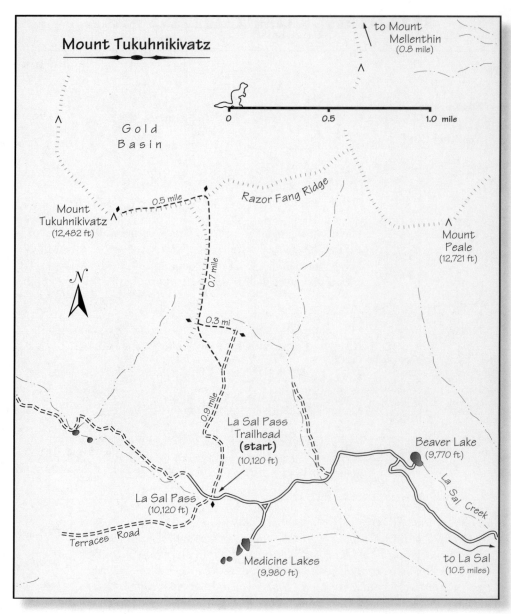

Mount Tukuhnikivatz

to Mount Mellenthin (0.8 mile)

Gold Basin

Razor Fang Ridge

0.5 mile

Mount Tukuhnikivatz (12,482 ft)

0.7 mile

0.3 mi

Mount Peale (12,721 ft)

N

0.9 mile

La Sal Pass Trailhead **(start)** (10,120 ft)

Beaver Lake (9,770 ft)

La Sal Creek

La Sal Pass (10,120 ft)

Terraces Road

Medicine Lakes (9,980 ft)

to La Sal (10.5 miles)

0   0.5   1.0 mile

Anyone who has visited Canyonlands or Arches National Parks in the early summer has probably gazed admiringly at the snow capped peaks of the La Sal Mountains. The sight of snow seems oddly out of place in the midst of the desert heat, but snow is usually visible on the higher summits of the La Sals well into July. Tradition has it that the

mountains were named by Silvestre Valez de Escalante, the Spanish missionary and explorer, who saw them during his expedition through Utah in 1776. He called them the Sierra La Sal, or "Salt Mountains" because he deemed it so unlikely that they could be covered with snow so late in the summer.

As small and isolated as the La Sal

Mount Tukuhnikivatz from the La Sal Pass Trailhead

Range is, it is actually the second highest mountain range in Utah. Only northern Utah's Uinta Mountains are higher. The highest point in the La Sals is Mount Peale (12,721 feet), but the most celebrated peak is the one with the most unpronounceable name: Mount Tukuhnikivatz. Tukuhnikivatz is prominently situated on the western side of the La Sals and can be easily seen from the desert canyon country around Moab. The exquisite red rock wilderness of Canyonlands and Arches is laid out in a vast panorama below the peak, and the resulting view from the top of Tukuhnikivatz on a clear sunny day is extraordinary. The mountain's tantalizing name is supposed to mean "The Place Where the Sun Sets Last" in the language of the Ute Indians.

Before you begin the hike, pause to look northward from the parking area at the top of La Sal Pass. Mount Peale is the broad peak on your right, and Tukuhnikivatz is the slightly lower but more pointed peak on the left. The two peaks are connected by a long summit ridge that runs in an east-west direction for about two miles. From the top of Tukuhnikivatz the ridge drops down at a 30 degree angle into a small saddle 500 feet below the summit of the mountain, and it is from that saddle that your final assent will be made. The best way to reach the summit ridge is to climb upward along the broad crest of the secondary north-south ridge that begins a half mile from the trailhead and ends at the saddle near the peak.

You will start by walking northward through the open meadow in front of the parking area along an old faintly visible jeep road. After a few hundred yards the jeep road bends to the left and then heads north again into the western side of a grove of spruce trees. The road stays in the trees for 0.2 mile and then emerges once more into another meadow. At this point you are at the foot of the secondary ridge that you must climb in order to reach the summit ridge. There is a vague trail leaving the jeep road and heading into the trees at the foot of the ridge, but the trail is difficult to find. Instead of wasting time looking for it just continue walking northward along the jeep road. The road follows the eastern side of the ridge for another 0.4 mile before it ends. When the road ends simply turn west and start climbing until you reach the crest of

Descending from the summit of Mount Tukuhnikivatz

the ridge. The crest of the ridge is about 500 feet above the road at this point. It is a steep, tiring climb, but at least there are no trees to hinder your progress.

When you reach the top of the secondary ridge you will find a trail that climbs along its crest to the summit ridge above. The route is still very steep but, again, there are few obstacles. The trail finally reaches the Peale-Tukuhnikivatz summit ridge 0.5 mile east of Mount Tukuhnikivatz, where once again you will be on relatively level ground. What a relief! The elevation is just over 12,000 feet, and the ground is covered with the grasses, mosses, and wild flowers of the Arctic-Alpine Tundra life zone. This area is part of the Mount Peale Research Natural Area, an area that was established in the 1980s to protect several species of endangered plants that occupy the above-treeline slopes of the La Sals. Try to tread gently across the tundra—especially if you are in a large group.

The route to the top of Mount Tukuhnikivatz from the summit ridge is quite obvious. Walking westward the grade soon

increases, and the pleasant carpet of plant life is replaced by a tortuous field of broken stones. There is no trail—just a lung busting climb up the last few hundred feet to the top of the talus covered peak.

From the top a large swath of some of the most interesting terrain in Utah is clearly visible. To the north, in Arches National Park, the Courthouse Towers rise dramatically from the desert floor like tombstones in a cemetery for giants. The Behind the Rocks area west of Moab is also clearly discernible, and the Colorado River Gorge that separates the Needles District from the rest of Canyonlands National Park meanders darkly through the maze of canyons, buttes, and mesas. In the words of Edward Abbey:

All around the peaks of the Sierra La Sal lies the desert, a sea of burnt rock, arid tablelands, barren and desolate canyons. The canyon country is revealed from this magnificent height as on a map and I can imagine, if not read, the names on the land.[4]

---

[4] Edward Abbey, *Desert Solitaire, a Season in the Wilderness*, Simon & Schuster, New York, 1968.

Little Wild Horse Canyon

★★★   day hike

Distance:	8.6 miles (loop)
Walking time:	5 hours
Elevations:	730 ft. gain/loss Little Wild Horse Canyon Trailhead (start): 4,940 ft. San Rafael Swell: 5,670 ft.
Trail:	There is no developed trail for this hike, but the route is very easy to follow. The middle 1.6 miles of the hike are along an old jeep road, and the rest is along the bottoms of two dry desert slot canyons. It is an easy walk, but carry plenty of water.
Season:	Spring, summer, fall, winter. Do not enter the canyons when rain threatens. Also, the road to the trailhead may occasionally be impassable after periods of heavy rainfall.
Vicinity:	Near Hanksville and Goblin Valley State Park
Maps:	Little Wild Horse Mesa (USGS) San Rafael Swell (Trails Illustrated, #712)
Information:	http://www.utahtrails.com/littlehorse.html (Utah Trails) http://www.blm.gov/utah/price/ (BLM, Price) phone: (435) 636-3600 (BLM, Price Field Office)

Drive south of I-70 on Highway 24 toward Hanksville for 24 miles, where you will see a paved road leaving on the right for Goblin Valley State Park. Take this road and follow the signs toward Goblin Valley. Two miles before you reach the state park (11 miles from Highway 24) you will come to a well marked junction where the road to Wild Horse Mesa begins. Turn right here and drive another 5.3 miles to the trailhead and parking area.

This dry, desert canyon hike follows two narrow slot canyons as they cut their way through the southeastern side of the San Rafael Reef. It is the most popular hike in the San Rafael Swell area, so don't be surprised if you encounter a lot of other people along the way. The route begins by following Bell Canyon from the south to the north side of the reef, and then returns through Little Wild Horse Canyon to the starting point. Both

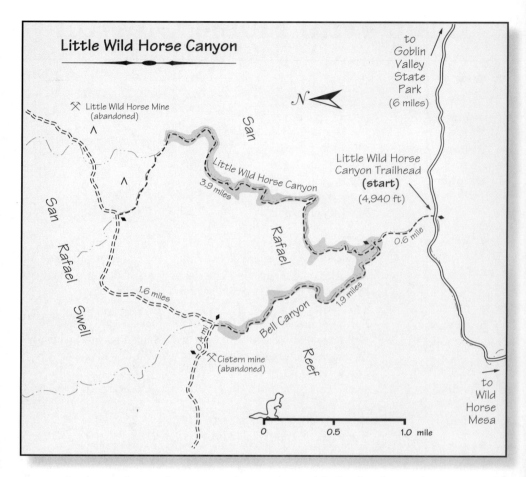

Little Wild Horse Canyon

to Goblin Valley State Park (6 miles)

Little Wild Horse Mine (abandoned)

San

Little Wild Horse Canyon

3.9 miles

Little Wild Horse Canyon Trailhead **(start)** (4,940 ft)

Rafael

0.6 mile

San

Rafael

Swell

1.6 miles

1.9 miles

Bell Canyon

0.4 mi.

Cistern mine (abandoned)

Reef

to Wild Horse Mesa

0   0.5   1.0 mile

canyons have some impressive narrows, but the narrows in the last half of Little Wild Horse Canyon are especially noteworthy. In one section the canyon meanders along for well over a mile with the distance between the sides rarely exceeding five feet. Walking down Little Wild Horse Canyon often feels more like exploring a cave that hiking in the desert. Children seem to get a particular thrill out of walking in the narrow passages, and this relatively easy hike is a good one for a family outing.

From the car parking area, the trail follows Little Wild Horse Wash northward toward the San Rafael Reef. After 0.4 mile you will see a small sign on the left side of

the wash indicating that you have entered the Crack Canyon Wilderness Study Area, and a few hundred yards farther the flat streambed is interrupted by a small dry waterfall. The easiest way around this obstacle is to climb slightly up the left side of the canyon and drop back to the bottom a short distance later near the confluence of Bell and Little Wild Horse Canyons. When you reach the confluence bear left into Bell Canyon.

The next section of the hike is an easy walk up the flat, sandy bottom of Bell Canyon. The canyon is quite narrow at first, but it steadily widens, finally breaking out of the San Rafael Reef and onto the San Rafael Swell some 1.9 miles later. Immediately after the canyon exits the San Rafael Reef

Bell Canyon

Little Wild Horse looks much like the northern end of Bell Canyon for the first 0.5 mile, but then the canyon suddenly drops down under a boulder and into its first section of narrows. This is an introduction to the long stretch of extremely tight narrows that begins about half way down Little Wild Horse. There may be water in a few places in the narrows if it has rained recently, but usually you won't have any trouble getting through with dry feet. There is no permanent water in either of the canyons, and the rainwater seems to drain out quite quickly. Needless to say, however, the canyons are no place to be if a storm threatens. The water can come up to the danger level as quickly as it goes down, and once inside the narrows there is no place to escape a flood.

After 3.3 miles Little Wild Horse Canyon emerges again at the confluence with Bell Canyon, and from there it is an easy matter to retrace your steps 0.6 mile back to the road.

you should see a jeep road crossing the sandy streambed. You will have to turn right onto the primitive road to reach Little Wild Horse Canyon, but first I suggest you turn left and walk for 0.4 mile to the site of the old Cistern Mine. The Cistern is an abandoned uranium mine that was developed in the 1950s. There are a number of interesting artifacts in the area, including a cabin that is still standing and the remains of an old truck. Whoever lived in the cabin must have had children, because there are also a few toys scattered around.

The road from the mouth of Bell Canyon to Little Wild Horse Canyon winds lazily eastward along the edge of the San Rafael Reef, climbing about 370 feet before dropping down again. After 1.6 miles it crosses a small wash that is a tributary of Little Wild Horse. Turn right off the road at this point, and follow the wash for 0.6 mile until it reaches the beginning of Little Wild Horse Canyon.

Little Wild Horse Canyon

Horseshoe Canyon

★★★

Distance: 7.4 miles (round trip)

Walking time: 4¼ hours

Elevations: 640 ft. loss/gain
Horseshoe Canyon Trailhead (start): 5,340 ft.
Great Gallery pictograph panel: 4,710 ft.

Trail: Well marked, well maintained

Season: Spring, summer, fall, winter. The canyon is quite hot in mid-summer, so carry plenty of water.

Vicinity: Canyonlands National Park, near Hanksville

Maps: Sugarloaf Butte *(USGS)*
Canyonlands Maze District *(Trails Illustrated, #312)*

Information: http://www.utahtrails.com/horseshoe.html *(Utah Trails)*
http://www.nps.gov/cany/ *(Canyonlands National Park)*
phone: (435) 259-2652 *(Hans Flat Ranger Station)*

Drive south from I-70 on Highway 24 for 25 miles. 0.6 mile beyond the turnoff to Goblin Valley State Park you will see a well marked gravel road leaving the east side of the highway for Roost Flats and Hans Flat Ranger Station. Turn left at this point. After 24.2 miles you will come to a signed fork in the road with the right fork leading to Hans Flat Ranger Station and the left fork to Horseshoe Canyon. Again you should turn left, toward Horseshoe Canyon. Another 5.1 miles will bring you to a smaller road, departing on the right, with a sign that says "Horseshoe Canyon Foot Trail". Follow this road for 1.8 miles to the trailhead..

Horseshoe Canyon contains what is probably the finest display of prehistoric Indian rock art in the United States. The famous Great Gallery, largest of several Horseshoe Canyon sites, is 200 feet long, 15 feet high and contains dozens of intriguing red, brown and white pictographs. The paintings are at least 2,000 years old, and possibly as old as 8,000 years. Rock art is notoriously difficult to date accurately, but from the style we can be reasonably certain that the work was done by the so called Archaic People who lived in the area before the arrival of the Anasazi and Fremont

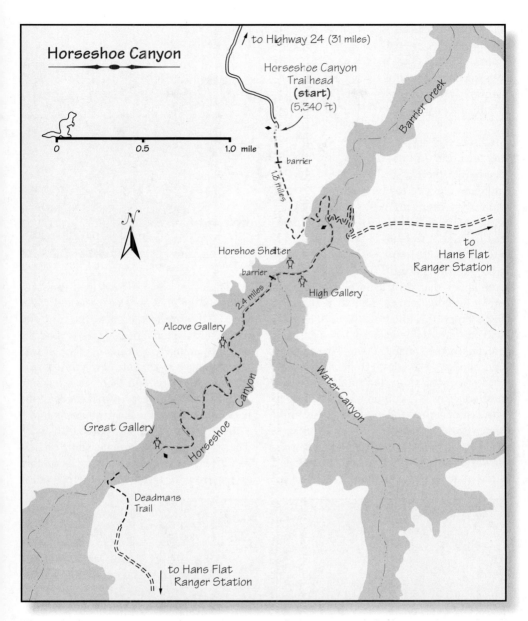

Indian cultures. Archaic clay figurines that closely mimic the pictographs have been found about nine miles away in Spur Fork, a tributary of Horseshoe Canyon, and the figurines have been dated to about 4700 B.C.

For years archaeologists have struggled to interpret the strange anthropomorphs that are depicted in the Great Gallery. In addition to many smaller figures, the huge panel contains about twenty life size human shapes, all of which have a strange mummy-like appearance. They lack arms or legs and often have huge insect-like eyes and bucket-shaped heads. Most intriguing of all is the figure known as the "Holy Ghost". This eight-foot-high painting stands out among the others because of its size and its ethereal appearance. Perhaps it was intended to portray a revered ancestor, or a mythical deity.

From the car parking area, the trail proceeds into the canyon along an old jeep road that was originally built in the 1920s by the Phillips Petroleum Company. Phillips was one of many oil

West rim of Horseshoe Canyon, near the trailhead

companies that drilled unsuccessfully for oil in the area during the first half of the last century. 0.2 mile from the trailhead you will pass an old iron gate that has since been erected to keep vehicles out of the canyon, and another 0.4 mile beyond the gate the trail passes an old water tank. The water tank was part of a pumping system built by sheep ranchers in the early 1940s to bring water up to the pastures above Horseshoe Canyon. The system never worked well, however, and it was abandoned after just a few years.

There are several fossilized dinosaur tracks in the slickrock near the old water tank. They are located near the trail 400 feet before the tank, or 200 feet beyond the point where the water tank first comes into view. Watch the left side of the trail as you approach the tank and there, in a flat slab of limestone just 3 feet from the side of the path, you can see the clear impression of a 3-toed monster that once passed this way. The track is 10 inches long and 8 inches wide. There are several more tracks another 20 feet from the trail, but the footprint near the trail is the most obvious one. Prior to 1997 it was also possible to see dinosaur tracks at another site on the canyon floor 0.2 mile above the Great Gallery Pictographs. However a flood in that year covered those tracks with debris and, to my knowledge, no other tracks are now visible inside the canyon.

Horseshoe Shelter pictograph panel in Horseshoe Canyon

As you continue

down into the canyon you can see another section of the old Phillips jeep road descending downward from the opposite rim. Until recently it was still possible to drive a jeep down that harrowing road, but in the late 1990s the road was damaged by floods to the extent that it is now impassible by any wheeled vehicle.

When you reach the bottom you must turn south and walk down the sandy streambed of Barrier Creek. This section of the trail was also once used by vehicles. When it was possible to descend into the canyon on the old Phillips Road cars could be driven the last 0.6 mile along the canyon floor to Water Canyon, where a barrier was in place. Now, however, you won't have to worry about encountering any vehicles in Horseshoe Canyon.

As you approach Water Canyon be sure to watch for the first two pictograph sites, one on each side of the canyon. The trail passes right by them. These sites, like the other two that you will see later, were painted by the Archaic People between 2,000 and 8,000 years ago. The third site is situated in a huge alcove on the west side of the stream, about 0.6 mile up-canyon from the first two. Unfortunately the alcove site has sustained substantial damage, both natural and man-caused, and it is not as impressive as the others.

Finally, 1.3 miles from the alcove site, or 3.7 miles from the beginning of the trail, you will come to the Great Gallery. This display of rock art has been called the Louvre of the Southwest, and, indeed, it is a phenomenal relic of the past. Dozens of intricate human and animal figures decorate the panel, mostly in red with some brown and white. The pigments were made from finely ground minerals, mostly hematite, and then mixed with a liquid base, perhaps animal tallow or vegetable juices, to form a crude paint. After thousands of years all traces of the base have disappeared, but the mineral coloring still adheres to the rock and the paintings remain preserved in astonishing detail.

The "Holy Ghost", Great Gallery pictograph panel in Horseshoe Canyon

Upheaval Dome

★★★

Distance:	8.1 miles (loop)
Walking time:	6 hours
Elevations:	1,500 ft. loss/gain Upheaval Dome Trailhead (start): 5,680 ft. Upheaval Canyon: 4,220 ft.
Trail:	This is one of the most popular trails in Canyonlands National Park. It is steep and rocky in a few places, but well marked with rock cairns and easy to follow.
Season:	Spring, summer, fall, winter. Canyonlands is very hot in the summertime and receives some snow in the winter. The best seasons for this hike are spring and fall.
Vicinity:	Canyonlands Island in the Sky District, near Moab
Maps:	Upheaval Dome *(USGS)* Canyonlands Island in the Sky District *(Trails Illustrated, #310)*
Information:	http://www.utahtrails.com/upheaval.html *(Utah Trails)* http://www.nps.gov/cany/ *(Canyonlands National Park)* phone: (435) 719-2313 *(Canyonlands National Park)*

Drive south of I-70 on Highway 191 for 20 miles until you see a paved road leaving on the right for Dead Horse Point and Canyonlands National Park. Turn here and drive for 21 miles to the Island in the Sky Visitor Center. Continuing past the visitor center for another 6.4 miles will bring you to another well marked junction where you must turn right. This road ends after 4.9 miles at the Upheaval Dome picnic area and trailhead.

Upheaval Dome is one of the most interesting geologic formations in Utah. At first glance the unusual circular structure appears to be a large crater, but geologically it more closely resembles an ancient dome. The strange formation consists of a huge circular pit, about a mile in diameter and 1,100 feet deep, surrounded by concentric rings of uplifted rock that was originally several thousand feet under the ground.

What kind of natural force could account for such a structure? Volcanic forces often

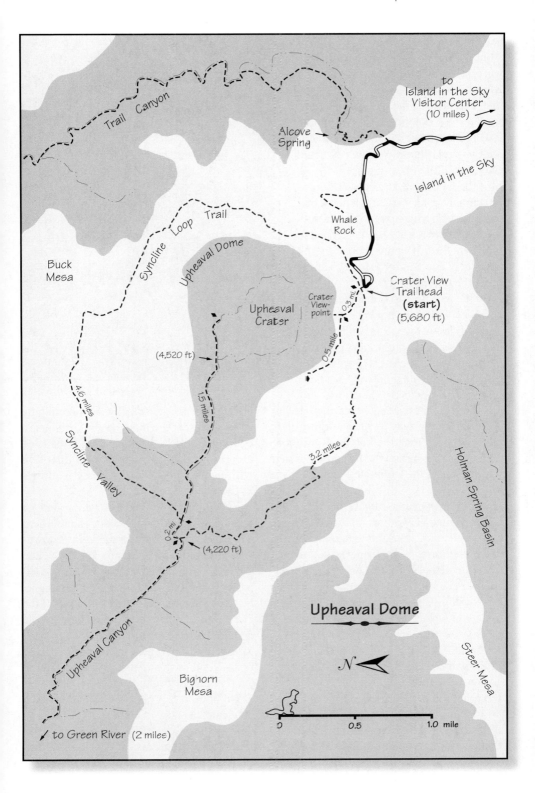

to
Island in the Sky
Visitor Center
(10 miles)

Trail Canyon

Alcove Spring

Island in the Sky

Syncline Loop Trail

Upheaval Dome

Whale Rock

Buck Mesa

Crater Viewpoint

Crater View Trailhead
(start)
(5,680 ft)

Upheaval Crater

0.3 mile

(4,520 ft)

0.5 mile

4.6 miles

1.5 miles

3.2 miles

Holman Spring Basin

Syncline Valley

0.2 mi

(4,220 ft)

Upheaval Canyon

Upheaval Dome

Bighorn Mesa

N

Steer Mesa

0   0.5   1.0 mile

to Green River (2 miles)

cause both uplifting and cratering, but it is highly unlikely that Upheaval Dome was created by a volcano. There is no evidence of volcanism anywhere in the area, and none of the rock in or around the dome is volcanic. A meteorite could have produced the crater, but it is difficult to explain how a meteorite could have caused the extensive uplifting. A third theory is that Upheaval Dome is the remnant of an ancient salt dome that was pushed up by subterranean forces millions of years ago and then eroded to its present form. But this theory doesn't adequately account for the crater at the top of the dome.

In the past the salt dome theory had the widest following among geologists. However new research, including a microscopic study of the sand grains at the bottom of the crater, suggests that Upheaval Dome may indeed have been formed by a meteorite. Scientists now hypothesize that the meteorite that struck Upheaval Dome was about one-third of a mile in diameter, and fell about 60 million years ago—long before the formation of the Green River or the Colorado Plateau.

A short trail leads from the parking area to several nice viewpoints on the south side of the crater rim. Be sure to take this walk before beginning your longer hike around the crater on the Syncline Loop Trail. From the rim a magnificent panoramic view of the crater will give you an appreciation for the geology of Upheaval Dome as well as show you where the hike will take you. The best viewpoint is the first one you will come to, only a quarter mile from the parking lot.

The Syncline Loop Trail intersects the viewpoint trail just a few feet from the parking area. This is the trail you will use for your eight-mile hike around Upheaval Dome. You can walk around the loop in either direction, but I recommend that you

Desert bighorn sheep in Upheaval Crater

circle the crater in a clockwise direction by turning west at the junction (left, if you are coming from the parking area). Walking around the loop in a clockwise direction will insure that the best scenery is always in front of you.

The trail stays on fairly level ground for about 0.8 mile as it skirts along the southern edge of the crater, but soon it begins a downward plunge that will eventually take you to the bottom of Upheaval Canyon. The trail is steep, but the scenic rewards are ample. Occasionally you can catch a glimpse of the Green River peering up through the twists and folds of the canyons below. Finally, after a descent of 1,000 feet, the trail reaches the bottom of a wash and then continues downward at a more gradual grade until it arrives at the bottom of Upheaval Canyon. When you reach the floor of Upheaval Canyon you will find a sign marking the trail to Green River, three miles away. You should turn right at this junction to stay on the Syncline

Loop Trail.

A short walk upcanyon from the Green River Trail Junction will bring you to the mouth of Syncline Valley, where you can usually find water. The trail then climbs about 100 feet to the top of a bench above Upheaval Canyon where you will see a sign marking the beginning of the spur trail that leads into the center of Upheaval Crater. You may want to make a side trip at this point; the trail into the crater is about 1.5 miles, one way. Inside the crater you will find a massive jumble of debris, including great piles of gray pulverized sand that was once a part of the White Rim geologic formation. It is this debris that has provided the strongest evidence to support the theory that Upheaval Dome was formed by a meteorite impact.

From the junction with the Upheaval Crater Trail the Syncline Loop Trail continues north into Syncline Valley. Again, there is usually water along this part of the hike, sometimes in large pools. After less than a mile the lower part of Syncline Valley ends in a box canyon, and the trail begins following a steep and rocky route up the valley's north side. Some scrambling may be necessary at this point, but once you reach the upper valley the trail again turns into a pleasant walk. There isn't usually as much water in the upper part of Syncline Valley as in the lower part, but it is still a green oasis in the desert canyon country. The path meanders for about a mile through the tamarisk and cottonwood trees, and then suddenly exits to the south through a large, unexpected break in the canyon wall. Hidden as it is from the outside world, Syncline Valley is the kind of place that would have made a perfect hideout for a band of outlaws at the turn of the last century.

Once you have climbed out of Syncline Valley through the narrow slot in the canyon wall you are back on top of the Island in the Sky. From there it is a relatively easy walk of about two miles through the juniper forest back to the trailhead and parking area.

Upheaval Crater

Murphy Trail

Distance:	9.0 miles (loop)
Walking time:	6 hours
Elevations:	1,390 ft. loss/gain
	Murphy Trailhead (start): 6,190 ft.
	Murphy Hogback: 5,200 ft.
	Murphy Wash: 4,800 ft.
Trail:	Good trail most of the way, but very steep and rocky for a half mile at the beginning and end.
Season:	Spring, summer, fall, winter. Canyonlands is very hot in the summertime and receives some snow in the winter. The best seasons for this hike are spring and fall.
Vicinity:	Canyonlands Island in the Sky District, near Moab
Maps:	Monument Basin, Turks Head (*USGS*)
	Canyonlands Island in the Sky District (*Trails Illustrated, #310*)
Information:	http://www.utahtrails.com/murphytrail.html (*Utah Trails*)
	http://www.nps.gov/cany/ (*Canyonlands National Park*)
	phone: (435) 719-2313 (*Canyonlands National Park*)

Drive south of I-70 on Highway 191 for 20 miles until you see a paved road leaving on the right for Dead Horse Point and Canyonlands National Park. Turn here and drive for 21 miles to the Island in the Sky Visitor Center. Continuing past the visitor center for another 6.4 miles will bring you to another well marked junction, where you must turn left toward Grandview Point. 2.5 miles from the last junction you will see a well marked dirt road leading off to the right toward Murphy Point. The trailhead is 0.5 mile from the pavement on this dirt road.

Hiking the Murphy Trail is an excellent way to gain an appreciation for the wild beauty and expanse of Canyonlands National Park. It is also a good way to sample some of the history of Canyonlands.

The trail was built during World War One by the Murphy brothers who grazed cattle on and below the Island in the Sky Mesa from 1917 until about 1920. This area was used extensively for winter grazing by local

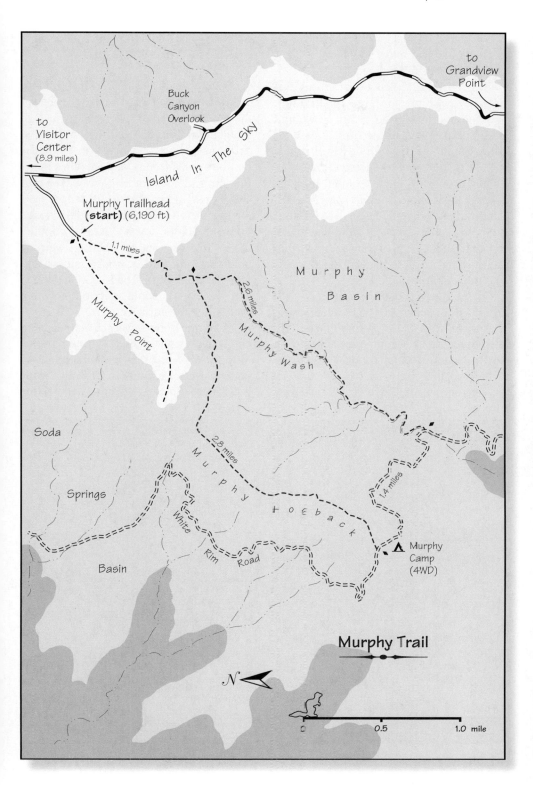

to Grandview Point

Buck Canyon Overlook

to Visitor Center (8.9 miles)

Island In The Sky

Murphy Trailhead **(start)** (6,190 ft)

1.1 miles

Murphy Basin

Murphy Point

2.6 miles

Murphy Wash

Soda

2.8 miles

1.4 miles

Springs

Murphy Hogback

White

Murphy Camp (4WD)

Basin

Rim   Road

Murphy Trail

N

0   0.5   1.0 mile

cattle ranchers during the first half of the last century, and many remnants of their occupation can still be seen.

The Island in the Sky district was also an active exploration area for uranium prospectors during the 1950s. Uranium ore is often found in the Chinle geologic formation above the White Rim Plateau, and during the nuclear energy craze of the 1950s prospectors came from all over the country to try their luck in Canyonlands. There are no active mines in the area now, but if you stand just about anywhere on the rim of Island in the Sky and gaze down into the canyon you can see parts of the old roads and trails built by the miners.

When the area became a national park in 1964 prospecting was no longer allowed, but 4-wheeling and bicycling on some of the old roads has become very popular. In particular, the 100-mile-long 4WD White Rim Road, that circles the Island in the Sky has become one of the parks best known at-

tractions. The middle 1.4 miles of this hike is along the White Rim Road.

From the parking area on Murphy Point the trail proceeds for 0.6 mile to the edge of the rim before plunging downward through a fault in the Wingate Sandstone. When you first look over the edge you may wonder how on earth anyone could get down there. But, miraculously, there is a way. The trail switchbacks down a series of ledges near the top, then finds a debris-scattered slope for the rest of the descent. Near the bottom there is one exciting part where the Murphy brothers built a wooden bridge across a ten-foot gap in the trail. The logs in the bridge are close to a hundred years old now, but they still seem sturdy enough.

When the trail reaches the bottom of the cliff it splits, with the left fork heading down Murphy Wash and the right fork going out onto the Murphy Hogback. The two trails will later be joined together by the White

Murphy Hogback - Murphy Wash Trail Junction

Rim Road, thus forming a loop that can be walked in either direction. From a practical point of view it doesn't really matter which trail you take first, but if it is still early in the day I suggest you turn right here onto the Murphy Hogback Trail and return on the Murphy Wash Trail; if it is near the middle of the day do the Murphy Wash segment first. The reason is that the most scenic part of the hike is along the Hogback, and you should walk this segment when the sun is lower in the sky. If the sun is directly overhead the geology of the shadowless canyons is not as interesting. I will assume here that you choose to proceed first onto the Murphy HogbackTrail.

The views from the Murphy Hogback are so impressive that upon reaching the White Rim Road many hikers choose to return the same way. Soda Springs Basin lies below the northwest side of the trail, where photogenic columns of Organ Rock reach up along the shores of the Green River and Turks Head butte forms the centerpiece of a long circular meander in the streambed. Farther to the south, across the hidden recesses of the Colorado River, are the orange-striped pinnacles of the Canyonlands Needles District. The view from the Hogback is an immense 360 degree panorama. Many of the same features can also be seen from other viewpoints above the rim, but it is not quite the same up there. Down on the Hogback you get the feeling that you are more than just an observer. You are somehow a part of it all.

Once you reach the White Rim Road turn left and walk southeast along the road for 1.4 miles until you see a sign marking the beginning of the Murphy Wash Trail. Murphy Wash is interesting in a less dramatic way. The sandy wash is more protected and receives more water that the exposed Hogback; hence the plant life is quite different there. Soon after leaving the road you will pass by a small spring which, as the animal tracks attest, attracts a good deal of canyon wildlife. As you near the top of the wash you will pass by an old corral, one of many left by the ranchers who worked the area before it became a national park. Finally, 2.6 miles after leaving the White Rim Road, the trail climbs out of Murphy Wash and rejoins the original trail for the climb back to the canyon rim.

Bicycling down the north side of the Murphy Hogback

Confluence Overlook

★

Distance:	10.4 miles (round trip)
Walking time:	6 hours
Elevations:	220 ft. gain/loss
	Big Spring Canyon Trailhead (start): 4,940 ft.
	Big Spring Canyon: 4,820 ft.
	Confluence Overlook: 4,920 ft.
Trail:	Easy, well marked trail
Season:	Summer, spring, winter and fall. This hike is very hot in the summer and cold in the winter. The best times are during the spring and fall.
Vicinity:	Canyonlands National Park, Needles District, near Moab
Maps:	The Loop, Spanish Bottom *(USGS)*
	Canyonlands Needles District *(Trails Illustrated, #311)*
Information:	http://www.utahtrails.com/confluence.html *(Utah Trails)*
	http://www.nps.gov/cany/ *(Canyonlands National Park)*
	phone: (435) 719-2313 *(Canyonlands National Park)*

Drive south of Moab on Highway 191 for 40 miles until you see a paved road on the right leading to the Needles District of Canyonlands National Park. (Don't confuse this road with the road to the Needles Overlook, 7 miles closer to Moab.) Turn right toward Canyonlands National Park and drive for another 35 miles to the Visitor Center. Continue past the Visitor Center on the paved Scenic Drive Road for 6.5 miles. The road finally ends at a small parking area on the rim of Big Spring Canyon where the hike begins.

Canyonlands, the largest of Utah's five national parks, is neatly split into thirds by the intersection of the Green and the Colorado Rivers. Both rivers have carved thousand-foot-deep canyons through the high surrounding desert, and the view of their confluence at the center of the park is one of Canyonlands' most impressive sights.

Both of the famous rivers have now been largely tamed by a series of dams built over the last sixty years, but from this prospective one can still see the same wild scene that

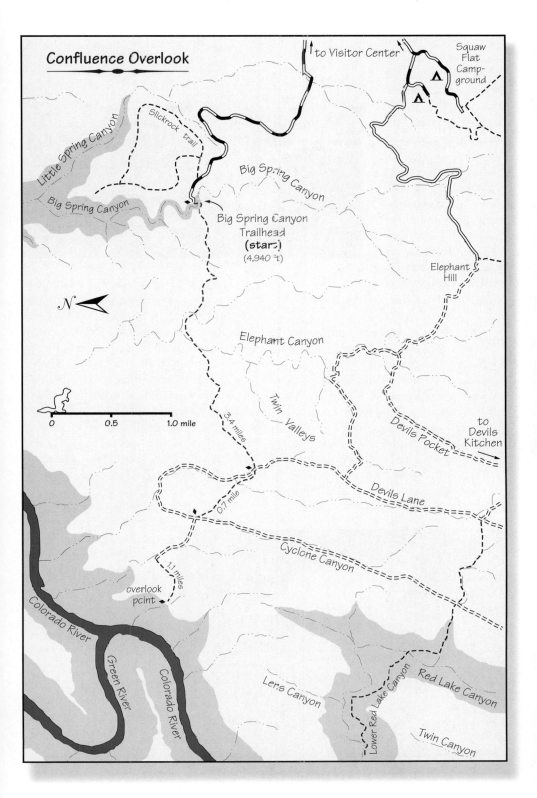

Confluence Overlook

to Visitor Center

Squaw Flat Campground

Little Spring Canyon

Slickrock trail

Big Spring Canyon

Big Spring Canyon

Big Spring Canyon Trailhead
(start)
(4,940 ft)

Elephant Hill

N

Elephant Canyon

Twin Valleys

Devils Pocket

to Devils Kitchen

3.4 miles

0 0.5 1.0 mile

Devils Lane

0.7 mile

Cyclone Canyon

1.1 miles

overlook point

Colorado River

Green River

Colorado River

Lens Canyon

Lower Red Lake Canyon

Red Lake Canyon

Twin Canyon

John Wesley Powell saw during his historical voyage down the Green and Colorado Rivers in 1869. In July of that year, while his party was camped on the north side of the confluence, Powell and one of his men climbed above the rivers to a point just south of the present day overlook trail. In the following passage, first printed in Scribner's Monthly in 1875, Powell describes what he saw:

Elephant Canyon, from the Confluence Overlook Trail

From the northwest came the Green in a narrow, winding gorge. From the northeast came the Grand [Colorado] through a canyon that seemed, from where we stood, bottomless.... Wherever we looked there was a wilderness of rocks – deep gorges where the rivers are lost below cliffs, and towers, and pinnacles, and ten thousand strangely carved forms in every direction, and beyond them mountains blending with the clouds.

From the parking area the trail immediately heads west and begins dropping into Big Spring Canyon, a tributary of the Colorado River that is about 120 feet deep at this point. Upon reaching the bottom of the dry canyon the trail follows the sandy streambed for 30 feet before starting up the other side. As it climbs out of the canyon the trail goes through the opening of a small natural arch called the "Keyhole", beyond which the Park Service has placed a steel ladder to help with the scramble to the canyon rim. The climb out of Big Spring is really the only strenuous part of this hike.

Soon after reaching the rim of Big Spring Canyon the trail begins a pleasant meander across the open desert. Then, after another mile it begins gradually dropping into Elephant Canyon. The trail descends through one of the eastern tributaries of the main canyon and then climbs a slickrock slope to the top of its western side.

Beyond Elephant Canyon the path winds through the Twin Val-

The Keyhole, near the rim of Big Spring Canyon

leys, a sandy expanse of desert punctuated by rocky arroyos and sagebrush-covered plains. Then, a half hour later, it descends slightly into the northern end of a another shallow canyon called Devils Lane. The trail crosses a primitive jeep road in the bottom of Devils Lane, and 0.7 mile later crosses the same jeep road again as it doubles back into Cyclone Canyon. At the point where the trail meets the jeep road the second time you will see a sign directing you down another spur road the branches off to the west.

After walking west along the spur for 0.6 mile you will come to a dead end where there is a small outhouse and a parking area for jeeps. Another Park Service sign points the way to the trail that will lead you the last 0.5 mile to the overlook point.

The Colorado River

After seeing the rivers from the overlook point, many hikers feel a great urge to descend into the canyon to the shore of the Colorado. The easiest way to get to the Colorado River is on the Lower Red Lake Canyon Trail, which descends from Cyclone Canyon 3.5 miles south of the overlook. To get there retrace your steps back to the place where the trail leaves the road in Cyclone Canyon. Then turn south and walk along the Cyclone Canyon jeep road for a distance of 2.4 miles until you see a sign marking the Lower Red Lake Canyon Trailhead on the west side of the road. It is 4.0 miles from Cyclone Canyon to the Colorado River along this trail. It is also possible to walk upstream along the Colorado River from the mouth of Lower Red Lake Canyon to the confluence – a distance of 3.6 miles.

If you want to hike to the Colorado via the Lower Red Lake Canyon Trail you had better pack for at least two days. However, if you have a four-wheel-drive vehicle you can easily visit the Colorado River and the confluence overlook in one day. A well-used jeep road from Elephant Hill to Cyclone Canyon will give you access to both the Lower Red Lake Canyon Trail and the Overlook Trail, allowing you to see everything with only about nine miles of hiking. (See page 256 for an explanation of how to get to Elephant Hill.)

Confluence of the Green River (left) and the Colorado River

Chesler Park Loop

Canyonlands National Park
overnight hike

Distance:	17.0 miles (loop)
Walking time:	day 1: 6 3/4 hours day 2: 6 hours
Elevations:	1,400 ft. gain/loss Elephant Hill Trailhead (start): 5,120 ft. Chesler Park: 5,600 ft. Druid Arch: 5,740 ft.
Trail:	This is almost entirely a slickrock trail, with stone cairns marking the way. The terrain is very rugged and you will be continually climbing over and around obstacles.
Season:	Spring, early summer, and fall. This is one hike you probably won't want to do in July or August. There is very little water or shade, and daytime summer temperatures are nearly always over 100 degrees F. Winter hikes are possible, but the high desert is often cold at night.
Vicinity:	Canyonlands National Park, Needles District, near Moab
Maps:	Druid Arch, The Loop *(USGS)* Canyonlands Needles District *(Trails Illustrated, #311)*
Information:	http://www.utahtrails.com/chesler.html *(Utah Trails)* http://www.nps.gov/cany/ *(Canyonlands National Park)* phone: (435) 719-2313 *(Canyonlands National Park)*

Drive south of Moab on Highway 191 for 40 miles until you see a paved road on the right leading to the Needles District of Canyonlands National Park. (Don't confuse this road with the road to the Needles Overlook, 7 miles closer to Moab.) Turn right, toward Canyonlands National Park, and drive for an-other 35 miles to the Visitor Center. You will have to stop there to obtain an overnight backcountry permit. From the Visitor Center just follow the signs to Elephant Hill where you will see the trailhead and parking area. The distance is 6.0 miles, with the last 3.0 miles unpaved.

Note: A fee of $15.00 is charged for hiking permits. A single permit will cover everyone in *your group, but the maximum group size is seven people. Most important, only 5 groups are allowed to camp each night in Chesler Park. The permits are issued at the Visitor Center on a first come-first served basis, but if you don't have an advance reservation you probably won't be able to get a permit. You can obtain a campsite reservation by fax or by mail, but you must contact the park at least two weeks before your intended stay. For more detailed information on how to make reservations call (435) 259-4351 between 8:00 a.m. and 12:30 p.m., Monday through Friday.*

If you can stand the high desert temperatures, the Needles District of Canyonlands is a hiker's paradise. The "needles" are a seemingly endless collection strange spires and pinnacles that decorate the landscape on the east side of the Colorado River. Nature has carved these odd sculptures from the Cedar Mesa Sandstone formation, a thick layer of sedimentary rock that was deposited under the Colorado Plateau some 270 million years ago. Today the formation generally lies several thousand feet below the surface, but when the Colorado River was formed 60-70 million years ago a process of erosion began in this area that eventually exposed the subterranean formation and produced the spectacle we see today.

Deep inside the rugged needles country lies Chesler Park, an unexpected refuge of flat, gentle grassland about a mile in diameter that is almost completely surrounded by the sandstone needles. There are five designated camping areas on the perimeter of the park, and one could hardly ask for a more beautiful place to spend a night or two. There are also several other interesting things to see within an easy walk from Chesler Park, including an impressive natural arch and an old cowboy camp. The one drawback that prevents Chesler from being a perfect hiking destination is the unavailability of water. Summer hikers should plan

Chesler Park

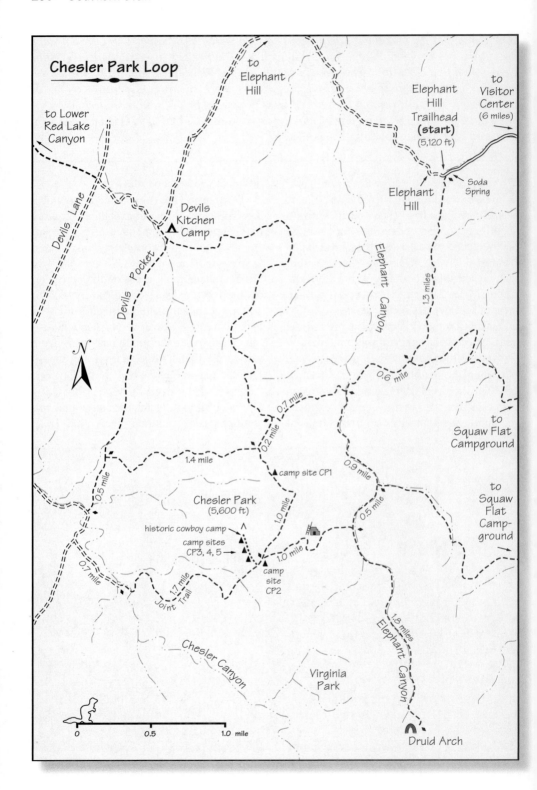

Chesler Park Loop

to Elephant Hill

to Lower Red Lake Canyon

Elephant Hill Trailhead **(start)** (5,120 ft)

to Visitor Center (6 miles)

Soda Spring

Elephant Hill

Devils Lane

Devils Kitchen Camp

Devils Pocket

Elephant Canyon

N

1.3 miles

0.6 mile

0.7 mile

0.2 mile

1.4 mile

camp site CP1

to Squaw Flat Campground

0.9 mile

Chesler Park (5,600 ft)

0.5 mile

historic cowboy camp

camp sites CP3, 4, 5

1.0 mile

1.0 mile

0.5 mile

to Squaw Flat Campground

0.7 mile

1.7 mile

Joint Trail

camp site CP2

Chesler Canyon

Virginia Park

Elephant Canyon

1.8 miles

0   0.5   1.0 mile

Druid Arch

The Joint Trail, Chesler Park

Bear right again and follow the trail into a small side canyon that provides a route out of the western side of the main canyon.

After crossing Elephant Canyon the trail continues southwest for another 0.6 mile to the long row of needles that define the northern edge of Chesler Park. Bear left at the third trail junction just before reaching the wall of needles and proceed through a small opening to the south side of the barrier. There you will see your first view of the northern side of the park.

Once you reach Chesler Park you should proceed directly to your assigned campsite so you can shed your backpacks before continuing with the hike. The Park Service allows camping in five places along the eastern edge of the meadow, but, in my opinion, the southern camp sites, CP3, CP4,

on consuming at least a gallon of water each day, and the nearest semi-reliable surface water is two miles away in Elephant Canyon. Be sure to carry a sufficient amount of water with you for this hike. Also, bear in mind that Chesler Park is a very popular destination among backpackers, so if you plan to stay in one of the backcountry campsites you must make reservations well in advance.

Day 1 (9.1 miles)

The route from Elephant Hill Trailhead to Chesler Park is only about 3.8 miles long, depending on which campsite you are assigned. The trail is almost entirely across slickrock marked by stone cairns. There is a great deal of up and down, and this makes the distance seem greater than it actually is.

The trail first climbs about 150 feet to get out of the shallow canyon where the road ends, and then proceeds in a southerly direction for the next 1.3 miles to a signed trail junction. Bear right at the junction and continue for another 0.6 mile to the rim of Elephant Canyon. From there the trail descends 150 feet, through a crack between two biscuit-shaped formations into the bottom of Elephant Canyon where you will come upon the second trail junction.

Chesler Park

and CP5 have the most to offer. To reach this area continue south from the last trail junction, along the eastern side of the park, until you meet another trail coming in from Elephant Canyon. Turn right here, onto the Joint Trail, and soon you will pass by the southern side of a rocky island in the center of the park. The camping area (marked by signs) is along the southwestern side of the island. This area was also the location of a campsite for cowboys who ran cattle in Chesler Park from the late 1800s until the early 1960s. You can still see the remains of their camp just north of the backpackers camping area.

After you have established your camp site leave your backpacks behind and check out the Joint Trail. Continue walking west from the camping area along the main trail for about 0.8 mile, where you will find a long, narrow flight of stone stairs that lead down into a dark, slender crack in the sandstone.

Joint Trail

The trail continues through the bottom of the three-foot crack, called a "joint" by old timers, for some 300 yards before emerging once again at the top of the slickrock. The Chesler Park hike is full of surprises, but for many the Joint Trail is the most exciting part of the trip.

Soon after emerging from the joint you will cross the dry streambed of Chesler Canyon and meet a jeep trail coming down from Elephant Hill. You will have to walk north along the jeep trail for a short distance to reconnect with the Chesler Park Trail and complete the loop back to your camp site. The sides of Chesler Canyon, through which the sandy road winds, are lined with hundreds of stone needles. Like giant terrestrial pin cushions, even the hills surrounding the canyon are packed with clusters of needles. After 0.7 mile on the jeep road you will see another sign marking the trail that returns to Chesler Park. Turn right here and then right again at the next trail junction. Finally, 1.9 miles from the road you will again arrive at the northeast corner of Chesler Park.

Day 2 (7.9 miles)

After breaking camp you should leave Chesler via the southeast exit to Elephant Canyon. About 0.2 mile before you arrive at Elephant Canyon you will have the opportunity to see an Anasazi Indian ruin. The ruin is a few hundred feet below the trail, in the bottom of a small canyon on the north side. You can't see the ruin from the trail itself, but just above the site there is a place where previous hikers have left the main path to walk to a viewpoint only 15 feet away that looks directly down onto it.

There is another trail junction in the bottom of Elephant Canyon. The northern path leads back to Elephant Hill where your car is parked. But before going back you should take off your backpack and make a side trip to Druid Arch, 1.8 miles south of the junction at the head of Elephant Canyon.

Druid Arch

You will probably see a few scattered water holes in the creek bed as you make your way up the canyon. This is one of the few places in the area where you can usually obtain water–a useful thing to know if you plan to spend more than one night in Chesler Park.

The trail climbs gradually up the canyon floor for the first 1.5 miles, and then, as it nears the end of the canyon, it starts making its way up the slickrock toward a bench below the canyon's eastern rim. Druid Arch is situated on the top of a long fin that projects into the box canyon from the south, and from the vantage point at the end of the trail you will be treated to a gorgeous panorama of the arch bathed in the morning sunlight with nothing but blue sky behind it. The appearance of the huge arch reminds many people of Stonehenge in southern England; hence its name.

From the Chesler Park trail junction, where you left your backpacks, the trail back to Elephant Hill continues down the bottom of Elephant Canyon for another 1.4 miles before reaching the trail used on the first day to reach Chesler Park. From that junction it is 1.9 miles back to the Elephant Hill Trailhead.

Alternative Routes

As the map suggests, there are many alternative routes for this hike. In my opinion it would be a shame to visit the area without (1) spending at least one night in Chesler Park, (2) experiencing the Joint Trail, and (3) seeing Druid Arch; and the route I have suggested will allow you to do those things with a minimum amount of walking.

If you have the time, another interesting route into Chesler Park begins at the Squaw Flat Campground rather than Elephant Hill. Beginning and ending the hike at the Squaw Flat Trailhead will add 2.1 miles to the outbound distance, and 2.7 miles (via Big Spring Canyon) to the return distance. The section of trail between Elephant Canyon and Big Spring Canyon is particularly interesting, with another cave-like crack to walk through and two strategically placed ladders to negotiate.

The Maze

★★★★

Canyonlands National Park
4WD vehicle required
overnight hike

Distance: 12.9 miles (loop)

Walking time:
day 1: 5¼ hours
day 2: 3¼ hours

Elevations: 1,560 ft. loss/gain
Chimney Rock Trailhead (start): 5,460 ft.
Harvest Scene Pictographs: 4,580 ft.
Maze Overlook: 5,160 ft.

Trail: The portion of the trail in the sandy bottom of the Maze is unmarked, but the route is not difficult to follow. The slickrock part of the trail above the Maze is marked with cairns. Some scrambling is necessary to reach the Maze Overlook, and a 25-foot length of rope is useful in raising and lowering backpacks.

Season: Spring, early summer, and fall. This hike is very hot in the summer and cold in the winter. The best times are during the spring and fall. The road to the trailhead may be impassable, even with a 4WD vehicle, after a heavy snow or rain.

Vicinity: Canyonlands National Park, Maze District, near Hite

Maps: Spanish Bottom, Elaterite Basin (*USGS*)
Canyonlands Maze District (*Trails Illustrated, #312*)

Information: http://www.utahtrails.com/maze.html (*Utah Trails*)
http://www.nps.gov/cany/ (*Canyonlands National Park*)
phone: (435) 259-2652 (*Hans Flat Ranger Station*)

Nearly all of the trailheads in this book can be reached with an ordinary car. The Chimney Rock Trailhead, however, is an exception; you must have a 4WD high clearance vehicle to reach this trailhead. Also, your vehicle should have a short wheel base. Full sized pickup trucks will have trouble getting around some of the turns and through some of the washes on the Chimney Rock Road. *There are several ways to reach Chimney Rock Trailhead, but all require 4WD vehicles. The route described here is the most feasible way, but it will still take you 6 hours of off-highway driving to get there! Be sure to carry plenty of fuel and water, and be prepared for unexpected emergencies.*

Before you start be sure to obtain a backcountry camping permit from the Park Service. You can do this over the telephone by calling the Hans Flat Ranger Station at (435) 259- 2652. Have a credit card ready; the cost is $15.00 per group for off-road camping. There are restrictions on the number of campers allowed in the Maze each day so, if possible, it is wise to get your permit in advance, especially during the peak spring and fall seasons. For more information on how to make advance reservations call the park headquarters in Moab at (435) 259-4351 between 8:00 a.m. and 12:30 p.m., Monday through Friday. Advance reservations must be made at least two weeks before the time of your visit.

To get to Chimney Rock Trailhead, first drive south from Hanksville on Highway 95 for 45 miles until you come to a bridge crossing the Dirty Devil River. 1.2 miles south of this bridge you will see a graded dirt road departing on the left. This is the road to the Maze. If you are coming from the other direction this road will be 1.0 mile north of the bridge across Lake Powell. The trailhead is 48 miles from Highway 95 by way of this road. The first 34 miles can be driven by almost any high clearance vehicle, but you will need a 4WD for the last 14 miles. The route is fairly straightforward, although there are a few forks where other less distinct roads join the main road. In these cases just stick to the better traveled route. Thirty miles from the highway, in a meadow called Waterhole Flat, you will come to a four way junction. Turn right here and follow the signs to the Doll House and Standing Rocks. Finally, 3.5 miles before reaching the Doll House, you will see a sign marking the Chimney Rock Trailhead and parking area.

The Maze District of Canyonlands National Park, separated from the rest of the park by the Green and Colorado Rivers, is one of the most rugged and remote desert

The Maze

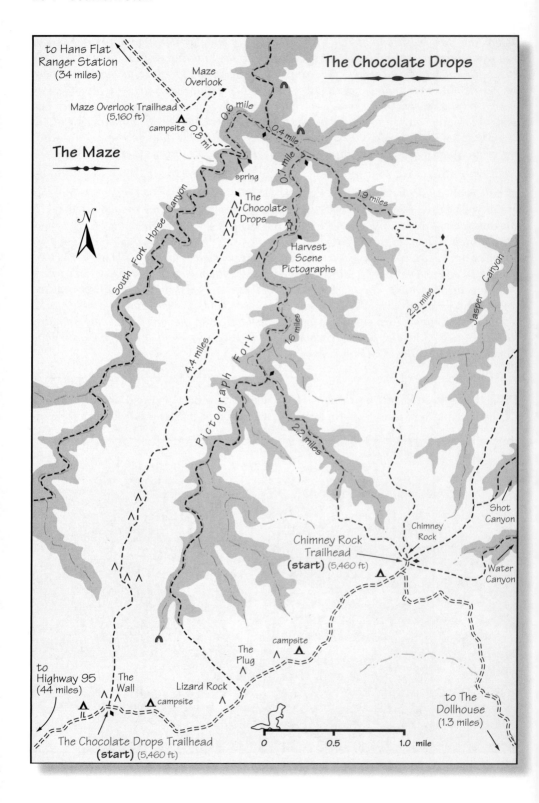

to Hans Flat
Ranger Station
(34 miles)

Maze
Overlook

Maze Overlook Trailhead
(5,160 ft)

campsite   0.8 mi

0.6 mile

0.4 mile

The Chocolate Drops

The Maze

0.7 mile

1.9 miles

spring

The
Chocolate
Drops

Harvest
Scene
Pictographs

N

South Fork Horse Canyon

4.4 miles

Pictograph Fork

1.6 miles

2.9 miles

Jasper Canyon

2.2 miles

Shot
Canyon

Chimney
Rock

Chimney Rock
Trailhead
(start) (5,460 ft)

Water
Canyon

campsite

The
Plug

Lizard Rock

to
Highway 95
(44 miles)

The
Wall

campsite

to The
Dollhouse
(1.3 miles)

The Chocolate Drops Trailhead
(start) (5,460 ft)

0   0.5   1.0 mile

The Chocolate Drops, as seen from the bottom of the Maze

through one of the canyons below. In addition, the route passes by the Harvest Scene Pictograph Panel, a fine example of Indian rock art produced by the Archaic Culture more than 2000 years ago. Many hikers complete the basic loop in one day, but spending an extra night in the canyons will allow you to include a side trip to the Maze Overlook, the best single place to see the Maze from above. Also, it would be a shame not to spend part of a day exploring a few side canyons before climbing back to the trailhead.

areas in the United States. As described above, just getting there requires six bone rattling hours of driving over a narrow unimproved road, the last fourteen miles of which cannot be completed without a 4WD vehicle. To their credit, the National Park Service intends to preserve the remoteness, and there are no plans to improve the access roads. Indeed, there could hardly be a more appropriate preamble to an experience in the Maze than the long journey across the open desert required to reach it; the rugged canyon country's isolation definitely adds to its appeal.

The Maze, which actually occupies only a small part the Canyonlands Maze District, includes about thirty square miles of land, etched and sliced apart by five major canyons and dozens of minor tributaries. How could such a small piece of land be carved into so many fissures? From the plateaus above it looks like a labyrinth with the top removed. A convoluted work of art, tenaciously sculpted by sixty million years of rainwater searching for a way to the Colorado River.

This loop hike features superb views of the Maze from the upper plateaus, as well as the experience of walking

Nuts and Bolts Formation

Trail to the Maze Overlook (Nuts and Bolts Formation on right)

Day 1 (8.4 miles)

There are four cairned trails leaving from the Chimney Rock parking area. The first trail on the left, bearing around the west side of Chimney Rock, leads to the bottom of Pictograph Fork. When you return to the trailhead at the end of the loop you will be on this trail. The second trail from the left passes by the east side of Chimney Rock and heads north across the plateau above Pictograph Fork. The hike starts on this trail. (The third and forth trails from the left lead to Shot Canyon and Water Canyon, respectively.)

As you walk northward across the slickrock from Chimney Rock you will see Petes Mesa directly in front of you. The large butte behind Petes Mesa is Ekker Butte. If you loose track of the cairns just stay high on the ridge as you continue toward Petes Mesa. When you get to within a half mile of the mesa, however, be sure to watch more carefully for the cairns so you will not miss the turn when the trail begins its descent down into the Maze. Also, be on the lookout for mountain sheep in this area. They are often sighted on the plateau near Petes Mesa.

Once you reach the bottom of the Maze you will be on the sandy floor of a small side canyon leading in a northwesterly direction. Soon you should see three large red rocks that look like a cluster of giant mushrooms growing out from the edge of the rim about a mile down the canyon. This odd formation, sometimes called the "Nuts and Bolts", lies just below the Maze Overlook.

Within fifteen minutes after you spot the Nuts and Bolts you will pass by another major canyon entering the drainage from the south. This is Pictograph Fork, the canyon containing the famous Harvest Scene Pictograph Panel. There are several other smaller side canyons in the area, but Pictograph Fork is the largest one. It is nearly 200 yards wide at the junction, with a 150-foot-wide span of slickrock in the center of the stream bed. Also the Chocolate Drops formation is clearly visible from the canyon mouth. This junction is a very pleasant place to stop for the night. There are several good campsites in the area and it is also a good base from which to take a side trip to the Maze Overlook.

Maze Overlook

If you got off to a late start you may want to wait and see the Maze Overlook in the morning. But if you plan to take photographs it is best to be there in the afternoon when the sun is in the west. Plan on about two hours for the walk from the mouth of Pictograph Fork to the overlook and back.

From the mouth of Pictograph Fork continue walking northwest along the floor of the Maze toward the Nuts and Bolts formation. After 0.4 mile the drainage ends at South Fork Horse Canyon. Turn left here and walk south for another 0.6 mile to a point where a break in the canyon wall provides access to the rim above. The cairned trail up to the rim begins on the end of a long toe of sandstone that protrudes into South Fork from the west rim. Look for the cairns marking the canyon exit point. Also, there is a spring in the canyon at the end of the toe, and there is usually a large pool of water in the stream bed at the point where the route starts up.

The trail from the bottom of South Fork to the Maze Overlook is an exciting one with some scrambling required. If you are carrying a backpack you should have a 25-foot length of rope with you to pull your pack up some of the pitches. If you exercise reasonable care the route is not dangerous, but there is just enough scrambling to make it fun. The trail heads straight up to a ledge just below the White Rim Formation, then turns north and traverses around the Nuts and Bolts to a break in the White Rim. From there it is an easy climb out to the top.

The view from the overlook point is one of the grandest views in Canyonlands National Park. The loneliness and serenity of this point, with the tortuous jumble of nature's handiwork in the canyons below is enough to inspire even the weariest of hikers. How and why could such a vista have been created? The complexity of the panorama astounds.

Given enough time, one must conclude that almost anything is possible. It has taken the forces of nature sixty million years to produce this scene. They began by washing away thousands of vertical feet of sedimentary rock that had been deposited during an earlier era to get down to the 270-million-year-old Cedar Mesa Sandstone, from which the Maze was sculpted. The excavation is ongoing, and is still not complete. Here and there one can see remnants of younger rock that still has not been entirely removed: Chimney Rock, the Chocolate Drops, Lizard Rock, the Standing Rocks. Everything else

Harvest Scene Pictograph Panel

has already been washed down and swept away by the relentless Colorado River. Presently the Maze itself is slowly being etched and chiseled away by the rain and the wind and washed to the sea by the river. The dramatic scene we see now represents only a brief interlude in the long evolution of the Colorado Plateau.

Day 2 (4.5 miles)

From the mouth of Pictograph Fork it is 0.7 miles up the dry canyon to the Harvest Scene Pictograph Panel. The panel is located at the bottom of the cliffs, about ten feet above the west side of the stream bed. You will find it about three hundred yards before you come to a thumb-shaped pillar of sandstone in the bottom of the canyon.

No reliable method has yet been developed for dating Indian rock art, but most archeologists believe that the Harvest Scene was painted by the Archaic People who lived in Utah from 8,000 to 2,000 years ago. These are the same people who produced the famous Great Gallery pictographs 18 miles to the north in Horseshoe Canyon (see page 240). The Archaic People, who predated the better known Anasazi and Fremont cultures, left few other remnants of their ancient society for us to study; hence archeologist have long struggled to interpret their art. But deciphering the paintings has proven just as difficult as dating them, and we still know little about what they mean. In this panel, one of the figures appears to be holding a sheaf of rice grass; hence the name Harvest Scene.

Continuing up the canyon from the Harvest Scene for another 1.6 miles will bring you to another junction with a major side canyon. The trail splits at this point. If you bear right you will be continuing up Pictograph Fork on a little used trail that finally ends on the east side of Lizard Rock. Most hikers, however, turn left at this junction and follow the cairns up an easier route to the rim that finally ends at the Chimney Rock Trailhead.

Sunset at Chimney Rock Trailhead

The Chocolate Drops

★

Canyonlands National Park
4WD vehicle required
day hike

Distance:	8.8 miles (round trip)
Walking time:	5 hours
Elevations:	540 ft. loss/gain Chocolate Drops Trailhead (start): 5,460 ft. Chocolate Drops: 5,080 ft.
Trail:	This is a slickrock trail, well marked by stone cairns.
Season:	Spring, early summer and fall. This hike is very hot in the summer and cold in the winter. The best times are during the spring and fall. The road to the trailhead may be impassable, even with a 4WD, after a heavy snow or rain.
Vicinity:	Canyonlands National Park, Maze District, near Hite
Maps:	Spanish Bottom, Elaterite Basin *(USGS)* Canyonlands Maze District *(Trails Illustrated. #312)*
Information:	http://www.utahtrails.com/chocolate.html *(Utah Trails)* http://www.nps.gov/cany/ *(Canyonlands National Park)* phone: (435) 259-2652 *(Hans Flat Ranger Station)*

See page 262 (The Maze) for a detailed description on how to reach the Chimney Rock Trailhead.

From the parking area at Chimney Rock Trailhead, drive back towards the highway for a distance of 3.0 miles, past Lizard Rock and the Wall, to another monolith on the north side of the road about 200 yards west of the Wall. As the road passes this monolith you will see a small parking area on the north side of the road. This parking area marks the beginning of the Chocolate Drops trail.

What shall we name those four unnamed formations standing erect above this end of The Maze? From our vantage point they are the most striking landmarks.... In a far-fetched way they resemble tombstones, or altars, or chimney stacks, or stone tablets set on end.[5]

---

[5] Edward Abbey, *Desert Solitaire, a Season in the Wilderness*, Simon & Schuster, New York, 1968.

When Edward Abbey first wrote these words he was standing on or near the Maze Overlook (page 267) looking at what we now call the Chocolate Drops. The Maze has since been protected as a part of Canyonlands National Park, and consequently it is still possible to share the feeling of wonderment that Abbey must have experienced fifty years ago.

see map
page 264

The Chocolate Drops formation consists of four vertical rectangular shaped columns of Organ Shale that rise almost 200 feet above the ridge separating South Fork Horse Canyon from Pictograph Fork Canyon. They are one of the most prominent landmarks in the Maze and can be seen from miles around. The trail described here also passes by a half dozen other pillars of Organ Shale on its way to the Chocolate Drops. These formations are all part of an area known as the Land of Standing Rocks.

Follow the cairns from the parking area around the east side of the large monolith beside the road, then on toward the other spires farther out on the plateau. All of these formations are the unlikely remains of a 200-foot-thick layer of Organ Shale that once covered Canyonlands. Now, however, the unrelenting forces of erosion have almost completely removed the crumbling rock from the area, and only a few pinnacles of red shale still remain. After about thirty minutes the trail passes by the next group of Organ Shale formations, including one particularly picturesque mound that is topped by an enormous balanced rock. So precarious is the capstone that it is hard to pass beneath it without unconsciously walking a little faster.

From the balanced rock to the first Chocolate Drop is about three miles. The route is well marked with cairns and not difficult to follow. It is generally an easy walk across level ground; however at one point some minor scrambling is necessary to get to the bottom of a low spot on the ridge. If you look to the right when you reach this point you will find an easy way down the slickrock to the bottom of the incline (about 50 feet lower), and beyond this point there are no additional obstacles.

As you walk northward along the ridge you can frequently peer into the bottom of Pictograph Fork on your right. At one point you can look directly down at the Harvest Scene Pictograph Panel (page 267). From the trail the panel is almost three-fourths of a mile away, however: too far to recognize any of the pictographs. When you finally reach the last Chocolate Drop on the end of the plateau you will also have a clear view of the trail down from the Maze Overlook.

The Chocolate Drops

Green and Colorado Rivers Overlook

★★   **Canyonlands National Park**
4WD vehicle required
day hike

Distance:	8.9 miles (round trip)
Walking time:	5 hours
Elevations:	300 ft. loss/gain Green and Colorado Rivers Trailhead (start): 5,100 ft. Green and Colorado Rivers Overlook: 5,000 ft.
Trail:	Easy, well marked
Season:	Spring, early summer and fall. This hike is very hot in the summer and cold in the winter. The best times are during the spring and fall. The road to the trailhead may be impassable, even with a 4WD, after a heavy snow or rain.
Vicinity:	Canyonlands National Park, Maze District, near Hite
Maps:	Spanish Bottom (*USGS*) Canyonlands Maze District (*Trails Illustrated, #312*)
Information:	http://www.utahtrails.com/colorado.html (*Utah Trails*) http://www.nps.gov/cany/ (*Canyonlands National Park*) phone: (435) 259-2652 (*Hans Flat Ranger Station*)

See page 262 (The Maze) for a detailed description on how to reach the Chimney Rock Trailhead.

Continue driving east from the parking area at Chimney Rock Trailhead for 3.8 miles. Near the end of the road, just in front of the Doll House rock formation, the road crosses a small wash where a sign marks the trailhead.

For colorful desert scenery it is hard to beat this popular hike. The normally light colored Cedar Mesa Sandstone has a rich red layer running through it in this area, which makes it much more colorful than the same formation in the nearby Maze. Beginning with the impressive Doll House, at the beginning of the trail, the rock formations along this hike are truly magnificent. They are particularly pretty in the late afternoon when the sunlight tends to enhance the red bands in the sandstone.

From the trailhead the trail winds northward, through clusters of sandstone formations similar to those found on the other side

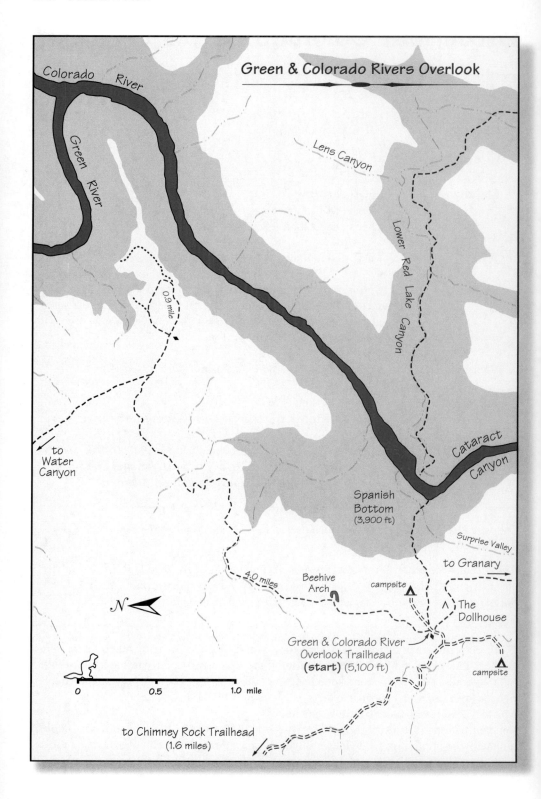

Green & Colorado Rivers Overlook

Colorado   River

Green   River

Lens Canyon

Lower Red Lake Canyon

0.9 mile

to
Water
Canyon

Cataract   Canyon

Spanish
Bottom
(3,900 ft)

Surprise Valley

to Granary

4.0 miles

Beehive
Arch

campsite

The
Dollhouse

Green & Colorado River
Overlook Trailhead
(start) (5,100 ft)

campsite

N

0   0.5   1.0 mile

to Chimney Rock Trailhead
(1.6 miles)

Green and Colorado Rivers Overlook Trail

ultimately back to the Chimney Rock Trailhead.

Continue east and soon the overlook trail splits into a 0.9 mile loop that goes past the overlook points. If you bear right here for another 0.4 mile you will arrive at the western rim of the Colorado River Gorge. The river is only about 400 yards away at this point, at the bottom of a nearly vertical wall. From there the path bends around to the west again, passing by a fine view of the Green River. You might want to do a little off-trail hiking before you leave this loop in order to achieve better views of the rivers. Soon after the trail leaves the Green River viewpoint it drops back into the meadow to complete the loop. From that point back to the trailhead is 4.0 miles.

of the Colorado in the Needles District of Canyonlands. Within 0.8 mile you will see the small Beehive Arch on your left. The trail winds down the slope a short distance and then back, passing right beside it.

About a mile beyond the arch start watching for pieces of flint scattered on the ground, particularly at the base of the sandstone cliffs on the left side of the trail. This glassy stone was brought here by prehistoric Indians from other locations in the park. Look carefully at the smaller pieces and you will see that most of them are actually flakes that have been chipped from larger stones. These flakes are especially prevalent in a few alcoves along the trail where prehistoric Indians must have worked, chipping the hard rock into points, scrapers, and other tools.

Halfway to the overlook point the trail skirts past the head of a large canyon. Although you can't see it from this perspective the Colorado River is below you, over a thousand feet down at the northern end of Cataract Canyon in an area called Spanish Bottom.

A mile beyond the canyon the trail enters a large open meadow, similar to Chesler Park in the Needles District. In the center of this meadow you will encounter another trail coming in from the northwest. This trail leads to Water and Shot Canyons, and

Green River, near confluence with the Colorado

Dark Canyon

★★★

Distance:	16.0 miles (with side trips)
Walking time:	day 1: 5 hours day 2: 5 hours
Elevations:	2,000 ft. loss/gain Sundance Trailhead (start): 5,620 ft. Dark Canyon: 4,000 ft. Lake Powell: 3,600 ft.
Trail:	The Sundance Trail into Dark Canyon is a slickrock trail, well marked by rock cairns. From the rim of the canyon to the bottom is a very steep descent, but little or no scrambling is necessary. Some scrambling is necessary to reach Lake Powell, but the route is not technically difficult.
Season:	Spring, summer, fall. The unpaved road to the trailhead is normally closed during the winter and after heavy rains.
Vicinity:	Near the Hite Marina on Lake Powell
Maps:	Indian Head Pass, Bowdie Canyon West *(USGS)* Manti-LaSal National Forest *(Trails Illustrated, #703)*
Information:	http://www.utahtrails.com/dark.html *(Utah Trails)* http://www.blm.gov/utah/monticello/ *(BLM, Monticello)* phone: (435) 587-1500 *(BLM, Monticello Field Office)*

Drive south of Hanksville on Highway 95 toward Lake Powell. Shortly after reaching the northern shore of the lake the highway crosses the Dirty Devil River, the Colorado River, and the road to the Hite Marina. 0.2 mile past the turnout to the Hite Marina, near milepost 49, you will come to a gravel road leaving the left side of the highway. This is the Horse Tanks Road (San Juan *County Road 2081). Make a note of your odometer reading and turn east onto the Horse Tanks Road. After 4.4 miles you will come to a junction; bear left here. At 7.4 miles you will pass Road 209a on your left; continue straight. At 7.7 miles you will see another road coming in from the right; again, continue straight. At 8.6 miles you will come to another junction where you must turn left. At 9.3 miles you will see another road taking off on the left; continue straight. At 11.0 miles, just across the road from Squaw and Papoose Rock you will see a smaller road on the left that leads 0.2 mile to the old trailhead. Continue straight for another 1.0 mile where you will see another road on the left that leads to the new Sundance Trailhead, built around 2003. Turn here and drive for the last 1.1 mile to the new trailhead. (The road from Highway 95 is rough in spots, but with care it can usually be driven by most passenger cars.)*

One can hardly visit this remarkable canyon without wondering about the dozens of other similar tributaries of Glen Canyon that were flooded by Lake Powell in 1964. Dark Canyon is more than 200 river miles upstream from Glen Canyon Dam; consequently it was spared most of the destruction that occurred in the lower canyons. What were the other canyons like before they were filled with water? What geological, biological, and archeological treasures did we loose? And what gems of natural beauty are now gone forever? A few of the canyons were photographed and studied before the man-made flood occurred, but many of them had never been visited by more than a few hundred people before they were erased from our maps and replaced with jagged blue lines. We cannot know how much we have lost, but if Dark Canyon is any clue the loss was substantial.

The hike described here touches only a few miles of Dark Canyon–the section just above Lake Powell. In my opinion, however, this is the most beautiful part of the canyon. There is a reliable stream here, and the greenery contrasts sharply with the pink sandstone and shale in the canyon walls. Near the bottom of the canyon is a fascinating layer of Honaker Trail Limestone that is chock full of well preserved 300-million-year-old fossils. Below that the picturesque

Dark Canyon

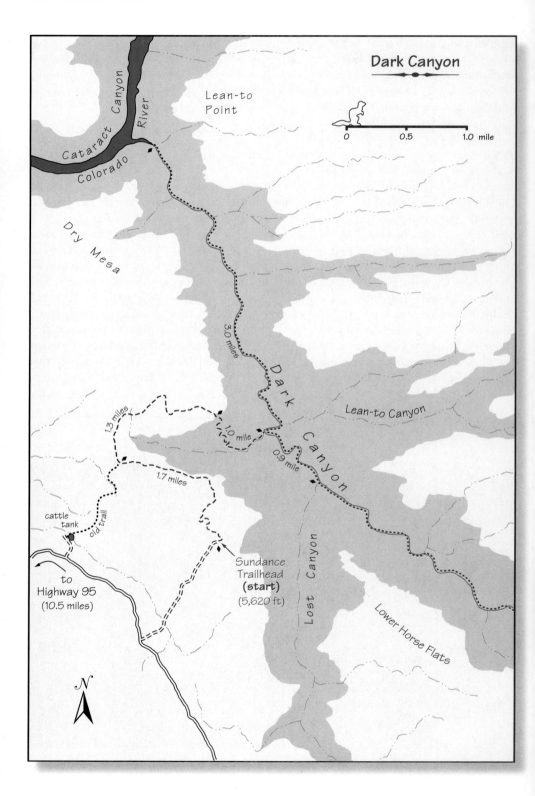

Dark Canyon

0   0.5   1.0 mile

Lean-to
Point

Cataract Canyon

Colorado River

Dry Mesa

Dark Canyon

3.0 miles

Lean-to Canyon

1.3 miles

1.0 mile

0.9 mile

1.7 miles

cattle
tank

old trail

to
Highway 95
(10.5 miles)

Sundance
Trailhead
(start)
(5,620 ft)

Lost Canyon

Lower Horse Flats

N

Dark Canyon, above Lost Canyon (after a flood)

scribed here. Unfortunately, however, the two trailheads are 63 miles apart.

Day 1 (8.0 miles)

For the first 1.7 miles the trail follows an old jeep road along the south side of a tributary of Dark Canyon. As it approaches the end of the secondary canyon the path leaves the road and bends around to the tributary's north side, finally reaching the rim of Dark Canyon 1.3 miles later.

The view from the rim of Dark Canyon is awesome. The canyon is 1,280 feet deep at this point, and the sensation is not unlike the feeling one gets when looking into the Grand Canyon: a feeling of grandeur, a feeling of immensity, and most of all a feeling of personal insignificance.

It is also abundantly clear from this vantage point that the climb down is going to be a steep one. The canyon bottom is only 1,750 horizontal feet from the

creek flows for several miles across a layer of smooth limestone adorned with a series of idyllic swimming holes and water slides.

Dark Canyon is over thirty miles long, and there are many other hiking opportunities along its length. The upper part of the canyon is part of the Manti-LaSal National Forest, and since 1984 it has been protected as the Dark Canyon Wilderness Area. The lower part, unfortunately, is on BLM land and is not part of the wilderness area. Another interesting hike through Dark Canyon begins in the wilderness area at Woodenshoe Canyon, near Natural Bridges National Monument, and exits 31 miles later on the Sundance Trail de-

Marine fossils in the Dark Canyon streambed

Dark Canyon

the dry, sandy streambed into Dark Canyon.

Once you reach the bottom of Dark Canyon the next order of business is choosing a suitable campsite. There are a few nice sites in the area where you first meet the water, and more sites upstream over the next mile. Beyond the confluence with Lost Canyon, however, there are fewer campsites. After a camp is established you will probably want to do some exploring. As discussed below, there is plenty to see both up and down the canyon.

Day 2 (8.0 miles)

Plan on 3 hours to climb back up the Sundance Trail and walk to your car. But before you leave be sure to take some time to look around. Many people spend four or five days enjoying the quiet beauty of Dark Canyon, but you should be able to see most of the highlights on a two-day trip.

rim and 1,280 vertical feet. If the trail had no switchbacks it would have to descend at an angle of nearly 40 degrees. Of course there are switchbacks, and the route down is about a mile long. Nevertheless it is a knee breaker, especially if you are carrying a heavy pack.

After the trail leaves the rim it drops slightly and then traverses west a short distance to a place where an ancient landslide has made it possible to get below the cliffs of the Cedar Mesa Sandstone into the previously mentioned side canyon. It then follows the rubble-filled slope down to the bottom of the canyon and turns east along

Side trips

The Sundance Trail meets Dark Canyon Creek in an area where three major canyons come together, so there are many opportunities for exploration in the area. Lean-to Canyon joins Dark Canyon 0.2 mile downstream from where the trail ends, and the junction with Lost Canyon is 0.9 mile upstream. Both of these side canyons are dry; hence few visitors bother to go very far into them. But if what you are looking for is solitude you might find them interesting.

The bottom of Dark Canyon above the confluence with Lost Canyon is particularly interesting. Here the creek flows over long stretches of hard, blue-gray limestone that has strange intrusions of chert imbedded in it. Occasionally another layer of limestone is also exposed just above the intruded layer that is a treasure-trove of marine fossils.

Youngs Canyon, a beautiful canyon with a stream and a waterfall at its mouth, is about 6.0 miles upstream from the Sundance Trail. The creek in the bottom of Dark Canyon ends about a mile above Youngs Canyon, so if you plan to continue beyond that point you will have to carry your own water.

The most popular side trip in lower Dark Canyon is the hike downstream to Lake Powell. The round trip from the Sundance Trail requires only about 3 hours, but some minor scrambling is necessary. For the first half hour it is an easy walk along the bottom of Dark Canyon. Several stream crossings are necessary, but there are no serious obstacles to impede the way. After about a half hour, however, you will encounter a series of pouroffs in the canyon that are increasingly difficult to get around. When you reach a point where you can no longer stay in the bottom of the canyon you will have to scramble up to a ledge about 15 feet above the right (east) side of the streambed. If you can't find a way up, just backtrack a ways until you see an easy way to climb to the ledge.

Once you reach the ledge you will see a fairly distinct trail that continues downstream above the creek. This trail continues for the next mile, climbing as high as 150 feet above the water. Finally you will come to a point where another large side canyon comes into Dark Canyon from the east, and it is here that the trail again descends to the canyon floor. Once the trail gets back to the floor of Dark Canyon just continue downstream for another 1.1 miles. After a half hour the stream becomes stagnant and the bottom of the canyon is covered with a thick, gooey mud that gets deeper and deeper as you proceed. This is the beginning of the lake. Unless the lake level is low, the last mile of Dark Canyon will be flooded, making it impossible to get to Cataract Canyon and the Colorado River without a boat.

Dark Canyon, below Lean-to Canyon

Natural Bridges Loop

★★★★

Natural Bridges National Monument
day hike

Distance:	8.6 miles (loop)
Walking time:	5 hours
Elevations:	490 ft. gain/loss
	Sipapu Bridge Trailhead (start): 6,200 ft.
	Kachina Bridge: 5,710 ft.
	Owachomo Bridge: 5,920 ft.
Trail:	The trail is mostly well maintained and easy to follow although it can be confusing in a few places–especially near Kachina Bridge. There are signs at all of the major trail junctions.
Season:	Spring, summer, winter, fall. The canyon is quite hot in mid-summer. Expect some rain in late summer.
Vicinity:	Natural Bridges National Monument, near Blanding
Maps:	Moss Back Butte *(USGS)*
	Manti-LaSal National Forest *(Trails Illustrated, #703)*
Information:	http://www.utahtrails.com/bridges.html *(Utah Trails)*
	http://www.nps.gov/nabr/ *(Natural Bridges Nat. Monument)*
	phone: (435) 692-1234 *(Visitor Center)*

Drive east from the Natural Bridges National Monument Visitor Center on Bridge View Drive. After about 2.5 miles you will see Sipapu Bridge Overlook on your right. Continue for another 0.5 mile to the Sipapu Bridge Trailhead and parking area.

The highlights of this hike are the three enormous natural bridges for which Natural Bridges National Monument was named: Sipapu, Kachina, and Owachomo Bridge. The canyon-bottom trail passes under all three while offering views of at least two other less-spectacular arches further up the side of the canyon walls. Also of interest are a number of Indian ruins within the canyon. The present-day park was used extensively by the prehistoric Anasazi Indians who lived here until about 1300 A.D.

From the Sipapu Bridge Trailhead the

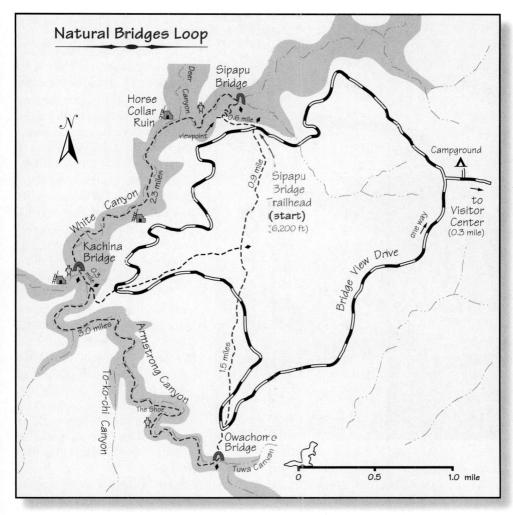

Natural Bridges Loop

Deer Canyon

Sipapu Bridge

Horse Collar Ruin

N

viewpoint

0.6 mile

White Canyon

2.3 miles

0.9 mile

Sipapu Bridge Trailhead (start) (6,200 ft)

Campground

to Visitor Center (0.3 mile)

one way

Kachina Bridge

0.3 mile

Bridge View Drive

3.0 miles

Armstrong Canyon

To-ko-chi Canyon

1.5 miles

The Shoe

Owachomo Bridge

Tuwa Canyon

0   0.5   1.0 mile

path immediately drops 440 feet in 0.6 mile to the creek bed under Sipapu Bridge. The trail is quite steep in places; the park service has constructed two metal staircases and three ladders to help with the descent. But don't be discouraged by the grade. Once you reach the bottom the trail is almost entirely on the canyon floor.

A short side trail branches off to the left about half way down for a magnificent view of Sipapu Bridge. Sipapu is the largest bridge in the monument, and this is the best place to photograph it. It rises an impressive 220 feet above the canyon floor, and with a

span of 268 feet it is only 10 feet shorter than Rainbow Natural Bridge, one of the largest natural bridges in the world.

From Sipapu the trail winds down the floor of picturesque White Canyon for another 2.3 miles to Kachina Bridge, passing several archaeological sites along the way. Look for a multitude of handprint pictographs just west of Sipapu Bridge; then, 0.7 mile below Sipapu, you will pass the park's most famous archaeological site: Horse Collar Ruin.

Horse Collar cannot be seen from the trail, but with a little effort it is not too dif-

Sipapu Natural Bridge

standing roofless dwellings on the southern end of the site that have doors shaped like horse collars.

Continuing down canyon for another 1.3 miles beyond the Horse Collar Ruin, past at least one more Anasazi granary and a small petroglyph panel, will bring you to Kachina Bridge, the second of the monument's three bridges. Only slightly smaller than Sipapu, Kachina spans 204 feet and is 210 feet tall. It is, however, a much younger, bulkier bridge–fully 93 feet thick at its crown. Kachina Bridge will still be standing many centuries from now.

Don't miss the petroglyphs near Kachina Bridge. There are dozens of them on the rock face just a hundred feet south of the bridge on the west side of the canyon. Kachina Bridge got its name from these petroglyphs, which remind some observers of the art that decorates Hopi kachina dolls. There are also the remains of two ancient granaries in the same area.

ficult to locate. It is situated about 30 feet above the canyon floor on a broken ledge along the northwest side of White Canyon. Look for the mouth of Deer Canyon, a major tributary that joins White Canyon from the north, and a shirt distance after passing the canyon junction you will come to the ledge. Getting up to Horse Collar Ruin requires some bushwacking and some scrambling, but the reward is well worth the trouble. Hidden in the back of a shallow alcove are the fragile remains of an ancient village that, although abandoned some 700 years ago, still contains several remarkably well preserved structures. The ruin was named after two particularly odd free

From Kachina Bridge it is very easy to take a wrong turn and get off the trail (as I

Anasazi granary near Kachina Natural Bridge

Owachomo Natural Bridge

did the first time I walked this loop). Don't bear right as you leave the area. Rather, follow the main path that bears left from Kachina Natural Bridge and goes up toward the canyon rim. After about 0.3 mile you will see a well marked junction in the trail with a sign directing you to Owachomo Bridge. At this point you are no longer in White Canyon; you have made the transition into Armstrong Canyon.

Owachomo Bridge is 3.0 miles down Armstrong Canyon from the trail junction near Kachina Bridge. This part of the trail is not as popular, and you are not likely to see other hikers until you reach Owachomo. There are not as many ruins of the Anasazi culture here, but at one point you can see quite an interesting collection of well preserved petroglyphs just above the right side of the trail. You are also much more likely to see deer and other wildlife during this part of the hike.

As the trail passes under Owachomo, you will immediately recognize it as the oldest of the three bridges.

Owachomo spans 180 feet, is 106 feet high, and is only 9 feet thick at its crown. It is a very shallow arch and gives the appearance that it could fall at any time. Its life span is, of course, impossible to predict, but it will probably not remain intact for more than another one or two centuries.

From Owachomo it is a short walk to the canyon rim, from where another trail leads 2.2 miles through the pinyon-juniper forest back to the Sipapu Bridge Trailhead where the hike began.

Kachina Natural Bridge

Grand Gulch - Bullet Canyon

shuttle car or bicycle required
3-day hike

Distance:	22.8 miles (plus 8.3 miles by car or bicycle)
Walking time:	day 1: 4 ¹/₄ hours day 2: 4 hours day 3: 5 ¹/₄ hours
Elevations:	1,080 ft. loss, 1,040 ft. gain Kane Gulch Trailhead (start): 6,440 ft. Bullet Canyon confluence: 5,360 ft. Bullet Canyon Trailhead: 6,400 ft.
Trail:	Parts of the trail are primitive and unmaintained, but the route is well marked and generally easy to follow. Getting out of Bullet Canyon can be tricky–especially with a heavy backpack. Inexperienced climbers may find a 25-foot length of rope useful for hauling packs up the slickrock in a few places.
Season:	Spring through early summer, fall. Water can be a problem in Grand Gulch after June. Much of the canyon contains running water in early spring, but the water soon dries up as the weather becomes hotter. By mid-June there are only occasional pools left, and by mid-July most of them have dried up. There is usually enough rain in late August and September to refill the pools and make hiking feasible again in the fall.
Vicinity:	Near Mexican Hat and Natural Bridges National Monument
Maps:	Kane Gulch, Cedar Mesa North, Pollys Pasture *(USGS)* Grand Gulch Plateau *(Trails Illustrated, #706)*
Information:	http://www.utahtrails.com/grand.html *(Utah Trails)* http://www.blm.gov/utah/monticello/ *(BLM, Monticello)* phone: (435) 587-1500 *(BLM, Monticello Field Office)*

Drive south from the junction of Highway 261 and Highway 95 (near Natural Bridges National Monument) toward the town of Mexican Hat. 3.9 miles from the junction you will arrive at Kane Gulch Ranger Station where the hike begins.

To get to Bullet Canyon Trailhead where the hike ends continue south from Kane Gulch

Ranger Station on Highway 261. After driving 7.2 miles you will see a clearly marked graded road on the right. Turn here and drive the last 1.2 miles to the trailhead.

Note: The BLM asks that all hikers in the Grand Gulch area register and obtain permits at the trailheads before entering the canyons. Day hikers will be charged $2.00/day for a permit or $5.00 for a 7-day pass, and backpackers will be charged $5.00/trip. During the peak seasons (March 1–June 15 and September 1–October 31) backpackers will be charged $8.00/trip and must pick up their permits between 8:00 a.m. and noon on the day of entry at the Kane Gulch Ranger Station. Only a limited number of backpacking permits are issued during the peak seasons, so reservations are recommended. Advanced reservations can be obtained by telephone at (435) 587-1510.

Grand Gulch is the premier area in Utah to see the ruins of the prehistoric Anasazi Indians. Their culture flourished in the canyon between 700 and 2000 years ago, and today dozens of cliff dwellings and other stone and mud structures remain to remind us of their occupancy. The most obvious ruins are from the so called Pueblo III culture of the thirteenth century, but more subtle remnants of the earlier Basketmaker culture that existed in the canyon from 200 to 700 A.D. are also present if one knows where to look.

By 1300 the Anasazi had deserted Grand Gulch and the surrounding canyons and moved southeast into the Rio Grande Valley of New Mexico. Precisely why they left is not known for certain, but drought, depletion of natural resources, and pressure from other nomadic Indians probably all played a

Split Level Ruin, Grand Gulch

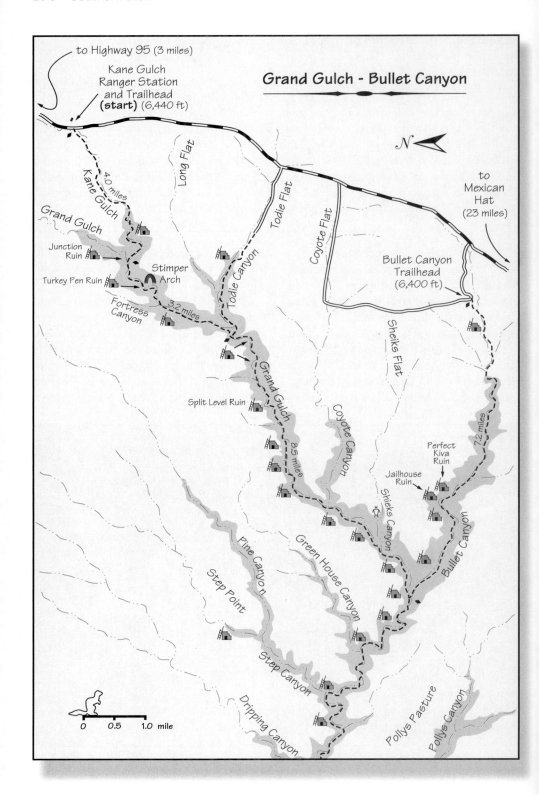

to Highway 95 (3 miles)

Kane Gulch
Ranger Station
and Trailhead
(start) (6,440 ft)

Grand Gulch - Bullet Canyon

N

Kane Gulch

4.0 miles

Long Flat

Todie Flat

Coyote Flat

to Mexican Hat (23 miles)

Grand Gulch

Junction Ruin

Turkey Pen Ruin

Stimper Arch

Todie Canyon

Bullet Canyon Trailhead (6,400 ft)

Fortress Canyon

3.2 miles

Sheiks Flat

Grand Gulch

Split Level Ruin

Coyote Canyon

8.5 miles

Perfect Kiva Ruin

7.2 miles

Jailhouse Ruin

Shieks Canyon

Bullet Canyon

Pine Canyon

Green House Canyon

Step Point

Step Canyon

Dripping Canyon

Pollys Pasture

Pollys Canyon

0   0.5   1.0 mile

role. For the past seven hundred years the Anasazi homes have stood in silence, clinging to the high canyon walls and causing the occasional canyon visitor to stare in wonder.

The first known white men to see Grand Gulch were the Mormons, who crossed Cedar Mesa in 1880. Soon afterward a series of amateur archaeologists begin to arrive in search of pots and other artifacts from the ruins. Between 1890 and 1897 at least nine expeditions entered Grand Gulch to dig for artifacts. The most famous of these was lead by Richard Wetherill, a rancher from southern Colorado who sold many Anasazi artifacts to the American Museum of Natural History in New York. Wetherill carved his name into the sandstone at several of the sites he excavated.

Needless to say, these early explorers did tremendous harm to the archeological record in Grand Gulch. Now, of course, it is against the law to remove artifacts from the canyons or to deface the ruins in any way. Please do not carry out pottery shards, corn cobs, flint flakes, or any other artifacts you may find laying on the ground. Also, do not climb on the ruins, and try to stay off the middens as much as possible. If everyone cooperates the wondrous Anasazi ruins of Grand Gulch will be there for many more years to come, and our children will have the opportunity to enjoy them as much as we do.

Day 1 (7.2 miles)

From the top of Kane Gulch the trail meanders gently downward for 3.8 miles before reaching the bottom of Grand Gulch. You should see your first ruin high on the southern wall of the Cedar Mesa Sandstone about an hour into the hike. This ruin is unusual in that it is on the north-facing rather than the south-facing side of the canyon. The Indians generally preferred to build their dwellings on the south-facing side where they received more winter sun.

Upon reaching the bottom of Grand Gulch you can't miss seeing the extensive Junction Ruin slightly upstream from the confluence. This area contains many fine camping sites under the cottonwood trees, and if you got a late start you may want to consider spending the night here.

Junction is one of the largest ruins in the canyon. It must

Junction Ruin

Pottery shards in Grand Gulch

rive at the mouth of Todie Canyon, where I suggest you make camp.

Day 2 (8.4 miles)

From Todie Canyon to Bullet Canyon, the suggested camp site for the second day, you will scarcely be able to walk a half hour without seeing a ruin of some sort. By my count there are at least eleven distinct ruins sites in the 8.4 miles between the two Canyons. Sometimes they consist of only a small granary or two, and at other times they include the remains of fifteen or twenty buildings. The first ruin is only a five minute walk from the mouth of Todie. Stay on the right side of the canyon as you walk downstream, and you will see it just as the stream bed swings around to the northeast.

The most impressive ruin in this section of the Grand Gulch is Split Level Ruin, so named because it includes a structure with two adjoining rooms, one higher than the other. Also notice, at this as well as other ruin sites, the presence of many kivas. The kivas are the low, round shaped structures, with a bench built into the wall and a fire pit near one side. The present-day Hopi Indians have similar structures in their pueblos, which leads many anthropologists to believe that they are modern descendants of the Anasazis.

As the trail approaches Bullet Canyon

have been home to many dozens of Indians when they lived in the canyon, and the number of stone buildings is impressive. It is also located near the stream bed and is quite accessible. Unfortunately, the midden in front of the ruin has been extensively excavated by amateur archaeologists and pot hunters over the years. As a result of all the digging, thousands of pottery shards, corn cobs and flints are now scattered about the ground's surface in front of the ruin. Enjoy the patterns and designs on them, but, again, please leave them where you find them so others can enjoy them too.

Turkey Pen Ruin, another large accessible site, is only 0.7 mile below Junction Ruin, and fifteen minutes beyond that you can see another less accessible ruin in an alcove above the cottonwood trees. Finally, 2.5 miles below Turkey Pen Ruin, you will ar-

Petroglyphs near Jailhouse Ruin, Bullet Canyon

you will see the wide, flat-bottomed canyon opening up on the left. The trail forks at Bullet Spring. There are no signs, however, so take care not to miss the turn. There are several excellent campsites within three hundred feet of the spring as you proceed into Bullet Canyon.

If you have time after pitching camp in Bullet Canyon you may want to spend an hour backtracking to Shieks Canyon (1.4 miles upstream from Bullet in Grand Gulch). There is an excellent panel of pictographs in the back of Shieks Canyon, 15 minutes from its mouth. There is also an interesting ruin on the north side of Bullet Canyon just a few hundred yards up from the confluence with Grand Gulch.

Day 3 (7.2 miles)

Most hikers complete this loop on the third day, walking up Bullet Canyon to the trailhead above the rim. There are at least five ruins to be seen in Bullet Canyon on the way up, but the most interesting one is Jailhouse Ruin, 2.4 miles from the canyon mouth. You will know you have arrived at Jailhouse Ruin when you see its unique pictograph consisting of two large white circles. The circles can be seen all the way across the canyon, but archaeologists have no idea what they were meant to represent. The ruin was named Jailhouse because of a small barred hole in the wall of one of its structures. The nearby Perfect Kiva Ruin is also interesting. It contains an extraordinarily well preserved kiva with a wooden ladder leading down into its interior. There are no restrictions against entering the kiva, but please take care not to damage it in any way.

As you proceed further up the canyon it soon narrows and becomes much more rocky. There are no ruins in upper Bullet Canyon, at least none that I have seen. The canyon bottom is completely unsuitable for farming here, so if the Indians did build any dwellings they would most likely be near the top of the rim. As you approach the top of the rim you will be walking on slickrock part of the time, and there are some areas where a bit of scrambling will be necessary. A short piece of rope is useful for lifting backpacks in one or two places so that you can climb unencumbered. Be sure to watch for rock cairns in the places where the canyon splits.

About ten minutes before you reach the top of the rim look up to the north at a square masonry tower that was built by the Anasazis on the very edge of the rim. Why would the Indians build a dwelling in such an exposed place? Perhaps it was a watch tower or a monitoring station to keep track of who was descending into the gulch. The parking area is about a quarter mile beyond the square tower ruin.

Upper Bullet Canyon

Grand Gulch - Collins Canyon

★ ★ ★ ★ ★

Distance: 29.9 miles
(plus 35 miles by car)

Walking time: day 1: 4 hours
day 2: 4 hours
day 3: 3½ hours
day 4: 5¼ hours

Elevations: 1,680 ft. loss, 370 ft. gain
Bullet Canyon Trailhead (start): 6,400 ft.
Bullet Canyon confluence: 5,360 ft.
Collins Canyon confluence: 4,720 ft.
Collins Spring Trailhead: 5,090 ft.

Trail: There are good trails down both Bullet Canyon and Collins Canyon. There is a primitive trail through most of Grand Gulch, but often it is easiest just to walk in the streambed.

Season: Spring through early summer, fall. Water can be a problem in Grand Gulch after June. Much of the canyon contains running water in early spring, but the water soon dries up as the weather becomes hotter. By mid-June there are only occasional pools left, and by mid-July most of them have dried up. There is usually enough rain in late August and September to refill the pools and make hiking feasible again in the fall.

Vicinity: Near Mexican Hat and Natural Bridges National Monument

Maps: Cedar Mesa North, Pollys Pasture, Red House Spring *(USGS)*
Grand Gulch Plateau *(Trails Illustrated, #706)*

Information: http://www.utahtrails.com/collins.html *(Utah Trails)*
http://www.blm.gov/utah/monticello/ *(BLM, Monticello)*
phone: (435) 587-1500 *(BLM, Monticello Field Office)*

Drive south from the junction of Highway 261 and Highway 95 (near Natural Bridges National Monument) toward the town of Mexican Hat. 3.9 miles from the junction you will arrive at Kane Gulch Ranger Station, where you must obtain a backpacking permit before entering the canyon. Continue south on Highway 261 for another 7.2 miles from the Kane

Gulch Ranger Station until you see a sign that says "Bullet Canyon Trailhead, 2 miles". Turn right here onto a graded dirt road and drive another 1.2 miles to the trailhead.

In order to get to the Collins Spring Trailhead, where the hike ends, you must return to the junction of Highway 261 and Highway 95 and drive west for 9.5 miles to Highway 276. Turn south on Highway 276 and continue for another 6.8 miles until you see a sign that says "Collins Spring Trailhead, 6 miles". Turn left here and follow a graded gravel road for 6.6 miles to the trailhead. 2.5 miles after leaving the pavement you will encounter a fork in the road where you should bear right. The last two miles of the road are quite rough in a few places, but with care most cars should be able to make it.

Note: The BLM asks that all hikers in the Grand Gulch area register and obtain permits at the trailheads before entering the canyons. Day hikers will be charged $2.00/day for a permit or $5.00 for a 7-day pass, and backpackers will be charged $5.00/trip. During the peak seasons (March 1–June 15 and September 1–October 31) backpackers will be charged $8.00/trip and must pick up their permits between 8:00 a.m. and noon on the day of entry at the Kane Gulch Ranger Station. Only a limited number of backpacking permits are issued during the peak seasons, so reservations are recommended. Advanced reservations can be obtained by telephone at (435) 587-1510

The Grand Gulch and its side canyons offer a number of interesting routes for extended backpacking in southeastern Utah. Personally, I have found the section of Grand Gulch, between Bullet Canyon and Collins Canyon, to be especially appealing. This portion of the Gulch is wilder and receives far fewer visitors than the section above Bullet Canyon, yet it contains many points of interest. Of course, the main attraction is the canyon's Anasazi Indian ruins. I have seen no fewer than twenty cliff dwelling and pictograph sites in this area, and I am certain many more could be found–especially if one takes the time to walk into some of the side canyons along the way.

The total distance of the hike described here, from Bullet Canyon Trailhead to Collins Spring Trailhead, is 29.9 miles. However Grand Gulch can also be accessed via the Government Trail (see page 300), which lies about halfway between

Bullet and Collins Canyons; hence it is possible to break the trip up into two shorter hikes. If you were to exit at Government Trailhead the total walking distance would be 21.4 miles, with a 12.6 mile shuttle. Alternatively, the distance from Government Trailhead to Collins Spring Trailhead is 15.4 miles and requires a 45.4 mile shuttle.

Grand Gulch ends at the San Juan River, 15.7 miles below Collins Canyon, and every year some ambitious backpackers hike

Anasazi ruin near the mouth of Deer Canyon

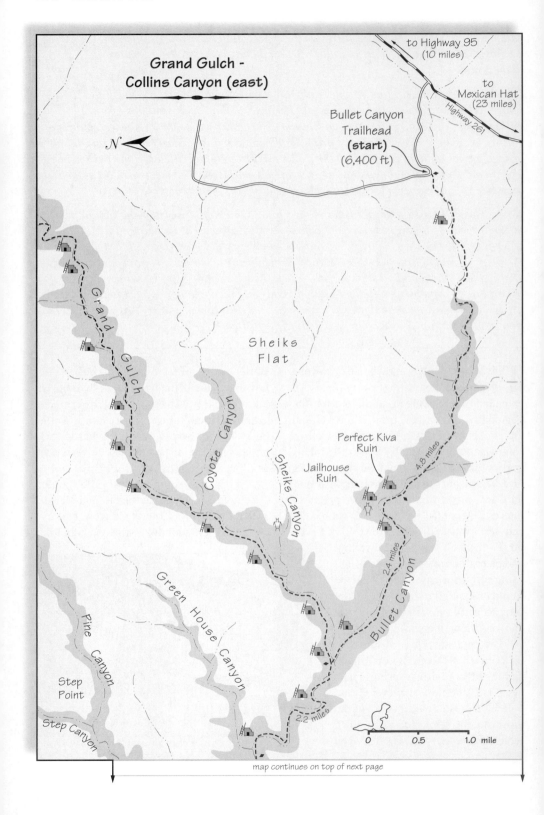

Grand Gulch -
Collins Canyon (east)

N

to Highway 95
(10 miles)

to
Mexican Hat
(23 miles)

Highway 261

Bullet Canyon
Trailhead
(start)
(6,400 ft)

Grand Gulch

Sheiks
Flat

Coyote Canyon

Sheiks Canyon

Perfect Kiva
Ruin

Jailhouse
Ruin

4.8 miles

Green House Canyon

Pine Canyon

Bullet Canyon

2.4 miles

Step
Point

Step Canyon

2.2 miles

0   0.5   1.0 mile

map continues on top of next page

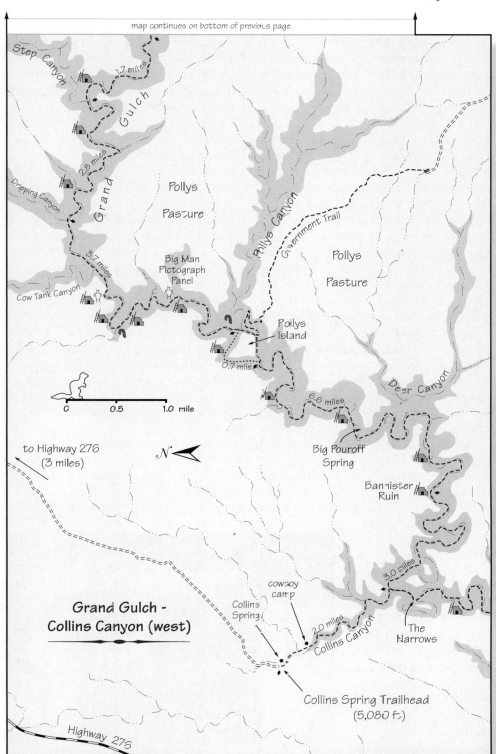

map continues on bottom of previous page

Step Canyon

1.7 miles

Grand Gulch

Dripping Canyon

2.8 miles

Grand

3.7 miles

Cow Tank Canyon

Big Man Pictograph Panel

Pollys Pasture

Pollys Canyon

Government Trail

Pollys Pasture

Pollys Island

0.7 mile

Deer Canyon

0   0.5   1.0 mile

6.6 miles

Big Pouroff Spring

to Highway 276
(3 miles)

N

Bannister Ruin

3.0 miles

Grand Gulch -
Collins Canyon (west)

cowboy camp

Collins
Spring

2.0 miles

Collins Canyon

The Narrows

Collins Spring Trailhead
(5,080 ft.)

Highway 276

the entire length of the canyon. This trip requires considerable planning, however, as the lower end of the Gulch is accessible only by boat.

Day 1 (7.2 miles)

From the trailhead the path meanders along the north rim of Bullet Canyon for 0.2 mile before suddenly turning south to descend into the upper reaches of the canyon. After loosing 120 feet of elevation the path turns west again to follow the dry streambed downward through an open forest of pinion pine and juniper. Soon you will see your first Indian ruin, a small stone tower that stands above the canyon on the edge of the north rim. It is clearly visible from the trail 0.5 mile below the point where the path first drops into Bullet Canyon. Its location seems to indicate that the 10-foot-square tower was some kind of an observation post built by the Anasazis to keep track of who was going in and out of the canyon.

You won't see any other ruins in Bullet Canyon for the next 3.8 miles, but there are several excellent ones in the lower part of the drainage. The next one you will en-counter is called the Perfect Kiva Ruin, and it is one of the few that have been given a name. Look for a place where a small side canyon comes in from the right, directly opposite an unusually steep cliff on the left. The trail splits in this area, and if you bear left you will miss the Perfect Kiva Ruin. Bear right along a trail that goes toward the small side canyon on the north side of Bullet. As you approach the side canyon you will notice a large, shaded south-facing al-cove about one-third of

the way up from the canyon floor on your left. Look closely and you will see a low square structure in the back of the alcove that appears darker than the surrounding rock. This structure was built by the Anasazi and is part of the ruin.

It is an easy climb of about 100 feet from the trail to the bottom of the alcove in which the Perfect Kiva Ruin is located. Your reward will be the remains of at least six rooms plus an intact underground kiva with a wooden ladder leading into it. It is rare to find a kiva in such good condition; hence seeing this one is a real treat. The round subterranean rooms were common in the Anasazi culture, but they all contained fire pits and most of them eventually succumbed to accidental fires. There are many of them in the Cedar Mesa area, but I only know of one other one, in Slickhorn Canyon, that has survived relatively undamaged.

Jailhouse Ruin is located just 0.2 mile further down-canyon from Perfect Kiva. Continue along the trail, staying close to the north side of Bullet Canyon, and within five minutes you should see two large white circles on your right near the base of the cliff. The circles are part of a pictograph panel above the Jailhouse Ruin.

Several unusual features make Jailhouse

Jailhouse Ruin

Anasazi ruin near Greenhouse Canyon

confluence, again on the right side of the canyon.

There is another fine campsite at the mouth of Greenhouse Canyon, 2.1 miles from the Bullet Canyon confluence, with good water availability. Greenhouse Canyon Spring lies about 300 yards upcanyon from Grand Gulch, but there is usually a nice pool of water at the canyon junction as well. There is also a small Indian ruin 100 feet above the junction, on the north side of the main canyon. This is a very pleasant place to stop, if only for a lunch break.

Ruin a particularly interesting one. It provides an excellent example of the "wattle and daub" method of construction occasionally used by the Anasazis. With this technique the wall is first framed with sticks and twigs, and then plastered with mud. One of the windows even contains a few exposed wattle sticks, giving it the appearance of a jail cell. Another interesting feature is the presence of a very small room that opens directly into the living area; it looks as if this room might have been a granary, or a "kitchen pantry".

You will pass by two more ruins in the next 2.4 miles between the Jailhouse Ruin and Grand Gulch–both of them are clearly visible from the trail on the north side of the canyon. Unless you got a very early start you will probably want to make camp when you reach Grand Gulch; there is an excellent campsite at the confluence with a reliable spring in the streambed of Bullet Canyon.

Day 2 (7.6 miles)

Most Grand Gulch hikers exit the canyon either at Kane Gulch or Bullet Canyon, so as you continue downstream from the mouth of Bullet you will probably see few if any other hikers. Yet, in my opinion, this is the most interesting part of the entire Grand Gulch. The next Indian ruin is 0.3 mile below the

Many of the ruins in Grand Gulch are located in areas where side canyons meet the main canyon. Just before the trail reaches

Anasazi ruin near Step Canyon

Hand prints near Cow Tank Canyon

the junction with Step Canyon, 1.8 miles downstream from Greenhouse Canyon, it passes below a ledge that contains three more interesting ruins. One of them is a two-story structure about 10 feet square by 12 feet high that is still largely intact

2.8 miles beyond Step Canyon the trail passes the mouth of Dripping Canyon and, after another 0.5 mile, Cow Tank Canyon. There is usually water in this area, and if it is late you might want to start looking for a place to camp. Both Cow Tank and Dripping Canyons have reliable springs about 0.8 miles up from the main canyon, but except in late summer there are usually intermittent pools in Grand Gulch itself. It is seldom necessary to walk far to find water.

If the spring runoff has finished and it doesn't look like rain you might want to consider camping right in the streambed. There is an excellent place to do this 0.4 mile down canyon from Cow Tank. Ten minutes after leaving the side canyon you will come to a sharp bend where the Gulch briefly turns north and then makes a hairpin curve back to the south. The northern canyon wall forms a sheer cliff, and if you look up you will see dozens of small red and white pictographs along a ledge about 50 feet from the bottom. The canyon floor is quite flat here, and you can lie on your sleeping bag and contemplate the dozens of handprints

and strange bucket-shaped pictographs above you. Many Anasazis undoubtedly slept in this very spot, and as you gaze at their art you can almost hear the prehistoric Indian children laughing and playing on the ledge. There is also a deep, shaded pool nearby that usually retains water for most of the summer.

Day 3 (6.4 miles)

0.7 mile down-canyon from your streambed campsite you can see a large natural arch high on the right side of the canyon. There are also two Indian ruins in the area—one about 300 yards upcanyon from the arch, on the same side of the canyon, and one about the same distance down-canyon on the opposite side. Arches must have held a mystical attraction for the ancient Anasazi, because they frequently chose to live near them. In some cases they even selected building sites that were greatly inferior, just so they could live in the vicinity of a natural arch.

Fifteen minutes after passing the natural arch you should start looking for the Big Man Pictograph Panel high on the left side of the canyon. (See photo on page 303.) The panel is located at the bottom of a 200-foot sheer cliff, facing west and framed by two long streaks of black desert varnish that flow down from the canyon rim. The bottom of the cliff is about 150 feet above the canyon

Pictographs near Cow Tank Canyon

Behind Polly's Island

is easy, and it will only add 0.3 mile onto the total distance. Watch for a secondary trail that leaves the streambed just below the natural arch and climbs up the sandy embankment in a westerly direction. Soon the trail breaks out of the undergrowth and proceeds around the back side of the island, across an open meadow of sagebrush and cactus. A million years ago this was the main channel of the Grand Gulch. But this section of the canyon has long since been bypassed, and is now filled with 30 feet of sand and other debris deposited over the centuries by the wind.

Look for an interesting Indian ruin opposite Polly's Island on the north east

floor, but if you are observant you can just see the Big Man's head peering down from behind the juniper trees at the foot of the precipice.

If you look carefully you will find a primitive hiker-made trail leading up from the streambed to the Big Man Pictograph Panel. There are also two more small Anasazi granaries hidden in the trees on the right side of the canyon within the next 0.4 mile below the pictographs.

The next major point of interest is Polly's Island, a 25-acre mesa that has been detached from the canyon rim by a dry meander in the streambed. Walk down-canyon from the Big Man Pictograph Panel for 1.4 miles and look for another natural bridge near the rim on the left side. Polly's Island is situated on the northwest side of the canyon, just beyond the natural bridge and opposite the confluence with Polly's Canyon. This is also where the Government Trail enters Grand Gulch and, as mentioned earlier, it is possible to exit the canyon and end the hike at this point. (See page 300.) The Government Trail leaves Grand Gulch 0.2 mile below Polly's Canyon.

An interesting diversion on this hike is to leave the main canyon and walk the long way around Polly's Island. The route

Grand Gulch

side of the rincon (see photo on page 16). The people who lived here had a fabulous view from their veranda, with the cliffs of Polly's Island rising above the meadow in front of them. I wonder if they grew corn in the flat meadow below their home? I wonder if any of them tried to find a way to the top of the Island, and if they were successful?

In my opinion, the most interesting Anasazi ruins you will see on this hike are at a site 1.4 miles down-canyon from Polly's Island. These ruins are all situated along a ledge about 300 yards long and 60 feet above the ground. The canyon runs due west at this point, and the ledge is on the south facing side of the canyon. One fork of the path runs along the north side of the canyon directly under the ruins, but they are also easy to spot if you happen to be walking in the streambed. The ledge

Ruin between Polly's Island and Big Pouroff Spring

is easily accessible from the east side, but only two of the ruins can be reached without some rock climbing skill. Unfortunately the best ruins are hard to get to, but even seeing them from the ground is a real treat. One of them is a multi-dwelling structure with four exterior doors in near pristine condition. But the most striking building is a round cylindrical-shaped structure, about ten feet high, with a small door near the bottom.

There is an excellent campsite near the cliffs on the opposite side of the canyon from these ruins, so if you want to spend more time studying them this might be a good place to stop. Otherwise, I suggest you continue on for another 1.3 miles and establish a camp at Big Pouroff Spring. Be

sure to keep an eye out for additional cliff dwellings as you walk; you should see at least two more small sites along the way.

You can't miss Big Pouroff; it is located right in the middle of the streambed, and when water is flowing in the Gulch it plunges over a 20-foot drop into a perpetual pool below. There is also a seep near the bottom of the pouroff, so even when the streambed is dry it is rare to find the pool completely empty. There is plenty of flat ground in the vicinity for a camp, but there are no trees near the pouroff so if you want shade you will have to camp away from the spring.

Day 4 (8.7 miles)

From Big Pouroff Spring to Bannister Ruin is 3.7 miles. There are at least four smaller ruins along the way, but Bannister is the last major ruin you will see on this hike. The unusual cliff dwelling is a multi-room structure where several families must have lived. A large part of it is fashioned with the wattle and daub method, and it is in excellent condition. Unfortunately it lies on the opposite side of the canyon from the trail, and it would be hard to reach even with a ladder. Most hikers are content to view it at a distance from the trail.

After Bannister Ruin the trail improves significantly. It is only 5.0 miles to the Collins Spring Trailhead, and many hikers visit Bannister as a day hike. This part of the trail is also frequently used by horseback riders. There is a spring 0.3 mile below Bannister Ruin, but beyond that you will notice a significant decrease in the amount of available water in the canyon as you continue.

From Bannister Ruin to the mouth of Collins Canyon is 3.0 miles, and it is another 2.0 miles up Collins Canyon to the trailhead. But if you have enough energy left when you reach the mouth of Collins Canyon you may want to make a 0.3-mile side trip to the Narrows before starting up. This slender section of the canyon was formed when the Grand Gulch long ago abandoned another one of its meanders to form a dry rincon in the streambed. The Narrows is the short section of canyon at the head of the rincon where the canyon narrows to a width of about 12 feet.

It is possible to walk around the dry rincon on the west side of the Narrows. The loop is 0.8 miles long, and a hiker-made trail makes it a relatively easy walk. The attraction in the rincon is more interesting pictographs. Most of them are located on the south facing walls near where the dry streambed exits and reenters the main canyon. (See page 310.)

The trail up Collins Canyon passes

one more point of interest before ending at the trailhead: an old camp where cowboys in the early 1900s stayed while tending their cattle. See page 309 for a description of the camp.

Finally, I should tell you how to find the spring at Collins Spring Trailhead; after four days on the trail you will probably appreciate knowing where you can find an ample supply of clean water! If you look down into Collins Canyon from the trailhead you will see that the actual drainage reaches the rim about two hundred feet east of where the trail comes up. Walk to the east side of the parking area and drop down 60 feet to the bottom of the Collins Canyon drainage, then turn south and walk down the bottom of the streambed. After 100 feet you will come to a pouroff in streambed with an alcove under it. Collins Spring is hidden in the back of the alcove.

Bannister Ruin

Big Man Pictographs

★★★

Distance:	10.6 miles (round trip)
Walking time:	6¼ hours
Elevations:	620 ft. loss/gain car parking area (start): 5,670 ft. Government Trailhead: 5,370 ft. Grand Gulch: 5,050 ft.
Trail:	The first 2.8 miles of trail is actually an old jeep road that has been closed to vehicles by the BLM. The 0.8 mile section of trail that descends from the canyon rim into Grand Gulch is a good trail, but there may be some confusion in finding the hiker-made trail on the canyon floor that leads to the pictographs.
Season:	Spring through early summer, fall. Spring or fall are the ideal times for this hike. The canyon is very hot in the summer and cold in the winter. The road to the car parking area is unpaved for the last 9 miles and may be impassable in wet weather.
Vicinity:	Near Mexican Hat and Natural Bridges National Monument
Maps:	Pollys Pasture (*USGS*) Grand Gulch Plateau (*Trails Illustrated, #706*)
Information:	http://www.utahtrails.com/bigman.html (*Utah Trails*) http://www.blm.gov/utah/monticello/ (*BLM, Monticello*) phone: (435) 587-1500 (*BLM, Monticello Field Office*)

Drive south from the junction of Highway 261 and Highway 95 (near Natural Bridges National Monument) for 3.9 miles to the Kane Gulch Ranger Station. Continuing south from the ranger station for another 9.6 miles will bring you to a junction where two dirt roads join the paved highway. Turn right (west) here onto County Road 245 and continue for 7.5 miles. You will encounter *major forks in the road in at least two places; in each case you should bear to the right. After you have driven 7.5 miles from the paved highway you will see a smaller dirt road branching off on the right with a sign that says "Government Trail". Turn here and drive the last 1.5 miles to the parking area beside a small cattle pond. The last 1.5 miles of road is very rocky, but with care most cars can make it.*

Note: The BLM asks that all hikers in the Grand Gulch area register and obtain permits at the trailheads before entering the canyons. Day hikers will be charged $2.00/day for a permit or $5.00 for a 7-day pass, and backpackers will be charged $5.00/trip. During the peak seasons (March 1–June 15 and September 1–October 31) backpackers will be charged $8.00/trip and must pick up their permits between 8:00 a.m. and noon on the day of entry at the Kane Gulch Ranger Station. Only a limited number of backpacking permits are issued during the peak seasons, so reservations are recommended. Advanced reservations can be obtained by telephone at (435) 587-1510.

Before you begin this hike, pause to examine the small pond near the car parking area. The pond is an oasis in the middle of a largely waterless tableland. Although it was constructed originally by local ranchers for the purpose of watering their cattle, it has since become a haven for birds, deer, and coyotes. If you arrived too late in the day to begin your hike, the pond is a delightful place to spend the night. Expect to be treated to an unforgettable outdoor performance by an orchestra of very talented frogs and birds. What better introduction to life on Cedar Mesa as it was during the time of the Anasazi.

The Big Man Pictograph Panel is a typical example of rock art produced by the Anasazi Basketmaker people who lived in Grand Gulch from about 100 B.C. to 750 A.D. Their art is frequently characterized by broad-shouldered anthropomorphs with body decorations like hair bobs, necklaces, sashes and belts. The Basketmakers did not possess the technological prowess of the later Puebloan Anasazi, who built the cliff dwellings we so admire today. They lived in simple pit houses and rock shelters a thousand years earlier. Yet, in spite of their technological inferiority, many anthropologists feel that the quality of the Basketmaker art is far superior to that of their more recent descendents.

Years ago it was possible to drive a jeep from the cattle pond all the way to the rim of Grand Gulch, where the Government Trail begins. The Grand Gulch is now designated as a Primitive Area, however, and the road beyond the pond is closed to all vehicles. Getting to Government Trail today requires a 2.8-mile walk along the former jeep road. The walk can be hot in the summer, but it is not without a measure of scenery. The road parallels Polly's Canyon, across a flat, open forest of juniper and pinion pine and lots of sagebrush. It is ideal rabbit country and, consequently, supports a large population of coyotes. After an hour's walk the road suddenly arrives at the canyon rim, where a

Grand Gulch, from Government Trail

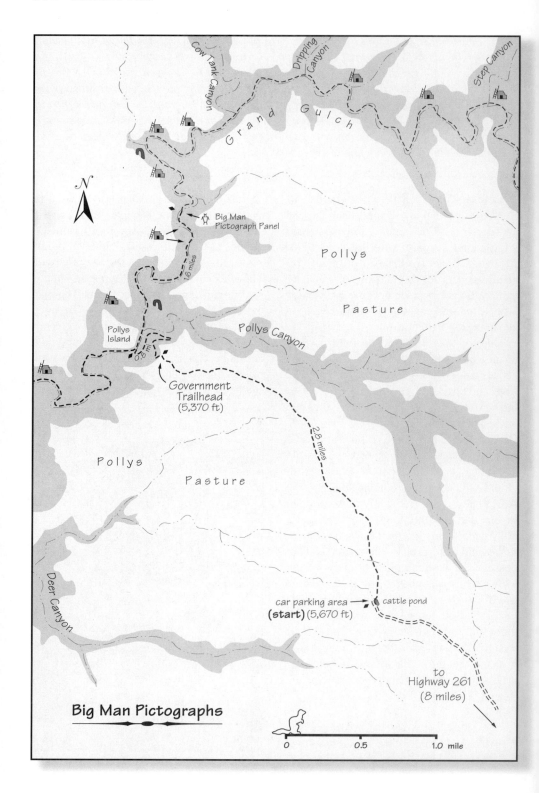

N

Cow Tank Canyon

Dripping Canyon

Step Canyon

Grand Gulch

Big Man Pictograph Panel

1.6 miles

Pollys

Pasture

Pollys Canyon

Pollys Island

0.8 mi.

Government Trailhead (5,370 ft)

2.8 miles

Pollys

Pasture

Deer Canyon

car parking area → cattle pond
(start) (5,670 ft)

to Highway 261 (8 miles)

Big Man Pictographs

0   0.5   1.0 mile

weathered wooden sign identifies the Government Trail.

The view from the rim into Grand Gulch is magnificent. Polly's Island, a huge piece of the mesa separated from the canyon walls by a dry meander in the streambed, rises directly to the west, while up and down the Gulch the bright green canyon floor borders the pink, convoluted walls of Cedar Mesa Sandstone.

Government Trail is only 0.8 mile long, and is the easiest of any of the five trails leading into Grand Gulch. It was probably built in the 1930s by the CCC workers to provide a way for ranchers to get cattle in and out of the canyon. The trail reaches the canyon floor at the base of Polly's Island, 0.2 mile south of the confluence with Pollys Canyon.

Once on the canyon floor it is an easy walk up the flat streambed of Grand Gulch to the Big Man Pictograph Panel. The Gulch is particularly pretty in this section, and there are numerous nice places to camp if you are so inclined. If you are observant you should be able to spot a small natural arch high on the east wall of the Gulch near the confluence with Polly's Canyon, and there are at least two Anasazi ruins on the canyon's west side as you approach Big Man.

The Big Man Panel is about 200 feet above the canyon floor and it is not visible from the trail, so it is easy to miss if you are not paying attention. About 1.2 miles upstream from Pollys Canyon you will see another large side canyon coming into Grand Gulch from the east. Beyond this point the streambed swings to the west to get around a bulge in the canyon's eastern wall. The Big Man Pictograph Panel is located precisely at the apex of this bulge, where the streambed straightens out again and then swings back to the east. If you watch carefully as you walk this section of the trail you should see footprints where other hikers have left the trail to climb up to the pictographs. The main trail follows the east side of the streambed in this area. If you see the trail crossing back to the west side it means you have gone too far.

When you see the pictograph panel it will become obvious why it was named Big Man. The central focus of the art is two life size human figures, one of which appears to be a woman and the other obviously a man. The explicit depiction of gender is a common characteristic of Basketmaker art, as are the handprints near the female figure.

Big Man Pictograph Panel

Lower Grand Gulch

★★★★ **3-day hike**

Distance:	23.0 miles (round trip to all points of interest)
Walking time:	day 1: 4½ hours day 2: 3½ hours day 3: 5½ hours
Elevations:	900 ft. loss/gain Collins Spring Trailhead (start): 5,090 ft. Collins Canyon confluence: 4,770 ft. Shaw Arch: 4,570 ft.
Trail:	Vague hiker-made trail through the bottom of Grand Gulch is often hard to follow, but the route is obvious.
Season:	Spring through early summer, fall. May is the ideal month for this hike, when the days are long, the temperatures are ideal, and water is not a problem. The water soon dries up as the weather becomes hotter and by mid-June only occasional pools are left. Even those pools are largely gone by mid-July, but there is usually enough rain in late August and September to refill them and make hiking into the canyon feasible again.
Vicinity:	Near Blanding and Natural Bridges National Monument
Maps:	Red House Spring, Slickhorn Canyon West (*USGS*) Grand Gulch Plateau (*Trails Illustrated, #706*)
Information:	http://www.utahtrails.com/lowergrandgulch.html (*Utah Trails*) http://www.blm.gov/utah/monticello/ (*BLM, Monticello*) phone: (435) 587-1500 (*BLM, Monticello Field Office*)

Drive west from Blanding for 34 miles to the junction with Highways 95 and 261. Continue west on Highway 95 for another 9.5 miles to the junction with Highway 276. Turn here and drive south on Highway 276 for 6.7 miles where you will see a sign marking the primitive road to the Collins Spring Trailhead on the left. The trailhead is located at the end of this road, 6.6 miles from the *highway. 2.5 miles after leaving the highway you will come to a fork in the road where you must bear right. The road gets quite rough in a few places, but with care most passenger cars with reasonably high clearance should be able to make it.*

Note: The BLM asks that all hikers in the Grand Gulch area register and obtain permits at the trailheads before entering the canyons. Day hikers will be charged $2.00/day for a permit or $5.00 for a 7-day pass, and backpackers will be charged $5.00/trip. During the peak seasons (March 1 – June 15 and September 1 – October 31) backpackers will be charged $8.00/trip and must pick up their permits between 8:00 a.m. and noon on the day of entry at the Kane Gulch Ranger Station. Only a limited number of backpacking permits are issued during the peak seasons, so reservations are recommended. Advanced reservations can be obtained by telephone at (435) 587-1510.

Grand Gulch, as mentioned on the preceding pages, is probably the best place in Utah to see artifacts of the ancient Anasazi Indians who lived in southeastern Utah from about 1200 B.C. until 1300 A.D. The canyon is full of their ruins, especially from the Pueblo III Period of the Anasazi culture that began around 850 years ago and lasted for some 150 years. It was during that time that they constructed their dwellings and granaries in the canyon cliffs throughout the four corners area of Utah, Colorado, Arizona, and New Mexico. The Grand Gulch contains a particularly high concentration of their artifacts, and a walk through the wild canyon amidst the ruins of the ancient Anasazi civilization can be an awesome experience.

The 80-mile-long Grand Gulch is too long to explore on a single backpacking trip, but fortunately there are several intermediate trailheads along the way that provide convenient entry and exit points for shorter trips. The most popular hike into Grand Gulch begins at the Kane Gulch Trailhead and ends at the Bullet Canyon Trailhead (see page 234). Another equally interesting but somewhat longer hike begins at the Bullet

Lower Grand Gulch

Ancient handprints in Lower Grand Gulch

Canyon Trailhead and continues down the Gulch to Collins Canyon (see page 290). Here I describe a third hike into the Grand Gulch that explores the lower part of the canyon below Collins Canyon.

This hike is different from the two previously described hikes into the upper reaches of the Grand Gulch in a few important respects. First, backpackers should be aware that there is generally less water in the lower reaches of the canyon than there is in the upper parts. Under normal conditions you won't find any running water at all along the route described here between Collins Canyon and Shaw Arch. The canyon floor is rarely completely dry, but unless there has been a recent rain you may have

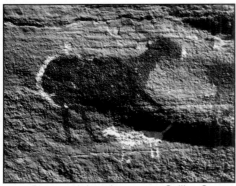

Pictograph in a rincon near Collins Canyon

to walk several miles between water holes. And when you do find water you will need to filter it or boil it before drinking. Look for small pools of muddy water in the backs of alcoves and other low shaded areas in the streambed.

Second, although there are a few small ruins below Collins Canyon, you won't find any of the large ruins sites that are present further up the canyon. What you will find is lots and lots of rock art: pictographs in white, red, orange, and brown representing birds, four-legged animals, and anthropomorphs, as well as hundreds of hand prints. The art appears to represent not only the Pueblo Period of Anasazi culture, but also the earlier Basketmaker Period. Some of the art is also in the Archaic style, produced by a culture that preceded the Anasazis over 3000 years ago.

Third, it will help you to locate the ruins and rock art in the canyon if you carry a compass, a watch, and a good map. Most people walk about 2 miles in an hour, and if you can determine the direction of the canyon with a compass it is usually easy to spot your location on a map. Also, bear in mind that ruins and rock art are almost always found on the south facing side of the canyon where the winter temperatures are warmer.

Day 1: (8.4 miles)

As you start down Collins Canyon it will soon become apparent that you are following an old cattle trail, probably built in the early 1900s when cattle ranching was a major industry in southeastern Utah. Just two minutes after leaving the trailhead you will come to a crudely marked junction where a short hiker-made spur trail departs on the left for Collins Spring. The spring, located under a 15-foot ledge in the center of the drainage, was originally developed by local ranchers to water their cattle.

0.4 mile below the trailhead the path passes an old campsite where cowboys once stayed while tending their livestock. Look for a shallow alcove behind the bushes just 30 feet to the left of the trail. In the back of the alcove you can still see an old feed storage bin as well as dozens of bottles, tin cans, and cooking utensils. It doesn't take much imagination to visualize the lonely nights that must have been spent here by the cowboys and their horses 50 miles from the nearest town.

Just 150 feet beyond the cowboy camp the trail encounters its first major obstacle: a 100-foot pouroff in the canyon floor with no easy way down. Here the ranchers used dynamite to blast out a descent route along the canyon's west wall. Beyond that point there are a few additional stretches of trail that had to be blasted, but today the descent through Collins Canyon is a fairly easy one. After loosing 320 feet over a distance of 1.7 miles from the trailhead you will arrive at the mouth of Collins Canyon. There you must turn right to continue down the sandy floor of the Grand Gulch.

Although most of the time the route through the lower Grand Gulch is very easy walking, you will occasionally be confronted with obstacles such as water barriers, rock fall, or heavy vegetation that make progress more difficult. In almost every case when an obstacle is imminent you will find a hiker-made bypass trail that climbs away from the canyon floor to get around the problem. These bypass trails are not always obvious, however, so be observant and watch both sides of the drainage for places where previous hikers have climbed out of the streambed

Cowboy camp in Collins Canyon

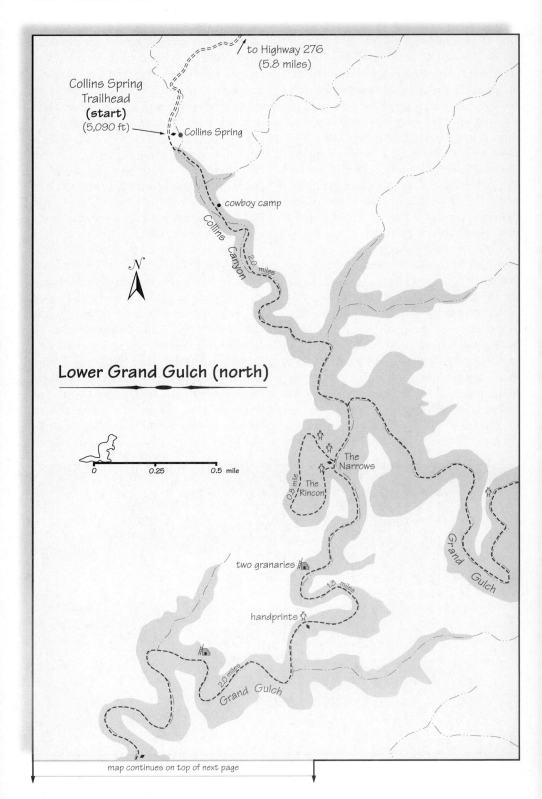

to Highway 276
(5.8 miles)

Collins Spring
Trailhead
(start)
(5,090 ft) → Collins Spring

cowboy camp

Collins Canyon

2.0 miles

N

Lower Grand Gulch (north)

0   0.25   0.5 mile

The
Narrows

0.8 mile

The
Rincon

Grand
Gulch

two granaries

1.3 miles

handprints

2.0 miles

Grand Gulch

map continues on top of next page

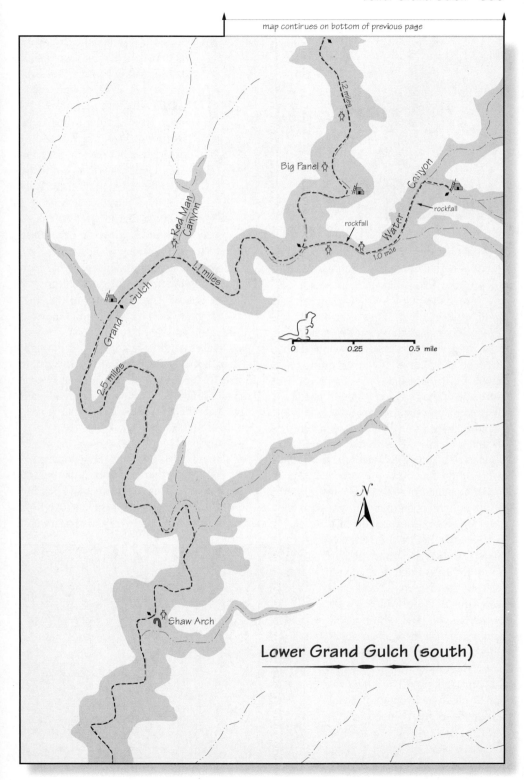

map continues on bottom of previous page

1.2 miles

Big Panel

Water Canyon

Red Man Canyon

rockfall

rockfall

1.0 mile

1.1 miles

Grand Gulch

2.5 miles

0   0.25   0.5 mile

N

Shaw Arch

Lower Grand Gulch (south)

Pictograph in the rincon near the Narrows

located. One of the granaries is in excellent condition, and it is interesting to note the careful plaster work on the inside of the structure that prevented mice from getting to its cache of food. Also, a great deal of effort was put into making the small opening that could be completely sealed simply by leaning a flat rock against it. I think that even after 700 years it would be difficult for a mouse to find its way into this granary.

to avoid obstacles. If you miss these detours the hike will become much more difficult.

0.3 mile below the confluence with Collins Canyon the Gulch briefly narrows to a width of just 12 feet. This short stretch, appropriately named the Narrows, is the result of an ancient breach in the canyon wall that changed the course of the streambed and created a dry meander, or rincon, on the west side of the canyon. I suggest you leave the main streambed at this point and walk into the rincon. The distance around the dry meander is only 0.8 mile, and you will find your first pictographs on the south-facing walls of the canyon as you proceed. There are small panels of rock art within 150 yards of the main canyon that you will pass both entering and exiting the rincon.

0.5 mile below the Narrows the streambed swings west into another large meander. After making the turn you should start watching the south-facing side of the canyon, and within a few minutes you will see two small side-by-side granaries on a narrow ledge about 150 feet above the canyon floor. The granaries can be easily reached for a closer look by retracing your steps 100 yards to the east, where there is a relatively easy way to climb up to the ledge where they are

Beyond the two granaries the canyon heads south again for 150 yards before beginning another long meander to the east. 0.5 mile later, as the streambed comes out of the loop and again turns south you will pass a large panel of handprints on the right side of the trail. The prints are clearly visible about 80 feet north of the streambed near the bottom of the south-facing canyon wall. I estimate there are close to 200 handprints on this impressive panel.

After passing the handprints the winding canyon heads south, then northwest, then southwest, then north for a total of 0.9 mile before turning to the west and passing beneath another ruin of an ancient dwelling. As before, this structure is located on a small

Pictograph in the rincon near the Narrows

Two granaries, Lower Grand Gulch

posed over the older ones. There must have been something very special about this site to have drawn so many people over such a long period of time. There are also several metates on the ledge below the panel where the Indian women once came to grind their corn.

The second pictograph panel fills the back of an alcove on the right side of the canyon. Often referred to as the Big Panel, it is the largest panel of rock art in Grand Gulch. Again, it presents an intriguing collection of birds, animals, and anthropomorphs. Some of the ghost-like figures look very much like the Barrier Canyon style pictographs that were drawn by the Archaic People more

ledge about 100 feet above the bottom of the canyon on the south-facing wall. The ruin consists of a single room about 10 feet square with a small door on the west side.

As you proceed down the Grand Gulch you will pass the weathered and broken remains of a few other granaries, but nothing so well preserved as the structures mentioned above. There are, however, some impressive pictograph panels further down canyon. You will pass the two best ones 1.5 miles and 1.7 miles, respectively, beyond the square ruin. The first panel is located high on a narrow ledge, about 30 feet above and 30 feet west of the canyon floor. It contains at least a dozen anthropomorphs as well as birds, animals, and abstract designs, all painted in shades of white, red, brown, and green. Many of the drawings are badly faded, and appear to have been painted many centuries before the more clearly defined ones. Also, many of the more recent drawings are superim-

Pictographs, Lower Grand Gulch

Big Panel pictographs

photo by Michael R. Kelsey

Canyon, a canyon that, as its name suggests, usually contains more water than the Grand Gulch. There is a lot of vegetation in this area and the streambed at the mouth of Water Canyon is only 6 feet wide, so if you are not paying attention it is easy to miss the confluence. Water Canyon is an interesting side canyon, and if you have the time you might want to spend a morning or afternoon exploring it. But I will talk more about that later.

than 3,000 years ago, but, unfortunately, archeologists still have not found a way to accurately date this art.

Just five minutes beyond the Big Panel you will come to a huge alcove on the east side of the canyon that extends for at least 150 yards. This alcove appears to have been an important site for the Anasazis when they lived in the canyon; there are signs of their occupation all along the floor of the alcove. Yet, interestingly, it faces due west, not south, and with the opposite canyon wall directly in front of it it only receives a couple of hours of sunlight in the mid-afternoon of each day. It would not have been a very comfortable location for a permanent settlement. Furthermore, the alcove has been extensively and crudely excavated, probably by one of the Wetherill expeditions in the 1890s. There are long furrows next to great mounds of dirt and rock throughout the alcove. My guess is that this was some kind of burial site for the ancients, and if that is the case the pot hunters must have hit the jackpot in this alcove. How shameful.

Another 0.4 mile beyond the burial alcove the trail passes the mouth of Water

Beyond Water Canyon there are fewer archeological sites in the Grand Gulch, although the canyon itself continues to be very photogenic. Another 1.1 miles will bring you to wide, shallow alcove above a sandy bench on the right side of the canyon. This bench contains another archeological site that was excavated in 1894 during one of the Wetherill expeditions. One of the workers is supposed to have left a dated signature somewhere at this site, but I was not able to find it. There are, however, several small ruins in the alcove.

If the weather is good and there is no flash flood danger, you will find the canyon floor near this ruin an excellent place to camp. There is a 150-foot wide expanse of slickrock in the streambed where you can sleep without getting sand in your sleeping bag, and also there is a semi-permanent pool of water nearby.

Day 2: (6.6 miles)

A good plan for the second day is to leave your backpacks at your campsite and walk 2.5 miles down-canyon to the Shaw Arch and back. There are no more significant Anasazi sites along the way, but the arch itself is exceedingly interesting and well worth the walk. There is some controversy about the Shaw Arch's name. Locals have long called it Grand Arch or Wetherill Arch, after Richard Wetherill who, in the 1890s, was probably the first white man to see it. But the USGS was persuaded to name it Shaw Arch after Merlin Shaw, a Mormon bishop who occasionally brought groups of boy scouts into Grand Gulch before his death in 1963. It is now labeled Shaw Arch on all USGS maps, even though the BLM still refers to it as Grand Arch. I don't know that the arch has ever been accurately measured, but I estimate its span to be about 120 long and 60 feet high. It is an arch, not a natural bridge, that was formed by a collapse in the sandstone wall between the Grand Gulch and one of its tributaries.

It is a shame that we will never know what the prehistoric Anasazis called the arch, because it obviously played an important role in their lives. They left hundreds of their hand prints on the walls on both sides of the arch, as well as petroglyphs on some to the fallen boulders below the opening. There are also several metates on the north side of the arch where Indian women once brought their corn to be ground into flour. Interestingly, one group of handprints on the side of the arch contains only smaller prints made by children perhaps 10-12 years old. It is as if a visit to the arch was somehow considered a rite of passage.

There is an excellent camping area just below the north side of Shaw Arch, and many hikers use this as a staging area for day hikes to Shangrila Canyon or the San Juan River. The river is located 6.7 miles below the arch at the mouth of Grand Gulch. The route is fairly free of obstacles as far as Shangrila Canyon, 3.5 miles below Shaw Arch, but beyond the Shangrila confluence you can expect to encounter at least one formidable obstacle of rockfall in the canyon.

Ruin below Red Man Canyon, Lower Grand Gulch

Shaw Arch

initially very easy; however after just 100 yards you will come to a rockfall where some brief scrambling is required. Before climbing over the rockfall stop and look up to the right. There is a small alcove about 60 feet above the east side of the canyon floor where you can see a few hand prints, a metate, and other signs of early human occupation. Then, immediately after climbing over the rockfall, you will come to a long slickrock bench that runs along the north side of the canyon for about 150 yards. Near the beginning of this bench, just 12 feet above the canyon floor, there is a small but impeccably well preserved panel of interesting petroglyphs.

0.4 mile from the confluence with Grand Gulch you will come to a fork where you must bear left to continue into the upper reaches of Water Canyon. This is a well vegetated area with lots of big cottonwood trees, and except in the very driest years you can always find water here. The area is a nice spot to establish camp before continuing your exploration of Water Canyon.

The good news is that water availability is generally not a problem in the vicinity of the Shangrila confluence. River runners coming down the San Juan frequently camp at the mouth of the Grand Gulch, and occasionally you will see other hikers who have been dropped off by boat at the mouth of canyon.

After returning from Shaw Arch and retrieving your backpacks it will be time to start planning your return journey to the Collins Spring Trailhead. I suggest you finish this day by walking back up the canyon 1.1 miles to Water Canyon, where there are several more points of interest as well as an another excellent campsite.

When you reach the mouth of Water Canyon turn east for the final half mile to the best campsite. Walking into the Water Canyon drainage from Grand Gulch is

Handprints near Shaw Arch

Water Canyon

Day 3: (8 miles)

Just a hundred yards north of your campsite you will encounter a large intimidating rockfall that must be negotiated before further progress up Water Canyon can be made. The rockfall is not insurmountable, but it does require a lot of tedious scrambling across a jumble of cabin-size boulders. There is another way around the rockfall, but most hikers will probably find it even more challenging than the scramble through the boulders. Looking up on the east side of the canyon you will see a long slickrock bench about 15 feet above the canyon floor, and if you can get up to the bench you can bypass the boulders and avoid most of the scrambling. But getting to this bench is not easy. Unless you are a mountain goat, the only way up is to climb a small tree that you will see leaning against the canyon wall 150 feet south of the rockfall. If you are extraordinarily good at climbing trees this 15-foot climb will give you access to the bench.

Just beyond the rockfall the canyon splits again. If you turn right at the fork and continue eastward for another 0.1 mile you will see the remains of what was probably an Anasazi kiva on another sandy bench against the north canyon wall. This D-shaped structure stands in isolation, but there are probably other artifacts elsewhere in the maze of Water canyon and its tributaries.

From the Water Canyon kiva back to Grand Gulch is 1.0 mile, and from there you can retrace your steps the last 6.5 miles back to the Collins Spring Trailhead.

Petroglyphs in Water Canyon

Slickhorn Canyon

★★

shuttle car or bicycle required
day hike

Distance: 10.1 miles (loop)
(plus 4.5 miles by car or bicycle)

Walking time: 7 hours

Elevations: 860 ft. loss, 950 ft. gain
First Fork Trailhead (start): 6,080 ft.
Trail Canyon confluence: 5,220 ft.
Trail Canyon Trailhead: 6,170 ft.

Trail: The trail is very primitive, unmaintained, and poorly marked. Also, there are a few sections near the beginning and end that are steep and rocky. Because of the difficulty of carrying a backpack down the rocky terrain, I recommend that you do this trail as a long day hike rather than an overnighter.

Season: Spring, summer, fall. Spring or fall are the ideal times for this hike. The canyons are very hot in the summer and cold in the winter. The road to the trailheads is unpaved and may be impassable in wet weather, but it is usually okay for most cars.

Vicinity: Near Mexican Hat and Natural Bridges National Monument

Maps: Pollys Pasture *(USGS)*
Grand Gulch Plateau *(Trails Illustrated, #706)*

Information: http://www.utahtrails.com/slickhorn.html *(Utah Trails)*
http://www.blm.gov/utah/monticello/ *(BLM, Monticello)*
phone: (435) 587-1500 *(BLM, Monticello Field Office)*

Drive south from the junction of Highway 261 and Highway 95 (near Natural Bridges National Monument) for 3.9 miles to the Kane Gulch Ranger Station. Continuing south from the ranger station for another 9.6 miles will bring you to a junction where two dirt roads join the paved highway. Turn right (west) here onto County Road 245. 2.6 miles after leaving the highway the road forks, *with the right fork leading to Grand Gulch and the left fork leading to Slickhorn Canyon. Make a note of your odometer reading at this junction and turn left (south). After 1.7 miles you will see the road to the First Fork Trailhead leaving on the right. This 0.4 mile road ends at the top of First Fork, where the hike starts. After 4.5 miles you will pass by the top of Third Fork Canyon, down which another trail leads to Slickhorn Canyon. After 5.8 miles you will come to a corral in the middle of a large meadow on your right. This corral marks the entrance to Trail Canyon, where the hike ends, and you should leave your shuttle car or bicycle here.*

Note: The BLM asks that all hikers in the Grand Gulch area register and obtain permits at the trailheads before entering the canyons. Day hikers will be charged $2.00/day for a permit or $5.00 for a 7-day pass, and backpackers will be charged $5.00/trip. During the peak seasons (March 1–June 15 and September 1–October 31) backpackers will be charged $8.00/trip and must pick up their permits between 8:00 a.m. and noon on the day of entry at the Kane Gulch Ranger Station. Only a limited number of backpacking permits are issued during the peak seasons, so reservations are recommended. Advanced reservations can be obtained by telephone at (435) 587-1510.

Slickhorn Canyon offers an alternative for those who are interested in the Anasazi Ruins of Cedar Mesa but want more solitude than Grand Gulch can offer. The ruins are not as extensive as those in Grand Gulch, but Slickhorn does have one bonus: an almost perfectly preserved kiva with the original roof still completely intact. The BLM has even provided a replica of an Anasazi ladder to give hikers access to the subterranean room through the opening in the roof. Also, the Slickhorn ruins do not appear to have been ravaged by Richard Wetherill and the other pot hunters of the late 1800s who excavated so many of the Grand Gulch ruins. Perhaps they didn't know about Slickhorn Canyon.

Like the Grand Gulch, Slickhorn Canyon runs in a southwesterly direction from the edge of Cedar Mesa to the San Juan River. There are a number of side canyons that join the main canyon from the east side, and it is through three of these side canyons, First Fork, Third Fork, and Trail Canyon, that most hikers find access to Slickhorn. The hike described here is a loop between First Fork and Trail Canyon.

From the parking area at the top of First Fork, begin by walking down the bottom of the drainage in a southwesterly direc-

tion. There are no signs and no maintained trail, but enough hikers use this route that a primitive trail is beginning to form. After a fifteen minute walk you will come to a small pouroff that you can easily get around by detouring a short distance into a shallow side canyon on the left. Another mile down-canyon will bring you to a much larger

Balanced Rock above the First Fork of Slickhorn

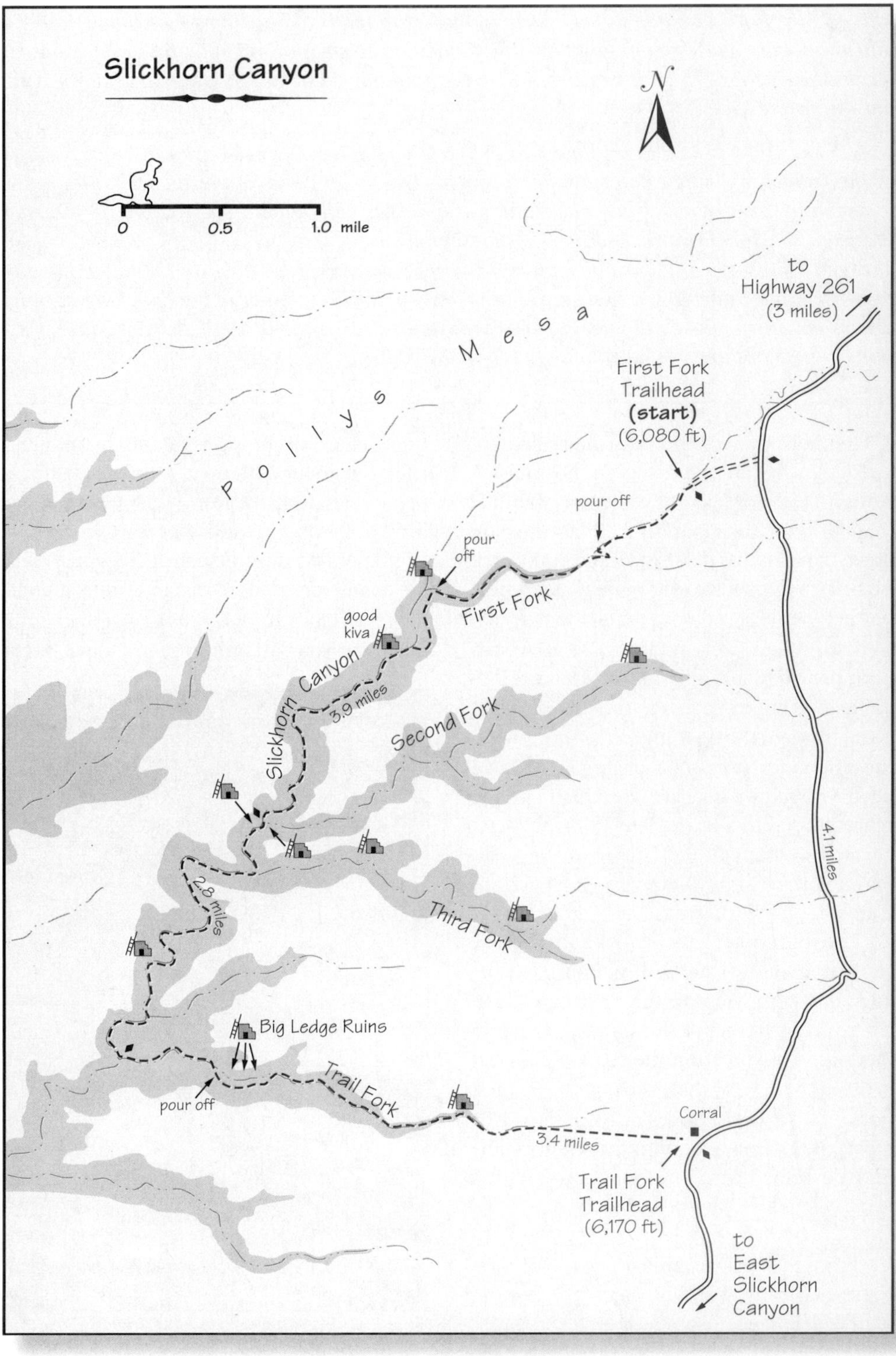

Slickhorn Canyon

0   0.5   1.0 mile

N

P o l l y s   M e s a

to
Highway 261
(3 miles)

First Fork
Trailhead
(start)
(6,080 ft)

pour off

pour
off

First Fork

good
kiva

Slickhorn Canyon

3.9 miles

Second Fork

2.8 miles

Third Fork

4.1 miles

Big Ledge Ruins

pour off

Trail Fork

Corral

3.4 miles

Trail Fork
Trailhead
(6,170 ft)

to
East
Slickhorn
Canyon

Entrance to the perfect kiva in Slickhorn Canyon

walk downstream for five minutes until you see a faint trail leading up to the alcove on the right. The ruin is not visible from the bottom, and there are very few cairns marking the assent; some scrambling is necessary but the climb is not difficult. You will certainly want to spend some time checking out this ruin as it is the one that contains the well preserved kiva mentioned earlier.

The Anasazi kivas are of special interest to anthropologists who study Indian cultures of the Southwest. Every Anasazi community seems to have had one of them, and the basic architecture has endured for centuries. Kiva-like structures have been around for at least 1300 years, and they still exist today in a few modern Indian cultures. The kiva in Slickhorn Canyon, though at least 700 years old, is almost identical to a modern Hopi kiva. Notice, for instance, the small hole in the center of the floor. Similar holes appear in

pouroff that cannot be dealt with so easily. This time you will have to climb up the south side of the canyon to a bench just below the top of the mesa that you can follow around the obstacle. Many hikers before you have taken this route, so look for the cairns they have left behind to guide you.

While you are on the bench be sure to look north into the short side canyon on the opposite side of First Fork; there is a small ruin near the top of the canyon wall. Also, take note of the large precariously balanced boulder that sits atop a pinnacle on the opposite side of the main canyon about 500 yards down-canyon from the pouroff. This balanced rock is approximately opposite the point where the trail again descends to the canyon floor.

The balanced boulder will also help you find your second ruin. Look carefully at the opposite canyon wall about 200 yards down-canyon from the balanced rock and you will see a large alcove half way up the side of the canyon wall. The ruin is in the back of this alcove. Once you reach the canyon floor

Slickhorn Canyon Trail

the seventh century pithouse kivas of Mesa Verde, as well as in present-day Hopi kivas. The Hopis, who call the hole a sipapu, or spirit hole, believe it is an entrance to the underworld. They believe that their ancestors entered and exited our world through a sipapu.

Below First Fork the trail through Slickhorn Canyon becomes much less rocky, and after 1.6 miles it opens up into a large, sandy meadow where it meets Second Fork, another canyon coming in from the left. There are two other ruins near the canyon floor at this confluence. The one on the west side of the canyon, a small granary, is particularly well preserved. 0.4 mile further downstream will bring you to the confluence with Third Fork. If you are interested in shortening your hike you can return to the top of the mesa through Third Fork. Doing this will shorten the hike by 2.0 trail miles and 1.3 road miles.

From the confluence with Third Fork, it is 2.4 miles of easy walking to Trail Canyon. Along the way you will pass at least one other ruin on the west side of the canyon and one other major side canyon coming in from the east. There are no signs, so be sure you turn into Trail Canyon and not the one before or after it. Just remember that Trail Canyon will be the fourth major side canyon you encounter coming into Slickhorn Canyon from the east.

About 0.6 mile up Trail Canyon there is another pouroff that must be detoured. If you see the pour off you have probably missed the way, and you will have to backtrack a short distance downstream to find a faint trail that climbs 100 feet up the south side of the canyon in order to get around the obstacle. Again, the way is marked by small cairns. As you pass above the pour off look across to the other side of the canyon at three small ruins perched precariously on a long, narrow ledge. These are the Big Ledge Ruins. Two of them look particularly interesting because they are build primarily of juniper logs rather than stone. What a chore it must have been to chop down all of those logs with stone tools and haul them to the high canyon ledge.

After the Big Ledge Ruins the trail again becomes very rocky as it climbs upward toward the mesa top. Occasional minor scrambling may be necessary, and if you are carrying a bulky backpack you will wish you weren't. Finally, after two miles, the trail breaks over the top of the rim into a large flat meadow of sagebrush. Continue walking eastward across the meadow and soon you will spot the corral where your shuttle car or bicycle is parked.

Granary in Slickhorn Canyon

Owl and Fish Creek Canyons

★★★   **overnight hike**

Distance:	16.1 miles (loop)
Walking time:	day 1: 6 hours day 2: 5 hours
Elevations:	1,340 ft. loss/gain Owl and Fish Creek Trailhead (start): 6,180 ft. Owl and Fish Creek Confluence: 4,840 ft.
Trail:	The trail is primitive and unmaintained, but it is well marked with rock cairns and easy to follow. Getting in and out of the canyons can be tricky, especially with a heavy pack. A twenty-foot piece of rope is useful for lowering backpacks down one small ledge at the top of Fish Creek Canyon.
Season:	Spring, summer, fall. Spring or fall are the ideal times for this hike. The canyons are very hot in the summer and cold in the winter. The road to the trailhead is unpaved for the last five miles and may be impassable in wet weather, but it is usually okay for most cars.
Vicinity:	Near Mexican Hat and Natural Bridges National Monument
Maps:	Snow Flat Spring, Bluff NW (USGS) Grand Gulch Plateau (Trails Illustrated, #706)
Information:	http://www.utahtrails.com/owl.html (Utah Trails) http://www.blm.gov/utah/monticello/ (BLM, Monticello) phone: (435) 587-1500 (BLM, Monticello Field Office)

Drive south from the junction of Highway 261 and Highway 95 (near Natural Bridges National Monument) for 3.9 miles to the Kane Gulch Ranger Station. Continue south from the ranger station on Highway 261 for another 1.1 miles where you will see a graded road leaving the pavement on the left. Turn here and drive another 5.3 miles to the Owl and Fish Creek Trailhead and parking area.

Note: The BLM asks that all hikers in the Grand Gulch area register and obtain permits at the trailheads before entering the canyons. Day hikers will be charged $2.00/day for a permit or $5.00 for a 7-day pass, and backpackers will be charged $5.00/trip. During

the peak seasons (March 1–June 15 and September 1–October 31) backpackers will be charged $8.00/trip and must pick up their permits between 8:00 a.m. and noon on the day of entry at the Kane Gulch Ranger Station. Only a limited number of backpacking permits are issued during the peak seasons, so reservations are recommended. Advanced reservations can be obtained by telephone at (435) 587-1510.

Southeastern Utah has one of the largest concentrations of Anasazi Indian ruins in the United States, and the area around Owl Creek and Fish Creek is one of the best places to see them. Most of the ruins in these two canyons are, unfortunately, located high on the cliffs in inaccessible alcoves. They are not generally obvious to the casual observer, and many hikers complete the loop having seen only one or two ruins.

You will have better luck in finding the Anasazi ruins if you know where to look. First, bear in mind that these canyons are cold in the wintertime, and the inhabitants preferred to build their homes where they could get as much winter sunshine as possible. That means on the south facing or north sides of the canyons. Rarely will you see a ruin on the south side of a canyon. Second, the Indians tended to live as close as possible to the land they were farming; consequently there are more ruins in those areas where the canyon bottom is wide and flat. In places where the canyon bottom is too narrow or rocky the Indians farmed above the rim, and in those locations the ruins are usually nearer to the top. When looking for cliff dwellings it helps to have a small pair of lightweight binoculars. I spotted seven ruin sites the first time I walked this loop, but two or three of them would have been impossible to identify without binoculars.

Indian ruins are not the only attraction this hike has. There is also plenty of inter-

Anasazi granary near confluence of Owl and Fish Creek Canyons

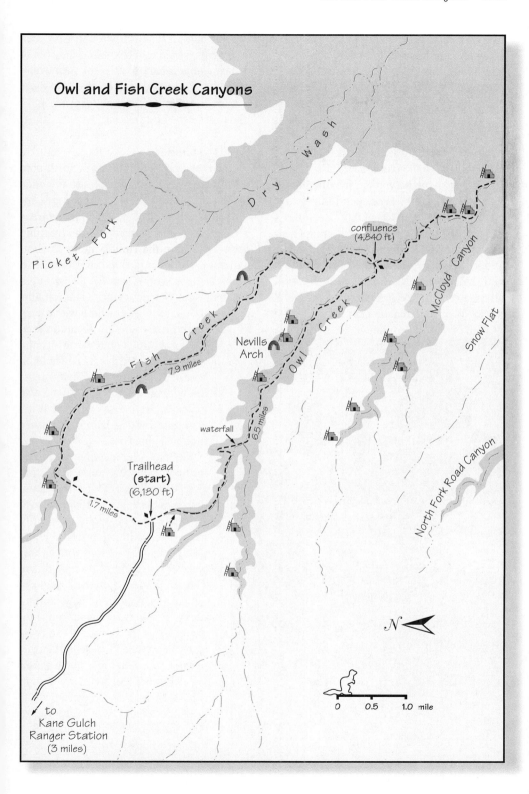

Owl and Fish Creek Canyons

Dry Wash

Picket Fork

Fish Creek

7.9 miles

Nevills Arch

Owl Creek

6.5 miles

confluence (4,840 ft)

McCloyd Canyon

Snow Flat

waterfall

Trailhead
(start)
(6,180 ft)

1.7 miles

North Fork Road Canyon

N

0   0.5   1.0 mile

to
Kane Gulch
Ranger Station
(3 miles)

esting scenery–especially in Owl Creek Canyon. The reddish colored Cedar Mesa Sandstone has been carved into an eye-catching display of pinnacles and spires and at least three natural arches. Neville Arch, about half way up Owl Creek Canyon, is particularly impressive. There are also a number of fine camp sites in both canyons–especially near the confluence.

The loop can be walked in either direction. The rangers recommend that hikers go down Owl Creek Canyon first, primarily because the trail down from the rim of Fish Creek Canyon is rather steep and rocky, and it is easier to climb out of that canyon with a pack than to climb into it. Personally, however, I feel it is better to begin at the top of Fish Creek and exit through Owl

Trail through Owl Creek Canyon

Creek Canyon. The trail along Fish Creek is sometimes vague, and when coming out of that canyon it is easy to miss the turn where the route leaves the streambed. Also there is more to see in Owl Creek Canyon, and I like to save the best for last.

Day 1: (9.6 miles)

From the parking area walk north on a well-trodden path for 1.7 miles to the edge of Fish Creek Canyon. The canyon rim, incidentally, is a good place to camp if you are getting off to a late start. Before dropping below the rim look carefully along the bottom of the cliffs on the opposite side of Fish Creek Canyon, and if you have sharp eyes you may spot your first ruin. The remains of a small, square stone dwelling with a door on the right side are located there. The structure is quite far away, and with the unaided eye it is difficult to positively identify it as man-made. But with binoculars you will be able to see the telltale pattern of brick work and the log beams that once supported the roof.

Shortly after leaving the rim the trail comes to a ten-foot ledge that can be troublesome getting down with a backpack. The best way to negotiate this obstacle, especially if you are hiking alone, is to lower your pack to the bottom with a short piece of rope before climbing down. The remainder of the trail down to the canyon floor is quite steep and rocky, but it is well marked with stone cairns. Take care not to twist an ankle. Once you reach the canyon floor the walking is much easier.

There are not as many Indian ruins in upper Fish Creek Canyon as there are along Owl Creek; hence the 7.9 mile walk down Fish Creek to the confluence with Owl Creek is

Neville Arch

rather uneventful. I was only able to see one other cliff dwelling along this section of the hike. The canyon is quite rugged, however, and there is some interesting scenery. There are also at least two unnamed natural arches in upper Fish Creek Canyon, but unless you watch the canyon walls carefully you may not see both of them. As you approach the confluence the canyon widens, the juniper forest thins out, and more cottonwood trees can be seen. The best camp sites are in the immediate vicinity of the confluence.

If you have time after pitching camp you may want to leave your pack behind and continue down into lower Fish Creek Canyon for a few miles. The canyon floor is wide and flat in this area and the walking is fast and easy along a good trail. There are a lot of ruins in lower Fish Creek, some of them quite well preserved and easy to get to. This area was probably extensively farmed by the Anasazis.

The first ruin in lower Fish Creek Canyon is located just above the confluence with McCloyd Canyon, about a half-hour walk from Owl Creek. Look to the left as the trail crosses a grassy meadow under a large, partially fallen cottonwood tree. It is not too difficult to climb up to this ruin, and a few pottery shards are still visible near it. Please don't remove anything, however. Such artifacts have far more meaning if they are seen in the wild where their original owners left them than they could ever have in your private collection. There are several other ruins in lower Fish Creek Canyon and also in McCloyd Canyon; you may want to spend an extra day in the area to examine them.

Day 2: (6.5 miles)

Today will be spent climbing out of Owl Creek Canyon. The first half of the trail is flat and easy, through an area that was undoubtedly farmed by the Anasazis. Again, the canyon walls have been carved into an impressive array of columns and monoliths that stand like sentinels above the canyon. The most impressive geologic formation, however, is Neville Arch, located 2.0 miles above the confluence. This huge arch, high on the canyon's north side, would be impressive in any setting, but seeing it in the wilderness of Owl Creek Canyon is especially memorable. There are at least three Anasazi cliff dwellings within a half-mile of the arch, and its presence surely played an important role in their lives. It is a pity that today we know nothing of what the arch meant to the canyon people, or even what they called it.

Soon after Neville Arch the canyon narrows, and the trail passes several small waterfalls as it slowly winds its way upward. There is usually not enough water in Owl Creek to present much of a spectacle at the falls, but they generally have at least a little water flowing over them. Two of the falls have fine swimming holes at the bottom— clear pools of water that have probably been a child's delight for thousands of years. The last fall, located about 2.1 miles from the arch, effectively blocks the canyon floor, forcing the trail to make a 0.4-mile detour into a side canyon to get around it.

Finally, as the trail climbs out onto the rim of Owl Creek Canyon it passes a hidden cliff dwelling with an exceptionally well preserved kiva as its centerpiece. Before 2006 the trail passed close by the ruin, but rock slides caused by heavy rains in that year forced the BLM to reroute the trail, and now this interesting archeological site is seldom seen. Look for it in a deep alcove just below the rim on the opposite side of the small side canyon where the trail makes its exit. The ruin is well protected from the wind and the rain, but it must have been bitter cold there in the winter as little sun ever reaches the alcove. Perhaps the Indians had their winter living quarters elsewhere and used this site primarily for grain storage and religious activities.

When you reach the rim you will find a good trail that continues in a northerly direction for another 0.3 mile to the parking lot where the hike ends.

Anasazi Kiva near where the trail exits Owl Creek Canyon

Road Canyon

★★★★   **day hike**

Distance:	11.4 miles (round trip)
Walking time:	6 ³/₄ hours
Elevations:	900 ft. loss/gain Road Canyon Trailhead (start): 6,305 ft. Seven Kivas Ruin: 5,440 ft.
Trail:	This rocky, unimproved trail is often mildly confusing, but the route is easy to follow. Most of the time you will be walking in the bottom of a dry, sandy wash. There is usually at least some water in isolated pools, but it must be treated before drinking.
Season:	Spring, summer, fall. Spring or fall are the ideal times for this hike. The canyons are very hot in the summer and cold in the winter. The road to the trailhead is unpaved for the last 3.5 miles and may be impassable in wet weather, but it is usually okay for most cars.
Vicinity:	Near Mexican Hat and Natural Bridges National Monument
Maps:	Cedar Mesa North, Snow Flat Spring *(USGS)* Grand Gulch Plateau *(Trails Illustrated, #706)*
Information:	http://www.utahtrails.com/roadcanyon.html *(Utah Trails)* http://www.blm.gov/utah/monticello/ *(BLM, Monticello)* phone: (435) 587-1500 *(BLM, Monticello Field Office)*

Drive south from the junction of Highway 261 and Highway 95 (near Natural Bridges National Monument) for 3.9 miles to the Kane Gulch Ranger Station. Continuing south from the ranger station for another 9.7 miles will bring you to a junction where you must turn left onto the road marked "Cigarette Spring". After 1.0 mile you will come to an unlocked wire gate where there is *an information board and trail register. Be sure to close the gate behind you and continue driving east on the Cigarette Spring Road for another 2.5 miles. Immediately after passing another road on the right you will see a spur leading to a parking area on the left. The trail begins on the northeast side of the parking area. (If you come to another gate on the Cigarette Spring Road you have driven 0.3 mile too far.)*

The BLM asks that all hikers in the Grand Gulch area register and obtain permits at the *trailheads before entering the canyons. Day hikers will be charged $2.00/day for a permit or $5.00 for a 7-day pass, and backpackers will be charged $5.00/trip. During the peak seasons (March 1–June 15 and September 1–October 31) backpackers will be charged $8.00/trip and must pick up their permits between 8:00 a.m. and noon on the day of entry at the Kane Gulch Ranger Station. Only a limited number of backpacking permits are issued during the peak seasons, so reservations are recommended. Advanced reservations can be obtained by telephone at (435) 587-1510*

Backcountry hikers can expect to find many surprises in southern Utah's redrock canyons, but few of them are as exciting as a close encounter with a 700-year-old cliff dwelling. The four corners area of Utah, Colorado, Arizona, and New Mexico contains literally thousands of dwellings and other structures that were left behind by the prehistoric Anasazi Indians; there were probably more people living in this region in the 1200s than there are today. The most famous Anasazi ruins are located at Mesa Verde National Park in Colorado, but for sheer numbers, Utah takes the prize. There are many more Anasazi archeological sites in southeastern Utah than in any of the other adjacent states.

Utah's Anasazi sites are scattered over a wide area that extends all the way from Green River to the Arizona border, but the very best place to see them is on the Grand Gulch Plateau. Here the forces of nature have carved dozens of meandering canyons into the Cedar Mesa Sandstone where water is at least sporadically available. The soil is fertile, the winters are relatively mild, and there are many deep alcoves in the sandstone walls of the canyons that provided shelter for the prehistoric Indians. The Anasazis found the canyons eminently suitable for their way of life, and today virtually every canyon on the Grand Gulch Plateau contains the remains of their stone and mud dwellings.

Grand Gulch itself is the longest and best-known canyon on the Grand Gulch Plateau, and there are several interesting hiking opportunities in Grand Gulch. But many lesser-known canyons in the area also have a great deal to offer. If you are looking for some interesting Anasazi ruins in a canyon that also offers a degree of solitude then Road Canyon would be a good choice. The trail into Road Canyon is more primitive and much less traveled, but there are at least four well preserved ruins sites in the canyon and several others in varying stages of decay.

From the parking area a well-defined trail heads out through the juniper trees for a distance of 0.4 mile before

Fallen Roof Ruin in Road Canyon

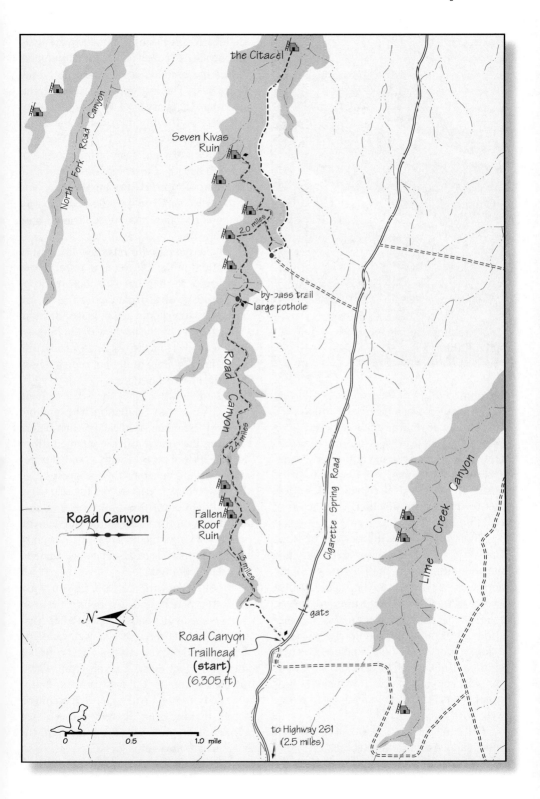

the Citadel

Seven Kivas
Ruin

North Fork Road Canyon

2.0 miles

by-pass trail
large pothole

Road Canyon

2.4 miles

Fallen
Roof
Ruin

1.3 miles

Cigarette Spring Road

Lime Creek Canyon

Road Canyon

N

gate

Road Canyon
Trailhead
(start)
(6,305 ft)

to Highway 261
(2.5 miles)

0   0.5   1.0 mile

Road Canyon

are located. A faint hiker-made trail along this bench, 150 feet above the streambed, passes the remains of at least three other structures. The last one is particularly interesting. It consists of two major rooms that were built using the "wattle and daub" method of plastering mud over a framework of sticks and twigs. One of the rooms appears to have had a secret compartment in the floor. Looking through the door you will see two small cubbyholes near the wall that look like they were once covered with slabs of rock.

The easiest way to return to the trail in the bottom of the canyon is to retrace your steps back to the first ruin before dropping back to the streambed. If you are observant you should see at least one more small granary on the north wall ten minutes down-canyon from the wattle and daub ruin. There are probably more, but they may not be visible from the trail.

3.1 miles after entering Road Canyon you will come to a junction with another major side canyon on the left. Just before reaching the junction the streambed drops down a 20-foot pouroff with a pool of water at the bottom; hence further progress along the canyon floor is impossible. In order to get around the pouroff the trail climbs 30 feet to a bench on the south side of the canyon and follows it for the next 0.3 mile to a point where it is possible to descend once again to the canyon bottom.

Look across the canyon as you walk along the bench, and just before the trail starts back down you will see another Anasazi dwelling at about the same elevation on the north side of the canyon. The ruin lies about 200 feet down-canyon from where the trail descends to the streambed, and if you study the opposite side of the canyon before making your descent you will see a hiker-made trail switchbacking up to the ledge where the ruin is located.

1.5 miles below the point where the trail

coming to the west end of Road Canyon. The trail then turns north and follows the rim of the canyon for a few hundred yards before starting down. After dropping 120 feet you will arrive at the bottom of a small side canyon that joins Road Canyon from the north. Walk down the tributary just a few feet to the canyon junction, and then turn east into Road Canyon.

The trail follows the bottom of Road Canyon for 0.7 mile before arriving below the first ruins in a small alcove near the northern rim of the canyon. These ruins, known as the Fallen Roof Ruins, are easy to see from the trail, and it is an easy 150-foot climb up from the canyon floor if you want a closer look. This site contains the best preserved of any of the ancient structures you will see on this hike. It includes four small rooms, three of which look like they were built only yesterday.

Before climbing back down to the trail you should walk east for another 250 yards along the bench where the Fallen Roof Ruins

returns to the streambed you will see another large side canyon entering from the north. Several large south-facing alcoves are visible in the northern canyon. At least one of the alcoves is supposed to contain another ruin, but I have not personally confirmed this.

The Seven Kivas Ruin is located just 0.2 mile beyond the last side canyon. This site is situated on a pile of rubble just 20 feet above the streambed in a large south-facing alcove. The site is about 150 feet long by about 30 feet wide and, as the name suggests, is the location of several kivas. The soil in this area is very sandy; hence the mortar that was used in the construction of the kivas is of very poor quality. Most of it has washed away over the centuries, leaving the walls of the structures in a sad state of decay. Two of the kivas still have intact roofs, but even those look as if they could cave in at any time. In one of them the BLM has inserted a support pillar to shore up the 700-year-old roof timbers.

Another option for the return journey to your car is to climb out the south side of Road Canyon and walk back along the Cigarette Spring Road to the beginning trailhead. 0.8 mile upcanyon from the Seven Kivas you will pass a primitive cairned trail that climbs out through a short side canyon to the south rim of Road Canyon. The trail ends at a stock pond, and from there a jeep road heads south for another 0.7 mile to the Cigarette Spring Road. When you reach Cigarette Spring Road turn west for the last 2.6 miles of road walking to your car.

When you reach the stock pond you might notice that there is yet another cairned trail that heads east along the south rim of Road Canyon. This is the trail to the Citadel, an extremely well preserved Anasazi ruin on the rim of the canyon 2.0 miles from the stock pond. The unique ruin is situated on the eastern end of a long, narrow peninsula of sandstone that protrudes eastward between Road Canyon and another one of its tributaries. The Citadel is definitely worth a visit if you have the time.

Seven Kivas Ruin

Mule Canyon

★★★   **day hike**

Distance: 9.0 miles (round trip)

Walking time: 5 hours

Elevations: 420 ft. gain/loss
Mule Canyon Trailhead (start): 5,980 ft.
Upper Mule Canyon: 6,400 ft.

Trail: There is an unmaintained trail throughout most of Mule Canyon. Very little scrambling is required and the brush is minimal, but you should wear wettable footwear as it is frequently necessary to cross the stream bed.

Season: Spring, summer, fall. The canyon is quite hot in midsummer and cold in winter.

Vicinity: Near Mexican Hat and Natural Bridges National Monument

Maps: Hotel Rock, South Long Point *(USGS)*
Grand Gulch Plateau *(Trails Illustrated, #706)*

Information: http://www.utahtrails.com/mule.html *(Utah Trails)*
http://www.blm.gov/utah/monticello/ *(BLM, Monticello)*
phone: (435) 587-1500 *(BLM, Monticello Field Office)*

Drive east on Highway 95 from the junction with Highway 261. After 8.6 miles you will pass the turnoff to Mule Canyon Roadside Ruins, and 0.5 mile later you will see a gravel road on the north side of the highway leading to Texas Flat. Turn left here and drive for 0.3 mile to the point where the Texas Flat road crosses Mule Canyon. You should see a sign marking the trailhead below the left side of the road as you climb up the northeast side of the canyon.

Note: The BLM asks that all hikers in the Grand Gulch area register and obtain permits at the trailheads before entering the canyons. Day hikers will be charged $2.00/day for a permit or $5.00 for a 7-day pass, and backpackers will be charged $5.00/trip. During the peak seasons (March 1–June 15 and September 1–October 31) backpackers will be charged $8.00/trip and must pick up their permits between 8:00 a.m. and noon on the day of entry at the Kane Gulch Ranger Station. Only a limited number of backpacking permits are issued during the peak seasons, so reservations are recommended. Advanced reservations can be obtained by telephone at (435) 587-1510.

The Anasazis occupied this area for about 550 years between 750 and 1300 A.D. They appear to have been a peaceful people who farmed the canyon lands throughout the four corners area, and judging from the number of archeological sites they left behind their population was substantial. In the last half of the thirteenth century the Anasazi people began to leave places like Mule Canyon, and by 1300 their communities had been completely abandoned. Why? A long drought that plagued the southwest between 1276 and 1299 was undoubtedly a major factor. Some archeologist believe another factor was the southern migration of Navajos and other nomadic tribes that came into the region at about that time.

The ruins you will see in Mule Canyon are between seven and nine hundred years old. They are not part of any national park, monument, or wilderness area, and they have never been excavated or restored in any way.

The opportunity to discover these ruins in this wild setting, with no rangers around telling you how to behave, is what makes Mule Canyon such an exciting place. But with that freedom comes great responsibility. The ruins are a precious national treasure and should be treated as such. View them with awe, but please do not deface them in any way, and do not steal any of the pottery shards or other artifacts you may find around them. Help preserve them so that others may also experience the magic of the canyon.

At the point where the trail enters Mule Canyon, the rim is only about 60 feet above the creek bed. The surrounding pinion-juniper forest is typical of the environment where Indian ruins are often found, but initially no ruins are evident. As you walk up the canyon it will begin to deepen, and you will notice occasional alcoves that have been eroded under the sandstone cliffs. These alcoves

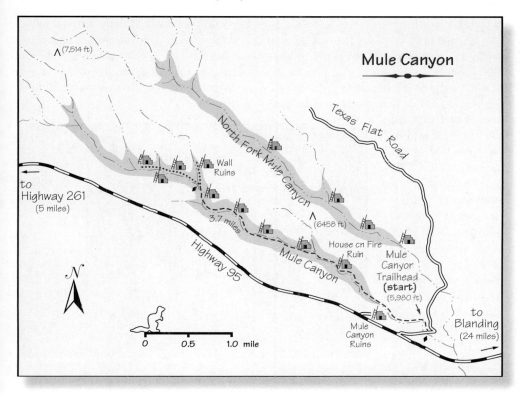

are the kinds of places often chosen by the Anasazis for their homes. Pay particular attention to the north side of the canyon as you proceed. The ancient Indians preferred to live on the north side because it receives more sun during the winter.

Finally, after walking 0.9 mile to a point where the canyon makes a short turn from west to north you should see your first ruin. It is only 100 feet from the north side of the trail, but it is partially hidden by the trees and easy to miss. This ruin consists of about 5 rooms, some of which are very well preserved. It is sometimes called the House on Fire Ruin because reflected sunlight illuminating the vertical fractures in the roof of the alcove remind some people of flames.

Another 1.0 mile up the canyon will bring you to the second ruin, a small structure with two walls and a window in a shallow alcove high on the north side of the canyon. You will come to it a short distance after passing a minor side canyon that comes in from the north.

Over the next 1.4 miles the trail passes beneath 3 more ruins as the forest gradually changes from pinion and juniper to ponderosa pine. The last ruin is located 200 feet above the east side of the canyon, just beyond another small side canyon that joins the west side of the main canyon. This ruin looks quite unimpressive from below, but if you will take the trouble to climb up for a closer look you will find it to be more extensive than expected. It also contains a small panel of petroglyphs.

The area below this ruin is a good place to camp if that is your intention. The canyon floor is wide and flat here, and the ground is shaded by on open forest of ponderosa pine. Also, there is usually plenty of water nearby.

0.2 mile more will bring you to another side canyon on the north side of the main canyon. Walk a short distance up this tributary and you will see what, in my opinion, are the most interesting ruins on this hike. There is a semi-permanent spring in the back of a shallow alcove on the west side of the short canyon, and directly across from the spring are a series of ancient dwellings known as the Wall Ruins. They are so named because some of the dwellings were constructed by building walls across the openings of caves in the cliff face. Two logs that protrude from one of the walls were possibly used by the Anasazis to anchor the ladders they needed to access the higher rooms.

There are at least two additional ruins within another mile up Mule Canyon, but beyond that I doubt if there are any more. Although Mule Canyon continues on for another three miles before arriving at the top of the rim, the higher reaches of the canyon were probably too cold for permanent Indian settlements.

House on Fire Ruin in Mule Canyon

Butler Wash

Distance:	Fishmouth Cave:	1.8 miles (round trip)
	Cold Springs Ruins:	1.8 miles (round trip)
	Monarch Cave Ruins:	1.5 miles (round trip)
	Wolfman Petroglyphs:	1.0 mile (round trip)
Walking time:	Fishmouth Cave:	1 hour
	Cold Springs Ruins:	1 hour
	Monarch Cave Ruins:	3/4 hour
	Wolfman Petroglyphs:	1/2 hour
Elevations:	700 ft. loss/gain (total for all 4 hikes)	
	Fishmouth Trailhead (start)	4,820 ft.
	Fishmouth Cave:	5,200 ft.
	Cold Springs Ruins:	4,760 ft.
	Monarch Cave Ruins:	4,750 ft.
	Wolfman Petroglyphs:	4,400 ft.

Trail: The trails from Butler Wash Road to these ruins are not maintained by the BLM, but they are all generally east to follow.

Season: Year round travel is possible, but these trails are very hot in the summer. Carry plenty of water

Vicinity: Near Blanding and Natural Bridges National Monument

Maps: Bluff NW, Bluff SW *(USGS)*

Information: http://www.utahtrails.com/butlerwash.html *(Utah Trails)*
http://www.blm.gov/utah/monticello/ *(BLM, Monticello)*
phone: (435) 587-1500 *(BLM, Monticello Field Office)*

Drive south from Blanding on Highway 191 for 4 miles to the junction with Highway 95. When you reach Highway 95 turn right, make a note of your mileage, and drive west toward Hanksville. 9.5 miles after leaving Highway 191 you will come to an unmarked graded dirt road on the left. This is San Juan County Road 262, also known as the Butler Wash Road, and all four of the following hiking trails are located along this road. The road can usually be driven by most passenger cars, although dry sand in the road can sometimes present a problem if it hasn't rained in a while. You can usually get better traction in the sand by letting some air

out of your tires (if you have a way of pumping them back up when you get back on solid ground). Butler Wash itself is generally dry except in early spring; however if you plan to camp in the wash be aware of the possibility of flash floods after a heavy rain.

B utler Wash is a shallow desert arroyo that runs for some 25 miles along the east side of a well known geologic monocline in Southern Utah called Comb Ridge. The wash ultimately drains into the San Juan River just south of Bluff, but the adjacent ridge continues on for another 100 miles, finally ending in the Navajo Reservation near Kayenta, Arizona. Comb Ridge is surrounded by desert, and water is a scarce commodity in the area. But the Navajo Sandstone that caps the desert ridge has given rise to hundreds of springs and seeps. Navajo Sandstone is not as dense as most other types of sandstone, and the microscopic spaces in the seemingly solid stone can store water that sometimes exits in the form of a spring at the base of the formation. Needless to say, these sources of water are an important part of the area's ecology.

A thousand years ago the water sources along the flanks of Comb Ridge attracted many Native Americans into the area, and some remnants of their ancient communities can still be seen today. Indian ruins left behind by the Anasazis 700 years ago can be found along the entire length of the Comb Ridge, but the area along Butler Wash is a particularly good place to see them. There are a number of sites in the canyons between Comb Ridge and Butler Wash that are relatively easily accessible from the Butler Wash Road; I will describe four short trails here that lead to some of the better known ones.

Fishmouth Cave (1.8 miles round trip)

Drive south from Highway 95 on the Butler Wash Road for 8.5 miles. There, 40 feet beyond a wire fence that crosses the road, you will come to a turnoff on the right that leads to the Fishmouth Cave Trailhead. Turn right at the turnoff and proceed the last 0.2

Fishmouth Cave

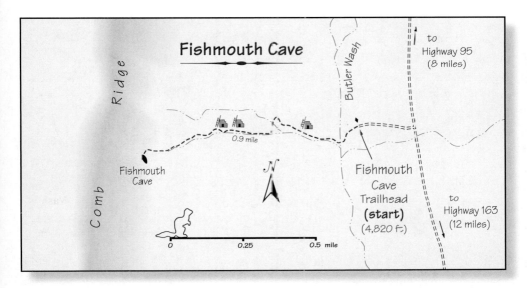

Fishmouth Cave

0.9 mile

Ridge

Butler Wash

to Highway 95 (8 miles)

Comb

Fishmouth Cave

Fishmouth Cave Trailhead **(start)** (4,820 ft)

to Highway 163 (12 miles)

N

0   0.25   0.5 mile

mile to the parking area and trailhead. Note the prolific growth of tumble weeds around Butler Wash. I definitely recommend long pants when hiking in this area if you want to avoid scratching your legs. Mosquitoes can also be a problem, especially in the spring before all of the water has dried up.

Fishmouth Cave is clearly visible from the parking area. Comb Ridge lies about a mile to the west, and halfway up the slick-rock ridge your eyes will be drawn to the prominent oval-shaped opening that defines the cave. It is obvious from this perspective that a bit of a scrambling will be required to reach the cave's entrance, but the elevation gain from the trailhead to Fishmouth is only 400 feet.

Initially the trail is just a continuation of the jeep road that leads to the trailhead. From the parking area the road proceeds past a BLM trail marker and swings to the left as it descends to the bottom of Butler Wash. Within 150 yards you will reach the bottom of the wash and cross into Fishmouth Wash, another minor tributary that continues on

in a westerly direction. The trail follows the smaller drainage for another 200 yards before climbing out the right side of the gully to the first ruins site. These first ruins are located at the base of a sandstone outcropping just above the north side of the wash. There are no intact structures here, just four or five broken walls that extend about five feet out from the sandstone cliff. They are, however, a precursor of what lies ahead.

Upon leaving the first ruins the trail meanders briefly before dropping back to

Ancient handprints in Fishmouth Cave

Fishmouth Ruin

the bottom of Fishmouth Wash. There are a number of cow trails in the area and there may be some confusion, so be careful not to get onto a trail that takes you too far to the north. There is a fence a few hundred feet north of Fishmouth Wash, and if you cross this fence you are on the wrong trail. Finally, 0.3 mile after leaving the first set of ruins the trail passes the second ruins site. These ruins are located in a large south-facing alcove on the north side of Fishmouth Wash. The alcove contains the ruins of at least a dozen dwellings and granaries, two of which are still in excellent condition.

Continuing up the trail for another 100 yards will bring you the another large alcove on the right side of the wash with yet another impressive collection of ruins inside. Note the fine quality of the stone work at this site. The person who built the structure on the west end of the alcove was a true craftsman; you can still see the peck marks where the stones of his walls were carefully shaped to perfection–without any metal tools! This alcove also affords a fine view of the open Fishmouth a third of a mile away.

The trail through the bottom of Fishmouth Wash continues westward from the last ruins site for another 0.2 mile before beginning the final scramble up to the mouth of the cave. There is not much of a trail for the last 150 yards of the climb, but the route is obvious and the scramble is not particularly difficult. Near the top you may notice the fallen remains of a granary, and there are a few handprints in the back of the cave. But the deep depression does not appear to have been permanently occupied.

Cold Springs Ruins (1.8 miles round trip)

The turnoff to the Cold Springs trailhead is located 5.1 miles south of the Fishmouth Cave turnoff or 13.6 miles south of Highway 95 on the Butler Wash Road (County Road 262). Note that County Road 230 departs from Road 262 at a junction 2.6 miles from the Fishmouth Cave turnout, and then rejoins 262 again 1.7 miles later. Be sure to bear

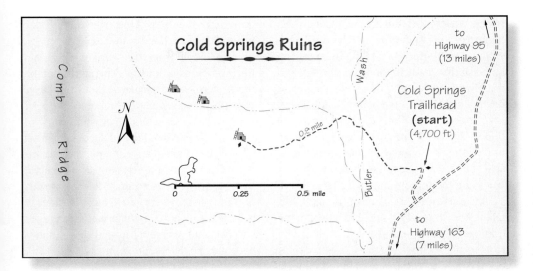

Cold Springs Ruins

Comb Ridge

N

to
Highway 95
(13 miles)

Wash

Cold Springs
Trailhead
(start)
(4,700 ft)

0.2 mile

Butler

0   0.25   0.5 mile

to
Highway 163
(7 miles)

right at each junction in order to stay on County Road 262. When you reach the Cold Springs turnoff turn right and drive the last 200 yards to the trailhead and parking area.

Although the BLM has erected a barricade to prevent vehicles from driving beyond the parking area, the jeep road to the trailhead actually continues in a west-erly direction for another 0.2 mile to the top of Butler Wash. Follow this road to its end, where you will see an obvious foot path that descends the last 200 feet into the cottonwoods and willows at the bottom of the drainage. The trail then threads its way through the vegetation for another 200 feet or so before climbing up the west side of

Kiva at Cold Springs Ruins

Butler Wash. After walking through the sagebrush for a few minutes you will cross another small gully before finally entering the wash that leads to the Cold Springs Ruins. The profusion of gullies and arroyos in the area could make navigation a confusing task, but be assured that the trail is easy to follow. The BLM does not actively maintain the trails along Butler Wash, but many hikers have gone before you to see the Cold Springs Ruins and the route is quite clearly marked.

A quarter-mile after entering Cold Springs Wash you will come to a fork in the drainage where you must bear right. The trail promptly climbs up the side of the right fork in order to get around a small pouroff and in another 150 yards you will arrive at the Cold Springs Ruins. These impressive ruins are located in a large south-facing alcove about 250 feet long and 30 feet high. Of particular interest near the east end of the alcove are the remains of a kiva that probably once served as the center of activity for the leaders of the community. There are also a fair number of grinding stones throughout

the complex where Anasazi women once ground the corn harvested from their crops.

But the feature that makes the Cold Springs Ruins unique is a spring or seep on the western end of the alcove that would have provided a convenient and reliable source of water for the residents throughout most of the year. The seep is located deep in the back of the alcove, and it appears that the Indians dug out a 15-foot diameter hollow beneath it to store the precious water. Furthermore this part of the alcove was walled off in order to protect the resource. Water was their key to survival, and very few Anasazi communities had such a convenient source.

Monarch Cave Ruins (1.5 miles round trip)

The turnoff to the Monarch Cave Trailhead is located 0.3 mile south of the Cave Springs turnoff or 13.9 miles south of Highway 95 on the Butler Wash Road. When you reach the Monarch Cave turnoff turn right and drive the last 200 feet to the trailhead and parking area.

The trail departs from the southwest

Walled off seep in back of Cold Springs Ruins

Monarch Cave Ruins

side of the small parking area and promptly plunges downward from the desert into a relative paradise of cottonwood trees and willows that define the bottom of Butler Wash. Once in the bottom of the drainage the excellent hiker-made trail enters the mouth of Monarch Cave Wash and follows it all the way to its end, 0.8 mile from the trailhead. The entire trail is through the bottom of a well shaded wash, making this one of the more pleasant hikes in the area. Monarch Cave Wash gets deeper and deeper as it approaches Comb Ridge, finally ending 0.5 mile from the summit of the ridge in a box canyon with a 200-foot cliff on its west side. There, in a deep wide alcove about halfway up from the floor of the canyon lie the Monarch Cave Ruins.

These ruins are, for me, the most interesting of the ruins in the Butler Wash area.

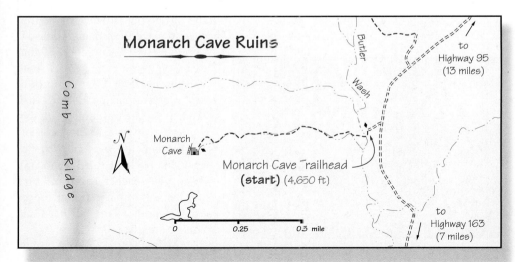

Wolfman Petroglyphs

When first viewed from the bottom of the canyon they almost look like the remains of an ancient castle. The builders showed considerable daring in building some of the structures right on the lip of the alcove, and although most of the walls are now badly eroded it appears that some of them may have extended all the way to the alcove's ceiling, 30 feet above the floor of the cave.

Monarch Cave must have been an extremely desirable place to live for its ancient inhabitants. The alcove is located in an easily defensible location above the canyon floor. The exterior dwellings even have a series of tiny openings where the residents could keep watch on the canyon below. And, although the alcove is easily accessible via a ledge on the north side, unwanted visitors could have been easily repelled. Look for

Pool below Monarch Ruin

the moki steps that have been chipped into the sandstone ledge on the north side of the alcove.

Even more important, the settlement had a reliable water source nearby. 100 feet below Monarch Cave, on the floor of the canyon, is a 30-foot diameter pool that probably contains at least some water throughout the year. The pool is fed from the streambed above the alcove, and whenever there is a substantial rain a waterfall must pour down in front of the alcove to the pool below. Such occasions must have created a lot of excitement for the people living behind the fall. There is also a small seep in the back of the alcove that would have provided some water.

Wolfman Petroglyphs (1.0 mile round trip)

The turnoff to the Wolfman Trailhead is located 6.1 miles south of the Monarch Cave turnoff, 20.1 miles south of Highway 95 or 1.0 mile north of Highway 163 on the Butler Wash Road. If you are traveling north from Highway 163 you will see the turnoff just 40 feet before the road crosses a fence and passes a BLM signboard. When you reach the turnoff turn west and follow the jeep road for the last 120 yards to the trailhead and parking area.

Initially the trail to the Wolfman

Wolfman Petroglyphs

panel is just a continuation of the jeep road that leads to the parking area. Start by following the primitive road in a westerly direction for 260 yards until it comes to an abrupt end on the rim of the Butler Wash gorge. If you have been on the other Butler Wash hikes discussed above you will be surprised at how much the character of the wash changes at it approaches its confluence with the San Juan River two miles downstream. Further upcanyon the wash is nothing more than a shallow desert gully, but here it is a 200-foot deep gorge. Looking across the canyon from your vantage point on the east rim you can see a prominent collection of Indian ruins below the opposite rim a few hundred yards further upcanyon. These ruins are easily accessible via a hiker-made trail that leads upcanyon from the Wolfman Petroglyph Panel.

When you reach the end of the jeep road you may be wondering which way to turn to begin your descent into the canyon. The continuation of the trail is not immediately obvious, but if you turn left and walk just 100 feet along the rim you will soon see a way to get to the bottom of the gorge. The trail follows a steep narrow ledge that was blasted out of the sandstone a century ago by local ranchers who needed a way to get their animals to water. Sheep ranching was a common industry at that time, and tens of thousands of sheep were grazed in Southern Utah. Water was always a problem in the

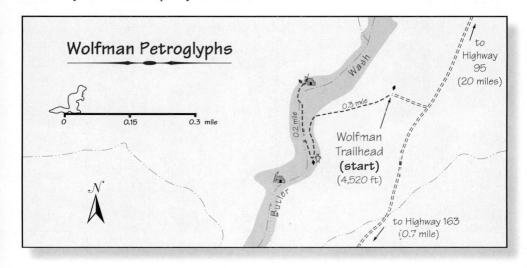

desert environment, and today it is not uncommon to find "sheep steps" like the ones in Butler Wash that were constructed so the ranchers could get their animals to the life giving liquid in the canyon bottoms. There is one obstacle at the top of the Butler Wash sheep steps. Some minor scrambling will be required to get around a large boulder that lies across the top of the trail, but beyond that it is an easy walk down the steps to the bottom of the wash.

Near the bottom of the steps the trail crosses the floor of a small alcove, and on the south side of the alcove you will find a thousand-year-old masterpiece of Indian rock art: the Wolfman Petroglyphs. This collection of petroglyphs, were probably made by the Anasazis who lived in these canyons for about 1500 years before their departure around 1300 A.D. Petroglyphs are notoriously difficult to date, however, and some or them could be much older. The Wolfman panel features several birds, human like figures, abstract designs, and two oval figures that have been interpreted as fertility symbols. The artwork is unusually fine and beautiful in its simplicity. It has un-

fortunately been marred by the presence of a dozen or so bullet holes, but I still consider it one of the best rock art panels in Utah.

From the petroglyphs the trail follows a bench above the streambed in a northerly direction for 100 yards before dipping down through a chute to the sandy floor of the canyon. The trail continues along the canyon floor for another 150 feet and then climbs out to another bench on the west side of the wash. Once on the west side you must scramble up a steeply eroded chute for another 20 feet to reach the south side of the shallow alcove where the Wolfman Ruins are located.

The Wolfman Ruins are not as well preserved as some of the other Butler Wash ruins, but they are nevertheless worth a visit. Suitable stone is harder to come by at this site, hence several of the structures are made mostly of mud. The best ruins are located on the northern end of the alcove, while some of the ones on the southern side look almost like natural heaps of earth. I suspect that they were built after workers on the north side had already exhausted the easily available supply of stone.

Wolfman Ruins

Cohab Canyon - Cassidy Arch

★★★

Capitol Reef National Park
shuttle car or bicycle required
day hike

Distance:	7.0 miles
	(plus 3.6 miles by car or bicycle)
Walking time:	4¹/₂ hours
Elevations:	1,040 ft. gain, 1,060 ft. loss
	Cohab Canyon Trailhead (start): 5,420 ft.
	highest point: 6,460 ft.
	Grand Wash Trailhead: 5,400 ft.
Trail:	Popular, well maintained trail
Season:	Spring, summer, fall, winter. There is snow on some parts of the trail during the winter months. During the summer months the trail is very hot. There is no water along the way so be sure to carry plenty.
Vicinity:	Capitol Reef National Park, near Fruita
Maps:	Fruita *(USGS)*
	Fish Lake/Capitol Reef Nat. Park *(Trails Illustrated, #213)*
Information:	http://www.utahtrails.com/cohab.html *(Utah Trails)*
	http://www.nps.gov/care/ *(Capitol Reef National Park)*
	phone: (435) 425-3791 *(Visitor Center)*

Drive south of the Capital Reef National Park Visitor Center for a distance of 3.4 miles to the turnout into Grand Wash. Take the dirt road into Grand Wash and drive for another 1.3 miles to the end of the road. This is the point where the hike ends and where you should leave your shuttle car or bicycle.

To get to the Cohab Canyon Trailhead, where the hike begins, return to the paved road at the head of Grand Wash and drive north toward the Visitors Center for a distance of 2.3 miles. You will see a sign marking the Cohab Canyon Trailhead on the right side of the road opposite the entrance to the campground.

Sixty-five million years ago, while forces inside the earth were pushing up the Colorado Plateau, a 100-mile-long wrinkle in the earth's mantle was formed in Southern Utah. Thousands of feet of subterranean sedimentary rock were forced upward as

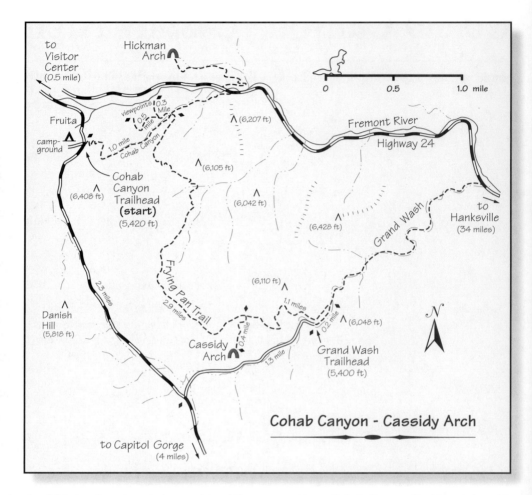

to
Visitor
Center
(0.5 mile)

Hickman
Arch

Fruita

camp-
ground

viewpoints 0.3
0.5 Mile
mile

1.0 mile
Cohab Canyon

∧ (6,207 ft)

Fremont River

Highway 24

∧ (6,105 ft)

Cohab
Canyon
Trailhead
(start)
(5,420 ft)

∧
(6,408 ft)

∧
(6,042 ft)

∧ (6,428 ft)

to
Hanksville
(34 miles)

Grand Wash

2.3 miles

Frying Pan Trail

2.9 miles

(6,110 ft) ∧

1.1 miles

Danish
Hill
(5,818 ft)

∧

0.4 mile

0.2 mile ∧ (6,048 ft)

Cassidy
Arch

1.3 mile

Grand Wash
Trailhead
(5,400 ft)

N

Cohab Canyon - Cassidy Arch

to Capitol Gorge
(4 miles)

0   0.5   1.0 mile

the fold developed, twisting and buckling to form a convoluted range of mountains we now call the Waterpocket Fold. Today, after a great deal of erosion, the mountains rise less than two thousand feet above the desert floor. What remains is a fairyland of geologic sculpture. The ancient mountains, most of which are now part of Capitol Reef National Park, have been carved into a tangle of hidden canyons, monolithic spires, and towering cliffs. The hike described here starts in the Fremont River Valley, near the pioneer settlement of Fruita, and crosses a portion of the Waterpocket Fold to Grand Wash. It offers a good representation of the unique landscape of the Waterpocket Fold.

From Cohab Canyon Trailhead the path begins by switchbacking up the clay benton-ite mounds of the Chinle Formation. Finally, after about 0.3 mile, it arrives at the base of the reddish cliffs that can be seen above the road. These sandstone cliffs are part of the 370-foot-thick geological formation known as the Wingate Sandstone. The trail then skirts around the west side of the cliffs and soon drops into a shallow, hidden drainage called Cohab Canyon. Cohab Canyon and its trail continue all the way to the Fremont River on the east side of the Waterpocket Fold, but on this hike you won't be follow-ing it that far.

About 0.6 mile after entering Cohab

Canyon you will come to a trail junction with a sign indicating the way to two overlook points. You should turn left here before continuing down the canyon and make a side trip to at least one of them. After 0.2 mile the overlook trail splits again, and you are given a choice between the north and the south overlooks. If you are interested in taking photographs take the south overlook trail (0.5 mile). It leads to a high vantage point above the Fruita area. Alternatively, if you bear right to the north overlook the trail soon ends on a slab of rock that overhangs the cliffs above the Fremont River with a shear 400 foot drop below.

When you are finished with the overlooks, backtrack to the Cohab Canyon Trail and continue onward for a short distance. After just a hundred yards you will come to another trail leaving Cohab Canyon on the right. This is the Frying Pan Trail, the one that will lead you to Grand Wash.

The Frying Pan Trail winds over a tortuous route along the top of the Fold, twisting between domes of sandstone and working its way around a series of gullies and ravines. In some places only rock cairns will tell you that you are still on the path, and you will probably wonder how you would ever be able to find your way through the obstacle course if you lost the trail.

Finally, after a long tiring climb you will reach the highest point on the Frying Pan Trail and start down again toward Grand Wash. Then, 1.5 miles later, you will see a sign marking the short spur trail across the slickrock that leads to Cassidy Arch. Cassidy Arch is a large and impressive natural arch that lies just minutes from the main trail. It was named after the outlaw, Butch Cassidy, who is thought to have used Grand Wash as an occasional hideout. The path ends on the plateau above the arch, and if you have a hiking partner and a camera it is easy to get a picture of someone standing on top of it. Getting to the bottom of the span, however, requires some rock climbing skill.

From the Cassidy Arch junction the Frying Pan Trail continues for another 1.1 miles before reaching the bottom of Grand Wash. Once you get to the bottom of the wash turn right and walk for another 0.2 mile to the end of the Grand Wash Road where your shuttle car is parked. If you look to the right as you drive back toward the Visitor Center you can see Cassidy Arch again from the bottom of Grand Wash. It should come into view about 0.5 mile from the end of the road.

Cassidy Arch

Chimney Rock - Spring Canyon

Capitol Reef National Park
shuttle car or bicycle required
day hike

Distance: 9.7 miles
(plus 6.9 miles by car or bicycle)

Walking time: 5¹/₂ hours

Elevations: 250 ft. gain, 1,080 ft. loss
Chimney Rock Trailhead (start): 6,050 ft.
highest point: 6,300 ft.
Fremont River: 5,220 ft.

Trail: Most of this hike is through the sandy bottom of a desert canyon. There is no maintained trail, but the route is easy to follow.
At the end of the hike it is necessary to ford the Fremont River.
This is usually not a problem, but if there has been a lot of rain
you should check the river before beginning the hike.

Season: Spring, summer, fall, winter. There is snow on some parts of the
trail during the winter months. The trail is very hot in the summer, with temperatures often exceeding 100 degrees F. There is
no reliable water along the trail, so be sure to carry plenty.

Vicinity: Capitol Reef National Park, near Fruita

Maps: Twin Rocks, Fruita *(USGS)*
Fish Lake/Capitol Reef Nat. Park *(Trails Illustrated, #213)*

Information: http://www.utahtrails.com/chimneyrock.html *(Utah Trails)*
http://www.nps.gov/care/ *(Capitol Reef National Park)*
phone: (435) 425-3791 *(Visitor Center)*

---

*Drive east of the Capital Reef National Park Visitor Center on Highway 24
for a distance of 3.9 miles, where you will see a small picnic area on the south
side of the Fremont River. This is where the hike ends, and where you should
leave your shuttle car. The hike begins 3.0 miles west of the Visitor Center
on Highway 24 at the Chimney Rock turnout on the north side of the road.*

Spring Canyon is a long, narrow desert
drainage on the northwestern side of

Capital Reef National Park. The canyon
begins just outside the park on the east-

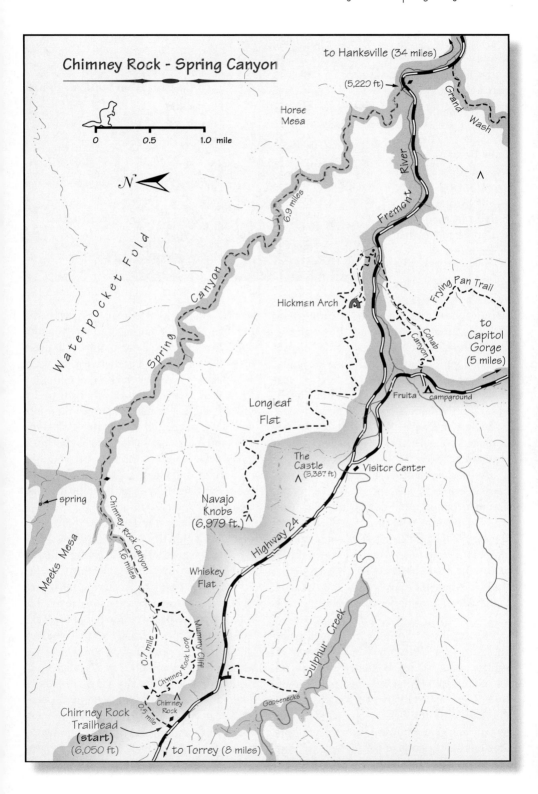

Chimney Rock - Spring Canyon

to Hanksville (34 miles)

(5,220 ft)

Horse
Mesa

Grand Wash

0   0.5   1.0   mile

N

Fremont River

6.9 miles

Frying Pan Trail

Spring Canyon

Hickman Arch

Cohab Canyon

to
Capitol
Gorge
(5 miles)

Waterpocket Fold

Long eaf
Flat

Fruita   campground

The
Castle
(3,387 ft)

Visitor Center

spring

Navajo
Knobs
(6,979 ft.)

Chimney Rock Canyon   1.6 miles

Highway 24

Meeks Mesa

Whiskey
Flat

Sulphur Creek

0.7 mile

Chimney Rock Loop

Mummy Cliff

Goosenecks

0.5 mile

Chimney
Rock

Chimney Rock
Trailhead
(start)
(6,050 ft)

to Torrey (8 miles)

ern slopes of Thousand Lakes Mountain and then meanders through the Waterpocket Fold for some twenty miles before draining into the Fremont River. The hike described here intersects Spring Canyon at its midpoint and follows the bottom of the gorge for its final seven miles.

This hike is particularly interesting from a geological

Chimney Rock Trail

point of view because it passes through so many different geologic strata. The trail begins in the Moenkopi Formation, then passes through the Shinarump, Chinle, Wingate, and Kayenta Formations, and finally ends in the center of the Waterpocket Fold at the base of the Navajo Sandstone. This sequence is unusual because the Navajo Sandstone is much younger than the preceding layers further upcanyon.

As you descend eastward through the canyon you will see successive layers of younger rock slanting downward along the walls to meet the older layers at the bottom. Because of the uplifting and subsequent erosion that created the Waterpocket Fold the exposed rock is oldest on the west side of the Fold where the hike begins–even though that area lies at a higher elevation.

The trail into Spring Canyon descends first through Chimney Rock Canyon, a shorter side canyon so named because of an impressive chimney-shaped pinnacle of Moenkopi Shale that rises from the desert floor near the trailhead. The path begins by winding gently upward from the parking area on the west side of Chimney Rock and

then around to its north side. After walking 0.5 mile and climbing 250 feet you will come to a junction where another trail takes off to the right. This alternative route veers south again to pass by the base of Chimney Rock and then rejoins the main trail 1.7 miles later. If you have the time you might want take this detour for a closer look at the monolith, but doing so will add about a mile to the total length of the hike. If you take the shorter route, to the left, you will reach the point where the two trails come together again after about 20 minutes.

After the second junction the trail descends gradually down Chimney Rock Canyon for about 1.6 miles before finally arriving at the junction with Spring Canyon. To reach the Fremont River you must turn right when you come to the main canyon, but if time permits or if you are doing this hike as an overnighter you may want to make a side trip to the canyon's best known spring. This spring lies about 1.0 mile upcanyon to the left. It is situated in an alcove just above a small pool of water under the north wall of the canyon. You will know you are near when you see a grove of large cottonwood trees. (Cottonwoods in the desert country of Southern Utah usually mark the presence of water.) This spring is why the canyon is called Spring Canyon.

From the point where the trail first meets Spring Canyon it is 6.9 miles to the Fremont River. There is no real trail, but the route is generally easy to walk. You will be following the sandy creek bed nearly all the way. There are some deer tracks in the canyon bottom, but the most interesting aspect of the hike is the geology. Much of the rock is a deep red color, and in the section of the canyon that passes through the Wingate Formation, the sandstone walls are sheer and smooth. You may be surprised to find frequent boulders of black volcanic rock. These worn boulders have been washed downstream by flash floods from a volcanic area near the top of the canyon. Now they lie in stark contrast to the reddish sandstone and shale of the Waterpocket Fold.

About half way through the gorge you will enter a half-mile section of narrows, where the canyon walls converge to a mere five feet apart. There are also two ten-foot pouroffs, or dry falls, in the bottom of this stretch of canyon. These falls are relatively easy to climb down and should not be a problem unless you are carrying a large backpack. But if they do present a problem, there is an alternative route around them. When you come to the first pouroff retrace your footsteps a few hundred feet back to a point where you can climb up to the ledge on the north side of the narrows. There you will find a primitive path that bypasses the obstacles before dropping back to the canyon floor.

Finally, just before you reach the end of the hike, the canyon widens and becomes less arid. The walls change from the ruddy, fissured Wingate and Kayenta Sandstone to the smooth, white cross bedded texture of the Navajo Sandstone. Soon you will round the last bend in the canyon and be confronted with your last obstacle—the Fremont River.

Under normal conditions fording the Fremont is no problem. It is seldom more than 18 inches deep. If there has been a lot of rain, however, its depth can easily rise to twice that. Find a stout stick to help you with the crossing. Walk slowly, taking small steps, and make sure the stick and one foot are firmly planted before moving your other foot. The stick should be positioned on your downstream side, with your right side facing upstream as you walk. Shortly after crossing the river you will arrive at Highway 24 and the ending trailhead.

Spring Canyon

Hickman Bridge - Navajo Knobs

Capitol Reef National Park
day hike

Distance:	11.0 miles (round trip to all points of interest)
Walking time:	7¹/₄ hours
Elevations:	1,900 ft. gain/loss
	Hickman Bridge Trailhead (start): 5,340 ft.
	Hickman Natural Bridge: 5,700 ft.
	Rim Overlook: 6,360 ft.
	Navajo Knobs: 6,979 ft.
Trail:	Generally well marked and easy to follow
Season:	Generally year round, although the higher parts of the trail are occasionally covered with snow in the winter.
Vicinity:	Capitol Reef National Park, near Fruita
Maps:	Twin Rocks, Fruita *(USGS)*
	Fish Lake/Capitol Reef Nat. Park *(Trails Illustrated, #213)*
Information:	http://www.utahtrails.com/hickmanbridge.html *(Utah Trails)*
	http://www.nps.gov/care/ *(Capitol Reef National Park)*
	phone: (435) 425-3791 *(Visitor Center)*

Drive east of the Capitol Reef National Park Visitor Center on Highway 24 for a distance of 2.0 miles. There you will see a well-marked turnout on the left that ends at the Hickman Natural Bridge Trailhead and parking area.

This hike is actually three hikes in one: Hickman Natural Bridge, the Rim Overlook, and the Navajo Knobs. Most people go only as far as the Hickman Natural Bridge, which is just 0.9 mile from the trailhead. This short hike has a great deal to offer. Not only will you see the natural bridge itself, but there is also a small Fremont Indian granary near the trail. Be sure to purchase a trail guide from the box near the trailhead before you start.

If you are looking for a longer hike you can continue on from Hickman Bridge to the Navajo Knobs for a total round trip distance of 11.0 miles. This extended hike gives you the opportunity to climb to the top of the

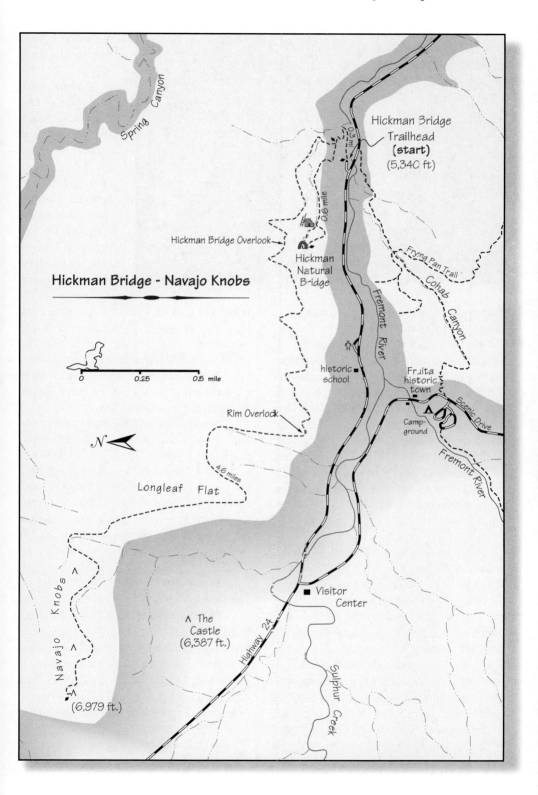

Spring Canyon

Hickman Bridge
Trailhead
(start)
(5,340 ft)

0.3 mi

Hickman Bridge Overlook

0.9 mile

Frying Pan Trail

Cohab Canyon

Hickman Bridge - Navajo Knobs

Hickman
Natural
Bridge

Fremont River

0   0.25   0.5 mile

historic
school

Fruita
historic
town

Scenic Drive

Rim Overlook

Camp-
ground

Fremont River

N

4.6 miles

Longleaf   Flat

Navajo Knobs

Visitor
Center

∧ The
Castle
(6,387 ft.)

Highway 24

(6,979 ft.)

Sulphur Creek

Hickman Natural Bridge

Hickman Bridge before continuing on.

From the junction the trail to Hickman Bridge meanders across the desert for 0.4 mile before coming to a small granary that was constructed by the Fremont Indians that inhabited this area some 700 years ago. It is located in a small alcove just above the right side of the trail. Watch the left side of the trail after leaving the alcove and about 0.1 mile further you will see a small pictograph panel that is covered with dozens of hand prints, again placed there by the prehistoric Fremont Indians.

0.6 mile from the trail junction the route passes under the natural bridge, a surprisingly scenic span 133 feet wide and 125 feet high. The bridge was named after Joe Hickman, a local teacher and activist who campaigned in the 1930s for the creation of Capitol Reef National Monument. The trail passes under the span then turns to the left to make a 0.2-mile loop that eventually runs back into the main trail. From there you can retrace your steps back to the junction and turn left onto the Navajo Knobs Trail.

The Navajo Knobs Trail first heads north toward a line of cliffs about 300 yards away, but before it actually arrives at the cliffs it turns to the west and continues to gain elevation only gradually. After 0.8 mile you will see a sign that says "Hickman Bridge Overlook", from where you can look down on the Hickman Bridge 100 feet below.

The trail continues its gradual climb for

Waterpocket Fold and enjoy the panorama below the south side of the uplift.

The Navajo Knobs Trail passes by the Rim Overlook Viewpoint 2.5 miles before ending at the Navajo Knobs, so if you are looking for an intermediate hike this might be a good place to turn around. The Rim Overlook is 600 feet lower than the Navajo Knobs and the view from there is not quite as dramatic, but it is still a worthwhile goal. It is situated directly above the historic town of Fruita, and it is fun to look down on the fruit orchards and historic buildings from above.

From the trailhead the well-used path follows the north side of the Fremont River for a few hundred feet, and then turns abruptly north to begin the climb out of the canyon. The trail climbs 120 feet to a plateau above the canyon floor before again finding relatively level terrain. Soon after reaching the plateau you will see a sign marking a trail junction where you must turn left for Hickman Bridge or right for the Rim Overlook and the Navajo Knobs. Bear left at the junction. Even if your ultimate goal is the Navajo Knobs, be sure not to miss another 1.3 miles as it winds along the base of the cliffs in a westerly direction. Finally, after gaining just over a thousand feet from the trailhead you will come to a sign marking the Rim Overlook. This is a great place to stop for lunch and enjoy the scenery. Fruita lies directly below the viewpoint on the shore of the Fremont River, and beyond the river the Waterpocket Fold extends south as far as the eye can see. If you have already done the Cohab Canyon hike (page 345) you will recognize Cohab Canyon on the west side of the Waterpocket Fold. You can also see a portion of the Cohab Canyon Trail climbing up into the rugged canyon from the campground.

The trail continues for another 2.5 miles beyond the Rim Overlook before ending at the top of the Navajo Knobs. The route keeps following the base of the cliffs for most of the distance, winding around the hills and valleys of slickrock as it follows the topology of the bench. The grade is never very steep, although it can be a long,

hot walk on a sunny day. There is very little shade and absolutely no water along the way, so hopefully you have brought along a hat, some sunblock, and something to drink.

For the last 0.5 mile the trail stays just below the south side of three prominent sandstone peaks that rise about 300 feet above the bench. These are the Navajo Knobs. After passing the first two knobs the trail finally makes an unexpected turn to the right and climbs the last 150 feet to the top of the westernmost knob.

This knob is not quite as high as the other two, but it is the easiest one to climb. It is also the one closest to the rim, which gives it the best view of the valley below. From there you can see an unbroken 20-mile stretch of Highway 24 as it winds past the Mummy Cliffs and Whiskey Flat toward the Fremont River. Looking north and east across the fantasy land of massive domes, stark monoliths and twisting canyons will give you an appreciation for how incredibly rugged the Waterpocket Fold really is.

Fruita, as seen from the Rim Overlook Viewpoint

Upper Muley Twist Canyon

★★★★★

Capitol Reef National Park
4WD vehicle required
day hike

Distance:	9.4 miles (loop)
Walking time:	6 hours
Elevations:	740 ft. gain/loss
	Upper Muley Twist Trailhead (start): 5,860 ft.
	end of Upper Muley Twist Canyon: 6,460 ft.
	top of Waterpocket Fold: 6,600 ft.
Trail:	There is no developed trail for this hike, but the route is not too difficult to follow. Initially it follows the bottom of a desert canyon, then it loops back across the slickrock of the Waterpocket Fold. Where needed, the route is well marked with stone cairns. There is no water, so carry plenty.
Season:	Spring, summer, fall, winter. Capital Reef is very hot in the summer and cold in the winter. The ideal times for the hike are spring and fall.
Vicinity:	Capitol Reef National Park, southern section
Maps:	Bitter Creek Divide, Wagon Box Mesa *(USGS)*
Information:	http://www.utahtrails.com/uppermuley.html *(Utah Trails)*
	http://www.nps.gov/care/ *(Capitol Reef National Park)*
	phone: (435) 425-3791 *(Visitor Center)*

Drive east of the Capital Reef National Park Visitor Center on Highway 24 for 9.1 miles until you see a paved road on the right leading to Notom and Lake Powell. Turn right onto this road and drive south for 33 miles to the junction with the Burr Trail Road. (The pavement ends after five miles, but the remaining gravel road is well maintained.) Turn right on the Burr Trail and drive up the switchbacks for another 3.2 miles where you will see a small sign on the right marking the dirt road that leads to Upper Muley Twist Canyon. Turn right onto this road. After 0.4 mile you will see a trail register and another sign advising you that to continue you will need a 4WD vehicle. The trailhead is another 2.4 miles along the 4WD road. Actually the road is not that bad; a 2WD pickup with high clearance can usually make it, but not an ordinary car.

No other hike in Capital Reef National Park offers as many scenic geological features as the loop through Upper Muley Twist Canyon. The canyon has been cut through a particularly interesting part of the Waterpocket Fold where the deep red Wingate Sandstone formation slopes down from the west and dips under the eastern wall of white Navajo Sandstone. The Wingate Sandstone in this area has a tendency to erode into arches, and if you are observant you will see at least five arches on the west side as you hike up the canyon. The return portion of the hike is along a high slickrock ridge of Navajo Sandstone above the eastern side of the canyon, and the views from the top are magnificent. From this vantage point you will be able to see a large part of the hundred-mile-long wrinkle in the earth's crust that geologists call the Waterpocket Fold.

From the end of the road at the bottom of Upper Muley Twist Canyon you should begin this hike by walking north along the Muley Twist streambed. Another trail on the right side of the parking area leads east to the Strike Valley Overlook, but don't be confused. This is not your trail. As you proceed be sure to scan the left side of the canyon occasionally, and after 1.6 miles you will see the first of five natural arches about 200 feet above the canyon floor. Another few hundred yards will bring you to a large crack in the canyon wall with the second arch above it. This one is called Saddle Arch, and it is the only one of the five that has been given a name. Just below Saddle Arch you should also see a sign on the right that marks the lower end of the Rim Trail. You will be joining the Rim Trail farther up Muley Twist, and this is where you will later drop back into the main canyon.

Continuing up the wash for another 1.3 miles will bring you to a break in the red Wingate Sandstone where, again, you should be able to see two arches. The arches are about 200 yards on either side of the break, but this time they are higher up on the side of the wall. The fifth and last arch is another 0.8 mile upcanyon. This one is just at the bottom of a slot canyon joining the main canyon from the left and, unlike the others, it is easily accessible.

Upper Muley Twist Canyon

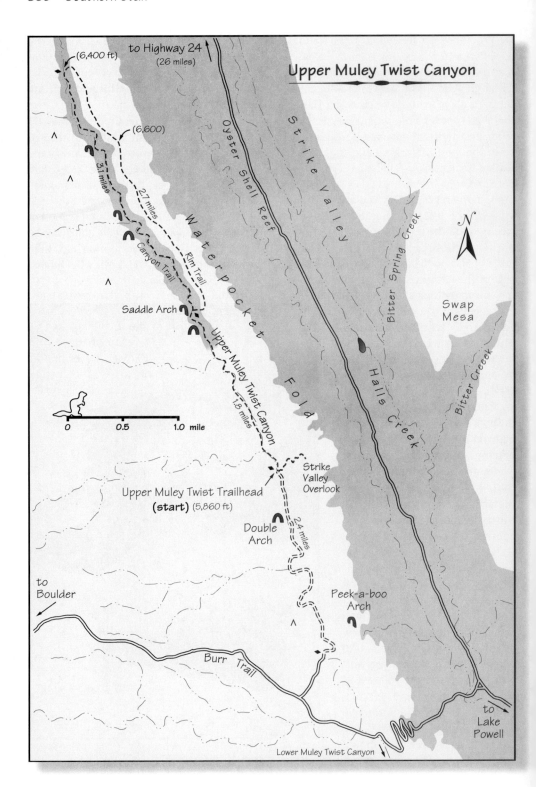

Upper Muley Twist Canyon

to Highway 24
(26 miles)

(6,400 ft)

(6,600)

3.1 miles

2.7 miles

Canyon Trail

Rim Trail

Saddle Arch

Upper Muley Twist Canyon

1.8 miles

0   0.5   1.0 mile

Oyster Shell Reef

Waterpocket   Fold

Strike   Valley

Bitter Spring Creek

Halls Creek

Bitter Creek

Swap Mesa

N

Upper Muley Twist Trailhead
(start) (5,860 ft)

Strike Valley Overlook

Double Arch

2.4 miles

Peek-a-boo Arch

to Boulder

Burr   Trail

to Lake Powell

Lower Muley Twist Canyon

Saddle Arch

comes upon you with no warning, and it is extremely impressive. One minute you are threading your way through the juniper forest, and the next minute you are on top of the world looking fifty miles down Strike Valley.

For the next two miles the view is nonstop. On one side of the slickrock ridge is Strike Valley, with

A short distance beyond the last arch the canyon narrows and is blocked by a pouroff. In order to avoid the obstacle the trail climbs up the right side of the canyon to a shelf about 100 feet above the streambed. Watch for the rock cairns that show the way. The trail stays high for 0.6 mile before dropping back down to the bottom of the wash. Then, after only 0.1 mile more, you will see another sign that says "Rim Trail". This is where you will finally leave the canyon.

It is very easy to loose the way climbing out of the canyon on the Rim Trail, so be sure to watch carefully for stone cairns. There are plenty of markers, and if you walk for more than a hundred feet without seeing one you are probably off the trail. Most of the cairns, however, are small and hard to spot. The trail goes straight up for a while and then doubles back through a break in the sandstone cliffs. Finally, after an altitude gain of only 200 feet, it breaks out onto the top of the Waterpocket Fold. The view

Tarantula Mesa and Swap Mesa beyond, and on the other side is the Wingate Formation that contains all of the arches previously seen. In between, the top of the Waterpocket Fold seems to go on forever in both directions.

After about an hour you will come to another small sign saying "Canyon Route", and from there the trail drops back down to the bottom of Muley Twist Canyon near the Saddle Arch. Again, pay attention to the rock cairns as it is easy to lose the way. From Saddle Arch, you will have to retrace your steps back to your car at the trailhead.

Looking north from the top of the Waterpocket Fold

Lower Muley Twist Canyon

Capitol Reef National Park
shuttle car required
overnight hike

Distance: 18.1 miles
(plus 5.0 miles by car)

Walking time: day 1: 6 hours
day 2: 4 hours

Elevations: 1,000 ft. loss, 200 ft. gain
Lower Muley Twist Trailhead (start): 5,640 ft.
Cowboy Camp: 4,770 ft.
The Post Trailhead: 4,860 ft.

Trail: There is no trail for most of this hike, but the route is easy to follow. You will be walking down the streambed of a desert canyon for the first day, then 5.6 miles back to The Post along an old abandoned wagon road. The walk is easy, but unfortunately there is no water. In hot weather you should carry 1.5 gallons of water per person just for drinking.

Season: Spring and fall. Summer hiking is possible, but it is very hot. The hike can also be pleasant during winter warm spells.

Vicinity: Capitol Reef National Park, southern section

Maps: The Post, Wagon Box Mesa *(USGS)*

Information: http://www.utahtrails.com/lowermuley.html *(Utah Trails)*
http://www.nps.gov/care/ *(Capitol Reef National Park)*
phone: (435) 425-3791 *(Visitor Center)*

After obtaining an overnight backpacking permit at the Capital Reef National Park Visitor Center, drive east on Highway 24 for 9.1 miles until you see a paved road on the right leading to Notom and Lake Powell. Turn right onto this road and drive south for 33 miles to the junction with the Burr Trail Road. (The pavement ends after five miles, but the remaining gravel road is usually well maintained.) Lower Muley Twist Trailhead, where the hike begins, is on the south side of the Burr Trail Road, 2.1 miles west of the Notom-Lake Powell Road.

To reach The Post Trailhead, where the hike ends, continue south on the road to Lake Powell for 2.3 miles past the Burr Trail Road. Here the road crosses over a cattle guard, beyond which you will see a small dirt road and a sign directing you to "Lower Muley Twist

Trailhead". This 0.6-mile-long road ends near a large corral, where you will see another sign marking the trailhead and where you should leave your shuttle car.

The silence of Muley Twist Canyon was briefly broken in the late 1800s, when it was discovered to be a feasible route for getting wagons through the formidable Waterpocket Fold of Southern Utah. Getting around the rugged, hundred-mile-long sandstone ridge had long been a major problem for travelers in the area–especially the Mormons who were trying to settle the southeastern corner of the Utah Territory. On their famous Hole in the Rock expedition from Escalante to Bluff in 1879 it took the Mormon settlers six months to travel around the southern end of the Waterpocket Fold, so when Muley Twist Canyon was discovered two years later it quickly became the preferred route. The narrow canyon was said to have so many hairpin curves it could "twist a mule"; nevertheless it was shorter and less hazardous than the notorious Hole in the Rock Trail.

Muley Twist Canyon was probably discovered by a man named Charles Hall, who operated a ferry service across the Colorado River thirty miles south of the canyon. Demand for his ferry increased dramatically for two years after his discovery, and his business thrived. However, in 1883 a new rail link across Utah was completed by the DRG&W Railroad, and communications between the eastern and western parts of the state were greatly simplified. Halls ferry service was shut down in 1884, and the winding trail through Muley Twist Canyon was rarely ever used again.

Day 1 (10.7 miles)

There are many short, steep canyons that descend from the top of the Waterpocket Fold to its eastern and western flanks. Muley Twist Canyon is unusual, however, because it runs in a southerly direction for a substantial

Lower Muley Twist Canyon

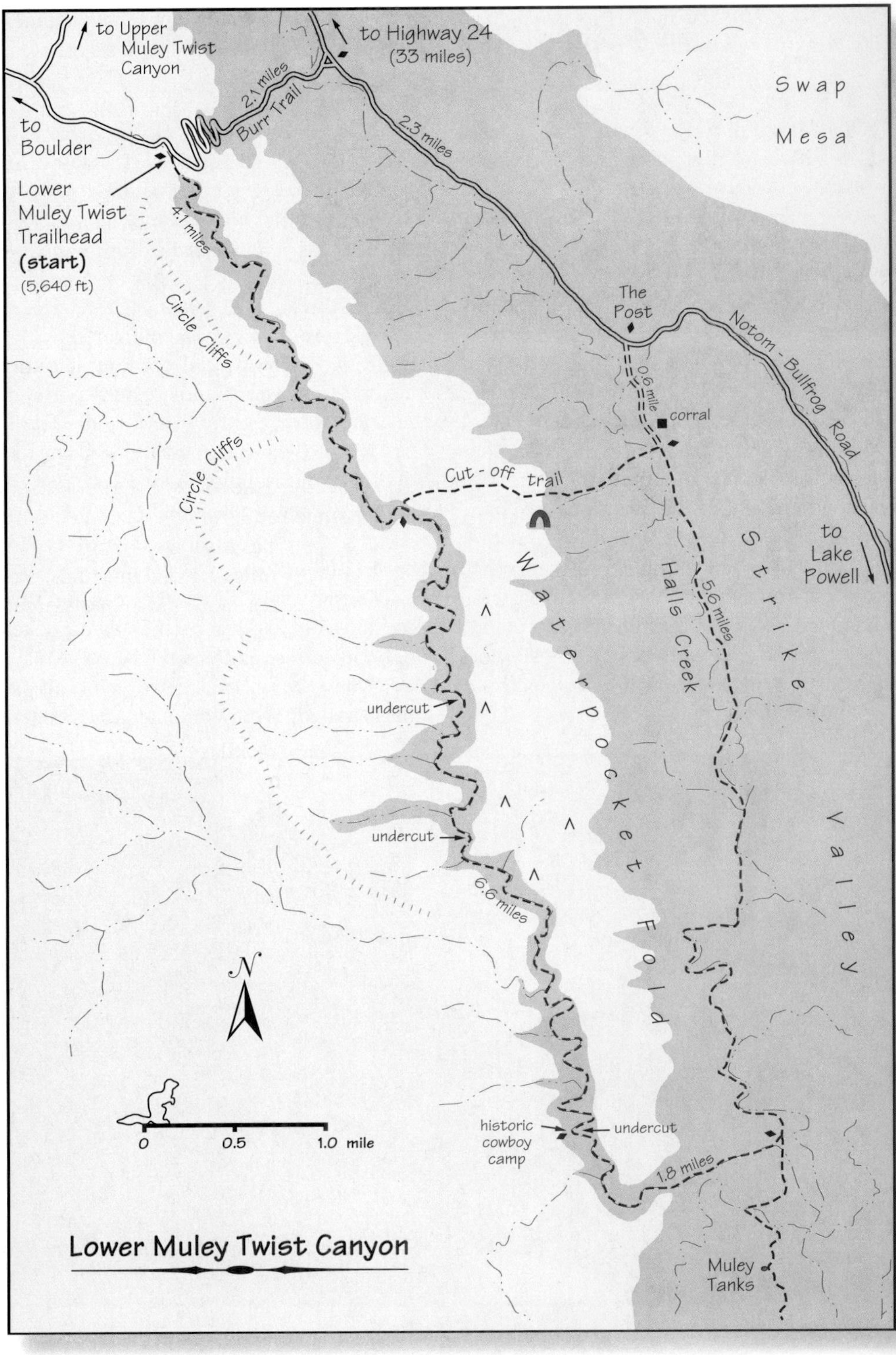

to Upper
Muley Twist
Canyon

to Highway 24
(33 miles)

2.1 miles

Burr Trail

2.3 miles

to
Boulder

Lower
Muley Twist
Trailhead
(start)
(5,640 ft)

4.1 miles

Circle Cliffs

Circle Cliffs

S w a p

M e s a

The Post

Notom - Bullfrog Road

0.6 mile

corral

Cut - off trail

to
Lake
Powell

Halls Creek

5.6 miles

S t r i k e

V a l l e y

W a t e r p o c k e t   F o l d

undercut

undercut

6.6 miles

N

historic
cowboy
camp

undercut

1.8 miles

0   0.5   1.0 mile

Lower Muley Twist Canyon

Muley
Tanks

First undercut in Lower Muley Twist Canyon

distance before turning east to exit the Fold. From its start at the Burr Trail Road, Lower Muley Twist Canyon descends down through the center of the Fold for some eleven miles before exiting into Strike Valley. As you walk down the canyon you will encounter several large side canyons coming in from the west. Bear to the left in each case to stay in Muley Twist Canyon.

After 4.1 miles you will come to a junction, where a wooden sign marks the Cutoff Trail leading to The Post. If you are looking for a shorter hike you can take this two-mile shortcut and avoid the bottom portion of Muley Twist. The most interesting part of the hike, however, is the part below the Cutoff Trail.

Continuing on past the Cutoff Trail you will notice many huge alcoves higher up the sides of the canyon. These would seem to be excellent places to find Indian ruins, but the scarcity of water makes it unlikely that Indians ever lived in the canyon.

1.7 miles below the Cutoff Trail the streambed makes a deep swing inward on the left side of the canyon, creating a huge undercut below the cliff above. For some 200 yards the trail continues under the overhang. The cave-like nature of the trail is enhanced by a 30-foot-high pile of rubble on the right side of the streambed that extends upward nearly to the roof of the alcove. This stretch of the trail feels like nothing so much as a subway tunnel.

1.4 miles beyond this tunnel the trail enters another similar undercut. The cool air inside the two alcoves is a welcome relief. At times there may also be pools of water in them, but don't expect to be so lucky during the hot months of summer.

Throughout most of Muley Twist Canyon there is no trace of the fact that it was once a major wagon route. Only in the Cowboy Camp, 6.6 miles below the Cutoff Trail junction can one still see a few relics of the pioneers that once passed through. The Cowboy Camp is in another large alcove that has been undercut into the west side of the canyon. This time, however, the wide, flat floor of the alcove is about ten feet above the streambed; hence it is an excellent camping area.

For over a century travelers and cowboys have broken their journeys at the Cowboy Camp, and now it contains abundant signs of human occupation. The collection includes a pile of old rusted tin cans, a few leaf springs from the wagons and, above all, graffiti. There are many dated signatures on the back of the alcove from the 1920s. Unfortunately the camp floor is also liberally sprinkled with old cow pies. There haven't been any cattle in the canyon for many decades, but the normal decay of organic material occurs very slowly in this dry desert country.

Day 2 (7.4 miles)

Soon after leaving the Cowboy Camp, Muley Twist Canyon finally turns east to begin the final leg of its journey through the Waterpocket Fold to Strike Valley. The towering canyon walls begin to come together, then their height gradually starts to diminish, and finally the impressive canyon is transformed into nothing more than an insignificant desert arroyo. About 0.2 mile after leaving the Fold you will see another trail crossing Muley Twist wash. This is the trail to Brimhall Arch, and you will have to turn left at this point to get back to The Post. Watch closely for the trail crossing because there are no signs at the junction.

After you have turned north onto the Brimhall Arch Trail it is an uneventful 5.6 miles back to The Post where your shuttle car is parked. Although the remainder of the trail closely follows the dry streambed of Halls Creek, there is generally no water along the way.

Muley Tanks

If you are desperate for water when you reach Strike Valley, there are two small water holes called the Muley Tanks 1.0 mile south of Muley Twist. To get there just turn right instead of left when you see the Brimhall Arch Trail and walk south until you see a sign directing you to the Muley Tanks. Don't expect a clear mountain spring, however. The tanks are little more than two muddy potholes at the bottom of a large slickrock runoff. As their name suggests the tanks are used primarily by pack animals, and the water is usually pretty wretched. If you really plan to drink it you had better have some way of filtering out the mud first.

Lower Muley Twist Canyon

The Pine Creek Box

★

Box - Death Hollow Wilderness Area
shuttle car required
day hike

Distance: 8.8 miles
(plus 11.1 miles by car)

Walking time: 5 hours

Elevations: 1,300 ft. loss
Upper Box Trailhead (start): 7,740 ft.
Deep Creek Confluence: 7,010 ft.
Lower Box Trailhead: 6,440 ft.

Trail: This hike follows a small, fast running creek down a narrow, tree-lined canyon. Frequent stream crossings are necessary, so wettable boots should be worn. There is no reliable trail for the first five miles and the ground cover is thick in places, so wear long pants.

Season: Late spring, summer and fall. Access to the trailhead is usually blocked by snow in winter and early spring.

Vicinity: Box-Death Hollow Wilderness Area, near Escalante

Maps: Posy Lake, Wide Hollow Reservoir *(USGS)*
Canyons of the Escalante *(Trails Illustrated, #710)*

Information: http://www.utahtrails.com/pinebox.html *(Utah Trails)*
http://www.fs.fed.us/dxnf/ (Dixie National Forest)
phone: (435) 826-5499 *(Escalante Interagency Visitor Center)*

Drive north from Escalante toward Boulder on the Hells Backbone Road (a graded gravel road). After 8.0 miles you will see a sign directing you to a primitive road on the right that leads to the Lower Box access. This is where the Pine Creek Trail ends, and your shuttle car should be left here. (Note: the primitive road to the Lower Box access is only 0.3 mile long, but it is very sandy. You may want to leave your shuttle car beside the main road to avoid the risk of getting stuck in the sand.)

The hike begins 10.8 miles further north on the Hells Backbone Road beside another sign that says "Upper Box access".

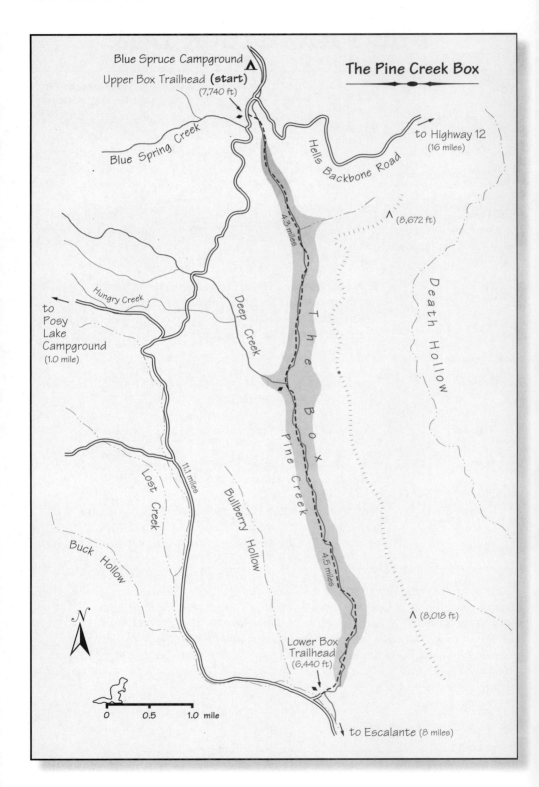

Blue Spruce Campground
Upper Box Trailhead **(start)**
(7,740 ft)

Blue Spring Creek

Hells Backbone Road

to Highway 12
(16 miles)

4.3 miles

∧ (8,672 ft)

The Pine Creek Box

Hungry Creek

Deep Creek

to
Posy
Lake
Campground
(1.0 mile)

The Box

Pine Creek

Death Hollow

11.1 miles

Lost Creek

Bullberry Hollow

4.5 miles

Buck Hollow

∧ (8,018 ft)

Lower Box
Trailhead
(6,440 ft)

N

0   0.5   1.0 mile

to Escalante (8 miles)

This hike is a very pleasant walk down an unusually scenic canyon of Pine Creek known as the Box. Conservationists fought hard to have this area included in the Utah Wilderness Act of 1984, but there was strong opposition from local ranchers and miners. The Box was ultimately included as part of the 25,750-acre Box-Death Hollow Wilderness Area, but only after the exclusion of the long, narrow plateau that separates the Box and Death Hollow. Now the map of the Box-Death Hollow Wilderness Area looks like a mitten, with Pine Creek running down the thumb. Cattle fences have been built to keep cows out of the Box, but the numerous cow pies in the canyon suggest that the effort hasn't been completely successful.

There is no trail from the road to the bottom of Pine Creek at the Upper Box access point. Just walk down the slope for a few hundred feet until you reach the creek, and then start following it downstream. There are bits and pieces of an unmaintained trail along the streambed, but for the most part you are on your own. Don't hesitate to walk across the stream if the terrain looks a little flatter on the other side, and don't work too hard at trying to keep your feet dry. You will be fording the creek many times before this hike is finished, so you might as will plunge in now and let your feet get used to the cold water.

The first few miles of the Box are particularly scenic, with steep cliffs coming down to the water's edge first on one side and then on the other. The banks of the creek are lined with spruce and occasionally Douglas fir. Fortunately no rock climbing is necessary, as there is always a passable route on at least one side of the canyon. Also, the water is seldom more that shin-deep at the crossing points.

After about 3.0 miles the canyon widens slightly and the rim becomes much higher.

After 4.3 miles you will meet Deep Creek, a tiny creek flowing in from the west. At this point you have lost about 730 feet of elevation, and you are a little less than half way through the hike. The canyon rim is about a thousand feet above you.

Below the Deep Creek confluence the forest gradually turns from spruce and Douglas fir to ponderosa pine, and the trail also gradually improves. You are more apt to encounter other hikers here—picnickers who have entered the Box from the lower trailhead. As the canyon widens the trail also becomes more and more sandy, the result of erosion on the sandstone cliffs that surround the Box.

Finally, 4.5 miles below Deep Creek, Pine Creek makes a sudden, dramatic exit through a slot in the cliffs out of the Box and onto Lost Creek Flat where your shuttle car is parked. Hell's Backbone Road is another 0.3 mile from the end of the trail.

The Pine Creek Box

Calf Creek

★★★★   **Grand Staircase - Escalante National Monument**
day hike

Distance:	5.4 miles (round trip)
Walking time:	3 hours
Elevations:	170 ft. gain/loss Calf Creek Trailhead (start): 5,340 ft. Lower Calf Creek Falls: 5,510 ft.
Trail:	Popular, well maintained trail. A trail guide is usually available at the trailhead.
Season:	Spring, summer, fall, winter. The trail is very hot in the summer, with temperatures often exceeding 100 degrees F.
Vicinity:	Near Escalante and Boulder
Maps:	Calf Creek (*USGS*) Canyons of the Escalante (*Trails Illustrated, #710*)
Information:	http://www.utahtrails.com/calfcreek.html (*Utah Trails*) http://www.ut.blm.gov/monument/ (*Grand Staircase-Escalante*) phone: (435) 826-5499 (*Escalante Interagency Visitor Center*)

Drive east from Escalante toward Boulder on Highway 12 for 16.3 miles to the Calf Creek Campground. The trailhead is near the back of the campground 0.4 mile from the highway. (Note: there is a charge of $2.00/vehicle for day use of Calf Creek Recreation Area. The campground is a pleasant place to spend the night, but if that is your plan you had better arrive early. It is very popular.)

Calf Creek Trail is the highlight of the Calf Creek Recreation Area, a delightful desert oasis maintained by the Bureau of Land Management. The canyon is a haven for birds, beaver, and other wildlife, and it was also once inhabited by the Fremont and Anasazi Indians. Take a booklet with you from the trailhead to help you spot some of the Indian pictographs and two granaries that were constructed by the Indians some 800-1000 years ago. Also, be sure to take a swimming suit to use in the pool at the bottom of Lower Calf Creek Falls.

The Calf Creek Trail winds along the west side of Calf Creek, a small desert stream surrounded by vertical walls of white and pink Navajo Sandstone. Not surpris-

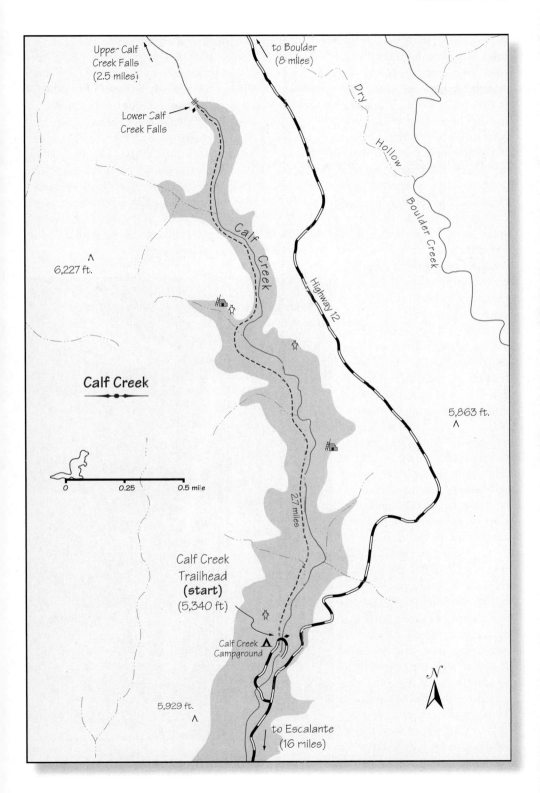

Upper Calf
Creek Falls
(2.5 miles)

to Boulder
(8 miles)

Dry

Hollow

Boulder Creek

Lower Calf
Creek Falls

Calf Creek

6,227 ft.

Highway 12

5,863 ft.

Calf Creek

0   0.25   0.5 mile

2.7 miles

Calf Creek
Trailhead
(start)
(5,340 ft)

Calf Creek ▲
Campground

5,929 ft.

N

to Escalante
(16 miles)

ingly, much of the trail is covered with loose sand. As the cliffs erode, the ancient beds of sand from which the Navajo Sandstone was originally made are slowly being returned to the canyon floor. The dominant trees in the canyon are pinion and juniper, although cottonwoods and box elders can also be found along the stream. Many of the latter species show damage from beaver; you can scarcely walk a hundred yards along the creek without seeing a beaver dam.

About 0.9 mile from the trailhead a small stone structure can be seen near the top of the cliffs across the river. This is the remains of a granary built by the Fremont or Anasazi Indians around 1100 A.D. to store the grain they grew on the canyon floor. Another half mile upstream, closer to the canyon floor, the Fremont Indians painted three large ceremonial human figures in red. The coloring of these pictographs is remarkably well preserved despite centuries of exposure to the sun and rain. Still more pictographs and another granary are visible in a small side canyon west of the creek about 1.6 miles from the trailhead.

Calf Creek Canyon was also briefly settled by white settlers in the early 1900s, and at one time there was a fence across a narrow part of the canyon where the homesteaders weaned their calves. A part of the fence can still be seen from the trail, and it was this early ranching activity that gave the canyon its name. Calf Creek was also locally famous for the tasty watermelons its farmers produced. Today, however, the farms and ranches have been long abandoned and very little evidence remains of the early homesteading activity.

Finally, after 2.7 miles, Calf Creek Canyon abruptly dead ends against a 130-foot-high vertical wall of Navajo Sandstone, making it obvious that the end of the hike has been reached. Here the creek emanates from the base of the Lower Calf Creek Waterfall. The setting is beautiful, with a sandy shore, large shade trees, and a clear pool below the fall. Most hikers stay awhile for a swim before heading back.

Lower Calf Creek Falls

Upper Calf Creek

★★★

Grand Staircase - Escalante National Monument
day hike

Distance:	8.2 miles (round trip to all points of interest)
Walking time:	5 ¹/₂ hours
Elevations:	880 ft. loss/gain Upper Calf Creek Trailhead (start): 6,520 ft. Upper Calf Creek Falls: 5,920 ft. top of Lower Calf Creek Falls: 5,640 ft.
Trail:	The trail to the upper falls is a well-marked slickrock trail. There is no trail for the 3.2 mile walk from the upper falls to the lower falls. The route is easy, but some serious scrambling and perhaps swimming will be required near the end.
Season:	Spring, summer, fall, winter. The trail is very hot in the summer, and there may occasionally be snow in the winter. Winter hikers rarely venture beyond the upper falls, since continuing on to the lower falls requires a great deal of wading.
Vicinity:	Near Escalante and Boulder
Maps:	Calf Creek *(USGS)* Canyons of the Escalante *(Trails Illustrated, #710)*
Information:	http://www.utahtrails.com/uppercalfcreek.html *(Utah Trails)* http://www.ut.blm.gov/monument/ *(Grand Staircase-Escalante)* phone: (435) 826-5499 *(Escalante Interagency Visitor Center)*

Drive east from Escalante toward Boulder on Highway 12 for 16.3 miles to the Calf Creek Campground. Check your odometer as you pass the turnout to the campground and continue driving north for another 6.0 miles. There you will see an unmarked, ungraded dirt road that turns off the pavement on the left. Take this road and drive for another 250 yards through the pinions and junipers to a parking area on the canyon rim. The trail starts at a trail register on the west side of the parking area.

This trail is usually taken by people who have already hiked to Lower Calf Creek Falls (page 368) and want to see more of this delightful canyon. The highlight of the trail

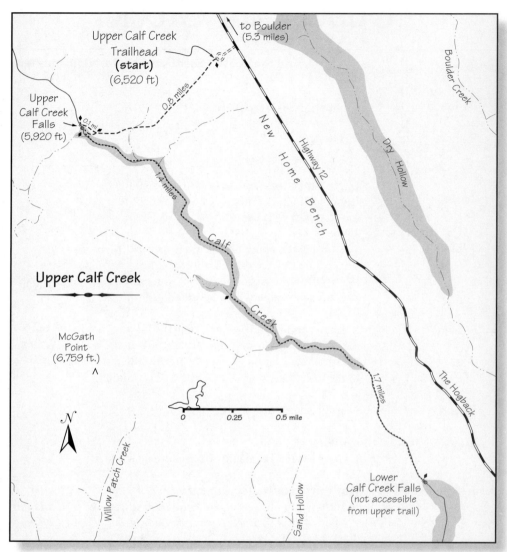

is Upper Calf Creek Falls, which is only 0.9 mile from the trailhead, and that is as far as most people go before turning around. If you have time, however, I urge you to walk downstream at least part of the way from the upper falls toward the lower falls before returning to your car. Unlike the trail through the lower half of Calf Creek Canyon there are no Indian granaries or pictographs to see along the way, but the thrill of walking through the lush, seldom-seen upper canyon will provide ample reward.

The trail begins its descent into Upper Calf Creek Canyon immediately after leaving the trailhead. As you walk downward you can gaze out across a vast sea of sandstone slickrock. What an unlikely place to find a babbling creek, in the midst of a seemingly endless desert of barren sandstone. But, oddly enough, the parched stone is really key to the existence of Calf Creek

Pools above Upper Calf Creek Falls

and other flowing streams in the area.

The fact is that the geologic formation surrounding Calf Creek, called Navajo Sandstone, is not as solid as it appears. When this formation was laid down some 180 million years ago the grains of sand were only loosely cemented together. Microscopic voids were left between the tiny particles. Now, because of these voids, some of the rainwater that falls onto the surface of the slickrock is able to seep ever so slowly downward and eventually reappear in the canyons below.

As you walk down into the canyon you will notice that much of the terrain is littered with black boulders of basalt. This debris came from a series of volcanic eruptions that occurred northwest of Boulder some 20 million years ago. The BLM has thoughtfully rolled most of the volcanic boulders to the side of the trail so they do not present a problem for hikers.

Most of the 600 feet of elevation loss to the canyon floor occurs in the first 0.4 mile

of the trail; beyond that the trail leaves the slickrock and levels out in a more sandy area. Continuing downward at a more gradual

Upper Calf Creek

rate, the trail next begins to turn to the right as it follows the rim of the Calf Creek gorge. Soon you will see the upper falls on the northeast side of the canyon, opposite a large alcove in the western wall. The trail splits here, with the right fork leading to the top of the waterfall and the left fork dropping on down to the bottom of the canyon.

Above the fall the stream flows through a series of small cascades and pools before suddenly plunging over the edge. It is worth spending some time here, especially if you have a camera. The contrast between the riparian streambed and the adjacent slickrock is stark. There is very little soil in the area, and the terrain changes from stark white sandstone to a lush green aquatic environment in just a few inches. The ponds are filled with tadpoles, but no fish.

Inside the gorge the trail soon ends on the south side of an 80-foot-diameter pond that defines the bottom of the waterfall. The setting is very similar to the scene below Lower Calf Creek Falls except that here the pond is lined with a carpet of thick, untrampled grass that grows right to the water's edge. The waterfall itself is about 110 feet high with a flow rate slightly less than that of the lower falls.

The 3.1-mile walk downstream from the upper falls to the top of Lower Calf Creek Falls is a memorable wilderness experience. Few people walk the entire distance, and the canyon is wild and pristine. The dense vegetation that lines the streambed generally makes walking along the shore impractical, but if you stay in the stream you will encounter few obstacles. The water is seldom more than a foot deep, and the creek is alive with 8-inch native brown trout that dart here and there in the shallow water as they hear you coming. How these fish initially migrated into this section of the creek between the two falls is a mystery.

As Calf Creek approaches the lower waterfall the canyon narrows, the gradient steepens, and the hike becomes more exciting. The fast running water in this area has carved out a series of pools and water slides, and some serious scrambling is required in a few places. Finally you will come to a small pool of relatively deep water that you can't get around without a short swim. Just beyond that pool lies the lip of the lower waterfall where the hike must end. There is no easy way to continue beyond the top of the waterfall.

Upper Calf Creek Falls

Escalante River

★★★★

Grand Staircase - Escalante National Monument
shuttle car required
overnight hike

Distance:	14.3 miles (plus 14.4 miles by car)
Walking time:	day 1: 4 hours day 2: 3¾ hours
Elevations:	530 ft. loss Escalante Town Trailhead (start): 5,730 ft. Death Hollow: 5,380 ft. Escalante River Trailhead: 5,200 ft.
Trail:	The route follows along the shore of the Escalante River. There is a sandy trail most of the way, but often it is easier to walk in the gravel filled streambed so be sure to wear wettable shoes. The water is seldom more than ankle deep.
Season:	Spring, summer, fall, winter. The best seasons for this hike are spring and fall. Escalante Canyon is very hot in the summertime, but you can always count on the availability of water.
Vicinity:	Near the town of Escalante
Maps:	Escalante, Calf Creek *(USGS)* Canyons of the Escalante *(Trails Illustrated, #710)*
Information:	http://www.utahtrails.com/escalante.html *(Utah Trails)* http://www.ut.blm.gov/monument/ *(Grand Staircase-Escalante)* phone: (435) 826-5499 *(Escalante Interagency Visitor Center)*

Drive east on Highway 12 from the center of Escalante Town for 1.2 miles until you see a small cemetery on your left. Turn off the highway here and continue past the cemetery on a small dirt road that leads to the city dump. After 0.4 mile you will come to a fork in the road where you must turn left for the final 0.5 mile to the Escalante Town Trailhead. Be sure to sign in at the trail register and obtain a free backcountry permit before you start.

Before beginning the hike you will need to place a shuttle car at the Escalante River Trailhead where the hike ends. To get there drive east toward Boulder on Highway 12 for 13.5 miles past the cemetery to the point where Highway 12 crosses the Escalante River (14.7

miles from Escalante Town, or 12.7 miles from Boulder). On the north end of the bridge you will see a turnout on the left that leads to the trailhead and parking area.

The 85-mile-long Escalante River is well known among Utah's backcountry enthusiasts. The small river and its dozens of side canyons contain some of the wildest, most scenic desert wilderness in the United States. It is a region of redrock canyons, sandstone arches, and Anasazi Indian ruins. The Escalante badlands contain hidden natural treasures guaranteed to give pause to even the most unenthusiastic of hikers. Sadly, none of the BLM managed Escalante drainage has yet been give the protection of a designated wilderness area, but in 1996 it was included in President Clinton's new Grand Staircase-Escalante National Monument.

Although the Escalante drains over 200 square miles of the Colorado Plateau, it is so remote that its existence wasn't even known until the middle of the last century. In 1866 it became the last major river to be discovered in the American West. It was named six years later in honor of the early Spanish explorer Silvestre Valez de Escalante who passed through Utah in 1776.

There are a number of hikes in the area that touch upon parts of the Escalante River, but the 14-mile section of the river described here is the most accessible. It is also a particularly interesting section, with fine examples of the sorts of things that make the Escalante drainage so interesting: petroglyphs, Anasazi ruins, natural arches, and slickrock pools.

Day 1 (7.3 miles)

From the trailhead near Escalante Town the trail winds down a small sandy hill for about 0.2 mile before intersecting the Escalante River. The trail reaches the river very close to its source, and at this point the Escalante is little more than a muddy wash lined with unsightly tamarisk trees and old tires that have washed down from the city dump. But don't despair. Within a mile the canyon becomes more pristine.

Soon after the river enters Escalante Canyon, near the junction with Pine Creek,

Escalante River

Escalante River petroglyphs

you will pass a gauging station used for measuring the water flow. From that point the trail often splits, giving you a choice of which side of the river to walk on. Just pick the easiest side, and don't bother trying to keep your feet dry. It is futile.

If you are interested in Indian artifacts try to stay on the north side of the river as much as possible because that is the side the prehistoric Indians along the Escalante preferred. The winter sun shines more directly on the north side of the canyon; hence it has less snow during the winter months. There are at least three small panels of prehistoric rock art within 2.2 miles of the gauging station. They are all situated on the north side of the canyon at the base of the cliffs in areas where the canyon runs due east and west. The first two sites are petroglyphs and the third is a badly damaged panel of pictographs in the back of a large alcove just above the water line.

The scenery gets better and better the farther downstream you walk. There are many good camp sites along the way, but if you plan to spend only one night in the canyon you should try to camp near the junction with Death Hollow. This side canyon is exceptionally pretty and, if time permits, you should try to spend at least a few hours exploring it before continuing down the Escalante.

Death Hollow is a 23-mile-long drainage

Escalante River

map continues on bottom of next page

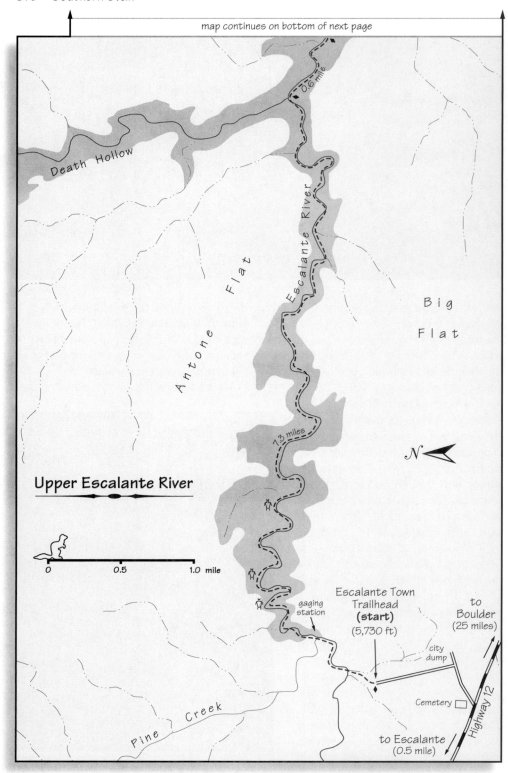

Death Hollow

0.6 mile

Escalante River

Antone Flat

Big Flat

1.3 miles

Upper Escalante River

N

0   0.5   1.0 mile

Escalante Town
Trailhead
(start)
(5,730 ft)

to
Boulder
(25 miles)

city
dump

gaging
station

Cemetery

Highway 12

Pine Creek

to Escalante
(0.5 mile)

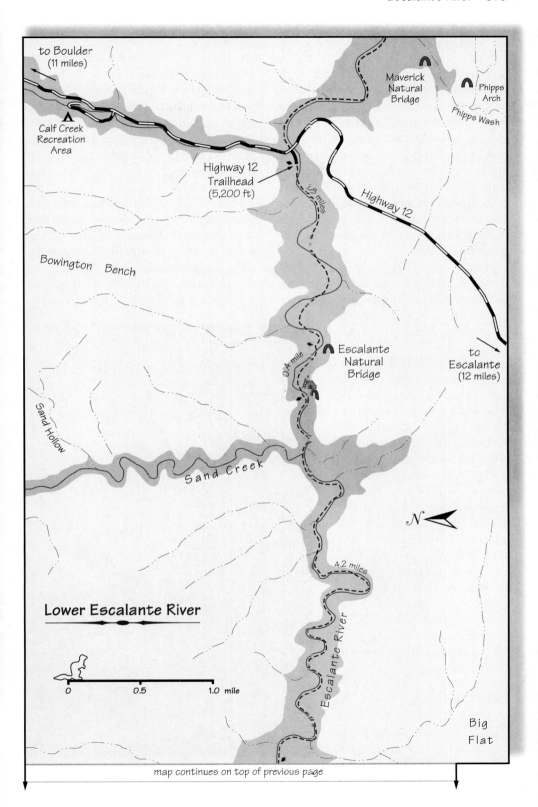

to Boulder
(11 miles)

Calf Creek
Recreation
Area

Maverick
Natural
Bridge

Phipps
Arch

Phipps Wash

Highway 12
Trailhead
(5,200 ft)

1.3 miles

Highway 12

Bowington   Bench

0.4 mile

Escalante
Natural
Bridge

to
Escalante
(12 miles)

Sand Hollow

Sand Creek

N

4.2 miles

Lower Escalante River

0   0.5   1.0 mile

Escalante River

Big
Flat

map continues on top of previous page

that begins near the Hells Backbone Road between Escalante Town and Boulder. The dry upper reaches of the hollow lie within the boundaries of Dixie National Forest and are part of the Box-Death Hollow Wilderness Area. The oasis-like Lower part of Death Hollow, however, lies within the jurisdiction of the Bureau of Land Management, and is not part of the designated wilderness area. Hopefully this situation will change in the future, but for now the most exquisite part of Death Hollow, along with the rest of the Escalante Basin, remains relatively unprotected.

Lower Death Hollow is best explored without a backpack. For the first mile the fast flowing stream rushes down the scenic canyon between patches of wild flowers and, unfortunately, poison ivy. It is best to wear long pants when walking through the foliage, or wade in the center of the streambed. After about a mile and a half the canyon begins to narrow noticeably, and you will encounter a series of pools and water slides. The best pools for swimming are about two miles upstream from the Escalante. The setting is idyllic: crystal-clear slickrock swimming holes, surrounded by pink sandstone cliffs and decorated with green foliage and yellow wildflowers. You might want to extend your hike by a day just to enjoy the attributes of the ill-named canyon. (See page 382 for a more detailed description of Death Hollow.)

Day 2 (7.0 miles)

From the mouth of Death Hollow, the Escalante River flows eastward for another 4.0 miles before coming to the junc-tion with Sand Creek, another possible side trip though not quite of the same caliber as Death Hollow. Beyond that, another 0.4 mile will bring you to Escalante Natural Arch, the first of two natural arches along this stretch of the river. It is situated high on the top of the canyon wall on the right side of the river. Impressive as this arch is, however, an even more thrilling sight is an Anasazi Indian ruin that lies just below the east side of the arch. The cliff dwelling is in the back of a large alcove about 150 feet above the canyon floor.

This ruin is extremely unusual because it lies on the south wall of the canyon and faces almost directly north. No winter sun ever shines into this alcove, yet 700 years ago it was home to a large family of Anasazis.

Death Hollow

It is quite obvious that they chose this site specifically because of its proximity to the stone arch above it. The arch must have had powerful magic for these Indians, and I can imagine that living below it must have filled them with an immense sense of well being. The location was important enough for them to forego all of the conventional wisdom of the day by living on the coldest side of the canyon.

While you are looking at the ruin notice the long jagged line that was painted on the cliff just above the largest dwelling in the alcove. One can only guess what the line represented or what its purpose was, but to me it appears to be some kind of spiritual shield separating the Indian home from the arch above–as if the arch's magic was so strong it was necessary to partially deflect it from the nearby house.

The next natural arch, usually referred to as Escalante Natural Bridge, is located on the same side of the canyon, 0.4 mile downstream from the first one. (see photograph on page 390.) There are no Indian ruins near this arch and, though impressive, it is in near perpetual shade and difficult to photograph. It does have one feature, however, that makes it quite interesting. The 200-foot-high span stands directly in front of a 150-foot-deep alcove in the cliff–like the grand entrance to a giant ballroom. A small trail leads through the portal and circles around the ballroom, providing an opportunity to view the sandstone arch from a different perspective. There are also a few old cowboy glyphs carved into the walls of the room, one of which is dated 1917.

Beyond the last natural arch

Escalante Canyon widens considerably as the trail winds over the last 1.8 miles to the trailhead at Highway 12. This part of the canyon is known as Phipps Death Hollow after a tragedy that occurred here in 1878. According to local folklore two cowboys named John Boynton and Washington Phipps were partners in a ranching operation along this stretch of the Escalante when Boynton shot and killed Phipps during an argument over a woman. So distraught was Boynton over what he had done that he saddled up and rode his horse to Escalante to give himself up. The authorities in Escalante gave him ten dollars and told him to report to the county sheriff in Parowan, but he must have had second thoughts along the way because he was never seen again.

Escalante Natural Arch

Death Hollow

Distance:	20.4 miles
	(plus 10.6 miles by car)
Walking time:	day 1: 3 hours
	day 2: 5 hours
	day 3: 3¾ hours
Elevations:	1,560 ft. loss
	Boulder Mail Trail parking (start): 6,760 ft.
	Boulder Mail Trailhead: 6,640 ft.
	Death Hollow–Escalante confluence: 5,380 ft.
	Escalante River Trailhead: 5,200 ft.

Trail: There is no reliable trail for most of this hike, however the route is very easy to follow. You will be walking through water much of the time, so wear wettable shoes. It may be necessary to float your backpack across a pool of water in one or two places, so you should also carry an air mattress and a watertight river bag to keep your gear dry. Also, you may occasionally have to walk through thick undergrowth, so wear long pants.

Season: Summer, early fall. You will be spending a great deal of time in the water on this hike, so it should be done in warm weather. The best time is from mid-June through September. Flash floods are possible, especially at the end of summer, so stay out of the canyon if it looks like rain. There is also a great deal of water in Death Hollow during the spring runoff from mid-May to mid-June. It is still possible to go through the canyon at this time, but you may have to do some swimming to get past the obstacles.

Vicinity: Near Boulder and Escalante

Maps: Boulder Town, Calf Creek, Escalante *(USGS)*
Canyons of the Escalante *(Trails Illustrated, #710)*

Information: http://www.utahtrails.com/deathhollow.html *(Utah Trails)*
http://www.ut.blm.gov/monument/ *(Grand Staircase-Escalante)*
phone: (435) 826-5499 *(Escalante Interagency Visitor Center)*

Drive south from Boulder on Highway 12 for 3.0 miles to the Hell's Backbone Road. (If you are starting in Escalante drive east on Highway 12 for 24.8 miles.) Turn onto Hell's Backbone Road and continue for another 0.2 mile, where you will see a small, unmarked road on the left leading to the Boulder Airport. Turn south here. After 0.4 mile you will arrive at the airport; con-
tinue on across the runway and in another 0.1 mile you will see the parking area for the Boulder Mail Trailhead on your left. The actual trailhead where the hike begins is another 1.0 mile down the road. Be sure to sign in at the trail register and obtain a free backcountry permit before you start.

The hike ends at the Escalante River Trailhead, which is on Highway 12 about half way between Boulder and Escalante. From Hells Backbone Road you must drive south on Highway 12 for 10.0 miles to the bridge that crosses the Escalante River. The Escalante River Trailhead and parking area are just on the north side of the bridge.

This is one of those special hikes that has something for almost everyone. The first part of the route follows the old Boulder Mail Trail, an historical trail characterized by wide vistas of slickrock desert with stunning views into Sand Creek Canyon and Death Hollow. The second part of the trail descends through the lower half of Death Hollow, a deep, wild, and watery canyon with scenery that is often spectacular. Finally, the trail leaves Death Hollow to follow a more serene section of the Escalante River past two natural arches and an Anasazi cliff dwelling to the trailhead near Calf Creek.

The first and last sections of the hike are easy, and can be done at almost anytime of the year. In Death Hollow, however, you will be walking in the streambed much of the time, and the difficulty is strongly dependent on how much water is present. Most of the year the water is never more than knee deep, but in some months hikers may have to swim to get across some of the pools. To be safe you should carry a river bag and an air mattress—just in case you have to float your pack across an unexpected pool of water. The worst time to hike through Death Hollow is during the spring runoff from mid-May through mid-June, when the creek is often flowing at 3-4 times its normal volume.

There can also be problems in August, the month that receives the most rain. Never venture into the canyon if it looks like rain, since there is an ever-present danger of flash floods. But the flow rate usually drops off quickly, so if it has not rained for a few days you can generally expect good conditions.

Boulder Mail Trail into Death Hollow

Day 1 (5.6 miles)

After leaving the road the trail winds across the McGath Point Bench in a south-westerly direction. The vegetation is primarily pinion pine and juniper, although there is not enough soil to support much of a forest.

Most of the route is over slickrock, and you must depend on cairns to show you the way. Initially the grade is level, but soon the trail starts downward as it begins its long descent into the Sand Creek drainage. The creek is located 1.8 miles from the trailhead.

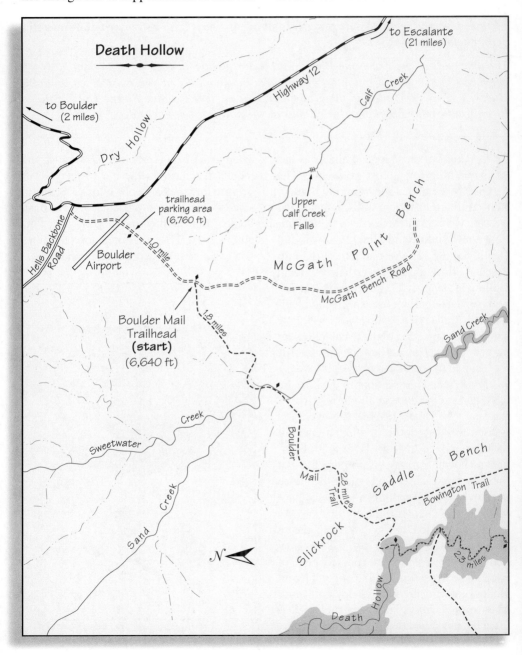

Death Hollow

to Escalante
(21 miles)

Highway 12

to Boulder
(2 miles)

Dry Hollow

Calf Creek

Hells Backbone Road

trailhead
parking area
(6,760 ft)

Upper
Calf Creek
Falls

McGath Point Bench

1.0 mile

Boulder
Airport

McGath Bench Road

Boulder Mail
Trailhead
(start)
(6,640 ft)

1.8 miles

Sand Creek

Creek

Sweetwater

Sand Creek

Boulder Mail Trail

2.8 miles

Saddle Bench

Bowington Trail

N

Slickrock

2.3 miles

Death Hollow

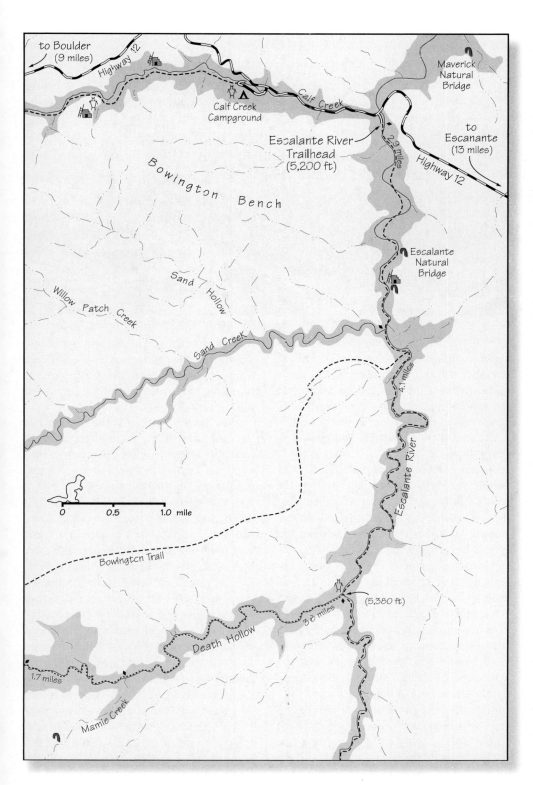

to Boulder
(9 miles)

Highway 12

Maverick
Natural
Bridge

Calf Creek

Calf Creek
Campground

Escalante River
Trailhead
(5,200 ft)

to
Escanante
(13 miles)

Highway 12

2.9 miles

Bowington Bench

Escalante
Natural
Bridge

Sand Hollow

Willow Patch Creek

Sand Creek

4.1 miles

Escalante River

0   0.5   1.0 mile

Bowington Trail

(5,380 ft)

3.8 miles

Death Hollow

1.7 miles

Mamie Creek

Looking down into Death Hollow from the Mail Trail

Sand Creek is a small perennial stream that runs through the bottom of a shallow, slickrock canyon. The trail crosses the creek soon after reaching it, and then follows its west side for 0.2 mile before climbing back to the top of the plateau. If you got off to a late start there are several good places to camp along the creek.

After climbing out of Sand Creek Canyon the path begins a long meander over the top of Slickrock Saddle Bench. The Mail Trail was once an important communications link between the towns of Boulder and Escalante, and you can still see the remains of an old telegraph line that ran beside the trail linking the two towns. The line was built by the U.S. Forest Service in 1910, and it was still in use as recently as 1955. It consists of a single galvanized iron wire strung across the desert on poles and live trees.

2.5 miles after leaving Sand Creek you will come to a fork where the Bowington Trail departs on the left. This trail is occasionally used as an alternative route to the Escalante River for pack animals. Bear to the right at the fork, and within a few minutes you will see the ground open up

in front of you as Death Hollow comes into view. Unlike the more mundane Sand Creek Canyon, Death Hollow forms a deep gorge in the slickrock plateau and the view from the top is dramatic.

Just before you reach the canyon rim the trail turns sharply to the right and then begins its descent. Before going down, however, you should drop your pack and spend ten minutes enjoying the view from above. If you leave the trail just before it turns to start down (near a large ponderosa pine tree) and walk straight ahead for a hundred yards you will come to an overlook point where there is an especially fine view into Death Hollow.

The route into Death Hollow follows a steep slickrock trail with about 640 feet of elevation loss. This section of the old Mail Trail must have been especially precarious for pack animals. It is said that the canyon received its name around the turn of the last century when a mule stumbled and fell into the gorge. Near the bottom the path passes by a large alcove that is a favorite campsite for backpackers. The alcove is located near the right side of the trail, about 100 feet above the canyon floor. There is a large flat area in the back of the recess, big enough to accommodate a small group of campers, and the site is well sheltered from the weather. If you prefer to be nearer the water there are also several nice sites on the canyon floor, or if you decide to walk further downstream you will have no trouble finding good campsites along the entire length of Death Hollow.

Day 2 (7.8 miles)

The 7.8 miles from the Boulder Mail Trail through Death Hollow to the Escalante River are the most exciting part of this hike. The hiker-made trail frequently plunges in and out of the streambed, dodging brush and boulders as it searches in vain for an easy way down the canyon. Occasionally you will encounter deep pools on the canyon floor, but there is usually an easy way around them. Under normal conditions you shouldn't have to cross any pools that are more than knee deep.

I have been in Death Hollow three times, and deep water never presented a serious obstacle to my progress. But I must add that conditions change from year to year in the canyon, and it is impossible to predict what one might encounter. Every few years a flash flood will roar down the gorge, washing all of the sand and rock from the potholes and turning shallow wading pools into deep swimming holes. So be prepared.

Death Hollow is not a place you would want to be during a flash flood, so always check the weather before entering the canyon, and stay out if it looks like rain. Flash floods are not particularly common, but there is ample evidence within the canyon to verify their existence (huge logs left stranded high above the streambed, flotsam stuck on the branches of trees). Most of the floods occur from mid-August to mid-September when

there are more thunderstorms, so if you are hiking during these months be especially careful. Also, try to avoid Death Hollow during the spring runoff. If you are hiking in late spring I can almost guarantee that you will have problems with deep water.

There is one more hazard in Death Hollow that should be mentioned: poison ivy. Poison Ivy is a bright green, usually shrubby plant that grows 2-3 feet high. Its leaves always grow at the ends of the stems in groups of three, and its pea-sized berries are yellowish white in color. For some reason there is a great abundance of poison ivy growing in the lower reaches of the canyon so be careful not to walk through it.

About fifteen minutes after reaching the bottom of Death Hollow the trail passes by a cairn on the right that marks the exit point

Death Hollow

of the Boulder Mail Trail. The old telegraph line crosses the canyon a short distance upstream. You may have also noticed an abundance of black volcanic boulders that have washed down the canyon from an old eruption to the north. The insoluble basaltic boulders are not easily eroded by the stream and they just keep moving down the canyon with each new flash flood. They are present in all the canyons of the Escalante drainage.

After 3.8 miles and countless stream crossings the trail passes by the mouth of Mamie Creek, roughly the halfway point of the hike. Below Mamie the canyon narrows in several places to a width of only 30 feet or less. The sandy bottom of the streambed is the easiest place to walk, but be on the lookout for quicksand. Quicksand most commonly occurs is places where the water is flowing very slowly or not at all, such as on the downstream side of a large boulder

Death Hollow

or other obstruction. It is not life threatening, but it can cause you to stumble and fall.

About halfway between the Mamie Creek confluence and the Escalante River the canyon walls narrow around a fast flowing waterslide on the canyon floor. Sliding down the smooth sandstone chute can be a lot of fun, but getting a backpack around it presents a problem. It is usually possible to get past the waterslide by crawling along a narrow shelf at the edge of the water, but this is hard to do with a pack and if you slip you will slide in. Alternatively, you can carry your pack around the chute on a ledge above the creek and lower it back down with a short piece of rope. Or, if all else fails you can always just go down the waterslide with your gear in a river bag and hope that it doesn't get soaking wet!

Finally, 1.9 miles below the waterslide, the trail reaches the Escalante River. There is a good place to camp in the grove of cottonwood trees on the opposite side of the Escalante, or if you prefer you can camp on the sandbar near the confluence. But before it gets dark you should take some time to examine the base of the cliff on the northeast side of the confluence. This area appears to have been occupied by the Anasazi in prehistoric times. The base of the cliff contains many badly eroded petroglyphs, including an easily recognizable impression of two desert bighorn sheep. I also saw a broken grinding stone while I was there.

Day 3 (7.0 miles)

The Escalante River is less wild than Death Hollow, and the 7.0-mile walk to the Boulder Highway is much more serene. Nevertheless, the Escalante has its own special beauty. Escalante Canyon is more open, with a wide, flat bottom, closed in on both sides by familiar walls of Navajo Sandstone. For 50 feet on either side of the river the ground

Death Hollow

is covered with dense thickets of tamarisk, willow, and cottonwood trees. But away from the river there are wide avenues of sagebrush covered desert. The trail avoids the river most of the time, but when the canyon narrows and the trail is forced back into the trees it is often much easier to walk right in the streambed.

4.8 miles below Death Hollow the trail passes the first major landmark along this section of the Escalante River: Escalante Natural Arch (see photograph on page 381.) The arch sits high on the south rim of the canyon, and is completely inaccessible from the bottom. Interestingly, there is an Anasazi cliff dwelling in an alcove just below the east side of the arch. The site faces north and would have been a very uncomfortable place to stay in the winter; nevertheless it looks as though the family that occupied the alcove was very well established. 700 years ago there were many Indians living along the Escalante. With its wide flat bottom and its reliable water supply the canyon must have been an ideal place for them to grow corn and squash. Although there are

many petroglyph sites along the river, the ruin near Escalante Natural Arch is one of the few remaining Anasazi dwellings. Most of the inhabitants must have lived in more

Escalante River

Escalante Natural Bridge

is well defined in this area, as many day hikers walk in from the highway to see the Escalante Natural Bridge. You should reach the Escalante River Trailhead and the end of the hike after about 45 minutes.

Upper Death Hollow

If you are the adventurous type and are looking for something more challenging than the hike described above you might want to consider entering Death Hollow from the upper trailhead on Hell's Backbone Road. To get there drive west from Highway 12 on Hells Backbone Road for 16.5 miles until you see a small Forest Service sign marking the Death Hollow Trailhead. (If you are coming from the other direction the trailhead is 4.5 miles east of the road to the Blue Spruce Campground.)

Upper Death Hollow is much different from the lower part of the canyon. In lower Death Hollow you will often be required to wade through pools of water, but they are seldom more than 3 feet deep. In the upper part of the canyon, however, the water barriers generally occur at the bottoms of deep V-shaped channels in the sandstone with sides so steep it is impossible to go around them. The slots can be up to 100 yards long, and the water in them is often too deep for wading. To make matters worse the narrow water-filled channels are frequently preceded by large chock stones that make it necessary to climb or slide down as far as 10 feet before splashing into the cold water.

How to get through these water barriers? In those places where wading is impossible most people swim and float their backpacks across on air mattresses. In a few places it is possible for one person to swim through the channel and then walk back over a ledge above the water and pull the backpacks up

temporary structures on the canyon floor.

The main trail continues eastward from the Escalante Arch along the north side of the river, but I suggest you pick up a lessor used trail near the Anasazi ruin on the south side of the river. This trail meets the river again 0.4 mile further downstream near the Escalante Natural Bridge, an even more impressive formation. The natural bridge lies in front a huge 200-foot diameter alcove that has been etched into the sandstone walls by a seep at the base of the sandstone cliff. The 15-foot-thick bridge is 200 feet high and spans across the entire width of the alcove. (Technically, since it was not formed by running water this formation is really a natural arch, not a bridge. But most maps still refer to it as Escalante Natural Bridge.)

East of the Escalante Natural Bridge the canyon widens out as the river makes three more long meanders before reaching Calf Creek and the Boulder Highway. The trail

Upper Death Hollow

you intend to exit at the Escalante River Trailhead.

The first part of this trail is very steep, loosing 500 feet in the first 0.3 mile. But after the initial drop it settles down to a more gradual rate of descent, finally reaching the bottom of the drainage 0.6 mile from the trailhead. From there a vague, often nonexistent trail follows the dry canyon floor for another 9.4 miles before finally coming to the first water.

Within 0.3 mile after reaching the first water you will arrive at the canyon's first serious obstacle, a waist-deep pool about 30 feet long. This pool is just a mild introduction to what lies ahead. Over the next 2.5 miles you will be forced to negotiate one watery barrier after another. The depth of the water will occasionally be over your head, but most of the time it is no more than chest deep. If you didn't have to worry about a backpack the barriers wouldn't really be a problem, but getting backpacks across the pools can be a difficult, time-consuming chore.

1.5 miles below the first barrier you will come to a narrow constriction where a huge chock stone has lodged, forming a 15-foot drop in the canyon floor. This particular obstacle would be enough to stop most people, but fortunately there is a way around it. If you will climb to the top of a 100-foot sandy ridge on the left side of the streambed you will see another side canyon coming in from the north. This is Right Fork, a major tributary of Death Hollow. Right Fork runs parallel to Death Hollow for a few hundred yards before intersecting the main canyon below the worrisome chock stone. By crossing the ridge into Right Fork and then walking to the confluence you can completely avoid the obstacle.

I should mention that there is an extraordinarily nice campsite in Right Fork Canyon.

with a 50-foot length of rope. Probably the easiest and fastest way to get through the deeper parts is to carry a river bag large enough for your entire backpack. This will allow you to float your gear through the channels and also use your pack as a flotation device to assist you in swimming.

Whatever you do, the most important thing is to plan ahead and be prepared for whatever you might encounter. Three essential items are 100 feet of rope, some way of keeping your gear dry, and some kind of flotation device for your backpack. Most important, you shouldn't attempt this hike alone. Two or three people working together will make the job of getting through the water barriers much easier, and if you get into trouble in the water someone with a rope can make all the difference. Allow 4 full days to get from the Hell's Backbone Road to the Boulder Mail Trailhead, or longer if

Upper Death Hollow

canyon changes dramatically. Gone are the narrow sandstone slots and stagnant water that caused so much trouble before. Instead you will find a pristine environment where the water is flowing and the canyon is filled with rich soil and lush vegetation.

As you approach the Mail Trail you will come upon a hiker-made trail that makes walking much easier. Finally, 18.2 miles after leaving Hell's Backbone Road you will arrive at the junction where the Mail Trail enters Death Hollow. Here you can either exit Death Hollow and walk to the Boulder Airport or continue down the canyon to the Escalante River along the route described earlier.

It is easy to miss the junction with the Boulder Mail Trail if you aren't paying attention, but if you are observant you shouldn't have any trouble. Just stay on the well-worn path and look for another obvious trail that leaves abruptly to the left and starts climbing up the east side of the canyon. Shortly after the junction the canyon makes a hairpin turn from east to west and passes under the old telegraph wire that is strung across the canyon about 30 feet above the ground.

When you drop into Right Fork you will find yourself on a broad, open veranda of flat slickrock–perfect for laying out sleeping bags and gazing at the stars. Several large water-filled potholes on the terrace support a large population of frogs, and the tiny animals seem to delight in serenading weary hikers each evening with their mournful songs of love.

The next 1.0 mile below the Right Fork campsite is the most difficult segment of the Death Hollow hike. There is more water in this part of the canyon, and the water-filled slots are also longer and deeper. At least two of the pools are over 100 yards long. Again, the water is seldom more than chest-deep, and the longest swim is no more than 60 feet. As before, however, the major problem is getting backpacks across the water.

Finally, about 3.0 miles above the point where the Boulder Mail Trail enters Death Hollow the character of the

Upper Death Hollow below Right Fork

Golden Cathedral

★★★★

Glen Canyon National Recreation Area
day hike

Distance:	9.5 miles (round trip)
Walking time:	6 hours
Elevations:	1,200 ft. loss/gain Egypt Trailhead (start): 5,620 ft. Escalante River: 4,530 ft. Golden Cathedral: 4,640 ft.
Trail:	The trail is generally easy to follow but can be confusing in places, especially the 0 9-mile portion along the Escalante River. Two fords of the Escalante are necessary, but the water is seldom more than a foot deep.
Season:	Spring, summer, fall, winter. Spring or fall are the ideal times for this hike. The canyons are very hot in the summer and cold in the winter.
Vicinity:	Near Escalante
Maps:	Egypt *(USGS)* Canyons of the Escalante *(Trails Illustrated, #710)*
Information:	http://www.utahtrails.com/neon.html *(Utah Trails)* http://www.nps.gov/glca/ *(Glen Canyon Nat. Recreation Area)* phone: (435) 826-5499 *(Escalante Interagency Visitor Center)*

Drive 5 miles east from the town of Escalante on Highway 12 until you see a sign marking the Hole in the Rock Road. Turn right here and drive south on this graded gravel road for another 16.3 miles where there is another road on the left and a sign that says "Egypt 10 miles". Turn left on the Egypt road and continue the last 9.8 miles to the trailhead at the end of the road.

The slickrock country that surrounds the lower Escalante River is a hiker's paradise of redrock canyons, natural arches, hidden springs, and Indian artifacts. Most of the hiking trails in the area lead into the canyon tributaries of the Escalante. More than twenty canyons drain into the river before it reaches Lake Powell, and nearly every canyon contains something special.

This hike will take you into two of the

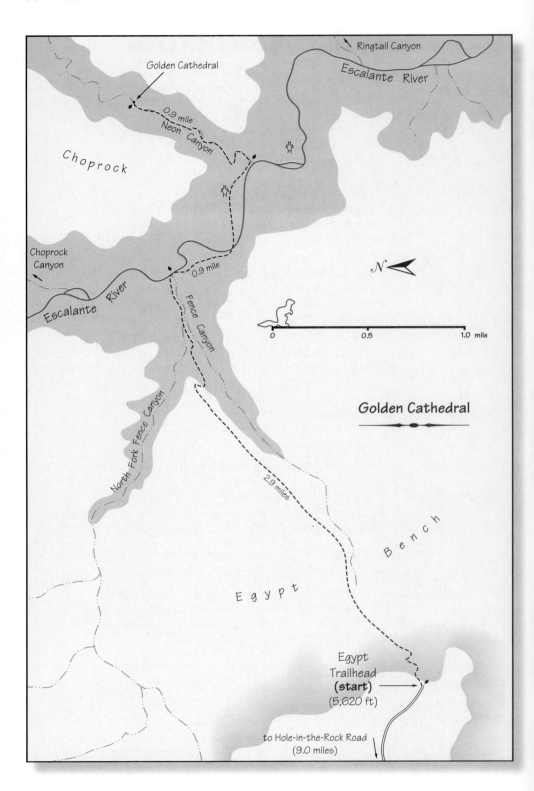

Golden Cathedral

Ringtail Canyon

Escalante River

Choprock

0.9 mile
Neon Canyon

Choprock Canyon

Escalante River

Fence Canyon

0.9 mile

N

0   0.5   1.0 mile

Golden Cathedral

North Fork Fence Canyon

2.9 miles

Bench

Egypt

Egypt
Trailhead
(start)
(5,620 ft)

to Hole-in-the-Rock Road
(9.0 miles)

Petroglyphs near Neon Canyon

the slickrock toward Egypt Bench below. Crude steps have been cut into the sandstone in a few places, and numerous scratches on the rock suggest that the trail has often been used by packhorses. The route descends 450 feet over 0.5 mile before finally leveling out onto the flat, sandy bench at the bottom of the Navajo Sandstone. From there you will see a hiker-made trail heading off in a northeasterly direction along the north side of Fence Canyon. Initially Fence is nothing more than a dry desert wash, but it quickly gains depth and within a mile the canyon floor steps down 200 feet over a pouroff that effectively prevents travel along the streambed.

1.9 miles after its descent to Egypt Bench the trail arrives at a point above the confluence of Fence Canyon and its northern fork. From there the path switchbacks down to the confluence and follows a small stream the last 0.2 mile to the Escalante River. A few minutes into the walk down Fence Canyon you will see a split in the trail where some hikers have climbed to a sandy ledge 15 feet above the north side of the creek. Turn left here to see a few remnants of an old cowboy camp that was once used by stockmen tending their animals in Fence Canyon. There was still a cabin here in the 1980s, but now all that is left is the foundation.

Fence Canyon meets the Escalante River just a few feet from where the old cabin used to be. At that point you must wade into the river and walk downstream about 100 feet before climbing back out on the same side of the water. You should see a well traveled trail at this point that follows the southwest side of the river. The trail stays on the river's southwest side for about 0.3 mile, then crosses to the northeast side. There are many hiker-made trails along both banks of the Escalante, but some of them are better than others. I have found the one described here to be the most straightforward.

canyons of the Escalante River drainage: Fence Canyon and Neon Canyon. Fence is a heavily vegetated canyon with permanent water that was once used by local cattle ranchers. It is a box canyon with no way out on its west side, so enterprising cattlemen once maintained a fence across its lower end to enclose their animals.

Neon Canyon is also a box canyon, but in this case the narrow gorge ends in a large sandstone alcove locally known as the Golden Cathedral. The roof of the undercut is penetrated by three large holes, and a soft diffusion of indirect sunlight illuminates the walls with a delicate yellowish glow. A permanent pond of water lies just inside the opening, and when the wind blows the walls shimmer in the water's reflected light.

From Egypt Trailhead the trail plunges almost immediately over the upper rim of the Escalante Basin to begin its descent down

Within 8 minutes after the trail crosses to the northeast side of the river you will be walking through a wide, open area that has obviously been heavily grazed in the past. The river runs due east here with low cliffs about 100 yards to the north. Watch the base of the cliffs and soon you will see an interesting panel of Indian petroglyphs. Unfortunately the panel has been partially defaced by some old cowboy graffiti, but some of the graffiti is also quite interesting. There are several dates inscribed in the rock, including one from 1881. (See photograph on page 17.)

Continue walking east along the north side of the river, and about 7 minutes after leaving the petroglyph panel the trail climbs up a small sand dune and turns left into the mouth of Neon Canyon. The river abruptly turns south at this point, so if you find yourself walking south you have gone too far.

Neon Canyon is a deep narrow gorge about 200 feet wide with sheer, 300-foot walls of Wingate Sandstone. The walk up the canyon floor is extremely pleasant, with ample shade and lots of greenery (watch out for the poison ivy). Other than a few boulders in the streambed near the end, there are no obstacles along the way and the elevation gain is minimal. After an easy walk of 0.9 mile you will arrive at your goal, the Golden Cathedral.

The Golden Cathedral is a magnificent natural alcove that has been etched into the walls of Neon Canyon by water seeping through the base of the sandstone cliffs. The cavity is roughly 150 feet in diameter by 80 feet high, and in its center a large pond of mirror smooth water reflects the reddish-orange walls. But the most notable feature of the Golden Cathedral is the openings in the ceiling. Like enormous chandeliers in the center of an opulent ballroom, the natural skylight casts a soft glow on the golden colored room below.

The Golden Cathedral is actually a natural bridge, and after a heavy rain water can often be seen pouring through the holes in the ceiling. It is also a popular destination for canyoneering enthusiasts, and climbers can occasionally be seen rappelling down through one of the holes to the pond at the bottom of the alcove.

The Golden Cathedral

Coyote Gulch

★★★★★

Glen Canyon National Recreation Area
4WD shuttle car useful
overnight hike

Distance: 11.8 miles
(plus 2.6 miles by car or foot)

Walking time: day 1: 4 hours
day 2: 4 hours

Elevations: 1,015 ft. loss, 1,110 ft. gain
Forty Mile Ridge Trailhead (start): 4,675 ft.
Jacob Hamblin Arch Trailhead: 4,770 ft.
Escalante River: 3,660 ft.

Trail: The most challenging part of this hike is the climb out of Coyote Gulch near Jacob Hamblin Arch. The climb involves scrambling up a 100-foot pitch of slickrock that ascends from the canyon floor at an angle close to 45 degrees. A 120-foot length of rope is useful here for raising backpacks. A compass is also useful for the last part of the hike, which involves a 2-mile cross-country walk from the canyon rim back to Jacob Hamblin Trailhead. Sneakers or other wettable shoes are the most practical footwear inside the canyon, as you will frequently be required to cross the streambed.

Season: Spring, summer, fall, winter. This area is very hot in the summertime and receives some snow in the winter. The best seasons for the hike are spring and fall.

Vicinity: Near Escalante

Maps: King Mesa, Stevens Canyon South *(USGS)*
Canyons of the Escalante *(Trails Illustrated, #710)*

Information: http://www.utahtrails.com/coyote.html *(Utah Trails)*
http://www.nps.gov/glca/ *(Glen Canyon Nat. Recreation Area)*
phone: (435) 826-5499 *(Escalante Interagency Visitor Center)*

Drive east of Escalante on Highway 12 for 5 miles until you come to the Hole In the Rock Road. Turn right here and drive south on this gravel road for 36.2 miles until you reach a well marked road on the left leading to Forty Mile Ridge (2.2 miles beyond Hurricane Wash). Turn left onto the Forty Mile Ridge Road and continue for 4.3 miles, where you will see another short spur that leads to a small corral and water tank on the left. This is where the hike ends. The road beyond this point is very sandy and may be impassable without a 4WD vehicle, but if you have a 4WD shuttle car leave it here. Continuing down the Forty Mile Ridge Road for another 2.6 miles will bring you to Forty Mile Ridge Trailhead where the hike begins. Be sure to sign the trail register before you start and obtain a free backcountry permit.

The Escalante River and its tributaries provide many of the most interesting hikes into the desert canyonlands of Southern Utah. Unfortunately the last 30 miles of the Escalante were flooded by Lake Powell after the construction of the Glen Canyon Dam in 1964, but enough attractions still remain to make the Escalante drainage a very special place for outdoor enthusiasts. Coyote Gulch, a side canyon of the lower Escalante, is one of the most popular hikes in the vicinity. With its impressive natural bridge, two arches and Indian artifacts, it is a particularly good place to sample the wonders of the Escalante drainage.

There are at least five ways to get in and out of Coyote Gulch; hence a number of variations of this hike are possible. Most people begin and end their hike at either the Hurricane Wash Trailhead or the Red Well Trailhead. The hike down Coyote Gulch to the Escalante River and back from either one of these trailheads makes a very pleasant, if somewhat long, backpacking trip. If you are the adventurous type, however, you will probably prefer the route described here. It does require a modicum of rock climbing ability, so if that makes you uncomfortable I suggest you end your hike at Hurricane Wash Trailhead rather than the Jacob Hamblin Arch Trailhead.

Day 1 (6.8 miles)

The Forty Mile Ridge Trailhead is locat-

Coyote Natural Bridge

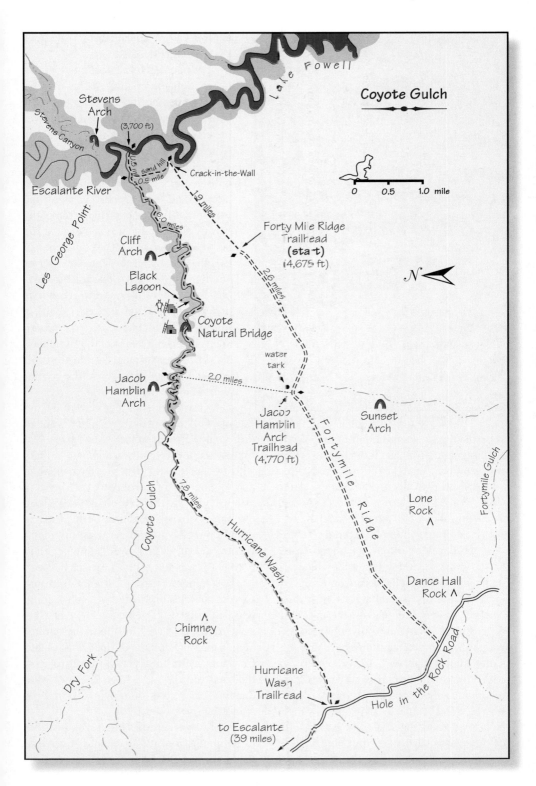

Lake Powell

Stevens
Arch

Stevens Canyon

(3,700 ft)

sand hill
0.8 mile

Crack-in-the-Wall

Escalante River

Les George Point

Coyote Gulch

0   0.5   1.0   mile

Cliff
Arch

6.0 miles

1.9 miles

Forty Mile Ridge
Trailhead
(start)
(4,675 ft)

2.6 miles

Black
Lagoon

N

Coyote
Natural Bridge

water
tank

Jacob
Hamblin
Arch

2.0 miles

Jacob
Hamblin
Arch
Trailhead
(4,770 ft)

Sunset
Arch

Fortymile Ridge

Coyote Gulch

7.8 miles

Lone
Rock
∧

Hurricane Wash

Dance Hall
Rock ∧

Fortymile Gulch

Chimney
Rock

Dry Fork

Hurricane
Wash
Trailhead

Hole in the Rock Road

to Escalante
(39 miles)

Trail from Forty Mile Ridge into Coyote Gulch

degrees east of true north, or 37 degrees east of magnetic north.

Your access into Escalante Canyon is through the "Crack-In-the-wall", a narrow opening in the sandstone cliff above the northwest side of a wide river meander. The crack is about 18 inches wide and fifty feet long. If you walk sideways down through this crack you will emerge at the top of an enormous pile of sand that extends nearly all the way from Coyote Gulch to the top of the Navajo Sandstone. Look down to the north and you can see the confluence of Coyote Gulch and the Escalante River about 0.6 mile away. The trail is obvious and easy to follow now. It winds downward over the sand for nearly a mile until it intersects Coyote Gulch about a half-mile west of the Escalante. As you descend a huge natural arch will soon come into view above the confluence. This is Stevens Arch.

After you reach the bottom of Coyote Gulch you will probably want to drop your backpack and take a side trip to see the Escalante River. It is only a 15-minute walk down the canyon. If you have the time and the inclination for more exploring it is also usually possible to wade or walk along the banks of the Escalante. The water is seldom more than two feet deep (although if the level of Lake Powell is higher than normal the water here may be much deeper).

Two hundred yards upstream from the Coyote Gulch confluence you will come upon another breathtaking view of Stevens Arch, the largest of the many natural arches in the Escalante drainage. Sculpted from a massive fin of Navajo Sandstone on the south side of , the huge 220-foot wide opening completely dominates the skyline above the river.

With some determination it is possible to climb up from the Escalante River into the eye of Stevens Arch. The route requires

ed on the top of a small knoll in the middle of a large sandy plateau. From there a broad, well-used trail leads across the desert in a northeasterly direction toward the Escalante River. For the first half mile the sandy trail is easy to follow, but soon the sand is gone and you will find yourself walking on slickrock. There are no footprints, of course, on the slickrock, so you will be following rock cairns until you reach the canyon rim.

There are occasional spaces of several hundred feet between cairns, but the route to the rim of Escalante Canyon is nearly a straight line so you shouldn't have any difficulty finding the way. Nevertheless, pay close attention to the cairns. If you don't arrive at precisely the right point on the canyon rim you won't be able to find your way down the Navajo Sandstone. A compass is useful for this part of the hike; your course from the trailhead should follow a line about 50

Waterfall near Cliff Arch

Continuing up Coyote Gulch you will pass two or three small waterfalls, and then as the streambed enters the Kayenta Formation the valley becomes wider and ascends more gently. Occasionally the trail climbs out of the streambed to circumvent a waterfall, but it never strays far up the side of the drainage. After about an hour you will see Cliff Arch coming into view high on the north side of the canyon. As the name suggests, the arch juts straight out from the sandstone cliff like a giant teacup handle. Slightly upstream from Cliff Arch is a gorgeous waterfall. The drop is only about fifteen feet, but the setting is magnificent.

From Cliff Arch to Jacob Hamblin Arch Coyote Gulch is at its best, with plenty of scenery and nice camp sites. This is about the halfway point of the hike, so you may want to start thinking about a camp site as you continue on.

Day 2 (5.0 miles)

Forty-five minutes or so after leaving Cliff Arch you should start watching for a particularly fine Fremont Indian pictograph panel on the north side of the canyon. It is located 1.6 miles beyond the arch in a large, sandy open area at the base of the Navajo Sandstone. Unfortunately, it is easier to spot the panel if you are walking in the opposite direction, so stop occasionally to look back. When you reach it you will see an obvious spur trail that branches off to the right and

bushwhacking through the tamarisk trees that line the east side of the river, followed by some strenuous scrambling up a steep talus slope below the arch. But many hikers have gone before you and you may see an occasional cairn along the route.

To reach the arch you must cross to the east side of the Escalante River just above the mouth of Coyote Gulch, and look for the one place where a break in the east canyon wall offers an assent route upward. After scrambling up the talus you will come to a slickrock bench along the base of the Navajo Sandstone formation that offers an easy walk for the last few hundred yards to the arch.

Pictographs in Coyote Gulch

a spring here and water seeps prodigiously from the porous sandstone to fill a small pond called the Black Lagoon. The pond is 30 feet across and looks to be about 5-10 feet deep at its deepest point. The Indians who lived in the canyon centuries ago must have visited the Black Lagoon often, because a line of toe holds has been chipped into the sandstone above the pond at the end of the trail. The steps don't appear to lead anywhere now, but perhaps there was once a granary on the bench above the water.

0.7 mile past the pictographs the trail passes under Coyote Natural Bridge, a 50-foot span of sandstone that arcs directly across the path. There is also another Indian ruins site in an alcove on the north side of Coyote Bridge. One of the dwellings can easily be seen from the upstream side of the bridge about 150 yards north of the trail.

Jacob Hamblin Arch, the last and most impressive of Coyote Gulch's sandstone arches, comes into view 1.7 miles above Coyote Natural Bridge. This arch is very imposing. The actual opening is only about 150 feet wide by 100 feet high—not extremely large as Utah's arches go. But the sandstone columns that support the arch are enormous, and the rock above the arch is at least 150 feet thick. It probably would not look so intimidating if it were located on the top of the mesa, but being confronted with this massive geological sculpture in the narrow confines of the canyon makes one feel as insignificant as an ant.

On the south side of Jacob Hamblin Arch, where the stream bends around the obstacle, the flowing water has scooped out an undercut in the canyon that is 500 feet wide, 300 feet high, and at least 200 feet deep. The acoustics in the center of this alcove are incredible. If you stand in the

climbs up a large sand dune to the base of the sandstone cliff. The ancient drawings are at the bottom of the cliff, 150 feet above the canyon floor and 100 yards north of the streambed. There is also a small ruin in the alcove just west of the pictographs. If you have sharp eyes you may see a few pottery shards and small corn cobs in the area. Please do not remove them, though. These treasures belong to the canyon, and are there for all to enjoy.

A hundred yards before reaching the Fremont pictograph panel the trail passes the mouth of a small heavily vegetated side canyon on the right that is also worth stopping to explore. An intermittent stream occasionally flows out of the small canyon, and there is a dense growth of joint weed at its mouth. Look carefully and you can see a primitive hiker-made trail that leads through the joint weed into the canyon. After only five minutes the trail ends beneath a large alcove at the back of the canyon. There is

Jacob Hamblin Natural Arch

amount of exposure is minimal and if you can get up the first 30 feet you should have no difficulty with the rest. Look carefully at the stone face near the bottom and you will notice several eroded depressions in the rock that can be used for toe holds. These holes were chipped out of the rock many centuries ago by ancient canyon dwellers that used this same route in and out of the gorge. A 120-foot length of rope will come in very handy at this point for pulling up backpacks and perhaps some of the less agile members of your party. If you don't feel comfortable with the climb you can also exit the canyon through Hurricane Wash which crosses the road 7.8 miles further upcanyon.

Once you reach the rim of the canyon walk due magnetic south for two miles to intersect the road along Forty Mile Ridge. The trailhead where you left your shuttle car is on the top of a small knoll that will come into view after about a mile.

center of the concave opening and strike two rocks together you can hear at least a dozen echoes that together sound like rolling thunder.

There are several nice camp sites in the vicinity of Jacob Hamblin Arch, and there is an excellent spring on the north side of the canyon 200 feet below the arch. This area is very popular with campers, and in an effort to keep the canyon clean the Park Service has constructed a pit toilet 200 feet below the spring on the south side of the canyon.

The route out of Coyote Gulch begins 20 feet west of the path to the toilet. From there it is possible to scramble up a long toe of sandstone that descends into the canyon from the south rim. The climb is not difficult, but it does require a small amount of rock climbing ability. The difficult part of the scramble lasts for about 100 feet; the

Climbing out of Coyote Gulch

Willow Gulch

★ ★ ★

Glen Canyon National Recreation Area
day hike

Distance:	7.2 miles (round trip)
Walking time:	4 hours
Elevations:	540 ft. loss/gain Willow Gulch Trailhead (start): 4,200 ft. Broken Bow Arch: 3,880 ft. Lake Powell: 3,660 ft.
Trail:	There is no trail for most of this hike, but the route is not difficult to follow. The portion of the hike below Broken Bow Arch is in a narrow canyon where there is a danger of flash floods, so don't venture beyond the arch if there is a chance of rain. Sneakers or other wettable shoes are the only practical footwear as you will frequently be walking in water.
Season:	Spring, summer, winter, fall. This area is very hot in the summertime and receives some snow in the winter. The best seasons for the hike are spring and fall.
Vicinity:	Near Escalante
Maps:	Sooner Bench, Davis Gulch *(USGS)* Canyons of the Escalante *(Trails Illustrated, #710)*
Information:	http://www.utahtrails.com/willow.html *(Utah Trails)* http://www.nps.gov/glca/ *(Glen Canyon Nat. Recreation Area)* phone: (435) 826-5499 *(Escalante Interagency Visitor Center)*

Drive east of Escalante on Highway 12 for 5 miles until you come to the Hole in the Rock Road. Turn right onto this gravel road, check your odometer, and drive south. After 34.7 miles you will pass a sign marking Hurricane Wash, then Fortymile Ridge after 37.1 miles, Dance Hall Rock after 37.8 miles, and Carcass Wash after 40.5 miles. When you reach Carcass Wash check your *odometer again and continue south. In another 2.2 miles you will see an unmarked road on the left. Turn here and drive east for 1.4 miles to the end of the road, where you will see a sign and trail registration box marking the Willow Gulch Trailhead.*

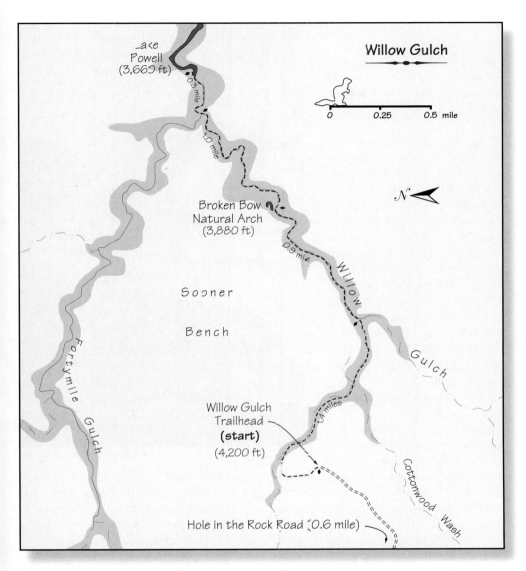

The attraction that draws most hikers to Willow Gulch is the magnificent Broken Bow Natural Arch. This improbable sandstone formation rises boldly from a low plateau on the north side of the streambed, where it can be seen clearly from a distance of several hundred yards. The triangular-shaped opening easily reminds one of a bow bent nearly double, but actually that is not how the arch got its name. It was given its present name in 1930 after an Indian bow was found underneath it.

Broken Bow Arch is located only 2.3 miles from the Willow Gulch Trailhead. It is a relatively easy hike to the arch, and many hikers turn around at that point. But in my opinion the hike from the arch on down to Lake Powell is almost as interesting as the arch itself. The character of the canyon changes dramatically in a surprisingly short distance, going from an open desert environment to a constricted environment of slickrock waterslides and sandstone narrows in less than a mile. Finally the canyon opens out again at the end, where a small plateau offers a fine view of Lake Powell.

From the parking area it may be difficult to see exactly where the trail starts, but if you walk in a northerly direction from the registration box, straight down the sandy slope, you will soon begin to see the trail. Look for Mortar Board Rock, a large sandstone boulder that looks like an upside-down Mexican hat about 150 yards from the trailhead. The trail passes within a few feet of the boulder, and then turns east for the descent into a short side canyon that eventually leads to Willow gulch.

This unnamed side canyon is interesting in its own right. It is dry and dusty with cliffs of Navajo Sandstone on both sides and a short stretch of nicely sculpted

Broken Bow Natural Arch

narrows in its center. The trail generally follows the right side of the canyon for 0.5 mile before dropping to the bottom of the streambed. Shortly after the trail reaches the bottom of the canyon you will come to an intersection where Cottonwood Wash enters from the right and another short canyon comes in from the left. You may be confused at this intersection as there are three possible routes to follow. Do not turn right or left, but continue straight through the intersection into the sandy wash that continues on the other side.

At this point you are in the lower part of Cottonwood Wash. Except in very wet years the canyon is bone dry, but, interestingly, it contains signs of beaver. Notice the stunted cottonwood trees struggling to find water

under the sand; many of them have been damaged by the wood-eating rodents. You can take that as an indication that there is water ahead, but it is surprising how far the beaver venture into the dry canyon.

0.4 mile after entering Cottonwood Wash the canyon widens again at the confluence with Willow Gulch. There are a great many willow trees in the area (hence the name), and you should finally see some water in the streambed. Turn left into Willow Gulch, but before continuing be sure to make a mental note of what the confluence looks like so you will know where to leave Willow on the return trip. What initially passed for a trail has long since disappeared by this time; consequently it is easy to miss the exit point from Willow Gulch when hiking out. If you do miss the turn you can still reach the Hole in the Rock Road by continuing up Willow Gulch. But if you do this you will have to road walk another 2.9 miles along the road to get from the head of Willow Gulch back to the trailhead.

You will pass a half-dozen small beaver dams as you walk down Willow Gulch. The easiest place to walk is generally in the bottom of the streambed, but the dams occasionally make detours necessary. The beavers are seldom seen, but their handiwork is everywhere. It is probably the pressure of overpopulation that causes some of them to venture up Cottonwood Wash in search of another place to build a home. Finally, a half-hour after entering Willow Gulch, Broken Bow Natural Arch should come into view.

Broken Bow is surely one of the most beautiful arches in the Escalante drainage. It curves gracefully away from the wall of the canyon in a way that is reminiscent of Rainbow Natural Bridge, one of the world's largest such formations. It is 170 feet high, with an opening 94 feet wide and 100 feet high. Its 70-foot-thick sides lend an element of strength to its grace, assuring us that it is going to be here for a long time to come. Best of all, it lies in an easily accessible area with no barriers on either side, so good photographic angles are easy to find. And its most photogenic side faces south, where it is in the sun for most of the day.

The Broken Bow Arch was sculpted from a fin of sandstone that once protruded into the canyon from the west wall. The stream has never actually flowed through the opening, and for this reason it is classified as an arch, not a natural bridge. It seems, however, that the fickle creek is intent on correcting this situation. As you walk through the streambed you can see the undercutting that has began as the water tries to straighten out its course and flow where Broken Bow now stands. The creek will probably someday be the instrument that destroys the arch.

The effects of water on sandstone become more and more apparent as you walk downstream from Broken Bow. The canyon becomes narrower, deeper, colder, and more devoid of plant life as you approach its mouth. In some sections the sensation is one of walking through a 20-foot diameter pipe that has been scoured smooth by the grinding power of water and sand. In other places it feels like you are walking along a racetrack with galleries for the spectators in the huge alcoves above. There are numerous waterslides along the way where the persistent stream has cut graceful channels into the smooth sandstone. And in one part of the canyon the water has carved out

Willow Gulch

a 200-foot-long section of narrows that is scarcely 4 feet wide

Thirty minutes below Broken Bow Arch you will come to Fortymile Gulch, another narrow, watery canyon that joins Willow Gulch from the north, and soon afterward the canyon ends at Lake Powell. When the lake is full the water may rise almost to the confluence with Fortymile Gulch, but by the end of summer the lake has usually receded 0.5 mile below the canyon junction. You will know you are getting close to the lake when you start seeing a thick layer of mud on the canyon floor. The mud contains the footprints of dozens of boaters who have landed and walked up Willow Gulch, but they seldom go more than a few hundred yards.

Fortymile Gulch

An interesting variation to this hike is to return to the Hole in the Rock Road through Fortymile Gulch and Carcass Wash (not shown on this map). That route is somewhat more difficult than the walk through Willow Gulch, however, so some additional planning is needed. First, the walking distance is 3.9 miles longer, bringing the total hiking distance around the loop to 11.1 miles. Second, there is more water and more obstacles in Fortymile Gulch, so progress is slower. There are at least two places in the lower part of Fortymile where it is necessary to wade or swim through deep pools of water that block the way. For this reason the hike should only be done in warm weather, and if you are carrying a camera you should have some means of keeping it dry. Finally, the Carcass Wash Trailhead is 3.6 miles by road from the Willow Gulch Trailhead, so some kind of a shuttle is necessary to get back to the starting point.

Carcass Wash is only one of three possible exit routes from Fortymile Gulch to the Hole in the Rock Road, but it is, by far, the easiest route. If you try to exit through Sooner Wash you will find a canyon full of chock stones, and if you continue up Fortymile Gulch you will soon find yourself in a box canyon with no apparent way out. Carcass Wash is the second major canyon you will see on the left as you walk up Fortymile.

It is easy to miss the turn from Fortymile Gulch into Carcass Wash, and for that reason it is probably better to do this loop hike in the reverse direction. If you start where Carcass Wash crosses the Hole in the Rock Road it is relatively straightforward to follow the canyon downstream to Fortymile Gulch and on to Willow Gulch. Regardless of the direction you are traveling, however, be sure to pay particular attention to the weather before entering Fortymile Gulch. A flash flood in this canyon could be deadly, so don't proceed if there is a chance of rain.

Lake Powell, near the mouth of Willow Gulch

Hackberry Canyon

★★

Grand Staircase - Escalante National Monument
shuttle car required
overnight hike

Distance: 22.0 miles
              (plus 19.7 miles by car)

Walking time: day 1: 6½ hours
               day 2: 5½ hours

Elevations: 1,340 ft. loss
              Round Valley Draw Trailhead (start): 6,100 ft.
              Mouth of Hackberry Canyon: 5,360 ft.

Trail: There is no trail for this hike, but the route is easy to follow.
          You will be walking down the streambeds of two desert can-
          yons. The first 2.2 miles through Round Valley Draw are in the
          bottom of a very narrow slot canyon and some scrambling will
          be necessary to get over several chock stones and other obsta-
          cles. A 30-foot length of rope will come in handy for lowering
          packs in a few places. Once you get through Round Valley
          Draw it is an easy walk down the sandy bottom of Hackberry
          Canyon. Unfortunately there is no water for the first 11.3 miles
          of this hike, so be sure to carry plenty. Some wading will be
          necessary for the last 6 miles, so wear wettable boots.

Season: Spring, summer, fall, winter. Spring or fall are the ideal times
          for this hike. The canyons are very hot and dry in the summer
          and cold in the winter

Vicinity: Near Kodachrome Basin State Park, south of Bryce Canyon
          National Park

Maps: Slickrock Bench, Calico Peak (*USGS*)

Information: http://www.utahtrails.com/hackberry.html (*Utah Trails*)
                http://www.ut.blm.gov/monument/ (*Grand Staircase-Escalante*)
                phone: (435) 644-4600 (*BLM, Kanab Field Office*)

Drive east of Bryce Canyon National Park on Highway 12 to the town of Cannonville, then turn south toward Kodachrome Basin State Park and Grosvenor Arch. 7.3 miles from Cannonville you will come to a junction where the Kodachrome Basin road turns abruptly to the left. Continue straight ahead here on the smaller gravel road toward Grosvenor

Arch and Highway 89. The gravel road winds across the desert for about 5 miles before climbing to the top of a ridge called Slickrock Bench, then drops down the other side. On the far side of Slickrock Bench, 6.8 miles from the Kodachrome Basin junction, the road dips through the bottom of a small wash called Round Valley Draw, and as you climb up the other side of the wash you will see another primitive dirt road departing on the right near a sign that says "Rush Beds". Turn right here and drive toward Rush Beds. This road is seldom maintained, but most cars should be able to handle it unless there has been a recent rain. The road parallels Round Valley Draw for a while, and then after 1.7 miles it dips down into the draw before veering south. The hike down Round Valley Draw to Hackberry Canyon begins at this point.

Before beginning the hike you will have to leave a shuttle car at the mouth of Hackberry Canyon, where the hike ends. To get there return to the Grosvenor Arch Road and drive south. After 2.8 miles you will pass the turnoff to Grosvenor Arch. Continuing past this turnout toward Highway 89 for another 15.2 miles will bring you to the confluence of Hackberry Canyon and Cottonwood Wash, where the hike ends. (Note: if you are coming from the south, the mouth of Hackberry Canyon is 14.6 miles from Highway 89 on the Cottonwood Wash Road. The Rush Beds Road is 32.6 miles from Highway 89.)

The Hackberry Canyon hike is well suited to those backpackers who enjoy remote areas with lots of solitude. It is in a rugged part of the state, between the Kaiparowits Plateau and the Vermilion Cliffs, where there are few good roads and fewer serious hikers. Unfortunately water is also scarce in this region, and the first 11.3 miles of the hike are waterless. Only after the gorge has cut nearly all the way through the Navajo

Hackberry Canyon

Sandstone to the top of the Kayenta Formation, does a spring finally appear to wet the stark white sand on the canyon floor. At this point the canyon begins to undergo a dramatic change as the colors of life are added to the black and white textures of upper Hackberry. In the next few miles even the walls of the canyon change their hue from the harsh white of the Navajo Sandstone to the softer reddish tones of the Kayenta Formation.

The plateaus above Hackberry have been used by cattle ranchers since the 1800s, and traditionally they have depended on the lower part of the canyon as a source of water for their animals. A couple of trails into the canyon are still occasionally used by local livestockmen, but human activity is only a small fraction of what it was in the early 1900s.

Day 1 (11.3 miles)

At the trailhead, where the Rush Beds Road crosses the top of Round Valley Draw, the drainage is very shallow and uninteresting. The fun begins, however, about 0.5 mile further down the streambed where, in order to continue, it becomes necessary to climb down into a 20-foot-deep crack in the bottom of the gully. The crack is only 12 to 18 inches wide—too narrow to negotiate with a backpack—so you will have to lower your pack in with a short rope before climbing down. The narrows continue for about 1.7 more miles before the canyon opens up again. In at least three more places you will meet interesting obstacles that have to be dealt with. Again, your rope will come in handy for lowering packs. At one point it is necessary to crawl through a small hole under a chock stone; at another your ability to get

through cracks will again be tested.

2.2 miles from the trailhead you may see a large stone cairn on the north side of the canyon floor. This marks the beginning of another trail coming down to Round Valley Draw from Slickrock Bench. Day hikers can exit the draw at this point and rim walk back to their car on the Rush Beds Road. The narrows end here, and the hike becomes an easy walk along the dry, sandy streambed. After another 1.0 mile you will arrive at the confluence with Hackberry Canyon.

Once you reach Hackberry Canyon turn left and proceed in a southerly direction until you reach water, 7.8 miles farther down the canyon. You will know you are getting close when you see a few small cottonwood trees growing in the sand. Then a short way

Entering Round Valley Draw

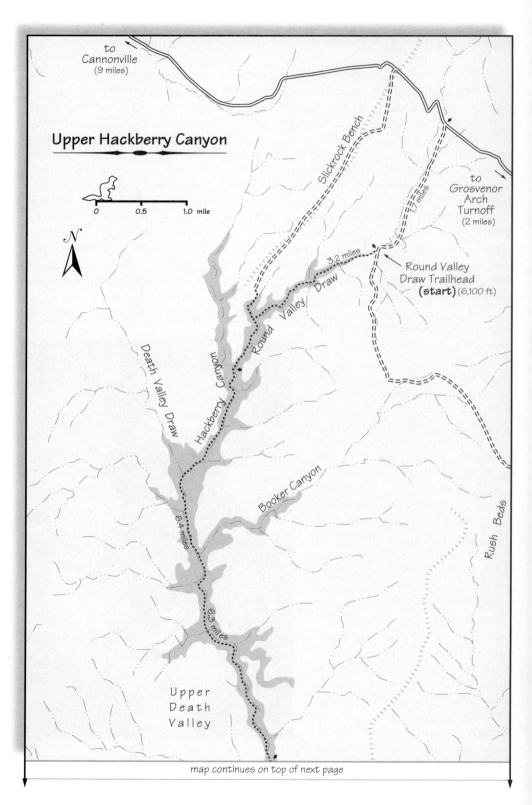

to
Cannonville
(9 miles)

Upper Hackberry Canyon

0   0.5   1.0 mile

N

Slickrock Bench

to
Grosvenor
Arch
Turnoff
(2 miles)

1.7 miles

3.2 miles

Round Valley Draw

Round Valley
Draw Trailhead
(start) (6,100 ft)

Death Valley Draw

Hackberry Canyon

Booker Canyon

Rush Beds

6.4 miles

6.3 miles

Upper
Death
Valley

map continues on top of next page

map continues on bottom of previous page

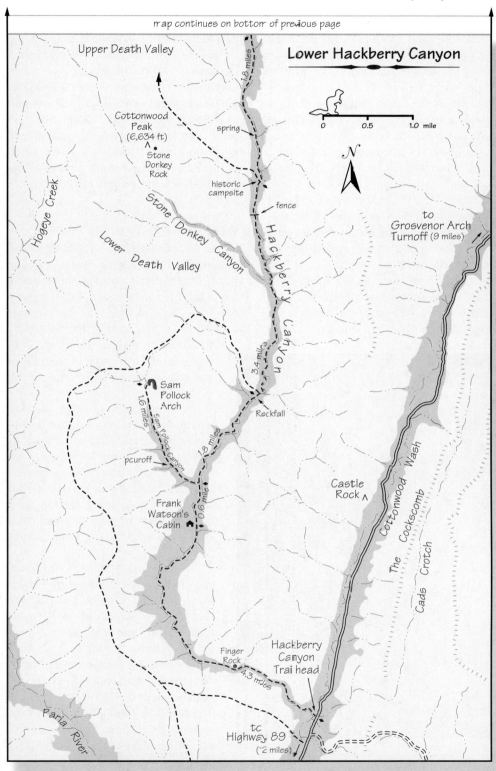

Upper Death Valley

Lower Hackberry Canyon

1.8 miles

Cottonwood
Peak
(6,634 ft)
∧
● Stone
Dorkey
Rock

spring

historic
campsite

fence

0   0.5   1.0   mile

N

Hogeye Creek

Stone Donkey Canyon

Lower Death Valley

Hackberry Canyon

to
Grosvenor Arch
Turnoff (9 miles)

3.4 miles

Sam
Pollock
Arch

1.6 miles

Sam Pollock Canyon

1.8 miles

Rockfall

pcuroff

Castle
Rock ∧

Frank
Watson's
Cabin

0.6 mile

The Cottonwood Wash

Cads Crotch

The Cockscomb

Finger
Rock
● 4.3 miles

Hackberry
Canyon
Trailhead

Paria River

tc
Highway 89
(~2 miles)

farther the sand will turn damp, and finally you will start to see small pools of water along the sides of the canyon. At about the point where the water first starts to flow, 0.6 mile below the first cottonwoods, there is a good camp site on a sandy knoll on the right side of the canyon. This site has been used by cowboys for at least a hundred years. It is also the trailhead for Upper Trail, an old cow path leading out of Hackberry Canyon to Death Valley. A short length of barbed wire fence at the top of the knoll, and a near-vertical cliff of Navajo Sandstone on the east side of the canyon will help you identify the site.

Like many place names in the West, there is an interesting story behind how Death Valley got its name. Cattlemen have long used this valley as a winter grazing pasture for their cattle. Their are no springs on the plateau, however, and the cattle depend on Upper Trail for their access to water. Oldtimers tell the story of how a cow once laid down and died on a very narrow part of the trail near the rim. The other cows were not able to get past the dead cow to go down the trail, and, as a result, many of them died of thirst on the plateau above. Since that time the pasture has been known as Death Valley.

Day 2 (10.1 miles)

As you continue down Hackberry Canyon from the campsite the water begins to flow a little faster, but the stream is seldom more than a few inches deep. Dense vegetation lines the banks, and the easiest place to walk is in the center of the flat, sandy streambed. Wading shoes are very useful for the remainder of the hike, as you will be in the water more than half of the time.

After about ten minutes you will pass another fence, built across the canyon floor to keep cattle from wondering downstream, and a mile farther on you will see Stone Donkey Canyon coming in from the right. Stone Donkey is a box canyon with no access to the top, but it has a nice spring near its mouth that adds to the meager flow in Hackberry Canyon.

1.9 miles below Stone Donkey Canyon there is a new feature in the canyon that was added in the fall of 1987. In that year a large rock slide came down from the west side of Hackberry, creating a dam across the canyon that backed up the stream for several hundred yards. A number of dead cottonwood trees reveal the size of the lake that was formed. The lake has subsided now, however, and it is not difficult to find your way across the rubble of the slide.

Hackberry Canyon

Sam Pollock Natural Arch

easy way up to a ledge above the pouroff. Once you are on this ledge you can walk upcanyon on a vague trail to a point just above the pouroff and then drop 15 feet back down to the stream-bed. The route is not difficult, but it is somewhat exposed at one point so be careful with your footing.

If you are observant you may see another trail descending into Hackberry Canyon from the west side a short distance upstream from the rock slide. This is the Lower Trail, another cow trail leading up to Death Valley. Nearby, the words "W.M. Chynoweth, 1892" have been scratched into the canyon wall. The Chynoweths were a prominent ranching family in Southern Utah, and the name appears more than once in the area's cowboyglyphs.

The next item of interest is Sam Pollock Canyon, 1.8 miles below the rock slide. If you have the time and energy you might want to drop your pack here and make a side trip into this canyon to see Sam Pollock Natural Arch (1.6 miles each way). The bottom part of Sam Pollock Canyon is filled with huge boulders from the cliffs above, and a lot of scrambling is necessary to get into the canyon. After getting through a half-mile of sandstone rubble you will be confronted with a 20-foot vertical pouroff that blocks the upper half of the canyon. But don't give up yet. About 200 yards below the pouroff, on the east side of the canyon, there is a relatively

Once above the pouroff it is an easy 1.1-mile walk up the streambed to the arch, located near the top of the canyon on the

Hackberry Canyon

Frank Watson's cabin

diameter on the west side of the water. At the foot of this boulder you should see a vague trail going up the side of the bank to the cabin which is hidden in the sagebrush only 100 feet away.

2.5 miles downstream from Watson's cabin Hackberry Canyon makes a sharp turn to the left and knifes its way through a ridge known as the Cockscomb before converging with Cottonwood Wash. For the last 1.8 miles the canyon narrows to twenty or thirty feet, with cliffs of Navajo and Kayenta Sandstone dropping precipitously from the convoluted Cockscomb to the waters edge. It is very scenic. Finally Hackberry Creek emerges from the ridge to join Cottonwood Wash and the road back to Kodachrome Basin.

north side. There are also more cowboy-glyphs in the vicinity of Sam Pollock Arch. In a small cave just north of the arch you can see a glyph scratched into the rock by another member of the Chynoweth family: "Art Chynoweth, 1912".

Continuing down Hackberry Canyon, be sure not to miss Frank Watson's cabin. Watson migrated to Utah from Wisconsin around 1910. Upon his arrival in Utah he changed his name, for reasons unknown, from Richard Thomas to Frank Watson, and for the next fifteen years he remained completely out of touch with his relatives in Wisconsin. Many people came west at that time to begin a new life, and newcomers were rarely questioned about their past. Watson went to work for a while in the nearby town of Pahreah (now a ghost town in Paria Canyon), and in about 1914 he built his cabin in lower Hackberry Canyon. The cabin is still in surprisingly good shape after all these years.

The Watson cabin can't be seen from Hackberry Creek, so it is easy to miss. It is located 0.6 mile downstream from the mouth of Sam Pollock Canyon on the edge of a sagebrush covered bench some fifteen feet above the west side of the streambed. As you walk downstream watch for a large red sandstone boulder about 15 feet in

Lower Hackberry Canyon

Buckskin Gulch

★★★

Paria Canyon - Vermillion Cliffs Wilderness Area
shuttle car required
overnight hike

Distance: 20.6 miles
(plus 15.5 miles by car)

Walking time: day 1: 7½ hours
day 2: 4½ hours

Elevations: 760 ft. loss, 180 ft. gain
Wire Pass Trailhead (start): 4,860 ft.
Paria River confluence: 4,100 ft.
White House Trailhead: 4,280 ft.

Trail: There is no trail for this hike, but the route is easy to follow. You will be walking along the bottoms of two narrow desert canyons. Occasionally there are deep pools of water in the canyon narrows, so be prepared with an air mattress or some other means of floating your backpacks across. You will also need a 30-foot length of rope to help you get down a rockfall near the end of Buckskin Gulch.

Season: Spring, summer, fall. Flash floods are common in Buckskin Gulch, so don't attempt this hike if there is a chance of rain. Be especially careful from late July through mid-September, when thundershowers in Southern Utah are more frequent.

Vicinity: Near Kanab and Page, Arizona

Maps: Pine Hollow Canyon, West Clark Bench, Bridger Point *(USGS)*

Information: http://www.utahtrails.com/buckskin.html *(Utah Trails)*
http://paria.az.blm.gov/ *(BLM, Paria Canyon-Vermillion Cliffs)*
phone: (435) 644-4600 *(BLM, Kanab Field Office)*

Drive east from Kanab on Highway 89 for 44 miles until you see a sign directing you to Paria Ranger Station, 0.1 mile south of the highway. From the ranger station there is a graded road leading to the White House Campground, 2.1 miles away, where the hike ends and where you should leave your shuttle car.

In order to get to the Wire Pass Trailhead, where the hike begins, return to Highway 89 and drive back toward Kanab for a distance of 4.9 miles until you see a gravel road on the left near a sign that says "House Rock Valley Road". Turn here and drive south for another 8.4 miles. About halfway along you will pass the Buckskin Trailhead, and finally you will come to a large parking area and a sign marking the Wire Pass Trailhead.

Note: Permits are now required to hike in Buckskin Gulch and Paria Canyon, and the BLM allows only 20 people per night to camp in Buckskin. Reservations can be obtained by calling (435) 644-4600 or (435) 688-3200. The cost is $5.00/day for each person, and the maximum group size is 10 people.

Buckskin Gulch is alleged by many veteran hikers to be the longest, narrowest slot canyon in the world. There are many other narrows hikes on the Colorado Plateau, but Buckskin is exceptional because of its length. The Buckskin narrows extend almost uninterrupted for over 12 miles with the width of the canyon seldom exceeding 20 feet. The walk through the dark, narrow canyon is truly a unique hiking experience.

The key consideration in planning a trip through Buckskin Gulch is water. How much water and mud is there in the canyon? And what is the probability that it will rain while you are inside it? The canyon was created by water, and water continues to shape it and change its character. As you walk along the sandy bottom you will continually be confronted with evidence of previous floods. Dozens of logs have been wedged between the canyon walls, and piles of huge boulders have been jammed into narrow constrictions. The characteristics change from year to year. One can never predict what the last flood might have taken away or left behind. According to BLM statistics there is an average of eight flash floods a year in

Paria Canyon and its tributaries. About a third of the floods occur during the month of August, so if you are planning a trip in late summer you should be especially cautious. Flash flood danger is lowest during the months of April, May, and June.

Day 1 (13.0 miles)

It is possible to begin this hike at either Buckskin Trailhead or Wire Pass Trailhead, but if you begin at Buckskin Trailhead the hike is 2.8 miles longer. If you begin the hike at Wire Pass you will have to walk 13 miles to the confluence campsite; whereas from Buckskin Trailhead the distance is 15.8 miles–more than a comfortable day's walk for most people.

From the Wire Pass parking area the

Buckskin Gulch

trail proceeds for a short distance along the south side of Wire Pass, then drops into the sandy bottom of the wash and descends eastward through the Cockscomb. At first the wash is so mundane it hardly seems an appropriate entry point to the world's best canyon narrows, but within a mile things begin to change drastically. The sandstone walls begin to rise and by the time you reach the mouth of Wire Pass, half an hour from the trailhead, your narrows experience is well underway. Buckskin Gulch widens slightly at the junction with Wire Pass and then quickly narrows again.

There are several petroglyphs of big horn sheep at the junction of the two canyons that you might want to look for before continuing. When you are finished check the sky once more, then turn south into Buckskin. There is no way out of the canyon until you reach the Middle Trail, 6.3 miles from the junction.

For the most part it is an easy walk along the bottom of Buckskin. The canyon floor is normally flat with very few large stones to impede your way. If it has rained recently there may be a layer of slippery clay mud covering the sand, but there is usually very little standing water for the first five miles. It is interesting to note the number of animals that accidentally fall into the steep narrow canyon from the desert above. Rattlesnakes are very common, and you will probably see one or two of them if you are observant. Most of them are babies, scarcely more than a foot long. Also, most of the time they are very lethargic, probably because of a lack of food in the canyon. You might also see a dead coyote—again, most likely a young one.

After you have gone about five miles you will enter a stretch of canyon where there are often large pools of stagnant water. Many of the pools contain rot-ting vegetation and are foul smelling. The largest of these pools has been named, appropriately enough, the Cesspool. Wading through the pools can be a revolting experience, but fortunately they are rarely more than thigh deep. Notice that there are no animals of any kind living in any of the stagnant pools: no tadpoles, no water skaters, no mosquito larva, nothing. Why? Similar pools farther down the canyon contain an abundance of life.

Shortly after leaving the last stagnant pool of water you will notice the canyon rim starting to get much lower, and soon you will come to the Middle Trail. The Middle Trail is not really a trail at all, but rather a route up which one can climb to the top of the north rim. The route is not well marked, but nevertheless easy to spot. It is located in a short, open section of the canyon where the walls are not steep and

Buckskin Gulch

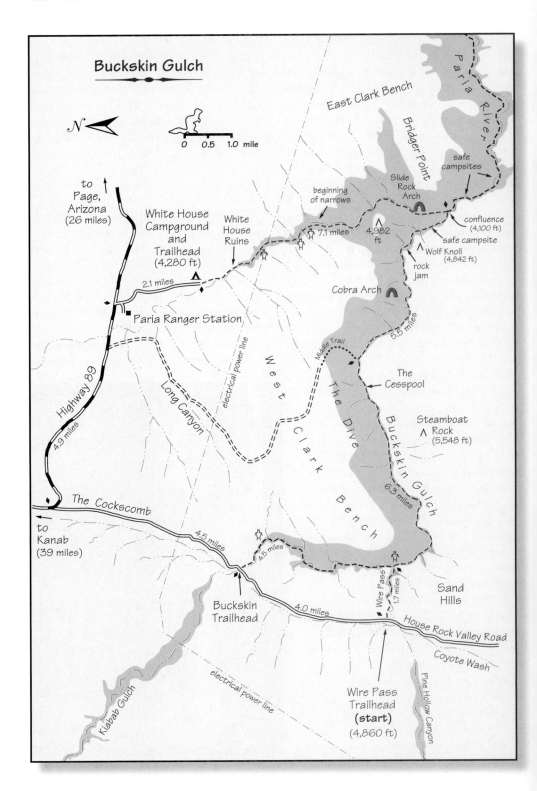

Buckskin Gulch

N

0   0.5   1.0 mile

to
Page,
Arizona
(26 miles)

White House
Campground
and
Trailhead
(4,280 ft)

White
House
Ruins

Paria Ranger Station

Highway 89

4.9 miles

2.1 miles

Long Canyon

electrical power line

W e s t   C l a r k   B e n c h

East Clark Bench

Paria River

Bridger Point

beginning
of narrows

Slide
Rock
Arch

safe
campsites

confluence
(4,100 ft)

7.1 miles

4,982
ft

safe campsite

Wolf Knoll
(4,842 ft)

rock
jam

Cobra Arch

5.5 miles

Middle Trail

The
Cesspool

The Dive

Steamboat
Rock
(5,548 ft)

Buckskin Gulch

6.3 miles

The Cockscomb

to
Kanab
(39 miles)

4.5 miles

4.5 miles

Buckskin
Trailhead

4.0 miles

Wire Pass

1.7 miles

Sand
Hills

House Rock Valley Road

Coyote Wash

Pine Hollow Canyon

electrical power line

Kanab Gulch

Wire Pass
Trailhead
(start)
(4,860 ft)

the rim is only 100 feet above the canyon floor. Look for the footprints of previous hikers going into a fault on the left. The assent is not a walk, but rather a scramble. Hikers with a modicum of rock climbing skill should have no trouble getting up, but don't try it with your backpack on. Better to leave your pack behind or pull it up after you with a short piece of rope. With a little route finding skill it is also possible to climb out to the south rim at this point.

If you got off to a late start you might want to use the Middle Trail to climb out of the narrows and make camp for the night. Unfortunately there is nothing but slickrock and sand above the canyon, and no water. But the flash flood danger makes it unsafe to spend a night inside Buckskin Gulch.

Soon after leaving the Middle Trail the narrows close in again, and the depth of the canyon continues to increase as you approach the Paria River. There are usually no more deep wading pools below Middle Trail, but after about four miles your progress will be stopped by a pile of huge rocks that have become wedged into a tight constriction in the canyon. This rock jam is Buckskin Gulch's most serious obstacle, and most people will need a rope to get safely around it. The standard route requires that you climb about 15 feet down the smooth face of one of the boulders. Previous hikers have chipped footholds into the soft sandstone, but unless you are very agile you will still need a rope to make a safe descent. Hikers often leave their ropes tied to the top of the pitch and you might be lucky enough to find a good one already in place. But BLM rangers regularly cut away any ropes that appear to be unsafe, so you had best have one of your own. Conditions change from year to year and, depending on what happened during the last canyon flood, you might find another easier route down the rock jam. But don't count on it.

Soon after you leave the rock jam you

Rock jam in Buckskin Gulch

will pass by a series of seeps in the Navajo Sandstone walls that supply a tiny flowing stream on the canyon floor. The fresh water is a welcome change from the stagnant, lifeless pools above Middle Trail. There is plenty of life in the water of the lower Buckskin, even including small fish.

About a mile below the rock jam, or 0.5 mile above the Paria River confluence, you will come to an excellent campsite. Look for a large grove of maple and boxelder trees growing in the sand above the streambed. There are several fine places to make camp under the trees on the benches of dry sand ten feet above the canyon floor. Since this area is the only place in Buckskin Gulch where it is possible to camp you may have trouble finding an unoccupied campsite, especially during the busy months of May and June. If you can't find a place here the next closest campsite is located about a mile away in Paria Canyon below the confluence.

Day 2 (7.6 miles)

It is only a ten minute walk from the Buckskin Gulch campsite to the Paria River confluence, where you must turn north up

Paria Canyon to complete the hike. The place where the two canyons come together is extremely impressive. The narrows here are much more open than the narrows of the Buckskin, but the reddish walls are shear and smooth. The presence of clean running water at the bottom of the 800-foot gorge also adds a touch of grandeur to the scene. The Paria is sometimes dry in midsummer, but there is always at least a trickle of water flowing out of Buckskin.

The next point of interest as you walk up the Paria River is Slide Arch, located about 0.7 mile above the confluence. This is not really an arch at all, but rather a large piece of sandstone that has broken away from the east wall and slid down into the river. Beyond Slide Arch the canyon walls start to become less shear and the canyon widens until it is eventually little more than a desert wash. There are a few hard-to-find panels of petroglyphs on the west side of the canyon as you approach the White House Trailhead. The first panel is about a mile before the point where the electrical power lines cross the canyon, and the last is just above the power line crossing.

Finally, you may want to pause for a few minutes at the White House Ruins. These are not Indian ruins, as many people think, but rather the site of an old home-steader's cabin. The cabin was originally built in 1887 by Owen Washington Clark, the same man for whom the West Clark Bench was named. Unfortunately it

burned down in the 1890s, and today there is little left but a pile of stones. The ruins are located on the east side of the Paria River, opposite a small side canyon on the west side about 0.3 mile below the trailhead.

Lower Paria Canyon

Many hikers combine the Buckskin Gulch hike with a hike through the lower part of Paria Canyon to the Colorado River. If you turn south at the Paria confluence instead of north you can walk all the way down the Paria River to Lees Ferry. This 30-mile walk makes a long but rewarding backpack trip with a great deal to see. There are several abandoned homestead sites and mining camps along the way dating back to the late 1800s. You will also see several impressive panels of Indian rock art, as well as one of the largest natural sandstone arches in the world. The distance by road from Lees Ferry back to the Paria Ranger Station is about 70 miles; hence two cars are needed for the hike.

Paria Canyon

The Wave

Paria Canyon - Vermillion Cliffs Wilderness Area
day hike

Distance: 5.2 miles (round trip)

Walking time: 3 hours

Elevations: 500 ft. gain/loss
                       Wire Pass Trailhead (start): 4,860 ft.
                       The Wave: 5,190 ft.

Trail: About half of this trail is over unmarked slickrock and can be
                       somewhat confusing. However if you follow the instructions
                       below you should have no trouble finding the Wave.

Season: Year round

Vicinity: Near Kanab and Page, Arizona

Maps: Pine Hollow Canyon, Coyote Buttes (Arizona) *(USGS)*

Information: http://www.utahtrails.com/thewave.html *(Utah Trails)*
                       http://paria.az.blm.gov/ *(BLM, Paria Canyon-Vermillion Cliffs)*
                       phone: (435) 644-4600 *(BLM, Kanab Field Office)*

Drive east of Kanab on Highway 89 for 39 miles until you see a gravel road
on the right near a sign that says "House Rock Valley Road". Turn right and
drive south on the House Rock Valley Road for a distance of 8.4 miles to the
Wire Pass Trailhead and parking area.

Sadly, the BLM has implemented a stringent set of rules that effectively prevent most people from ever being able to do this hike. The Wave is located in a special
BLM management area called North Coyote Buttes, and only 20 people are given permits
to enter the area each day. Ten of the permits are issued by way of an on-line reservations
lottery that is held on the first day of each month; the other ten are issued at 9:00 each
morning on a walk-in basis at the Grand Staircase-Escalante National Monument Visitor
Center in Kanab.

If you wish to participate in the on-line reservations lottery you must submit your application four months before the month of your intended visit. You will then receive an email
on the first day of the following month to inform you if your application was successful. If
you wish to apply for a walk-in permit you must show up at the National Monument Visitor
Center on Highway 89 just east of Kanab on the day before your intended visit. Drawings

are held at 9:00 each morning and permits are issued to the successful applicants. As this book goes to press the cost of a permit is $7.00/person, but the cost as well as the rules are frequently revised. If you are planning a trip to the Wave I urge you to go to the BLM website at www.blm.gov/az/st/en/arolrsmain/paria/coyote_buttes.html and read the most recent BLM regulations.

Be warned that during the peak April-October season there are often dozens of people lined up at the National Monument Visitor Center for walk-in permits, and the odds of getting on-line advance reservations are no better. The BLM website states that only about ten percent of the applicants seeking permits through its lottery system for the Spring and Fall seasons are successful. The result of these stringent rules is that many people hike to the Wave illegally. One way the BLM discourages illegal hikers is by making it as difficult as possible to find the Wave. There are no signs at or near the trailhead that even mention the Wave, and the middle half of the trail is completely unmarked. Past hikers have attempted to mark the route with stone cairns, but these cairns are systematically removed almost as fast as they are erected. You will be given a detailed map that shows how to find the Wave if you are lucky enough to get a permit, but not before.

For all of the publicity it has received, one might reasonably expect the Wave to be an enormous geological sculpture that stands alone, like Ayers Rock, in the middle of the desert. Actually it is a relatively small hollowed-out cove on the side of a sandstone hill, not much more than a half acre in size. Nevertheless, the Wave is extremely

The Wave

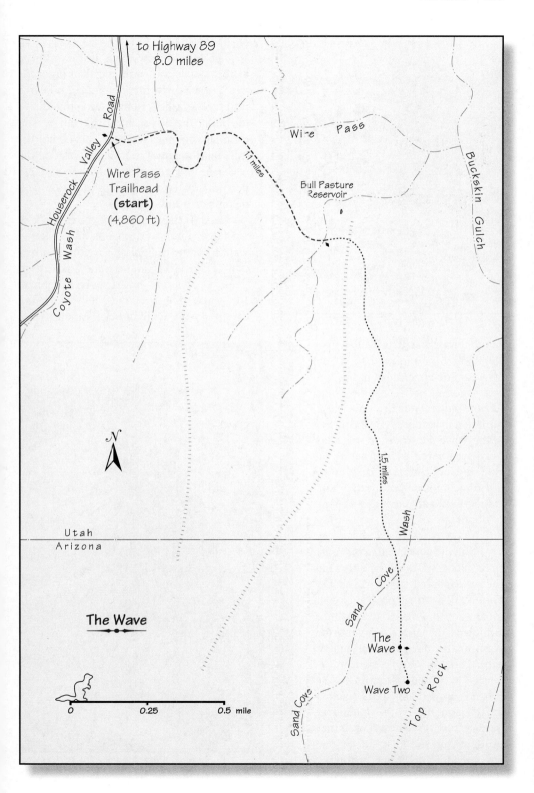

to Highway 89
8.0 miles

Houserock Valley Road

Wire Pass

Wire Pass
Trailhead
(start)
(4,860 ft)

Coyote Wash

1.1 miles

Bull Pasture
Reservoir

Buckskin Gulch

N

Utah
Arizona

1.5 miles

Wash

The Wave

Sand Cove

Sand Cove

The
Wave

Wave Two

Top Rock

0   0.25   0.5 mile

Top Rock (the Wave is in the yellow circle)

of the Wave Trail.

The trail climbs about 100 feet to the plateau above the wash and then proceeds in a southeasterly direction for 0.2 mile to a trail register (the first indication that this is the trail to the Wave). From the trail register the route continues southeast for another 0.4 mile until it comes to a sandy wash on the west side of a long rocky ridge. From there the trail turns east and climbs over a low pass on the north end of the ridge.

Once you have crossed to the east side of the ridge you must turn right and continue walking along its flank in a southerly direction. There is no trail here and no cairns to guide you, but that should not be a problem. Just walk south over the slickrock, being careful not to gain or loose elevation. If you

photogenic, and it is well worth the short hike required to see it. Its aesthetic appeal lies in the fact that the layers of sandstone in the Coyote Buttes area present a huge variation in hardness and color, and at the Wave the stratified stone has been weathered by the wind and rain into an amazing display of curving, multicolored bands and ridges that no artist could ever hope to duplicate.

From the parking area the route to the Wave starts out by following the well marked trail to Buckskin Gulch. The trail proceeds east along the side of a sandy wash for 5 minutes, then drops down into the wash just as the streambed makes a turn to the south. Follow the wash for another five minutes as it bends around and starts heading north again, then within a hundred yards you will see a well used trail climbing up the east side of the streambed. This is the beginning

Formation near the entrance to the Wave

see a lot of cairns it probably means that you have gone too low. As I stated earlier, there are few cairns along the correct route. About 10 minutes after turning south you will come to an old fence, and if you are following the route correctly you should cross the fence very close to its western end.

1.2 miles after turning south you will come to an arroyo called Sand Cove Wash. The slickrock gives way to sand in this area, so it is easier to see the tracks left by previous hikers. Following these tracks across the wash you will come to a hiker-made trail that climbs up a sand dune and continues a short distance to the Wave. The Wave is 0.3 mile south and 200 feet higher than the bottom of Sand Cove Wash.

Another way to pinpoint the location of the Wave is to study the slickrock hill, called Top Rock, on the south side of Sand Cove Wash. Long before you arrive at the wash you will see a dark vertical crack near the summit of Top Rock. The Wave is located in smaller dark area on the side of the hill just below and to the right of the crack. (See photograph on previous page.)

Although the Wave is the most prominent feature in the Coyote Buttes Area, it is not the only formation worth seeing. Just 300 yards south of the Wave there is another interesting formation that some people are now calling Wave Two. To reach Wave Two just climb to the top of the Wave, turn right, and proceed along the slickrock at the same elevation for 4-5 minutes.

The rugged landscape around the Wave and Wave Two is littered with many other interesting sandstone sculptures, and if time permits a little independent exploration can be highly rewarding. Try walking south for a few hundred yards beyond Wave Two along the west side of Top Rock. You might also want to check out two clusters of buttes called the North and South Teepees. They are located east of Top Rock, about 1.0 mile southeast of the Wave.

Wave Two, just south of the Wave

Fairyland Loop

★★

Distance:	8.6 miles (loop)
Walking time:	5¼ hours
Elevations:	950 ft. loss/gain Fairyland Trailhead (start): 7,760 ft. Fairyland Canyon: 7,150 ft. Rim Trail: 8,100 ft.
Trail:	Excellent, well marked trail
Season:	Summer to mid-fall. The trail is covered with snow during the winter months. Also the road to Fairyland Point is used as a cross-country ski trail in the winter.
Vicinity:	Bryce Canyon National Park
Maps:	Bryce Canyon (*USGS*) Bryce Canyon National Park (*Trails Illustrated, #219*)
Information:	http://www.utahtrails.com/fairyland.html (*Utah Trails*) http://www.nps.gov/brca/ (*Bryce Canyon National Park*) phone: (435) 834-5322 (*Visitor Center*)

Drive north from the Bryce Canyon National Park Visitor Center for one mile, then turn right and drive for another mile to Fairyland Point. The trail begins near the parking area at the end of the road. If you are staying in the park at North Campground it may be more convenient for you to begin this hike on the Rim Trail, near the amphitheater on the south end of the campground.

The area below the rim of Bryce Canyon National Park is a fantasyland of strange and wonderful geologic formations. Stone spires and pinnacles with fanciful names like the "Chinese Wall" and "Seal Castle" surround the trails, making them delightful places to hike. The Fairyland Loop Trail provides a fine opportunity to examine some of these natural sculptures, and as it is somewhat of the beaten path it is not as crowded as other trails in the park.

The stone sculptures of Bryce Canyon, whimsically called "hoodoos", have been eroded from a thick layer of soft sedimentary rock called the Claron Formation that was deposited in Utah some 60 million

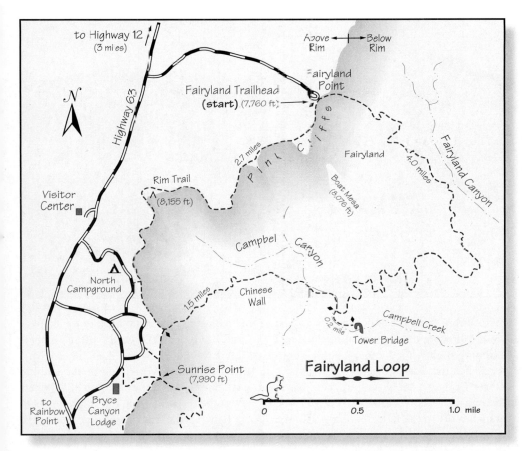

years ago. As the canyon rim erodes new hoodoos are formed; they begin first as tall thin fins, then serrate to form pinnacles and spires. The colors are caused primarily by iron and manganese impurities in the rock that oxidize into colorful hues of red, pink, orange, yellow, and purple. The carving action is still continuing, and it is estimated that the rim of Bryce Canyon is receding at the rate of about one foot in 65 years. In another hundred thousand years it will have receded by a third of a mile, and a whole new display of artwork will be ready for viewing in nature's gallery.

The trail descends immediately from Fairyland Point, winding down the north side of Boat Mesa for a distance of 1.5 miles to Fairyland Canyon. the lowest point on the

Fairyland Loop Trail

Fairyland Loop Trail

hike. From there the trail turns south and west, following the contour of the land and climbing slightly for another 2.5 miles until it reaches the Tower Bridge trail junction. Tower Bridge, a small natural bridge, is at the end of a short, well marked trail that branches off to the left. It is only 0.2 mile from the main trail, and it makes a nice lunch stop. From the Tower Bridge trail junction the path starts its climb back to the canyon rim. It winds to the west, with Campbell Canyon on the right and the Chinese Wall on the left, finally arriving at the canyon rim 1.5 miles later after a climb of 770 feet.

At the top of the rim the trail intersects the Rim Trail. Turn right here and walk along the rim for 2.7 miles back to the Fairyland Point parking lot.

Fairyland Loop Trail

Queens Garden

★★★★

Bryce Canyon National Park
day hike

Distance:	3.0 miles (loop)
Walking time:	2 hours
Elevations:	550 ft. loss/gain Sunset Point Trailhead (start): 8,000 ft. Queens Garden: 7,600 ft.
Trail:	Excellent, well marked trail
Season:	Summer to mid-fall. The trail is covered with snow during the winter months.
Vicinity:	Bryce Canyon National Park
Maps:	Bryce Canyon, Bryce Point (*USGS*) Bryce Canyon National Park (*Trails Illustrated, #219*)
Information:	http://www.utahtrails.com/queens.html (*Utah Trails*) http://www.nps.gov/brca/ (*Bryce Canyon National Park*) phone: (435) 834-5322 (*Visitor Center*)

This hike begins in Bryce Canyon National Park at Sunset Point, 1.5 miles south of the Visitor Center on Highway 63.

Bryce Canyon National Park is one place where you can see a lot of fantastic scenery in a very short time. There are numerous trails below the rim, especially in the area between Sunrise Point and Bryce Point, and several variations of this hike are possible. The route I will describe here descends below the rim through a narrow gorge called Wall Street Canyon. It then follows the Queens Garden Trail through an area that is filled with the weird and colorful geologic formations, called "hoodoos", that have made Bryce Canyon famous. Finally, the trail exits the canyon at Sunrise Point and turns to follow the rim back to Sunset Point where the hike began. Much of the route followed inside the canyon can also be seen from the rim trail, so you can enjoy Bryce Canyon's unique geology from two different perspectives.

There are two separate trails descending

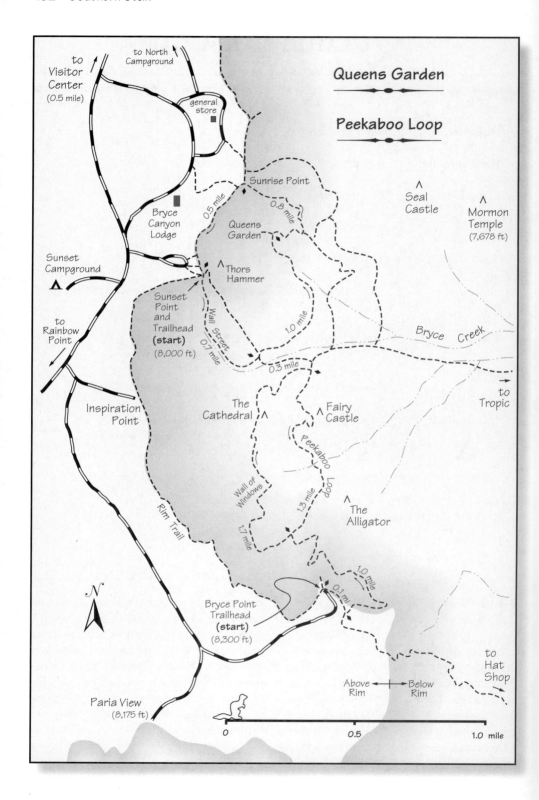

to Visitor Center (0.5 mile)

to North Campground

Queens Garden

Peekaboo Loop

general store

Sunrise Point

0.5 mile

0.8 mile

Seal Castle

Mormon Temple (7,678 ft)

Bryce Canyon Lodge

Queens Garden

Thors Hammer

Sunset Campground

Wall Street

1.0 mile

Bryce Creek

to Rainbow Point

Sunset Point and Trailhead **(start)** (8,000 ft)

0.7 mile

0.3 mile

to Tropic

Inspiration Point

The Cathedral

Fairy Castle

Peekaboo Loop

Wall of Windows

1.3 mile

The Alligator

Rim Trail

1.7 mile

N

1.0 mile

0.1 mi

Bryce Point Trailhead **(start)** (8,300 ft)

to Hat Shop

Paria View (8,175 ft)

Above Rim　Below Rim

0　　0.5　　1.0 mile

Queens Garden

into Bryce Canyon from Sunset Point: the Wall Street Trail and the Navajo Trail. The trails are both about the same length, and they meet at a point 0.7 mile below the rim. You can begin this hike by taking either trail, but personally I prefer the Wall Street Trail. There is some very nice scenery along the Navajo trail, but the Wall Street Trail offers the experience of walking down a narrow, deeply shaded canyon with towering cliffs and hoodoos on each side. It was, of course, metaphorically named after Wall Street Canyon in Manhattan, where New York's towering skyscrapers line the narrow road below.

Near the bottom of Wall Street Canyon you will see a sign directing you up a small side canyon where there is a natural arch. The arch is only a 2-minute walk off the main trail. After loosing 520 feet of elevation the main trail levels out and soon passes another trail on the right that leads to the Peekaboo Loop. Continue straight here and within a minute or so you will come to another junction where the Navajo Trail departs on the left. Again, continue straight ahead here on the trail that will take you to Queens Garden.

After leaving the Navajo Trail the Queens Garden Trail continues north for another 1.0 mile at a very gentle uphill grade until it passes the Queens Garden spur trail on the left. Turn here and walk the last 100 feet into a small amphitheater surrounded by a whimsical collection of hoodoos that have been named after European and Egyptian queens. It is a picture postcard scene, perfectly decorated with trees and rock formations as only nature can do.

After leaving Queens Garden the grade increases somewhat as the trail climbs the last 400 feet to Sunrise Point on the canyon rim. This is a very scenic area, with lots of hoodoos rising from the canyon floor. The trail meanders through a forest of pinnacles, passing through two short man-made tunnels along the way. If you are observant you may also see two small natural arches as you approach the rim.

Finally, the 0.5-mile walk back along the rim from Sunrise Point to Sunset Point provides an interesting opportunity to look back down into Bryce Canyon. Several segments of the Queens Garden Trail are clearly visible from the rim trail.

Peekaboo Loop

★★★

Distance: 5.2 miles (loop)

Walking time: 3 1/4 hours

Elevations: 1,100 ft. loss/gain
Bryce Point Trailhead (start): 8,300 ft.
Wall of Windows: 7,700 ft.

Trail: Excellent, well marked trail

Season: Summer to mid-fall. The trail is covered with snow during the winter months.

Vicinity: Bryce Canyon National Park

Maps: Bryce Point *(USGS)*
Bryce Canyon National Park *(Trails Illustrated, #219)*

Information: http://www.utahtrails.com/peekaboo.html *(Utah Trails)*
http://www.nps.gov/brca/ *(Bryce Canyon National Park)*
phone: (435) 834-5322 *(Visitor Center)*

Drive south from the Bryce Canyon Visitor Center for 1.6 miles until you see the turnoff for Inspiration and Bryce Points. Turn left here and follow the signs the last 2.0 miles to the Bryce Point parking lot where you will see the trailhead.

The Peekaboo Loop Trail is actually an equestrian trail used by the Park Service for twice-daily guided trail rides. Consequently, you are likely to see horses and mules while walking this trail. (If you are interested in a trail ride contact Canyon Trail Rides at (435) 679-8665.) Some hikers may not appreciate the sight and smell of the manure that the animals inevitably leave on the trail, but personally I feel a certain nostalgia in seeing the graceful animals in this beautiful canyon country. The valley east of the rim was used by cattle ranchers long before the national park was created.

The hike I describe below starts at Bryce Point, but it is also possible to begin the walk at Sunset Point. From there you can descend below the rim through Wall Street Canyon or on the Navajo Trail and arrive at the northern end of Peekaboo Loop 1.0 mile

Bryce Amphitheater from Bryce Point

later. The total walking distance of the hike if you begin at Sunset Point is 5.0 miles.

Whichever route you choose, when you reach the beginning of the loop I suggest you turn left and walk around it in a clockwise direction. The Wall of Windows, which is the highlight of the Peekaboo Loop, should be approached from the south, its most impressive side. If you are interested in photographing the Wall of Windows the best lighting is before noon, while the sun is in the east.

see map
page 432

Bryce Point, where this hike begins, is probably the most impressive overlook point in the park, so be sure to check out the view from there before beginning the hike. The view into the Bryce Amphitheater is particularly impressive at sunrise. The Peekaboo Loop Trail lies at the bottom of the amphitheater just north of Bryce Point, and from the overlook you can see most of the route you will be following on this hike.

The trail begins on the north side of the parking lot and proceeds in an easterly direction for a short distance before intersecting the Under the Rim Trail. There you must turn left to begin your descent into the canyon. Notice the gnarly, centuries-old bristlecone pines growing along the trail as you descend down the switchbacks. They are the trees with the fox tail-like branches, covered with long needles. Soon the trail passes through a short tunnel and then continues in a northwesterly direction below the north side of Bryce Point. Finally, about 30 minutes after leaving the trailhead you will arrive at a junction that marks the southern end of the Peekaboo Loop Trail.

Bear left at the junction and soon you will pass a horse corral and pit toilets where the Peekaboo Loop trail rides typically stop for a midday break. Unfortunately the horses and mules don't use the pit toilets, so as you proceed be careful where you step! From there the trail continues meandering in a northerly direction for another 15 minutes before arriving on the south side of the famous Wall of Windows.

The Wall of Windows is a thin vertical fin of sedimentary rock that is slowly eroding into a long line of hoodoos. The uneven erosion along the sides of the fin has caused about a dozen windows of various sizes to open up, allowing daylight to stream down onto the trail below. After reaching the wall the path turns to the northeast and parallels the ridge for a few hundred yards, giving hikers a fantastic view of the unusual formation before crossing to its north side.

After leaving the Wall of Windows the trail passes through another man-made tunnel and continues on for another 15 minutes to the Cathedral, an impressive hoodoo-studded butte that rises above the right side of the path. From the Cathedral it is another 0.5 mile to the north end of the loop. At this point you will come to a short connecting trail that leads to the Navajo Loop Trail and on to Sunset Point. In order to complete the Peekaboo Loop, however, you must bear right at this junction.

The next item of interest along the east side of the Peekaboo Loop Trail is the Fairy Castle, another collection of colorful hoodoos just 0.4 mile south of the junction. There the trail climbs to the crest of a long ridge, ultimately passing just 100 yards from the base of the Fairy Castle.

After leaving the Fairy Castle the route passes through yet another short tunnel before continuing the last 0.9 mile to the southern end of Peekaboo Loop. From there you can retrace your steps the last 1.1 miles back to the parking lot at Bryce Point.

Wall of Windows

Riggs Spring Loop

★

Distance:	8.0 miles (loop)
Walking time:	6½ hours
Elevations:	1,635 ft. loss/gain Rainbow Point Trailhead (start): 9,115 ft. Yovimpa Pass: 8,355 ft. Riggs Spring: 7,480 ft..
Trail:	Excellent, well marked trail
Season:	Summer to mid-fall. The trail is usually covered with snow from mid-November until mid-June.
Vicinity:	Bryce Canyon National Park
Maps:	Rainbow Point, Podunk Creek *(USGS)* Bryce Canyon National Park *(Trails Illustrated, #219)*
Information:	http://www.utahtrails.com/riggs.html *(Utah Trails)* http://www.nps.gov/brca/ *(Bryce Canyon National Park)* phone: (435) 834-5322 *(Visitor Center)*

This hike begins at Rainbow Point, 17 miles south of the Visitor Center at the end of the scenic drive road in Bryce Canyon National Park.

The Riggs Spring Trail, like many of the trails in Bryce Canyon National Park, was built by the Civilian Conservation Corps (CCC) in the mid-1930s. It is located near the southern boundary of the park, far removed from the popular viewpoints near Bryce Canyon Lodge, and its original purpose was to give fire suppression crews access to that more remote area. More recently it has become a popular recreational trail. There are several nice views of Bryce Canyon's famous rock formations along the way—the Pink Cliffs, viewed from Yovimpa Pass, are particularly photogenic—but the main attraction is the forest itself. At the higher elevations you will be in a dense for-

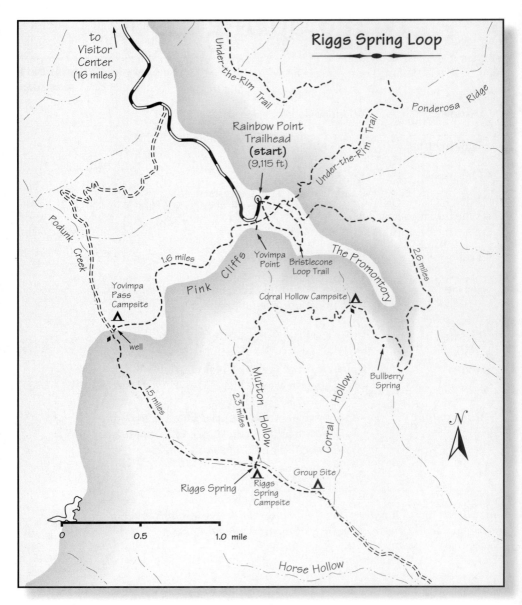

est of Engelmann spruce, Douglas fir, white fir, and an occasional bristlecone pine, and below the rim the forest gradually changes to ponderosa pine. The loop can be easily completed in one day, but it can also be done as a short, relaxing overnighter. The Park Service has constructed four primitive campsites in the area to accommodate backpackers.

There are several trails leaving Rainbow Point and the trail to Riggs Spring is not clearly marked, so be careful not to take a wrong turn at the beginning. Start out by following the Bristlecone Loop Trail near the rest rooms on the east side of the parking area. After just a few hundred feet the path forks; take the left fork. A few hundred feet later you will come to a four-way junction with trails leading to Yovimpa Point, the Bristlecone Loop, and the Under the Rim Trail. Turn left here along the Under the Rim Trail. The path will immediately begin loosing elevation, and after another hundred yards you will come to the third trail junction. This time there is a sign directing you to bear right for Riggs Spring. As the trail descends it makes a wide swing to the east to get around The Promontory, then after 1.8 miles it turns west and doubles back under the Pink Cliffs. Once you are under the cliffs the trail dips in and out of three small drainages before turning south to follow the Mutton Hollow Drainage for the last 0.9 mile to Riggs Spring. You will pass by the Corral Hollow Campsite 2.3 miles before you get to the spring.

Riggs Spring itself is surrounded by a grove of huge 150-foot ponderosa pines with nice grassy areas for pitching a tent. The spring, however, is barely a trickle and some might be discouraged by the quality of the water. It is badly silted and has a rusty color. Best to filter it before drinking. Except for the water quality one could not ask for a more pleasant place to spend the night, but if you plan to do this hike as an overnighter be sure to obtain a backcountry camping permit from the visitor center before starting out.

From Riggs Spring it is 1.5 miles back to the top of the Pink Cliffs at Yovimpa Pass. The trail climbs steadily upward but the elevation gain is only 875 feet. The Park Service maintains a small well just below the pass, and you will see a dirt access road to the pass coming in from the north. The trail turns east at the pass, and generally follows the rim above the Pink Cliffs back to Rainbow Point. There are a number of fine views along the trail; at one point you will be directly above

Mutton Hollow looking south toward Riggs Spring 1.4 miles away. The Park Service has buried a pipe line under the trail to get water from the well below Yovimpa Pass to the rest rooms at Rainbow Point, and occasionally you will see short sections of the pipe that are no longer buried. That is, however, only a small distraction along the scenic trail.

Be sure to watch for bristlecone pines near the edge of the rim. These ancient trees are often found in high, exposed areas where other trees don't do well, and they frequently live for more than 3,000 or even 4,000 years. They are easy to identify because of the way the needles grow all along the branches, giving them the appearance of fox tails. The needles are generally about 1 1/2 inches long with each bud producing a bundle of four or five needles.

Riggs Spring Trail

Rattlesnake Creek-Ashdown Gorge

 ★★★

Distance:	9.8 miles
	(plus 19 miles by car)
Walking time:	6 hours
Elevations:	3,460 ft. loss
	Rattlesnake Trailhead (start): 10,460 ft.
	Coal Creek: 7,000 ft.
Trail:	The trail is poorly maintained, but generally easy to follow. The last 3.4 miles of the hike involve wading through a shallow, rocky creek in the bottom of the Ashdown Gorge, so be sure to wear wettable boots. Sneakers and sandals are not recommended.
Season:	Midsummer to mid-fall. The higher elevations are usually covered with snow from mid-November through June, making the trail difficult to follow.
Vicinity:	Cedar Breaks National Monument, near Cedar City
Maps:	Brian Head, Flanigan Arch *(USGS)*
Information:	http://www.utahtrails.com/ashdown.html *(Utah Trails)*
	http://www.fs.fed.us/dxnf/ *(Dixie National Forest)*
	phone: (435) 865-3200 *(Cedar City Ranger District)*
	phone: (435) 586-0787 *(Cedar Breaks Visitor Center)*

Drive east on Center Street in Cedar City. Check your odometer as you cross Main Street and continue east on Highway 14 into Cedar Canyon. After you have driven 7.8 miles you will see a large pullout area on the left side of the road. This is where the hike ends and where you should park your shuttle car. The parking area is about 100 feet above a concrete spillway that has been constructed at the bottom of Coal Creek.

To get to Rattlesnake Trailhead where the hike begins continue driving up Cedar Canyon for another 14 miles following the signs to Cedar Breaks National Monument. After you reach the Visitor Center drive north for another 5.0 miles toward Brian Head Ski Resort. The well marked trailhead is located on the west side of Highway 143, just 100 feet beyond a boundary fence that marks the northern perimeter of Cedar Breaks National Monument.

This diverse hike has something for almost everyone–from high alpine wilderness to a walk through a narrow river gorge. There are also several nice views of the Cedar Breaks Amphitheater along the way. Finally, during most of the summer you will be unlikely to meet other hikers on this trail, and the solitude makes it an even more pleasant way to spend a day.

Although the hike can easily be completed in one day many people prefer to extend it to an overnight backpacking trip. There is plenty to see. Ashdown Creek originates in the Cedar Breaks Amphitheater, about 1,500 feet below the Visitor Center, and a nice side trip is to walk upstream along the creek into the amphitheater. The Park Service does not allow camping in this area, however, so if you intend to do this you should establish a camp on the west side of the park boundary.

From Rattlesnake Trailhead the route meanders gently downhill in a westerly direction along the northern boundary of Cedar Breaks National Monument. The trail is faint in a few places, but it is well defined by blaze marks on the trees and occasional cairns. Short spur trails leave the main trail in at least two places for viewpoints along the rim. Be sure to take advantage of these side excursions.

After about 1.5 miles you will see Snow Ridge just south of the trail, so called because of the white

rock along the top of the ridge. Here the route suddenly becomes steeper as it cuts down below the ridge on its way to Stud Flat. Stud Flat, a large rolling meadow above the confluence of Tri Story Canyon and Rattlesnake Creek, is extremely photogenic and a good place for a brief rest stop. Be sure to spend some time enjoying the view because soon you will be in the bottom of a heavily timbered canyon.

From the western side of Stud Flat the trail continues dropping down into Rattlesnake Canyon, reaching the creek after a descent of some 600 feet. If you are inter-

Cedar Breaks Amphitheater

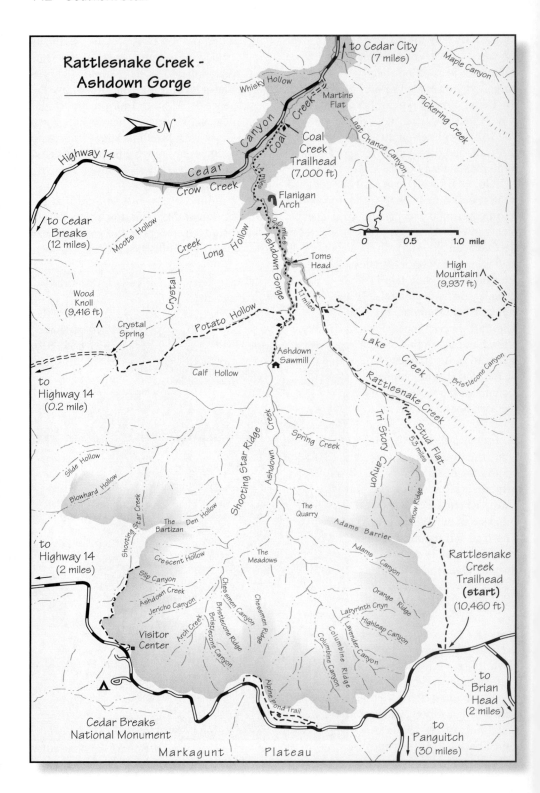

Rattlesnake Creek - Ashdown Gorge

N

to Cedar City (7 miles)

Maple Canyon

Whisky Hollow

Martins Flat

Pickering Creek

Cedar Canyon

Coal Creek

Coal Creek Trailhead (7,000 ft)

Last Chance Canyon

Highway 14

Crow Creek

1.4 miles

Flanigan Arch

to Cedar Breaks (12 miles)

Moots Hollow

Crystal Creek

Long Hollow

0.9 mile

Ashdown Gorge

Toms Head

High Mountain (9,937 ft)

Wood Knoll (9,416 ft)

Crystal Spring

Potato Hollow

1.1 miles

Lake Creek

Bristlecone Canyon

to Highway 14 (0.2 mile)

Calf Hollow

Ashdown Sawmill

Rattlesnake Creek

Stud Flat 5.3 miles

Slide Hollow

Blowhard Hollow

Shooting Star Creek

Shooting Star Ridge

Ashdown Creek

Spring Creek

Tri Story Canyon

Snow Ridge

The Quarry

Adams Barrier

to Highway 14 (2 miles)

The Bartizan

Den Hollow

Crescent Hollow

The Meadows

Adams Canyon

Rattlesnake Creek Trailhead (start) (10,460 ft)

Slip Canyon

Ashdown Creek

Jericho Canyon

Arch Creek

Chesmen Canyon

Bristlecone Canyon

Bristlecone Ridge

Chesmen Ridge

Orange Ridge

Labyrinth Cnyn

Highleap Canyon

Lavender Canyon

Columbine Ridge

Columbine Canyon

Visitor Center

Alpine Pond Trail

to Brian Head (2 miles)

to Panguitch (30 miles)

Cedar Breaks National Monument

Markagunt   Plateau

0   0.5   1.0 mile

Ashdown sawmill

photo by TK421

original homestead is still owned by the Ashdown family of Cedar City. Please respect their property if you visit this historic site.

It is only 3.4 miles from the east entrance of Ashdown Gorge to the end of the hike, but before proceeding into the gorge you should reassess the weather. If there is any chance of rain, stay out! Ashdown Creek drains a large area that includes the entire Cedar Breaks Amphitheater, and the water level of the creek can rise very quickly during a rainstorm. There is no way out of the narrowest sections of the gorge, so if it looks like rain, don't take a chance.

If the weather looks bad, there is another route that leads to Highway 14 without entering the gorge. Just continue following the trail across Ashdown Creek. The trail soon crosses a jeep road and then continues in a

ested in camping along Rattlesnake, there is a particularly good campsite about 0.7 mile downstream from the point where the trail first reaches the water. Finally, after following the creek for 1.6 miles you will come to a trail junction where a sign identifies the High Mountain Trail on the right. Here the Ashdown Gorge Trail leaves Rattlesnake Creek, climbing slightly up the south side of the stream and swinging around in a wide turn to the east to meet Ashdown Creek. As you leave Rattlesnake be sure to start looking for a strong, straight stick to use as a walking stick over the last section of the hike through Ashdown Gorge. The trail crosses Ashdown Creek on the eastern end of the gorge, 1.1 miles after leaving Rattlesnake Creek.

As stated earlier, Ashdown Creek also forms a natural route into the Cedar Breaks Amphitheater below the rim of Cedar Breaks National Monument. If you wish to make a side trip into this area it is about 2.1 miles upstream from the beginning of Ashdown Gorge to the national park boundary. 0.5 mile along the way you will pass the remains of a century-old sawmill that is still remarkably well preserved. The mill was constructed in 1898 by George Ashdown on 320 acres of homesteaded land. Although the mill is now almost entirely surrounded by the Ashdown Gorge Wilderness Area, the

Toms Head, Ashdown Gorge

photo by TK421

Ashdown Gorge

The next point of interest is Flanigan Arch, a large natural arch located 20 minutes downstream from Tom's Head along Ashdown Creek. Unfortunately the arch is difficult to spot and many hikers miss it. Watch for a black cabin-size boulder lying in a flat, rocky open area above the south side of the stream-bed. The river runs directly magnetic west at this point. If you are walking on the left side of the creek when you see the boulder you can briefly spot the 100-foot span high above the rim on the opposite side of the canyon.

From Flanigan Arch it is another 1.4 miles through the western portion of Ashdown Gorge to Highway 14. Ashdown Creek becomes Coal Creek as it exits the gorge, and after passing the Long Hollow and Crow Creek tributaries on the left you will see the highway above the south shore of the stream. When you reach the concrete spillway in the streambed you will find a short jeep road leading up to the pullout where your shuttle car is parked.

southerly direction up Potato Hollow. After 2.9 miles the trail reaches Crystal Spring, where it meets another jeep road that leads to Highway 14. The total distance from Ashdown Creek to the highway by this route is 3.9 miles. Unfortunately, however, the trail meets the highway 5.8 miles upcanyon from the pullout where your shuttle car is parked.

For most people the highlight of this hike is the final 3.4-mile walk through Ashdown Gorge. From the east entrance the gorge gradually deepens until the walls on either side reach a height of 600 feet. After 1.0 mile you will pass by the junction of Lake Creek and Ashdown Creek. Notice the 100-foot-high limestone monolith, locally known as Toms Head, at the confluence.

Upon reaching Toms Head you might want to take a side trip up Lake Creek before continuing down the gorge. Lake Creek is joined by Rattlesnake Creek 0.6 mile upstream from its confluence with Ashdown Creek, and there are two 20-foot waterfalls at the intersection of the two tributaries.

photo by TK421

Lake Creek Waterfall

Zion Narrows

★★★★★

Distance: 17.3 miles
(plus 38 miles by car)

Walking time: day 1: 6¹/₂ hours
day 2: 6 hours

Elevations: 1,410 ft. loss
Chamberlain Ranch Trailhead (start): 5,830 ft.
Big Spring: 4,790 ft.
Temple of Sinawava: 4,420 ft.

Trail: Except for a few miles at the beginning and the end of this
hike there is no trail. You will be wading in the North Fork of
the Virgin River most of the time, so be sure to wear wettable
boots. Sandals and sneakers are not recommended. During the
dry season the water is usually no more than knee deep, but it
can get much deeper.

Season: Summer to mid-fall. It is imperative to check with the Park Service before beginning this hike. For safety reasons access to the
Zion Narrows is strictly regulated and permits are required, even
for day hikers. The best times of year are midsummer, after the
spring runoff has subsided, and early fall. Thunder storms are
more frequent in late summer; hence there is a greater danger of
flash floods at that time.

Vicinity: Zion National Park

Maps: Temple of Sinawava, Clear Creek Mountain, Straight Canyon *(USGS)*
Zion National Park *(Trails Illustrated, #214)*

Information: http://www.utahtrails.com/zionnarrows.html *(Utah Trails)*
http://www.nps.gov/zion/ *(Zion National Park)*
phone: (435) 772-0170 *(Zion backcountry office)*

*Chamberlain's Ranch, where the hike begins, is 31 miles from the Zion Canyon Visitor
Center. Drive first to the Zion National Park east entrance, then continue on Highway 9 for
another 2.5 miles until you see a paved road departing on the left. Take this road and drive
north for 18 miles (unpaved after the first two miles) to a bridge across the North Fork of the*

Virgin River. Turn left on the north side of the bridge and drive 0.3 mile to a gate on the edge of the Chamberlain Ranch property. The gate is not locked, but please be sure to close it after you. A half mile beyond the gate the road again comes to the river. Park your car here and begin your hike by crossing the stream on foot and following the road on the south side of the river.

The hike ends at the Temple of Sinawava, 7.0 miles north of the visitor center. During the summer months the Park Service operates a free shuttle bus that runs frequently between the Temple of Sinawava, the visitor center, and Springdale. You should leave your shuttle car either at the visitor center or in Springdale.

Note: The Zion Adventure Company operates a convenient shuttle service for hikers to most of the national park's trailheads; the charge for a ride to Chamberlain's Ranch during the summer hiking season is $35.00/person. The shuttle leaves Springdale at 6:30 and 9:30 every morning, but be sure to make reservations in advance as the service is very popular. For more information or reservations call (435) 772-1001.

This is probably the best known hike in Utah. The watery North Fork Virgin River Canyon offers a welcome respite from Southern Utah's hot summer weather, and the scenery within the canyon is truly spectacular. There are only about three months of the year, however, when conditions are suitable for the hike, and a fair amount of planning is required for a successful trip.

The most important consideration is the weather. Flash floods are a constant danger in narrow slot canyons like the Zion Narrows, and you shouldn't begin this hike unless the forecast is good. The North Fork Virgin River drains several hundred square miles, and during a thunder storm the water level inside the canyon can rise several feet in a matter of minutes. At least five hikers have already drown in the Zion Narrows after being caught in flash floods, and because of this danger the Park Service allows backpackers to spend only one night in the canyon.

A maximum of 40 overnight hikers in are permitted to enter the

Zion narrows each day; for a group of 3-7 people the cost of a permit is $15.00. Reservations for 24 of the daily permits can be made online up to three months in advance at *http://zionpermits.nps.gov/.* The remaining 16 permits are issued at the visitor center on a walk-in basis one day in advance. This hike is very popular during the summer and fall seasons, so if you plan to get a walk-in permit I suggest you show up at the visitor center when it opens at 7:00 a.m. and go directly to the backcountry office to get a permit for the following day. Camping is allowed at

Bulloch's Cabin

only 12 sites along the North Fork of the Virgin River, and only two of the campsites can accommodate the maximum group size of 12 people. Consequently it is easier to get permits for groups of 6 or fewer people.

Day 1 (11.1 miles)

Cross the North Fork Virgin River at the car parking area on Chamberlain's Ranch and continue following the jeep road on foot above the south side of the river. This is a beautiful hiking area with rolling hills, scattered trees and large grassy fields along the river, but bear in mind that it is all private property accessible to hikers only by prior agreement with the owners. You won't actually be on National Park Service land for nearly seven miles. The owners have requested that hikers not camp on their land and not walk across their fields or disturb their cattle. If the ranchers' private property is not respected there could come a day when hikers are no longer allowed access into this area, so please follow the rules.

After walking 2.5 miles along the jeep road you will come to Bulloch's Cabin, an old abandoned homestead on the south side of the road. Remarkably, the cabin is still in reasonably good condition. There are also a few pieces of old farming machinery lying about the area. The road finally ends 0.3 mile beyond Bulloch's Cabin, and a trail continues along the river. Soon the river begins its descent into the canyon which you will follow all the way to the end of the hike.

North Fork Canyon is a canyon full of surprises, and for the rest of the day you can count on being awed and inspired over and over

again. Frequently the canyon will appear to end at the base of an impenetrable cliff a hundred feet ahead, but it always turns at the last minute to find a way around the obstacle. Often you will see large trees and other debris that have been washed into the canyon by previous flash floods. But the way around these obstructions is usually easy and very little scrambling is necessary. Because of the large number of hikers that pass through the canyon the easiest route is generally well defined.

You will come to the first long stretch of really good canyon narrows near the park boundary about three miles after you first enter the canyon. The canyon rim at this point is 800 feet above the streambed, and

North Fork Canyon below the Chamberlain Ranch

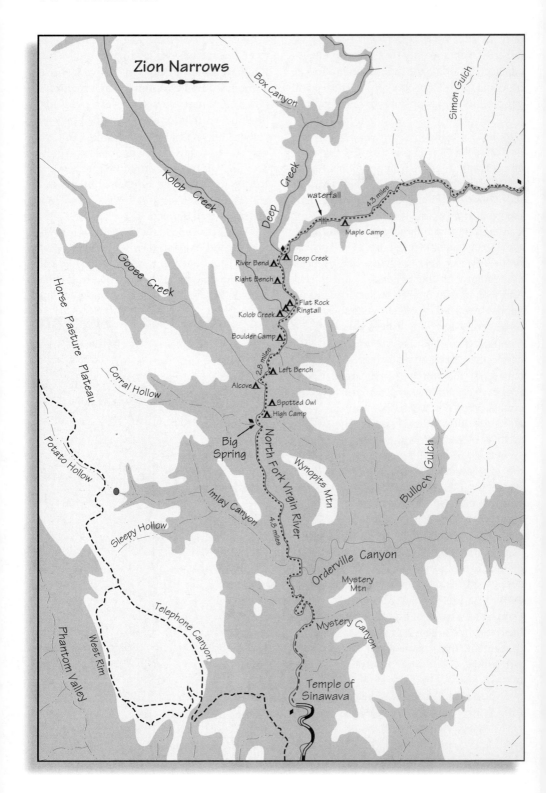

Zion Narrows

Box Canyon

Simon Gulch

Kolob Creek

Deep Creek

waterfall

4.3 miles

Maple Camp

Goose Creek

River Bend ▲   ▲ Deep Creek

Right Bench ▲

Flat Rock
▲ Ringtail
Kolob Creek ▲ ▲

Horse Pasture Plateau

Boulder Camp ▲

2.8 miles

Corral Hollow

▲ Left Bench

Alcove ▲

▲ Spotted Owl

▲ High Camp

Potato Hollow

Big
Spring

North Fork Virgin River

Wynopits Mtn

Bulloch Gulch

Imlay Canyon

Sleepy Hollow

4.8 miles

Orderville Canyon

Telephone Canyon

Mystery
Mtn

Phantom Valley

West Rim

Mystery Canyon

Temple of
Sinawava

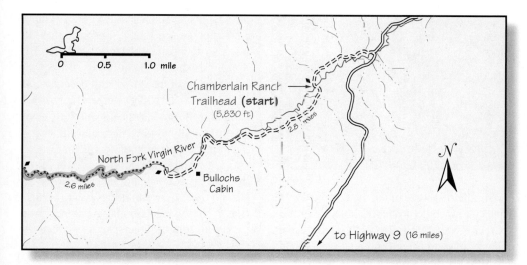

the walls at the bottom are often no more than fifteen feet apart. The first campsite, Maple Camp, is also located in this area, at a well marked location on the left shore about 8 feet above the water.

The next point of interest in the canyon is a small waterfall. About 1.6 miles below Maple Camp the stream suddenly plunges over a 20-foot dam in the canyon floor. Occasionally a daring hiker will take off his backpack and jump over the fall into the pool below, but to do so is foolhardy. First of all it is impossible to see what rocks might lie below the boiling water, and second, it is hard to imagine a more inconvenient place to sustain an injury. Don't take the chance. There is an easy way around the waterfall on the south side of the canyon.

Deep Creek joins the North Fork at a wide confluence 0.8 mile below the waterfall. Beyond this point you will notice a large change in the flow rate of the river; about two thirds of the water flowing through the Zion Narrows comes from Deep Creek. This canyon offers a popular side trip and you may want to spend some time exploring, especially if your assigned campsite is the Deep Creek Camp located at the confluence.

The other ten campsites are all located

in the next 2.5 miles downstream from Deep Creek. Unfortunately the Park Service does not allow hikers to stipulate which site they

Zion Narrows

Big Spring

near campsite number 10, the Alcove Camp.

Below Goose Creek you will pass the last two campsites before coming to Big Spring, about 45 minutes away. Big Spring is a large gushing spring that cascades out of the cliff face 10 feet above the river. It is the most dramatic spring you will see on this hike, but between here and the end of the trail you can count on seeing many other smaller springs. This stretch of river passes through the geologic boundary between the Navajo Sandstone and the Kayenta Formation. The Navajo Sandstone is a porous rock with microscopic spaces between the

want, but if I were given the opportunity to pick one I would probably choose the Kolob Creek Camp 0.9 mile below Deep Creek. This campsite is located on a high shaded bench, just south of the Kolob Creek confluence. The site is very pretty, but what makes it especially attractive is its proximity to Kolob Canyon, the most interesting of all the Zion Narrows side canyons. If you have a few extra hours to spend exploring on your way through the narrows this is a good place to spend it. Kolob Canyon is one of the best examples in Utah of a deep, narrow slot canyon.

Day 2 (6.2 miles)

The next side canyon you will pass is Goose Creek Canyon, which merges into Zion Canyon 1.3 miles below Kolob Creek. Goose Creek also provides a good opportunity for side trips. It is a wider canyon than Kolob, with more vegetation in the bottom. Goose Creek joins the North Fork on the west side of the river

Zion Narrows

constituent particles of sand that allow water to seep down from the plateaus above, while the Kayenta Formation contains layers of clay and mudstone that effectively halt the water's downward penetration. When the water reaches the Kayenta Formation hydrostatic pressure from above pushes it out into the canyons where it is seen as spring water.

Big Spring also marks the beginning of the two-mile section of canyon commonly known as the Zion Narrows. This part of the canyon is distinguished by its sheer thousand-foot walls that rise above the river with little or no sandy shore between. There is no high ground here; hence it is not a place you would want to be during a storm. Under certain conditions the water can rise very quickly, and people have died in the past from flash floods in this section of the canyon. When no storms are imminent, however, the danger is minimal. Just use common sense and don't enter the narrows if the sky looks like rain.

About the time you reach the mouth of Orderville Canyon, 2.3 miles below Big Spring, the Zion Narrows widens again and you will find a well-used trail to follow on the sandy shore of the river. Also at this point you will begin to see day hikers from the Temple of Sinawava—hundreds of them. The remaining 2.7 miles of trail, from Orderville Canyon to the road, is the most popular part of Zion Canyon, and on a typical summer afternoon you will pass more than a thousand people splashing in the water along this stretch of the canyon. Finally, for the last mile you will be walking on the Gateway to the Narrows Trail, a paved walkway leading back to the trailhead at the Temple of Sinawava.

Zion Narrows

East Rim Zion Canyon

★ ★ ★ ★

**Zion National Park
shuttle car required
overnight hike**

Distance:	17.9 miles, including side trips to most points of interest (plus 15 miles by car)
Walking time:	day 1: 6 hours day 2: 3³/₄ hours
Elevations:	1,190 ft. gain, 2,560 ft. loss East Entrance Trailhead (start): 5,720 ft. Cable Mountain: 6,500 ft. Weeping Rock Trailhead: 4,350 ft.
Trail:	Very popular, well maintained trail
Season:	Late spring through mid-fall. The higher parts of the trail are usually covered with snow from mid-November to mid-May.
Vicinity:	Zion National Park
Maps:	Temple of Sinawava, Springdale East, The Barracks, Clear Creek Mountain *(USGS)* Zion National Park *(Trails Illustrated, #214)*
Information:	http://www.utahtrails.com/eastrimzion.html *(Utah Trails)* http://www.nps.gov/zion/ *(Zion National Park)* phone: (435) 772-0170 *(Zion backcountry office)*

After obtaining an overnight backpacking permit at the Zion Canyon Visitor Center drive 11 miles east on Highway 9 to the park's east entrance. Just before you reach the entrance gate you will see a narrow road leaving on the left for the trailhead, 0.2 mile north of the highway.

The hike ends at Weeping Rock, 5.3 miles north of the visitor center. During the summer months the Park Service operates a free shuttle bus that runs frequently between Weeping Rock, the visitor center, and Springdale. You should leave your shuttle car either at the visitor center or in Springdale.

Note: The Zion Adventure Company operates a convenient shuttle service for hikers to most of the national park's trailheads; the charge for a ride from Springdale to the East Entrance Trailhead during the summer hiking season is $22.00/person. For more information or reservations call (435) 772-1001

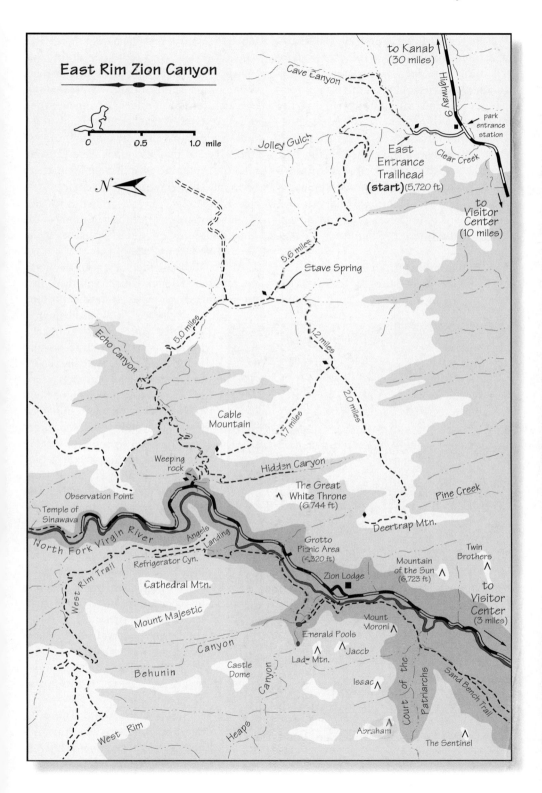

East Rim Zion Canyon

0   0.5   1.0 mile

N

to Kanab
(30 miles)

Cave Canyon

Highway 9

park
entrance
station

Jolley Gulch

East
Entrance
Trailhead
(start)(5,720 ft)

Clear Creek

to
Visitor
Center
(10 miles)

3.6 miles

Stave Spring

5.0 miles

Echo Canyon

1.2 miles

2.0 miles

Cable
Mountain

1.7 miles

Weeping
rock

Hidden Canyon

Observation Point

The Great
White Throne
(6,744 ft)

Pine Creek

Temple of
Sinawava

North Fork Virgin River

Angels
Landing

Deertrap Mtn.

Grotto
Picnic Area
(4,320 ft)

West Rim Trail

Refrigerator Cyn.

Cathedral Mtn.

Zion Lodge

Mountain
of the Sun
(6,723 ft)

Twin
Brothers

to
Visitor
Center
(3 miles)

Mount Majestic

Emerald Pools

Mount
Moroni

Canyon

Lady Mtn.

Jacob

Behunin

Castle
Dome

Isaac

Court of the Patriarchs

Sand Bench Trail

Canyon

West   Rim

Heaps

Abraham

The Sentinel

Zion National Park is probably the best all around hiking area in the state of Utah. The trails here are very popular, so if it is solitude you are looking for this is the wrong place. But you will certainly find plenty of breathtaking scenery and interesting geological formations. The East Rim Trail, especially when walked in the direction suggested here, is a very pleasant way to sample what Zion has to offer. Very little climbing is required, the temperatures are not extreme, and the scenery just keeps getting better and better all the way to the end.

Day 1 (10.8 miles)

From the East Entrance Trailhead the hike begins by following Clear Creek for about 1.5 miles and then turns north into Cave Canyon. You will soon notice that much of the trail is along an old wagon road. Before Zion National Park was created this area was used extensively by ranchers and loggers. Once it reaches Cave Canyon the trail begins to ascend gradually to the top of the tableland that surrounds Zion Canyon, and after another mile it doubles back to give you a fine view from the mesa top down into Clear Creek Canyon. From this vantage point you can easily see the beginning of the trail, 400 feet below, threading its way along the side of Clear Creek.

Next, the trail veers again to the north to get around Jolley Gulch, and then, free of any further obstacles, it meanders along the contours of the mesa in a westerly direction toward Stave Spring. About 0.1 mile beyond Stave Spring you will see a fork in the trail, where you should turn left toward Cable Mountain. Soon you will cross a small, unnamed stream, beyond which you might want to begin looking for a camp site. There are a number of nice spots along this section of trail. Please be aware, however, that you should not camp right next to the water and you should be out of site of the trail.

There are two interesting side trips here to consider, either after establishing camp on the first day or before you put on your backpacks on the second day. Depending on how far from the Stave Spring trail junction you camped, Cable Mountain is about 2.0 miles away and Deertrap Mountain about 2.5 miles.

Cable Mountain, the most interesting of the two side trips, is a high promontory, about 2,100 feet

East Rim Trail

above the Virgin River, with an unimpeded view of Angels Landing and the West Rim. It is called Cable Mountain because in the early 1900s, before Zion National Park was formed, the Zion Cable Company operated a tram from the top of Cable Mountain to the bottom of Zion Canyon. The tram was used primarily for lowering lumber from the mesa top to the canyon floor, where it was loaded onto wagons and hauled to nearby towns like Springdale and Rockville. Quite a bit of the original structure can still be seen on the edge of the mountain, although the tram hasn't been operated for eighty years.

The second side trip you might want to consider while you are on the mesa top is the walk to the Deertrap Mountain Overlook. Deertrap Mountain, which is situated high above the Zion Lodge, offers a fine view of the Court of the Patriarchs and Lady Mountain on the other side of the Canyon. You can easily walk to either one of these viewpoints and back in a couple of hours.

Day 2 (7.1 miles)

The trail from Stave Spring to Weeping Rock is one of the most scenic walks in Zion. It is only 5.0 miles long, and all downhill. It will only take a few hours to complete the trip, so if you haven't taken the side trip to Cable Mountain or Deertrap Mountain yet you should definitely do so before starting down. The trail to Weeping Rock passes directly beneath Cable Mountain on the way down, and it is all the more interesting if you have also seen it from the top.

The trail first heads north into the back of

Echo Canyon, and then turns west as it descends to the bottom of Zion Canyon. The scenery starts getting very interesting after about 1.5 miles. Echo Canyon gets narrower and narrower as you go down; in places the canyon is only 20 feet wide and everywhere there are water-carved etchings in the rock. Finally the side canyon breaks out into the main canyon about 500 feet above the Virgin River, and the trail switchbacks the rest of the way to the bottom.

0.6 mile after entering Echo Canyon you will pass another junction where the trail to the East Rim Observation Point climbs northward out of Echo Canyon. Observation Point offers another possible side trip, but if you have already been to the top of Cable Mountain you will note that the view from there is quite similar.

Finally, 0.6 miles before reaching the bottom of Zion Canyon you will pass the trail to Hidden Canyon—another highly recommended side trip. Hidden Canyon is a narrow slot canyon, similar to the lower reaches of Echo Canyon, that cuts back into the East Rim for about a mile. Depending on how much exploring you want to do, it will take an hour or less to check it out. Note: camping is not allowed in Hidden Canyon.

Looking across Zion Canyon from Cable Mountain

West Rim Zion Canyon

 ★★★★

Zion National Park
shuttle car required
overnight hike

Distance: 15.4 miles
                            (plus 42 miles by car)

Walking time: day 1: $2^1/_2$ hours
                         day 2: $5^1/_2$ hours

Elevations: 3,140 ft. loss
West Rim Trailhead (start): 7,460 ft.
Potato Hollow: 6,780 ft.
Grotto Picnic Area: 4,320 ft.

Trail: Very popular, well maintained trail

Season: Late spring through mid-fall. The higher parts of the trail are usually covered with snow from mid-November to June.

Vicinity: Zion National Park

Maps: Kolob Reservoir, The Guardian Angels, Temple of Sinawava *(USGS)*
Zion National Park *(Trails Illustrated, #214)*

Information: http://www.utahtrails.com/westrimzion.html *(Utah Trails)*
http://www.nps.gov/zion/ *(Zion National Park)*
phone: (435) 772-0170 *(Zion backcountry office)*

To get to the West Rim Trailhead, where the hike begins, drive south from the park entrance for 14 miles on Highway 9 to the town of Virgin. In Virgin you will see a sign marking the road to Kolob Reservoir. Turn here and drive north for another 21 miles until you see a sign directing you to Lava Point on the right. Proceed on the gravel road toward Lava Point for 1.0 mile to *another junction where you must turn left on a dirt road that drops down to the West Rim Trailhead, 1.3 miles further.*

The hike ends at the Grotto Picnic Area, 4.3 miles north of the visitor center. During the summer months the Park Service operates a free shuttle bus that runs frequently between the picnic area, the visitor center, and Springdale. You should leave your shuttle car either at the visitor center or in Springdale. Be sure to obtain a backcountry camping permit at the visitor center before driving to the West Rim Trailhead.

Note: The Zion Adventure Company operates a convenient shuttle service for hikers to *most of the national park's trailheads; the charge for a ride from Springdale to the West Rim Trailhead during the summer hiking season is $39.00/person. For more information or reservations call (435) 772-1001.*

The diversity of this hike, combined with the magnificent views of Zion Canyon from the West Rim, make it one of the most enjoyable trails in the park. Horse Pasture Plateau, where the trail begins, is a long flat finger of sandstone that protrudes from the Kolob Plateau, on the northern park boundary, into Zion Canyon. The path meanders gently downward through the ponderosa pine and pinon-juniper forests of the plateau, dropping 740 feet over a distance of 9.7 miles before descending abruptly into the canyon. Spectacular views from the West Rim begin about six miles from the trailhead, where the route skirts the edge of Phantom Valley, and peak 3.5 miles later at Cabin Spring. Beyond Cabin Spring the trail drops into Zion Canyon and winds through another 4.7 miles of slickrock and canyon country before reaching the North Fork of the Virgin River.

Only nine groups of hikers are permitted to camp along the West Rim Trail each day; the cost of a permit is $15.00 for a group of 3-7 people. Reservations for four of the nine backcountry campsites can be made online up to three months in advance at http://zionpermits.nps.gov/. The remaining five sites are assigned at the visitor center on a walk-in basis one day in advance. This hike is very popular during the summer and fall seasons, so if you plan to get a walk-in permit I suggest you show up at the visitor center when it opens at 7:00 a.m. and go directly to the backcountry office to get your permit and campsite assignment for the following day. Only two of the sites can accommodate the maximum group size of

West Rim Trail

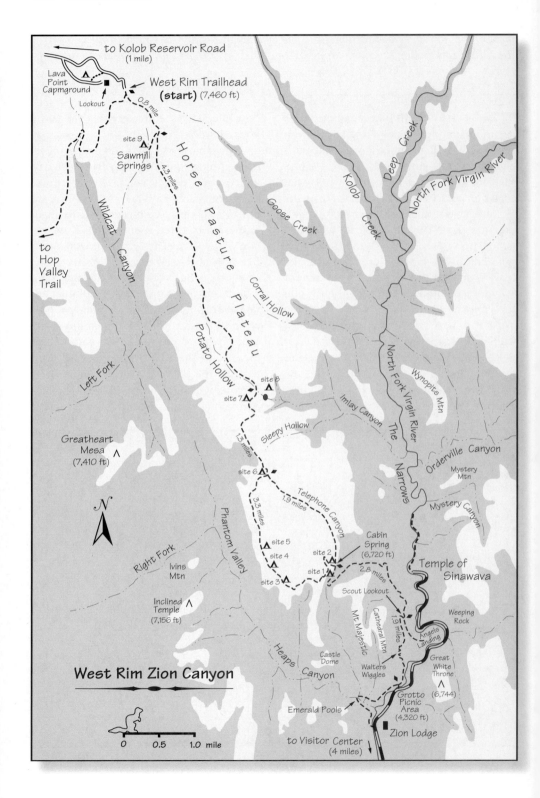

to Kolob Reservoir Road (1 mile)

Lava Point Campground

Lookout

West Rim Trailhead **(start)** (7,460 ft)

0.8 mile

site 9

Sawmill Springs

4.3 miles

Horse Pasture Plateau

Deep Creek

North Fork Virgin River

Kolob Creek

Goose Creek

Wildcat Canyon

to Hop Valley Trail

Corral Hollow

Potato Hollow

Left Fork

site 8

site 7

Imlay Canyon

North Fork Virgin River

Wynopits Mtn

Orderville Canyon

Sleepy Hollow

1.3 miles

Greatheart Mesa (7,410 ft)

site 6

Mystery Mtn

The Narrows

Mystery Canyon

Telephone Canyon

1.9 miles

3.3 miles

N

Phantom Valley

site 5

site 4

site 2

Cabin Spring (6,720 ft)

Temple of Sinawava

2.8 miles

Right Fork

Ivins Mtn

site 3

site 1

Scout Lookout

Weeping Rock

Inclined Temple (7,156 ft)

Mt Majestic

Cathedral Mtn

1.9 miles

Angels Landing

Heaps Canyon

Castle Dome

Walters Wiggles

Great White Throne (6,744 ft)

West Rim Zion Canyon

Emerald Pools

Grotto Picnic Area (4,320 ft)

Zion Lodge

0   0.5   1.0 mile

to Visitor Center (4 miles)

12 campers, so it is easier to get permits for groups of 6 or fewer people.

Day 1 (5.1 miles)

In contrast to the canyons below the rim, the top of Horse Pasture Plateau is remarkably flat. The West Rim Trail meanders along the plateau for nearly ten miles, depending on your choice of routes, with little hint of the rugged terrain that lies ahead. 0.1 mile from the trailhead you will come to a fork with the Wildcat Canyon Trail branching to the right, and 0.7 mile farther another trail branches off to the right for Sawmill Springs. Keep to the left in both cases. The trail descends very gradually in a southerly direction through an open forest of ponderosa pine, turning slowly to pinion and juniper as altitude is lost.

About 3.5 miles from the Sawmill Springs trail junction you will begin dropping into Potato Hollow, a shallow drainage that flows into Imlay Canyon on the east side of the plateau. Potato Hollow is a delightful place to spend a night; the Potato Hollow Campsites 7 and 8 are the best ones you will find on this hike. A large grove of quaking aspen surrounds the depression, and a small pond on its southern side is a favorite afternoon watering hole for wildlife. As a bonus, the nearby rim of the plateau presents some fine views across Imlay Canyon.

Day 2 (10.3 miles)

About a mile below Potato Hollow the trail crosses Sleepy Hollow, where you will be treated to a panorama of Phantom Valley. Look for Greatheart Mesa, one of the landmarks of the park, on the opposite side of the valley. Another 0.3 mile will bring you to another trail junction where a decision has to be made. The Telephone Can-

yon Trail, on the left, is the shorter route to Cabin Spring, but unless you are in a terrible hurry you should bear to the right here and follow the rim trail. It is 1.4 miles longer but much more scenic.

The rim trail skirts the southeastern side of Horse Pasture Plateau, passing campsites 5, 4, and 3, and affords almost continual views of Phantom Valley and Heaps Canyon below. Telephone Canyon is a more densely forested route that cuts through the center of the plateau to meet the rim trail again at Cabin Spring.

Cabin Spring is a good place to stop for lunch. The spring itself is quite unimpressive. It was named after a Park Service cabin that once stood nearby but unfortunately burned down in the 1970s. From the rim near Cabin Spring, however, you can see

Looking into Zion Canyon

a long stretch of the trail below, and it is interesting to gaze down into the slickrock canyon country and trace out the route you will follow below the plateau.

Beyond Cabin Spring the trail begins to descend almost at once, making two long switchbacks down the sandstone cliffs into the canyon below. After loosing about 900 feet you will arrive at a point directly below and to the east of the spring; look back and see the water-streaked cliffs beneath it. Immediately to your right is Mount Majestic and, behind that, Cathedral Mountain. You will spend the next two miles skirting around these two formations to reach Refrigerator Canyon.

After you have walked 2.8 miles from Cabin Spring you will see a spur trail on the left heading for the top of a rocky peak known as Angels Landing. If you have the time, Angels Landing is a side trip that shouldn't be missed. The top is only 0.5 mile from the main trail, and the view is absolutely incredible. The river winds around a huge 180 degree bend in the canyon, and on the road, 1,470 feet below, cars creep like ants on their way to and from the Temple of Sinawava. The Great White Throne, probably the most famous of Zion's landmarks, rises 3,420 feet above the canyon floor on the opposite side of the river.

A word of caution about the "trail" to Angels Landing. Some scrambling is necessary and, although the park service has installed rails and support chains on a few of the more exposed sections, the route is not for the faint of heart. Small children and people who suffer from vertigo should not attempt this hike. Angels Landing is especially dangerous when it is wet or windy. Also, the top of the ridge is frequently struck by lightning, so

avoid it during stormy weather.

If you decide not to attempt Angel's Landing, at least pause to enjoy the view from Scout Lookout near the trail junction. Leaving Scout Lookout, the trail drops straight down into Refrigerator Canyon over a series of no less than 21 switchbacks. These switchbacks, whimsically called Walter's Wiggles, were cut from the rock cliff in 1926 so that tourists could reach the viewpoints above. Viewed from a distance they look more like a rope ladder or a spider's web than a trail.

Finally, after following the bottom of Refrigerator Canyon for about a half mile, the trail emerges on the west side of the inner canyon and threads its way down to the river 1.9 miles from Scout Lookout.

Walter's Wiggles

The Subway

★★★★

Distance:	9.1 miles (round trip from Left Fork Trailhead)
Walking time:	6 hours
Elevations:	1,150 ft. loss/gain Left Fork Trailhead (start): 5,100 ft. lowest point: 4,640 ft. Subway: 5,330 ft.
Trail:	Unmaintained hiker-made trail. The route is easy to follow, but there is considerable boulder hopping to contend with along the creek. Wear wettable shoes because you will be crossing the stream many times. As described below, if you intend to explore the upper Subway you should carry 60 feet of rope or nylon webbing (wide nylon webbing is preferred).
Season:	June through early October. Because of the danger posed by flash floods you should not enter the Subway if there is a chance of rain. Be especially careful in late August and September when thunderstorms are more common.
Vicinity:	Zion National Park
Maps:	The Guardian Angels *(USGS)* Zion National Park *(Trails Illustrated, #214)*
Information:	http://www.utahtrails.com/subway.html *(Utah Trails)* http://www.nps.gov/zion/ *(Zion National Park)* phone: (435) 772-0170 *(Zion backcountry office)*

Drive south from the Zion National Park south entrance for 14 miles to the town of Virgin. As you enter Virgin you will see a sign marking the road to Kolob Reservoir. Turn here and drive north for another 8.2 miles, until you see a sign marking the Left Fork Trailhead. The trailhead and parking area are located just off the right side of the road.

Note: Permits are required for this hike, and only 80 people are allowed to visit the Subway each day. 60 of the permits are issued by way of a lottery/reservation system, and the remaining 20 are issued on a "walk-in" basis. You can join the permit lottery by filling out an online application at http://zionpermits.nps.gov/ up to three months before the month

of your intended trip. If you want to get one of the 20 walk-in permits I suggest you join the line at the Zion Visitor Center no later than 7:00 a.m. on the day before your intended trip. The ranger at the backcountry country desk starts issuing the permits at 8:00 a.m. and they usually go quickly. The maximum group size is 12, and a small fee is charged according to how many people are in your group.

This hike is considered by many outdoorsmen to be Utah's premier canyoneering experience–especially if it is done as a one-way hike from the Wildcat Canyon Trailhead (see page 467). The route from Wildcat Canyon is more technical than the hike up Left Fork Creek described below, but either approach will take you to the section of canyon commonly referred to as the Subway. The canyon narrows that comprise the Subway are actually only 400 yards long, but the scenery within that short section of canyon is truly spectacular. Many of the photographic prints for sale in Southern Utah's art galleries were taken there, and if you are a landscape photographer the Subway should be high on your list of places to see.

From the Left Fork Trailhead an excellent trail sets off in a northeasterly direction through the pinion and juniper trees toward the south side of Tabernacle Dome. The path crosses a shallow drainage after 5 minutes, then continues on for another 0.4 mile to the northern rim of Great West Canyon. The canyon is 400 feet deep at this point, and from the rim you can clearly see the trail snaking its way down the side to meet the Left Fork of North Creek at the bottom. Water can always be found in

Left Fork so it is not necessary to carry a great deal of water on this hike, but it must be filtered or treated before drinking.

Once on the canyon floor the route follows the stream all the way to the Subway. There is a reasonable trail much of the way, but it occasionally fades away or gets lost in the rocky areas, so be prepared to do some scrambling and bushwhacking. Also, don't

Left Fork of North Creek

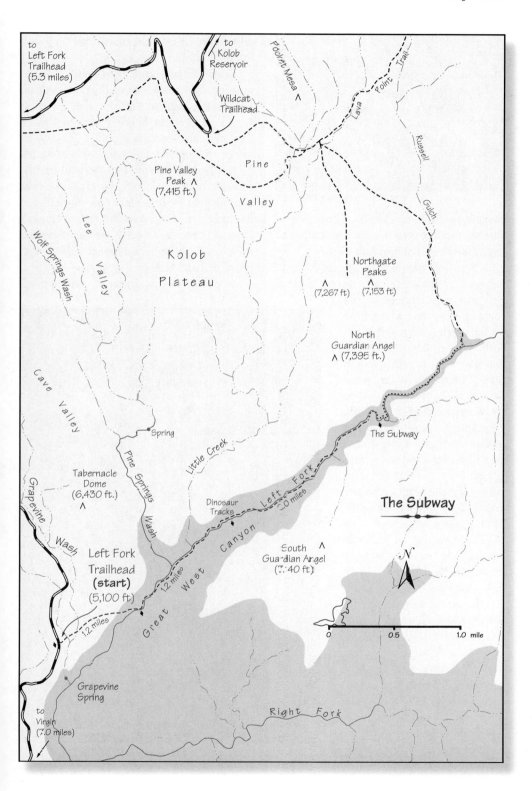

to
Left Fork
Trailhead
(5.3 miles)

to
Kolob
Reservoir

Pocket Mesa ∧

Wildcat
Trailhead

Lava Point Trail

Russell Gulch

Pine

Pine Valley
Peak ∧
(7,415 ft.)

Valley

Lee
Valley

Wolf Springs Wash

Kolob
Plateau

Northgate
Peaks

∧
(7,267 ft)

∧
(7,153 ft)

North
Guardian Angel
∧ (7,395 ft.)

Cave Valley

Spring

Little Creek

The Subway

Pine Springs Wash

Tabernacle
Dome
(6,430 ft.)
∧

Dinosaur
Tracks

Left Fork

2.0 miles

Grapevine Wash

The Subway

Left Fork
Trailhead
(start)
(5,100 ft)

1.2 miles

West   Canyon

Great

South
Guardian Angel
(7,340 ft)

∧

N

1.2 miles

0   0.5   1.0 mile

Grapevine
Spring

to
Virgin
(7.0 miles)

Right   Fork

Dinosaur Tracks beside Left Fork

other point of interest: fossilized dinosaur tracks.

Watch for two large flat slabs of crumbly grayish-white mudstone on the north side of the creek. Together the two slabs of rock form a panel about 20 feet wide and 40 feet long that has been tilted up at a 30-degree angle. The panel faces the stream about 20 feet from the water, and the trail passes directly between it and the creek. Look carefully at the stone slabs and you will see that they are covered with dinosaur tracks! Dozens of the tracks are impressed into the rock, each about 10 inches long with the characteristic three toes.

Some minor scrambling is still required

hesitate to cross the stream from time to time in search of the easiest route. Often the easiest route is in the stream itself.

0.5 mile upstream from the point where the trail first meets the canyon bottom you will see a break in the north canyon wall where Pine Spring Wash flows into the Left Fork. Unfortunately, however, the main trail is on the south side of Left Fork at this point so you will probably not see the water rushing down from Pine Spring. A short distance further upstream Little Creek also flows into the north side of Left Fork, but the trail does not cross to the north side of the canyon floor until it is above the Little Creek confluence.

The section of canyon around Pine Spring Wash and Little Creek is littered with thousands of black basaltic boulders from an old volcanic eruption, and the trail has a difficult time finding an obstacle-free route through this area. A great deal of scrambling is necessary. The boulder field ends, however, about 0.4 mile upstream from Little Creek, and just beyond the last basaltic boulder you will come to an-

Entrance to the Subway

upcanyon from the dinosaur tracks, but in general there are fewer major obstacles to contend with and the scenery just keeps getting better. Occasional outcroppings of shale in this area form low stairsteps in the streambed, and the creek flows through a series of delightful cascades as it tumbles down the barriers. These cascades are particularly impressive over the last mile of this hike where the creek cuts through the boundary separating the Navajo Sandstone from the underlying Kayenta Formation.

Finally, 3.0 miles upstream from the point where the trail first meets Left Fork Creek, you will come to a place where the canyon floor is paved with a 100-foot-wide sheet of gently sloping slickrock. The smooth sandstone is covered with a carpet of moss that is kept green and alive by a thin veneer of water trickling down the slope. The route follows the wet shimmering slickrock for a distance of several hundred feet, then bends 90 degrees to the right to enter the section of the canyon known as the Subway.

At this point there is no mistaking the scene before you. The famous keyhole-shaped entrance to the Subway lies 200 feet ahead. There are many photographs of this odd formation in the Zion Visitor Center, and it will be instantly recognizable to many hikers. The symmetrical opening is 40 feet wide at the bottom with a 10-foot slot in the top—a natural subway tunnel without the train or the tracks.

As you proceed into the Subway you will notice a string of potholes that have been dissolved from the sandstone by the unceasing presence of water. The liquid-filled voids are up to 10 feet in diameter and 5 feet deep, and are arranged along the slickrock floor like a string of watery glass beads.

200 feet beyond the keyhole forma-

tion the streambed enters a deep meandering channel that ends a short distance later at the base of a 15-foot waterfall. There is more to see above the waterfall in the upper Subway, but unfortunately it is nearly impossible to climb above the waterfall without help. For most people this will be the end of the hike. With a little advanced planning, however, there still might be a way to get into the upper Subway.

During the summer months you can usually count on meeting several groups of hikers that have descended into the Subway from the top of the Kolob Plateau, a more difficult route that requires some swimming and rope handling skills. These groups typically reach the upper Subway around noon or shortly after, and if you happen to be below the waterfall when one of them arrives the

Rappelling into the Lower Subway

The Upper Subway

rock. There is a 6-foot vertical section at the bottom of the pitch that presents a problem for some people, but if you lean back against the rope and walk up rather than trying to pull yourself up the ascent isn't too difficult.

If your rope is only 30 feet long you will have to tie one end to the belay point and abandon it when you climb back down. If your rope is 60 feet long, however, you can pass it through the belay point without a knot and then pull it down after you when you return to the bottom of the pitch. One other hint: it is easier to climb hand-over-hand with wide nylon webbing than with rope.

If you happen to get stranded above the waterfall without a rope don't despair. There is another way down. There is a place a few feet downstream from the waterfall where you can easily slide down a 4 feet drop into the icy water below. If you don't have a rope but you are with one or two friends that can give you a boost, you may also be able to get up to the upper Subway from there.

chances are good that you will find a friend willing to help you up. If you leave the Left Fork Trailhead by 8:00 a.m. you should have plenty of time to enjoy the scenery and still make it to the Subway before all of the climbers have descended below the waterfall.

The other requirement is that you carry at least 30 feet of rope or nylon webbing in your pack. Then all you need to do is throw the rope up to a person at the top and ask him to tie it onto something for you before he comes down. Most people climb into the upper Subway from a point 100 feet downstream from the waterfall. There you will find a 60-degree pitch of slickrock with a permanent belay point bolted into the sandstone at the top. The pitch is only 30 feet long, and once a rope has been tied or passed through the belay point it is relatively easy to walk hand-over-hand up the slick-

After climbing the pitch just described you must cross the top of the waterfall to the left side of the stream in order to continue on into the upper Subway. You will soon enter a part of the canyon very different from your earlier experience. Gone are the photogenic pools of clear water and the moss-covered flowstone. Instead you will enter a dark, foreboding place with no plant life and almost no sunshine. There is no way out of the narrow prison-like vault except the way you came in. The walls of sheer sandstone are overhung and stained with long purplish-black streaks of desert varnish. Occasional flash floods assure that nothing grows in the cavern-like narrows. The streambed is scoured clean and any plant that might try to gain a foothold will eventually be washed away.

The upper Subway is a particularly eerie place to be in alone. The first time I was there my thoughts were equally divided between studying the marvels of nature and wondering what it would be like to be locked in a dungeon. My concerns were real enough that I took the time to walk back and pull up my rope for fear that some prankster might come into the lower Subway and pull it down. The canyon twists and turns several times and finally ends 200 yards later at the base of Keyhole Falls, another small water-fall. This time there is no way to continue.

Wildcat Canyon Trailhead

The hike described above is the easi-est way to see the Subway; however if you are the adventurous type you might prefer to begin this hike at the Wildcat Canyon Trailhead. From there it is possible to drop down into the Subway from above and follow Left Fork Creek back to the road. The total walking distance of that hike is 9.6 miles– slightly longer than the round trip hike from Left Fork Trailhead described above. The Wildcat Canyon Trailhead is also located on the Kolob Reservoir Road, but it is 7.9 miles

north of the Left Fork Trailhead so if you chose to start at Wildcat Canyon you will need a shuttle car.

Unlike the trail up Left Fork, the route down from the Wildcat Canyon Trailhead to the Subway has several technical challenges. Short rappels are required in two places, so you will need some rope handling skills and a 60-foot length of nylon webbing or rope. You will also be required to swim across at least two small pools of water, so it is wise to carry a river bag for your gear. Finally, do not attempt this hike unless the weather is warm and sunny. The water is always cold and unless you wear a wet suit there is no way to stay dry.

From the trailhead the Wildcat Canyon Trail heads off in an easterly direction across the Kolob Plateau for 1.0 mile before arriv-ing at the Hop Valley Trail junction. Bear left here and continue another 0.2 mile through an open forest of Ponderosa Pine to a second junction where you must turn right onto the Northgate Peaks Trail. After walking south for just 100 yards on the Northgate Peaks Trail you will see another trail departing on the left next to a sign marking the route to the Subway.

Up to this point the terrain is relative-ly flat, but soon after leaving the Northgate Peaks Trail the path veers to the southeast and begins dropping down a long sloping expanse of slickrock into Russell Gulch. Gone is the sandy trail, but you will have no trouble following the route. Many people before you have come this way, and the trail

Entering Russell Gulch

is well marked with stone cairns.

After dropping off the rim into Russell Gulch the trail meanders southward through the depression for 2.3 miles before finally arriving at the confluence of Russell Gulch and Left Fork. In order to continue you must climb down to the canyon floor at this point and turn right into Left Fork Canyon. Unfortunately, as the trail nears the confluence it is 150 feet above the streambed, and there appears to be no easy way to get to the bottom of the sheer canyon walls. If you carefully follow the cairns, however, they will lead you to a narrow cleft in the sandstone cliff where there is a feasible route down to the canyon floor. Once you reach the bottom of Russell Gulch continue south for another 60 yards to the confluence and then turn right into Left Fork Canyon.

The next 1.1 miles below the confluence of Russell Gulch and Left Fork presents a series of watery challenges that increase in difficulty as you penetrate deeper into the canyon. At first the obstacles are nothing more than small water-filled potholes that can usually be skirted without getting wet. But soon the canyon begins to narrow, and after about 15 minutes you will come to a 30-foot-long pool of cold water that completely fills the bottom of the gorge. The only way to get across it is to swim. This is just the first of several more pools you will encounter. Some of them can be avoided by scrambling around the canyon walls, but it is often easier to just take the plunge and wade or swim through.

Finally, just before reaching the Subway, you will be confronted with the last serious obstacle: Keyhole Falls. Keyhole Falls is a small 10-foot-high waterfall that seems to have been strategically placed above the east entrance of the Subway for no other reason than to keep people out. The canyon is only a few feet wide at the top of the waterfall, and the only way forward is to do a free rappel over the lip of the pouroff. The drop is not very high and there is a good belay point at the top of the fall, but the rappel is almost directly under the unceasing flow of icy water.

When you reach the bottom of Keyhole Falls you will be in the upper Subway, and the most difficult part of the hike is behind you. As described above, one more rappel is required to get from the upper Subway to the lower Subway, but this last pitch is a simple 30-foot drop down a dry 60-degree incline. From there it is an easy walk down Left Fork Creek to the Left Fork Trailhead.

Left Fork Creek above the Subway

Hop Valley and Kolob Arch

★★★★

Zion National Park
shuttle car required
overnight hike

Distance:	14.3 miles (plus 43 miles by car)
Walking time:	day 1: 6³/₄ hours day 2: 4¹/₂ hours
Elevations:	1,290 ft. loss, 1,000 ft. gain Hop Valley Trailhead (start): 6,350 ft. Kolob Arch Viewpoint: 5,400 ft. La Verkin Creek Trailhead: 6,060 ft.
Trail:	Popular, well maintained trail
Season:	Late spring through mid-fall. Winter snows often close the roads to the trailheads from mid-November to May. Also, the trail is quite hot in July and August.
Vicinity:	Kolob Canyons Section of Zion National Park
Maps:	Kolob Arch, The Guardian Angels *(USGS)* Zion National Park *(Trails Illustrated, #214)*
Information:	http://www.utahtrails.com/kolob.html *(Utah Trails)* http://www.nps.gov/zion/ *(Zion National Park)* phone: (435) 586-9548 *(Kolob Canyons Visitor Center)*

Drive south of Cedar City on I-15 for 18 miles to Exit 40, then leave the highway and drive east for another 0.5 mile to the Kolob Canyons Visitor Center of Zion National Park. You will need to get a backcountry camping permit here for an overnight hike into the park. After you have obtained your permit continue driving beyond the Visitor Center for another 3.7 miles to Lees Pass, where the La Verkin Creek Trailhead is located. The trailhead marks the end of the hike, and you should leave your shuttle car in the nearby parking lot.

To get to Hop Valley Trailhead, where the hike begins, return to I-15 and drive south for 13 miles to the junction with Highway 17. Turn here and follow the signs to Zion National Park for 12 miles through La Verkin to the town of Virgin. In Virgin you will see a sign identifying the road to Kolob Reservoir. Turn left onto this road and drive for 13.4 miles, until you see the sign directing you to the Hop Valley Trailhead on your left.

Note: The Zion Adventure company in Springdale operates a shuttle service between the two trailheads during the summer hiking season. Their shuttle leaves Springdale each morning at 7:00 a.m. and arrives at the Hop Valley Trailhead at 8:40 a.m. From there it proceeds to the La Verkin Creek Trailhead, arriving at 9:40 a.m., and back to Springdale. The cost: $39.00 per person. For more information or reservations call (435) 772-1001.

Kolob Arch is the second longest natural arch in the world. Accurate measurement of its size is difficult because of its location, high above the canyon floor, but recent calculations place its span at about 287 feet. This is only three feet shorter than Landscape Arch, the world's longest span, in Arches National Park (see page 212). The arch is situated near the top of the Navajo Sandstone cliffs on the north side of La Verkin Creek, about 700 feet above the trail. It faces east, so the best time to see and photograph Kolob Arch is in the morning before about 10:00 a.m.

There are three possible ways to walk to Kolob Arch, but the Hop Valley Trail, suggested here, is the most scenic approach. This trail starts on the Kolob Plateau, south of La Verkin Creek, and proceeds down the colorful Hop Valley Canyon to its confluence with La Verkin. The canyon is about 200 yards wide, with a flat, grassy bottom boxed in on both sides by towering cliffs of red sandstone. A shallow stream, fed by runoff from a half dozen side canyons, keeps the bottom of the narrow valley green, while in the distance one can see a picturesque maze of mesas and canyons that surround the confluence of Hop Valley and La Verkin Creek.

Unfortunately, the Hop Valley experience is degraded by the presence of several dozen range cows. This valley was grazed long before Zion National Park was established, and cattle are still grazed here. As of this printing, 3,477 acres of land within the published boundaries of Zion National Park

Hop Valley

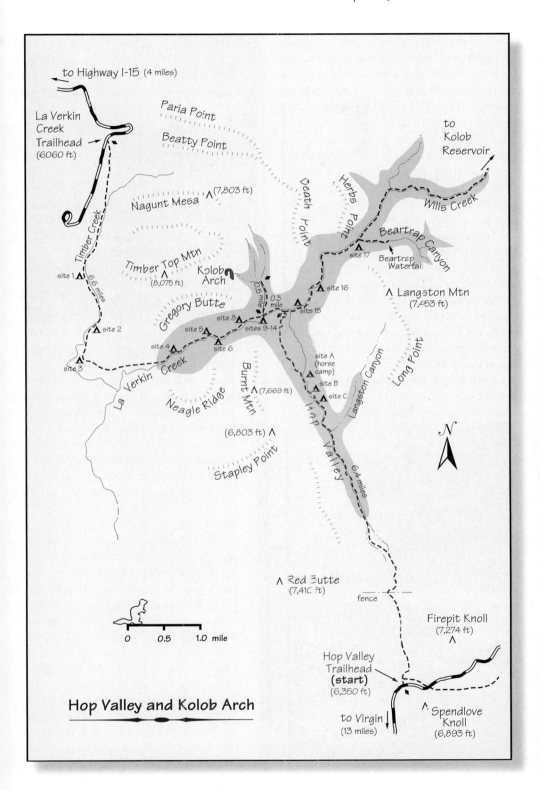

to Highway I-15 (4 miles)

La Verkin
Creek
Trailhead
(6060 ft)

Paria Point

Beatty Point

to
Kolob
Reservoir

Death Point

Herbs Point

Wilis Creek

Nagunt Mesa ∧ (7,803 ft)

Beartrap Canyon

site 17

Beartrap
Waterfall

Timber Creek

Timber Top Mtn
∧
(8,075 ft)

Kolob
Arch

∧ Langston Mtn
(7,453 ft)

site 1 ∧

6.6 miles

site 16

Gregory Butte

0.5 mile

0.3
mile

site 15

∧ site 2

site 8

site 5

sites 9-14

Long Point

site 4

site 6

La Verkin Creek

Burnt Mtn

site A
(horse
camp)

Langston Canyon

site 3

Neagle Ridge

∧ (7,669 ft)

site B

site C

(6,803 ft) ∧

Hop Valley

Stapley Point

6.4 miles

N

∧ Red Butte
(7,410 ft)

fence

Firepit Knoll
(7,274 ft)
∧

Hop Valley
Trailhead
(start)
(6,350 ft)

0   0.5   1.0 mile

Hop Valley and Kolob Arch

to Virgin
(13 miles)

∧ Spendlove
Knoll
(6,893 ft)

are still privately owned by local ranchers. The National Park Service has been trying to solve this problem for years, but like most other federal problems the solution requires money. The degree to which the Hop Valley ecosystem has been damaged by the cattle is starkly apparent about a mile before La Verkin Creek, where a fence has been erected to keep cattle out of the lower end of the valley. Beyond this barrier the diversity in plant species increases dramatically, the creek bed becomes deeper and more clearly defined, and the presence of birds and other wildlife becomes noticeable once again.

Only 19 groups of hikers are permitted to camp in Hop Valley and the Kolob Canyons each day; the cost of a permit is $15.00 for a group of 3-7 people. Reservations for 7 of the 19 backcountry campsites can be made online up to three months in advance at http://zionpermits.nps.gov/. The remaining 12 sites are assigned at the visitor centers on a walk-in basis one day in

La Verkin Creek

advance. If you plan to get a walk-in permit during the peak summer season I suggest you show up at one of the visitor centers no later than 8:00 a.m. the day before your intended departure and go directly to the backcountry office to submit your request. Only one of the sites can accommodate the maximum group size of 12 backpackers, so it is easier to get permits for groups of 6 or fewer people.

Day 1 (6.9 miles)

From the Hop Valley Trailhead the trail passes through 1.4 miles of open pinion-juniper forest before coming to a fence near the beginning of Hop Valley Canyon. This fence marks the beginning of an inholding of privately owned land. Beyond the fence the trail begins descending gradually into Hop Valley, finally reaching the canyon floor after about 1.5 miles. As you proceed down the canyon the floor becomes wider and flatter until, after another 1.5 miles, it reaches its maximum width of about 300 yards. Finally, 4.8 miles from the trailhead, you will cross the northern

Hop Valley

boundary of the Hop Valley grazing area, where another fence spans the bottom of the canyon to keep cattle out of La Verkin Creek. Make sure you close the gate behind you as you cross through the fence.

Soon after leaving the grazed portion of Hop Valley, the trail leaves the valley floor and climbs slightly into a forested area below the west wall. Then, 0.3 mile before reaching La Verkin Creek the trail breaks out of the trees and begins a series of switchbacks down into La Verkin Canyon. Just before reaching the creek you will see another trail coming down the canyon from Willis Creek. Turn left here and walk for 0.4 mile to the short spur trail that leads to Kolob Arch.

As mentioned earlier, Kolob arch is located directly west of the viewpoint; hence the best time to see it is in the morning when the sun is in the east. For that reason a good place to end the first day's walk is near the spur trail that leads to the arch. You should try to reserve one of the six campsites near the trail junction when you apply for your permit.

Day 2 (7.8 miles)

The first item of business on the morning of the second day is to see the Kolob Arch. The viewpoint is only a 10-minute walk from the trail junction near La Verkin Creek. Unfortunately, however, the viewpoint at the end of the trail is still 600 yards from the arch, and because of the rough terrain it is almost impossible to get more than 200 yards closer. Without a good frame of reference the arch does not seem as big as it really is, and you may be mildly disappointed. Nevertheless, it is huge, spanning 287 feet .

From your campsite, the trail to Lees Pass continues down La Verkin Creek for about 1.6 miles before veering off to the north The trail finally leaves the creek near the remains of an old corral that was used years ago when cattle were still being grazed here. 1.3 miles later the trail encounters Timber Creek, a tributary of La Verkin, and continues north toward Lees Pass. Finally, 0.9 mile before arriving at the trailhead, the trail leaves Timber Creek and climbs the last 470 feet to the parking lot.

Kolob Arch

Middle Fork Taylor Creek

★★★

Distance:	5.4 miles (round trip)
Walking time:	3 hours
Elevations:	490 ft. gain/loss Taylor Creek Trailhead (start): 5,530 ft. Double Arch Alcove: 6,020 ft.
Trail:	Generally good trail, although parts of it are occasionally washed out by flash floods.
Season:	Spring, summer, fall. The trail is often covered with snow during the winter months.
Vicinity:	Kolob Canyons Section of Zion National Park
Maps:	Kolob Arch *(USGS)* Zion National Park *(Trails Illustrated, #214)*
Information:	http://www.utahtrails.com/taylor.html *(Utah Trails)* http://www.nps.gov/zion/ *(Zion National Park)* phone: (435) 586-9548 *(Kolob Canyons Visitor Center)*

Drive south of Cedar City on I-15 for 18 miles to exit 40, then turn east onto the Kolob Canyons Road. Within 0.2 mile you will come to the Kolob Canyons Visitor Center, where you must pay a small entrance fee to enter Zion National Park. This is also a good place to buy books and maps and ask any questions you might have. The Taylor Creek Trailhead is 1.9 miles further east from the visitor center on the Kolob Canyons Road. There is a small parking lot near the trailhead on the left side of the road, and trail brochures are available at a cost of $1.00.

The Kolob Canyons section of Zion National Park offers visitors a splendid opportunity to enjoy Zion's unique redrock canyons without enduring the crowds of people that are usually present in Zion Canyon. Of particular interest to hikers are the Finger Canyons of the Kolob. These scenic canyons are deeply etched into the western side of the Kolob Plateau, and from above they look like so many fingers clawing their way into the plateau's rouge colored sandstone. None of the canyons are more than a few miles long, but they are notable because of their sheer walls. Typically the cliffs are over a

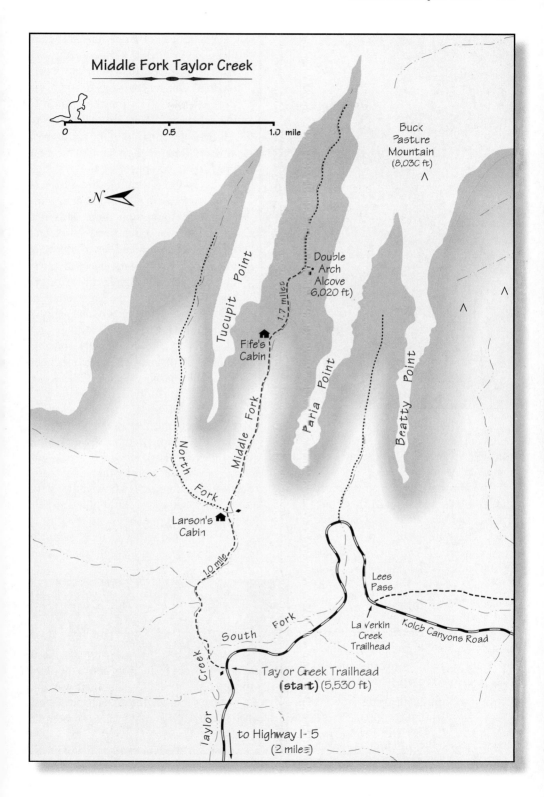

Middle Fork Taylor Creek

0   0.5   1.0 mile

N

Buck
Pasture
Mountain
(8,030 ft)
∧

Tucupit Point

Double
Arch
Alcove
6,020 ft)

1.7 miles

Fife's
Cabin

Middle Fork

Paria Point

Beatty Point

∧

∧ ∧

North Fork

Larson's
Cabin

1.0 mile

Lees
Pass

La Verkin
Creek
Trailhead

Kolob Canyons Road

South   Fork

Creek

Taylor Creek Trailhead
(start) (5,530 ft)

Taylor

to Highway I-15
(2 miles)

Middle Fork Taylor Creek

then continues in an easterly direction along Taylor Creek. Very soon the trail crosses to the north side of the creek, the first of many crossings to come, but it never strays far from the bottom of the drainage. There is usually at least a little water running in the streambed, although late in the summer the flow may dry up completely.

You will be walking through a low montane forest of ponderosa pine, white fir, juniper, and pinion pine. This area was heavily logged during the first half of the last century and few of the trees are older than 50 years, but fortunately the vegetation has made a remarkable comeback and now the area seems as pristine as ever. There are few signs of the earlier destruction.

After 1.0 mile you will come to another confluence where Taylor Creek splits into its north and middle forks. There is a primitive hiker-made trail branching off to the left that goes about 2.0 miles to the back of the North Fork. You are likely to meet far fewer people along the North Fork of Taylor Creek, and for that reason some prefer that hike. Also, backcountry camping is allowed along the North Fork, but you must obtain a permit first from the visitor center.

There is an old settler's cabin beside the trail just a few hundred feet north of where

thousand feet high, rising nearly vertically through the Navajo Sandstone Formation that underlies the plateau.

The Fingers can all be accessed from the Kolob Canyons Road that runs along Timber and Taylor Creeks a half mile to the west. There are six of them in all, and their rugged beauty is enough to make the heart of any outdoorsman beat a little faster. The most popular hikes are into the canyons formed by the North, Middle, and South Forks of Taylor Creek. Of the three, Middle Fork Taylor Creek Canyon is the only one that contains a maintained trail. In my opinion this hike is also the most interesting one, and it is the one I will describe here.

From the road the trail drops down about 60 feet to the confluence of Taylor Creek and the South Fork,

Arthur Fife's cabin

the North Fork and the Middle Fork meet. The cabin was built by a farmer named Gustav Larson some twenty-five years before the area became part of Zion National Park. Larson raised pigs which he periodically hauled 23 miles to market in Cedar City. His nearest neighbor was a professor named Arthur Fife, who taught at the agricultural college in Cedar City. Fife built his cabin a mile further up the Middle Fork on the left side of the streambed. Both cabins were erected around 1930.

Middle Fork Canyon begins about 300 yards upstream from the Larson cabin, and by the time you reach the Fife cabin the canyon will have narrowed to just a few hundred feet. Fife raised goats on his property, and he built a fence across the canyon in order to contain his animals. There is now no trace of Fife's fence, but both his and Larson's cabins are still in remarkably good condition. The Fife cabin is right by the trail, but if you are walking in the streambed, as many people do, you might miss it. It is located about 20 feet from the left bank of the creek in a heavily shaded grove of trees.

The trail ends at the Double Arch Alcove, 0.7 mile beyond Arthur Fife's cabin. This alcove is a large cave, about 150 feet deep and 150 feet in diameter, located 20 feet above the streambed on the south side of the canyon. Like most sandstone alcoves, this one was formed by a seep in the side of the cliff. Water seeping out from the canyon wall weakens the sandstone and eventually causes it to crumble away. A great deal of water is still seeping out of the Double Arch Alcove, and, judging from the size of the cave, the seep has been active for many thousands of years. The alcove was named after two

blind arches (arches that have not yet been completely formed) that are located on the cliffs above.

If you still have energy left when you reach the Double Arch Alcove it is possible to continue up Middle Fork Canyon for another 0.8 mile before the walls close in and make further progress impossible. 0.2 mile above the alcove the canyon is blocked by an ancient rockslide, but if you are willing to do some scrambling you can easily climb around the right side of this obstacle. After climbing about a hundred feet to the top of the slide the canyon floor flattens out again and widens into a small hanging valley. From there you can continue another 0.6 mile or so before further progress becomes impossible.

Double Arch Alcove

Pine Valley Mountains

Pine Valley Mountains Wilderness Area
shuttle car or bicycle useful
overnight hike

Distance: 15.7 miles
                        (plus 1.5 miles by foot, bicycle, or car)

Walking time: day 1: $5^3/_4$ hours
                     day 2: 8 hours

Elevations: 4,410 ft. gain, 4,580 ft. loss
                   Whipple Trailhead (start): 7,050 ft.
                   Whipple Valley: 9,320 ft.
                   Hidden Valley: 8,980 ft.
                   Browns Point Trailhead: 6,880 ft.

Trail: Generally well marked, easy to follow trail

Season: Water availability can be a problem on this hike. In the early summer there is usually abundant water at several points along the trail, but by mid-July most of the water has dried up. You might also have problems if you attempt the hike too early in the year. Most of the snow is usually gone by June 1, but before then the route may be muddy and hard to follow. The best month is June.

Vicinity: Near Cedar City and Saint George

Maps: Signal Peak, Grass Valley *(USGS)*
                   Cedar Mtn., Pine Valley Mtn. *(Trails Illustrated, #702)*

Information: http://www.utahtrails.com/pinevalley.html *(Utah Trails)*
                   http://www.fs.fed.us/dxnf/ *(Dixie National Forest)*
                   phone: (435) 652-3100 *(Pine Valley Ranger District)*

Drive west from Cedar City on Highway 56 for 36 miles to the Beryl Junction. Turn left here and continue driving south for 24 miles on Highway 18 to Central, where you will see a well marked road leading to Pine Valley on your left. Turn here and drive to the town of Pine Valley 8.3 miles west of Central. Once you reach Pine Valley Town you will see a sign directing you to the Pine Valley Recreation Area. Turn here and proceed east for 1.5 miles to the recreation area entrance gate, where you must pay $2.00 per car to enter. (If you intend to use one of the campgrounds the entrance is free.)

1.3 miles beyond the entrance station you will see a paved road on the right that leads to the Pines Campground and beyond. Browns Point Trailhead is at the end of this road, 0.5 mile past the Pines Campground or 0.6 mile from the main road. This is where the hike ends. To get to the Whipple Trailhead where the hike begins you must return to the main road and continue upcanyon for another 0.2 mile until you come to the road to Blue Springs Campground. The Whipple Trailhead is on this road, 0.4 mile above Blue Springs Campground or 0.6 mile from the main road.

The Pine Valley Mountains of southwestern Utah are located on the eastern side of the Great Basin Geologic Province. Like most other ranges in the Great Basin Province they are very dry and contain no significant lakes. They do, however, contain a number of small creeks and meadows which, at least during the early weeks of summer, are extremely scenic. Unfortunately, most of the water disappears soon after the winter snow has melted. The best time to attempt this hike is during the month of June, when the meadows are usually green and full of water. As midsummer approaches they soon dry up and the hike becomes much less appealing.

Although this hike is only 15.7 miles long it has a great deal of elevation gain, and many people prefer to spend a second night along the trail. If you elect to do this you will have no trouble finding good campsites along the Summit Trail between Whipple Valley and Nay Canyon. You can camp near water at Whipple Valley, South Valley, Hop Canyon, Hidden Valley or Nay Canyon.

Day 1 (5.3 miles)
From Whipple Trailhead the trail starts

Whipple Trail

upward almost immediately and climbs steadily over the first two miles through a forest dominated by subalpine fir and Engelmann spruce. You will want to stop frequently to enjoy the magnificent views of Pine Valley Town below and the hills that surround it. Finally, after an elevation gain of some 1,300 feet, the trail dips 200 feet down into Hop Canyon, where you should be able to fill your canteens before continuing the climb. After Hop Canyon it is uphill again–another 1,100 feet of steady climbing until you reach Whipple Valley, just east of the summit ridge.

Whipple Valley is a picture-perfect alpine meadow about 100 yards wide and 500 yards long with a small creek running through the middle. If you got off to a late start you might want to select a campsite on the edge of Whipple Valley. There are plenty of ideal spots along the sides of the grassy meadow. In the spring it is filled with wildflowers nourished by the melting snow, but snow is the only source of water and the meadow quickly dries out after the snow is gone. Water is plentiful in early June, but by midsummer it has usually disappeared. If there is no water in Whipple Valley try walk-

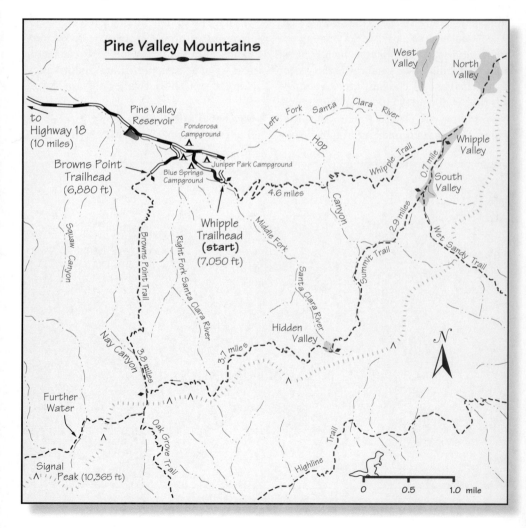

ing northwest for another half mile up the drainage toward West Valley. This is the headwaters of the Left Fork of Santa Clara River and there is sometimes water here after Whipple Valley has dried out.

Pine Valley

As you enter Whipple Valley you will notice a sign indicating that you have reached a trail junction. This is the point where Whipple Trail meets the Summit Trail, a 35-mile-long pack trail that runs in a northeast-southwest direction along the summit ridge of the Pine Valley Mountains. If you have an extra day to spend you might want to establish a camp here and spend some time exploring the nearby North Valley and West Valley meadows, both within a mile of the junction. In order to complete this loop hike, however, you will have to turn right at the junction and follow Summit Trail in a southerly direction until you reach Browns Point Trail, 7.3 miles away.

The Summit Trail is not as well defined as Whipple Trail and you may have trouble following it for the first mile. The route is easy, though, so don't worry too much if you can't find the trail. Just walk south along the Whipple Valley drainage until you come to the southern end of the meadow. Continue following the drainage through the trees and within 0.3 mile you will break out into another meadow called South Valley. You should be able to pick the trail up again as you continue south along the western edge of South Valley.

South Valley is every bit as beautiful as the better known Whipple Valley, and the

water supply is slightly more reliable. It is another two-hour walk to the next comparable campsite, so unless you got off to a very early start you will probably want to spend the night in South Valley. Near the trail about half way through the meadow the creek bed winds around a big boulder, forming a shaded pool that seems to hold water until later in the summer. There is also plenty of flat ground in the area, making it a good place to set up camp. Furthermore, this meadow seems to be a favorite evening hangout for deer, so if you are quiet and observant you will probably see some wildlife before the sun sets.

Day 2 (10.4 miles)

As you approach the southern end of South Valley the trail seems to disappear again. Finally, just before you reach the trees you will see another sign that says "Wet Sandy Trail" with an arrow pointing to the left. This is not the trail you want. Stop at the sign and look due magnetic south at the edge of the meadow about 100 yards in front of you. If you look carefully you will see another trail, the Summit Trail, entering the trees on the south end of the meadow. There are also well defined blaze marks on the trees where the trail leaves the meadow. Once you enter the woods the trail is again quite will defined.

Immediately after you leave South Valley the Summit Trail again begins to climb. Over the next 2.9 miles you will first gain 220 feet in elevation, then drop 420 feet, then gain 400 feet, then loose 420 feet before finally reaching what, in my opinion, is the most beautiful meadow of all: Hidden Valley. Located at the foot of a rocky outcrop near the headwaters of the Middle Fork of Santa Clara River, Hidden Valley is indeed well hidden. The meadow is small, only 100 yards in diameter, and it is completely surrounded by tall, stately Engelmann spruce. You will hardly know it is there before you walk into it. Adding to the effect, Summit Trail exits the meadow through a partially hidden five-foot-wide crack in the rock barrier on its western side—a perfect secret entrance to an outlaws' hideout. If you are looking for quiet seclusion there are no better places to camp than Hidden Valley.

Continuing its up-and-down route, the Summit Trail climbs nearly a thousand feet above Hidden Valley and then drops 320 feet back down into Nay Canyon, where you will come to the Browns Point Trail. Nay Canyon generally has water in early summer, and it is a good place to camp or refill your canteens.

In order to complete this loop you must leave the Summit Trail at the Nay Canyon Junction and take the Brown Point Trail back to the Pine Valley Recreation Area. Again, however, if you have an extra day to spend there are a number of points of interest further up the Summit Trail. Continuing south on Summit Trail for 1.3 miles from the junction will bring you to Further Water, a good water source and a popular camping area. Two miles from the junction Summit Trail passes within 0.2 mile of Signal Peak (10,365 ft.), the highest point in the Pine Valley Mountains. The peak is about 370 feet above the path, and there is no trail to the summit. The climb, however, is not particularly difficult.

From its junction with the Summit Trail, the Browns Point Trail follows the bottom of Nay Canyon for 0.7 mile before climbing 400 feet back up the ridge on the east side of the canyon and then following the ridge the rest of the way to the bottom. The total amount of elevation loss along the trail from the junction is a knee busting 3,120 feet, but you will be compensated by fine views of the valley below. You can see Pine Valley for almost the entire distance.

South Valley

Public Lands Agencies

National Park Service

Arches National Park
www.nps.gov/arch/
P.O. Box 907
Moab, UT 84532
(435) 719-2299

Bryce Canyon National Park
www.nps.gov/brca/
P.O. Box 640201
Bryce Canyon, UT 84764
(435) 834-5322

Canyonlands National Park
www.nps.gov/cany/
2282 SW Resource Blvd.
Moab, UT 84532
(435) 719-2313 (Headquarters)
(435) 259-2652 (Hans Flat Ranger Station)

Capitol Reef National Park
www.nps.gov/care/
HC-70 Box 15
Torrey, UT 84775
(435) 425-3791

Cedar Breaks National Monument
www.nps.gov/cebr/
2390 West Highway 56, Suite #11
Cedar City, UT 84720
(435) 586-0787

Dinosaur National Monument
www.nps.gov/dinc/
4545 E. Highway 40
Dinosaur, CO 81610
(970) 374-3000

Escalante Interagency Office
755 West Main Street
Escalante, UT 84726
(435) 826-5499

Glen Canyon National Recreation Area
www.nps.gov/glca/
P.O. Box 1507
Page, AZ 86040
(928) 608-6200

Hovenweep National Monument
www.nps.gov/hove/
McElmo Route
Cortez, CO 81321
(970) 562-4282 ext. 10

Natural Bridges National Monument
www.nps.gov/nabr/
HC 60 Box 1
Lake Powell, UT 84533
(435) 692-1234 ext. 16

Rainbow Bridge National Monument
www.nps.gov/rabr/
P.O. Box 1507
Page, AZ 86040
(928) 608-6200

Timpanogos Cave National Monument
www.nps.gov/tica/
R.R. 3, Box 200
American Fork, UT 84003
(801) 756-5238

Zion National Park
www.nps.gov/zion/
Springdale, UT 84767
(435) 772-3256

U.S. Forest Service

Ashley National Forest
www.fs.fed.us/r4/ashley/

> Duchesne Ranger District
> 85 West Main
> Duchesne, UT 84021
> (435) 738-2482

> Flaming Gorge Ranger District
> 25 West Highway 43
> Manila, UT 84046
> (435) 784-3445

> Roosevelt Ranger District
> 650 West Highway 40
> Roosevelt, UT 84066
> (435) 722-5018

> Vernal Ranger District
> 355 North Vernal Avenue
> Vernal, UT 84078
> (435) 789-1181

Dixie National Forest
www.fs.fed.us/dxnf/

> Cedar City Ranger District
> 1789 N. Wedgewood Lane
> Cedar City, UT 84721
> (435) 865-3200

> Escalante Ranger District
> 755 West Main Street
> Escalante, UT 84726
> (435) 826-5499

Pine Valley Ranger District
196 E. Tabernacle, suite 40
St. George, UT 84770
(435) 652-3100

Powell Ranger District
225 East Center
Panguitch, UT 84759
(435) 676-9300

Fremont River Ranger District
138 South Main
Loa, UT 84747
(435) 836-2811

Fishlake National Forest
www.fs.fed.us/r4/fishlake/

Beaver Ranger District
575 South Main
Beaver, UT 84713
(435) 438-2436

Fillmore Ranger District
390 South Main
Fillmore, UT 84631
(435) 743-5721

Fremont River Ranger District
138 South Main
Loa, UT 84747
(435) 836-2800

Richfield Ranger District
115 East 900 North
Richfield, UT 84701
(435) 896-9233

Manti-La Sal National Forest
www.fs.fed.us/r4/mantilasal/

    Ferron Ranger District
    115 West Canyon Road
    Ferron, UT 84523
    (435) 384-2372

    Moab Ranger District
    62 East 100 North
    Moab, UT 84532
    (435) 259-7155

    Monticello Ranger District
    496 East Central
    Monticello, UT 84535
    (435) 587-2041

    Price Ranger District
    599 West Price River Drive
    Price, UT, 84501
    (435) 637-2817

    Sanpete Ranger District
    540 North Main Street
    Ephraim, UT 84627
    (435) 283-4151

Uinta-Wasatch-Cache National Forest
www.fs.usda.gov/uwcnf

    Supervisor's Office
    88 West 100 North
    Provo, UT 84601
    (801) 342-5100

    Heber Ranger District
    2460 South Highway 40
    Heber City, UT 84032
    (435) 654-0470

    Nephi Office
    740 South Main
    Nephi, UT 84648
    (435) 623-2735

    Pleasant Grove Ranger District
    390 North 100 East
    Pleasant Grove, UT 84062
    (801) 785-3563

    Spanish Fork Ranger District
    44 West 400 North
    Spanish Fork, UT 84660
    (801) 798-3571

    Evanston Ranger District
    1565 S. Highway 150, Suite A
    Evanston, WY 82930
    (307) 789-3194

    Kamas Ranger District
    50 East Center Street
    Kamas, UT 84036
    (435) 783-4338

    Logan Ranger District
    1500 East Highway 89
    Logan, UT 84321
    (435) 755-3620

    Mountain View Ranger District
    321 Highway 414
    Mountain View, WY 82939
    (307) 782-6555

    Ogden Ranger District
    507 25th Street
    Ogden, UT 84401
    (801) 625-5112

    Salt Lake Ranger District
    6944 South 3000 East
    Cottonwood Heights, UT 84121
    (801) 236-3400

Bureau of Land Management

Cedar City Field Office
www.blm.gov/ut/st/en/fo/cedar_city.html
176 East D.L. Sargent Drive
Cedar City, UT 84721
(435) 865-2401

Escalante Interagency Office
755 West Main Street
Escalante, UT 84726
(435) 826-5600

Fillmore Field Office
www.blm.gov/ut/st/en/fo/fillmore.html
95 East 500 North
Fillmore, UT 84631
(435) 743-3100

Grand Staircase-Escalante Nat. Mon.
www.blm.gov/ut/st/en/fo/grand_staircase-
escalante.html
669 South Highway 89A
Kanab, UT 84741
(435) 644-1200

Henry Mountain Field Station
380 South 100 West
Hanksville, UT 84734
(435) 542-3461

Kanab Field Office
www.blm.gov/ut/st/en/fo/kanab.html
669 South Highway 89A
Kanab, UT 84741
(435) 644-1200

Moab Field Office
www.blm.gov/ut/st/en/fo/moab.html
82 East Dogwood
Moab, UT 84532
(435) 259-2100

Monticello Field Office
www.blm.gov/ut/st/en/fo/monticello.html
365 North Main Street
Monticello, UT 84535
(435) 587-1500

Price Field Office
www.blm.gov/ut/st/en/fo/price.html
125 South 600 West
Price, UT 84501
(435) 636-3600

Richfield Field Office
www.blm.gov/ut/st/en/fo/richfield.html
150 East 900 North
Richfield, UT 84701
(435) 896-1500

Salt Lake Field Office
www.blm.gov/ut/st/en/fo/salt_lake.html
2370 South 2300 West
Salt Lake City, UT 84119
(801) 977-4300

St. George Field Office
www.blm.gov/ut/st/en/fo/st__george.html
345 East Riverside Drive
St. George, UT 84790
(435) 688-3200

Vernal Field Office
www.blm.gov/ut/st/en/fo/vernal.html
170 South 500 East
Vernal, UT 84078
(435) 781-4410

Index

   Although most of us now live in cities, we are all descended from a people that lived much closer to the earth. Our early ancestors lived their entire lives in the natural world, and they understood it in ways that we cannot. But there is still something in our genes that yearns to learn more about the world they knew. Get out of the city. Go out and experience, if only for a day, the timeless beauty and the mystery of nature. It will calm your soul and bring new meaning to your life.

-- David Day